T0305553

Global Imbalances and Financial Capitalism

The past few decades have witnessed the emergence of economic imbalances at the world level and within the euro zone. The failure of mainstream economics to accurately predict financial crises, or model the effects of finance-led growth, highlights the need for alternative frameworks.

A key text, *Global Imbalances and Financial Capitalism: Stock-Flow-Consistent Modelling* demonstrates that Stock-Flow-Consistent models are well adapted to study this growth regime due to their ability to analyse the real and financial sides of the economy in an integrated way. This approach is combined with an analysis of exchange rate misalignments using the Fundamental Equilibrium Exchange Rate (FEER) methodology, which serves to give a synthetic view of international imbalances. Together, these models describe how global and regional imbalances are created, as well as suggest appropriate tools through which they may be reduced. The book also considers alternative economic policies in the euro zone (international risk sharing, fiscal federalism, eurobonds, European investments, a multispeed euro zone) alongside alternative monetary policies. In particular, it examines the possibilities of using SDR (Special Drawing Rights) as a reserve asset to be issued to fight a global recession, to support the development of low-income countries, or as an anchor to improve global monetary stability.

This text will be of interest to students, scholars, and researchers of economic theory and international monetary economics. It will also appeal to professional organisations that supervise international relations.

Jacques Mazier is Professor Emeritus at the University Sorbonne Paris Nord, CEPN-CNRS, France.

Routledge Frontiers of Political Economy

Inequality and Governance
Andreas P. Kyriacou

A New Approach to the Economics of Public Goods
Thomas Laudal

Marx's Capital after 150 Years
Critique and Alternative to Capitalism
Edited by Marcello Musto

The Political Economy of Prosperity
Successful Societies and Productive Cultures
Peter Murphy

Macroeconomic Measurement Versus Macroeconomic Theory
Merijn Knibbe

Hayek's Market Republicanism
The Limits of Liberty
Sean Irving

The End of Individualism and the Economy
Emerging Paradigms of Connection and Community
Ann E. Davis

Profit, Accumulation, and Crisis in Capitalism
Long-term Trends in the UK, US, Japan, and China, 1855–2018
Minqi Li

Global Imbalances and Financial Capitalism
Stock-Flow-Consistent Modelling
Jacques Mazier

For more information about this series, please visit: www.routledge.com/books/series/SE0345

Global Imbalances and Financial Capitalism

Stock–Flow–Consistent Modelling

Jacques Mazier

with Vincent Duwicquet,
Luis Reyes, Jamel Saadaoui,
and Sebastian Valdecantos

LONDON AND NEW YORK

First published 2020
by Routledge
2 Park Square, Milton Park, Abingdon, Oxon OX14 4RN

and by Routledge
605 Third Avenue, New York, NY 10017

First issued in paperback 2021

Routledge is an imprint of the Taylor & Francis Group, an informa business

Publisher's Note
The publisher has gone to great lengths to ensure the quality of this reprint but points out that some imperfections in the original copies may be apparent.

British Library Cataloguing-in-Publication Data
A catalogue record for this book is available from the British Library

Library of Congress Cataloging-in-Publication Data
Names: Mazier, Jacques, author.
Title: Global imbalances and financial capitalism: stock–flow–consistent modelling / Jacques Mazier; with Vincent Duwicquet, Luis Reyes, Jamel Saadaoui and Sebastian Valdecantos.
Description: 1 Edition. | New York: Routledge, 2020. |
Series: Routledge frontiers of political economy |
Includes bibliographical references and index.
Identifiers: LCCN 2019059174 (print) | LCCN 2019059175 (ebook)
Subjects: LCSH: Economic development–Econometric models. |
Foreign exchange rates–Econometric models. |
Capital movements–Econometric models.
Classification: LCC HD75.5 .M395 2020 (print) |
LCC HD75.5 (ebook) | DDC 338.9/27–dc23
LC record available at https://lccn.loc.gov/2019059174
LC ebook record available at https://lccn.loc.gov/2019059175

ISBN 13: 978-1-03-223604-9 (pbk)
ISBN 13: 978-1-138-34558-4 (hbk)

DOI: 10.4324/9780429437786

Typeset in Bembo
by Newgen Publishing UK

Contents

Contributors

Vincent Duwicquet, Senior Lecturer, University of Lille, CLERSE-CNRS, France

Luis Reyes, Finance Lecturer, Kedge Business School, Marseille, France

Jamel Saadaoui, Senior Lecturer, University of Strasbourg, BETA-CNRS, France

Sebastian Valdecantos, Assistant Professor, National University of General San Martin, Buenos Aires, Argentina

Introduction

Jacques Mazier

The aim of the book is to study different features of the finance-led regime that has settled in most industrialized countries since the late 1980s. Capital accumulation is driven by the financial rate of return and periodic crises appear as its normal adjustment mode. Recurrent global imbalances are another component of this growth regime with both a real and financial dimension. They are observed at the world level (US deficits facing Asian surpluses) and regional level (intra-European imbalances). Economic policies have been active to fight against crises, especially after 2008. The worst have been avoided but the mechanisms remain almost unchanged. These questions will be discussed using rather simple macroeconomic models at the national and international levels. The case of the European Union (EU), where the crisis of the euro zone has presented strong specificities due to the inconsistency of the monetary union, will be examined more in detail.

Since 2010 a long, though moderate, recovery has been observed in the United States, but the movement has been less pronounced in the EU and in Japan. China has almost succeeded to escape the 2008 crisis thanks to a huge demand support plan based on credit. China is shaping the world economy but, since the election of Donald Trump, the intensity of the trade war has escalated. Exchange rate policy has always been important for China and remains a possible answer. Special attention is paid to it. However, the future is uncertain. A slowdown can be expected in 2020 at the world level and yet another financial crisis cannot be excluded. The growth regime seems unsustainable, especially in the United States in spite of the room for manoeuvre given by the oil sector boom. The mechanisms at work before 2008 have not changed radically. This is all the more worrying given that the traditional economic policy tools have reached their limits. Public debt is high virtually everywhere, interest rates are close to zero in many countries, the balance sheets of central banks have increased considerably thanks to quantitative easing. In this context, although multilateralism is no longer fashionable, a global reform of the international monetary system based on an enlargement of the role of the Special Drawing Rights (SDR) deserves to be discussed.

Regarding the theoretical background, the financial crisis has shown the inability of mainstream models to explain it, in particular the so-called Dynamic

Stochastic General Equilibrium (DSGE) models. More realistic assumptions have been integrated in these with asymmetric information, sticky prices or credit rationing, but their main assumptions remain based on the single representative agent maximizing a utility function. Since these are supply-side models, they take little or no account of finance and are based on unreliable hypothesizes, which makes them rather unsuitable to explain growing world imbalances. The framework used in this book is different. It is macroeconomic without micro foundations, based on national accounts both in real and financial terms, Stock Flow Consistent (SFC) and mainly demand-led. Agents react to disequilibria on the basis of partial adjustment functions. Macroeconomic relations describe how the economic system can be reproduced from period to period inside the accounting framework (see Nikiforos and Zezza, 2017 for a survey). Following a Kaleckian perspective, long run evolution appears as a progressively changing component of short run sequences (Kalecki, 1965). According to the periods and the structural characteristics, real and financial business cycles or divergent evolutions can occur. SFC modelling is well suited to take into account the interaction between the real and the financial sectors which is a key issue of our times. Balance sheet constraints and revalorization effects, with capital gains or losses, are explicitly described. This SFC approach focuses on the macroeconomic forces at the domestic and international levels but remains mainly theoretical, even if simulations based on calibrations are made. In order to give a more empirical light on global imbalances the Fundamental Equilibrium Exchange Rate (FEER) methodology is used in complementarily. The FEER is defined as the level of exchange rate which allows the economy to reach simultaneously internal and external equilibrium. This approach allows a synthetic estimation of the equilibrium current accounts and of the exchange rate misalignments.

Since the burst of the financial crisis of 2008 several references have been made to Minsky (1986). In the Minskyan framework, the surge in investment during the upswing takes place thanks to an increase in external financing, which leads to the endogenous fragility of firms. The decrease in risk perceived by investors, that is, the reduction of investors' liquidity preference on financial markets, fosters a rising debt share in the firms' balance sheet. But this process ends because of an endogenous reversal of the liquidity preference which corresponds to a reversal of collective opinion in financial markets. As a consequence, credit risk is revised upward, which generates the fall in investment. When investors in financial markets start having doubts about the value of collateral, liquidity preference starts rising and this generates a fall in prices on financial markets. These doubts generate a revaluation of credit risk. Investors run towards liquidity, which thus leads firms to run strong insolvency risks since the refinancing of debt becomes difficult. A complete modelling of Minsky's analysis would be very complex and does not exist. However, we will see how some of the Minskyan mechanisms can be incorporated within the SFC approach.

The closest theoretical takes place via Godley and Lavoie (2007a) and Taylor (2004). Godley and Lavoie have laid the foundations of macroeconomic

SFC modelling. In the same theoretical framework, we pay more attention to empirical results, including econometric ones, and to calibration of the models, especially in the European case. The international dimension is more developed than in Godley and Lavoie's book but this question has been treated more in detail in several other articles (Godley and Lavoie (2007b) for the European case; Lavoie and Daigle (2011) for the introduction of expectations; Lavoie and Zhao (2010) for the treatment of Chinese exchange rate policy). Taylor (2005) is also a founding work. Compared to previous publications by the author, this one focuses more, from the outset, on social accounting matrices with their associate balance sheets and on macroeconomic SFC modelling. But his modelling technique is in continuous time, which has the disadvantage of demanding simplifications (sometimes quite important) in order to carry on the computations. By contrast, our modelling is in discrete time and relies more on simulations to study the properties of the models. In spite of a broad agreement with Taylor, we have one divergence on a specific point, the determination of exchange rates, as it will be developed more in detail.

Hein (2012) is another important reference. It is a systematic study of the finance dominated capitalism and its crises, which provides many stimulating results. However, some points seem debatable. First, most of the models studied in large detail are in a closed economy. This can be considered quite acceptable as a first step, but it can hardly be argued that they are meaningful to discuss international imbalances and coordinated economic policies. Second, the finance dominated economy is formalized in a very simplistic way. There is no price of equities, no difference between productive capital and financial capital or between the economic rate of profit and the financial rate of return. The balance sheet of firms and banks is described in an overly simplistic way. Strangely, there are no financial dynamics in this finance dominated economy. In contrast, we develop more elaborated models, first at the financial level with an analysis of the dynamics of equity prices and of the rate of interest, second at the international level with multi-country models and various exchange rate regimes. Simulations help manage these more complete SFC models.

The main themes of the book are the following. In a first part we will present the basic elements of the methodology used: SFC modelling for a closed economy, multi-country SFC model and FEER approach. At the same time a first look at the operating mode of the finance-led regime and of the world imbalances since the 1990s will be given. Chapter 1 is dedicated to a simple SFC model in a closed economy in order to provide a reference model for the other chapters of the book. Based on the French case, the main stylised facts of the finance-led regime are recalled. Simulations are used to reproduce some of the characteristics of the cycles of the 1990s and 2000s with the price of equities clearing the market. Chapter 2 provides an evaluation of the global imbalances using the notion of FEER. Current imbalances and exchange rate misalignments are estimated since the 1980s for the main countries (the

United States, China, the Eurozone, Japan, the United Kingdom and the rest of the world). The main economic policy guidelines are reviewed within this framework. Chapter 3 analyses macroeconomic adjustments at the world level using a three-country SFC model (the United States, Europe, the rest of the world). This model also serves as a reference model for the other chapters of the book. Different exchange rate regimes are compared and used to analyse the global imbalances since the 1980s: the hybrid dollar standard with fixed dollar–yuan parity and a floating euro, a more elaborated Chinese central bank policy with reserves diversification, various regimes with more flexible dollar–yuan parity.

In a second part we focus on the European challenges. Chapter 4 assesses the European integration since the early blocking of the European Monetary System (EMS) at the beginning of the 1980s. Intra-European exchange rate misalignments are estimated following the FEER approach as they have been a key issue at the time of the EMS, but also within the monetary union. The main drawbacks of the European economic policy from the Single Market program in the 1980s to the launching of the monetary union is given particular attention. The single currency trap since the burst of the financial crisis in 2008 and the reforms undertaken in emergency are analysed. The inconsistency of a monetary union between heterogeneous countries, almost without any adjustment mechanism except wage deflation, are highlighted. The risk of a status quo has led to many alternative proposals which are examined in Chapter 5: fiscal federalism, European unemployment insurance system, eurobonds and public debt mutualisation, enlargement of the European financing in favour of southern countries, European investment programs. Simulations with an SFC model of the monetary union will show that these alternative economic policies could have either an efficient stabilising role (fiscal federalism, investment programs) or a more limited one (European stability mechanism, debt mutualisation). But in most cases, they will appear politically unlikely or hardly feasible. This persistent blocking leads to the discussion of a more radical alternative framework where the possibility of intra-European exchange rate adjustments would be reintroduced thanks to new monetary regimes: a multi-euro system or a euro bancor system. These regimes will be detailed and simulated with a four-country model (north Europe, south Europe, the United States and the rest of the world) in Chapter 6.

In a third part, without analysing all the threats to which is confronted the world economy, we focus on monetary issues. The future of monetary cooperation in East Asia is explored in Chapter 7 using four-country models (China, Japan, East Asia and the rest of the world). A rough description of the East Asian monetary regimes observed in the past is given (dollar-pegged regime, hybrid regime with more flexible East Asian exchange rates and more managed regime for the yuan). In a forward-looking framework, long-term scenarios are discussed: a rather unlikely yuan zone, a yuan block where the yuan–East Asia parity could be managed, Asian Currency Unit (ACU) regimes with various forms of ACU, an Asian bancor regime. In the last chapter, we analyse to which extent a global reform of the international monetary system based on a deepening of the Special Drawing Rights (SDR) could contribute to stabilise the world economy and reduce the large global imbalances. Alternatives will be proposed for the emission criterion of SDRs (with regular or countercyclical emission) and for the distribution criterion of SDRs (according to each country quota or to each country's demand for reserves). A final part concludes.

Part I

Finance-led regime and global imbalances

A first glance

1   A simple finance-led SFC model

Jacques Mazier and Luis Reyes

Introduction

The finance-led growth regime corresponds to the current stage of capitalism. It first settled in the United States and the United Kingdom at the beginning of the 1980s and spread in most of the countries with national specificities (Aglietta, 1998; Boyer, 2000). The main characteristic of this regime is the new corporate governance that prioritizes shareholders and financial accumulation at the expense of productive investment, with a large use of leverage effects. Rising income inequality has come along with these trends. These transformations have generated macroeconomic instability and weak growth despite the recovery of profits high levels. Financial accumulation and increasing inequalities limit domestic demand which can only be sustained by rising indebtedness. This regime is regulated by periodic financial crisis with an instability mainly caused by over-indebtedness and wealth effects. SFC models are well suited to study this growth regime as they analyse the real and financial sides of the economy simultaneously, taking into account the balance sheet constraints and revaluation effects.

This chapter, based on Mazier and Reyes (2014), presents a simple SFC model for a closed economy. First, we describe the stylised facts for France which is a representative country of the finance-led growth regime. Second, we give account of the most relevant works on SFC models and their ability to describe the real and financial cycles, with a discussion on firms' closure either via debt or by new issuance of equities. Third, the model is presented rather in detail, given that the same structure is used in the other chapters of the book. Fourth, the dynamics of the model are studied with the help of simulations and shocks on the real and financial sides. Their capacity to take into account financial cycles and over-indebtedness, typical of the finance-led growth, may thus be analysed.

Stylised facts

Liberal reforms implemented in the decade of the 1980s and 1990s have had major consequences in the way economies behave today, both at a national level and world-wide. National economies have suffered a drastic transformation in the capital structure of the non-financial sector, largely increasing their dependence on financial instruments which, instead of boosting investment, have generated slow growth. Income distribution has evolved in favour of capital owners at the expense of workers, leading to rising inequality, which has further contributed to the slowdown of economic activity via depressed purchasing power of workers. Indeed, globalisation has played an increasingly important role in this process. Nevertheless, in the remaining of this chapter we focus on a closed economy, leaving the aspects of an open economy for further chapters. We want to highlight the way non-financial companies accumulate capital and are financed, proposing a model which takes into account their most important liabilities explicitly, with the price of equity determined explicitly in the model.

The following figures are for France, which is a good example of a financialized economy. We consider that, beyond national specificities, the overall trend is similar in other major advanced economies. Table 1.1 shows the main variables of a simplified balance sheet for non-financial companies.

Figure 1.1 shows two definitions of the rate of capital accumulation of non-financial companies. The first is the usual rate of accumulation $\Delta K/K_{-1}$ (K stands for fixed capital at constant prices, $\Delta K = K - K_{-1}$) which follows a cyclical path with four peaks (1980, 1990, 2000, and 2007). Following each recession, the recovery was limited (4% in 1990, 3% in 2000 and 2007) and did no last until the fall of 2009. Since the crisis of the 1970s and early 1980s the French economy has not succeeded in building a sustained growth regime. The second definition is the financial rate of accumulation $\Delta Ee/Ee_{-1}$ (Ee stands for equities held) which exhibits financial cycles. However, unlike the previous variable, during the 1990s the recovery of the rate of financial rate of accumulation has been much stronger, reaching 8% in 2000. After the fall of 2002 the recovery was also significant. In 2008 the rate of financial accumulation was still close to 6% just before the crisis and shows a sharp decline afterwards. This opposite comovement of the two rates of accumulation, financial and non-financial, is a

Table 1.1 Non-financial companies' balance sheet

	Assets	*Liabilities*
Fixed capital	*pk K*	
Land	*pl Kl*	
Total capital	*pkt Ktot*	
Loans		*L*
Equities	*pe Ee*	*pe E*
Net wealth		*Ve*

Source: Authors' construction.

Notes:
pk K: fixed capital (produced non-financial assets).
pl Kl: land (non-produced non-financial assets).
pkt Ktot: total capital (total non-financial assets).

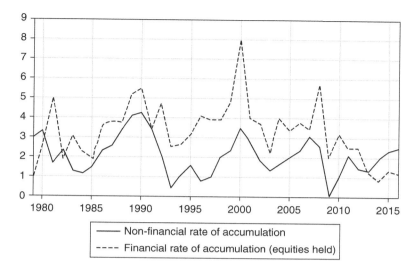

Figure 1.1 Firms' financial ($\Delta Ee/Ee_{-1}$) and non-financial rate of accumulation ($\Delta K/K_{-1}$), %.

Source: Own calculations based on data from *INSEE*'s *Comptes de Patrimoine* (non-financial accumulation) and *Banque de France*'s *Comptes Financiers* (financial accumulation).

first illustration of the finance-led growth regime that has settled since the end of the 1980s.

The analysis of the profit rate, measured as the ratio of gross operating surplus to the stock of productive capital ($Pro/pk\ K_{-1}$), provides further evidence (Figure 1.2). After the deep blow suffered due to the crisis of the late 1970s the profit rate was restored at the end of the 1980s and remained at a rather high and stable level until 2008. Despite the fragility of the comparison, this level was close to what had been observed during the 1960s, the period of high growth in France (Mazier et al., 2016, p. 53). Contrary to what is expected, this recovery of profitability did not lead to a permanent recovery of the non-financial rate of accumulation.

This kind of temporary disconnection can be considered as another piece of evidence of the financial growth regime, where financial accumulation is preferred over the productive one. Two factors have contributed to this upswing in the rate of profit. The first one is the improvement of the productivity of capital measured in constant prices (Y/K_{-1}) which increased consistently until 2007, and reflects a rather good efficiency in the accumulation process (the dashed line in Figure 1.2). Growth in capital productivity at current prices ($pY/pk\ K_{-1}$) has been more modest, and has even slightly declined since the 2000, thanks in part to the relative price effect (p/pk). The second and main factor explaining the restoration of the rate of profit has been the sharp decrease of the labour share during the 1980s and its stabilization around a rather low level afterwards.

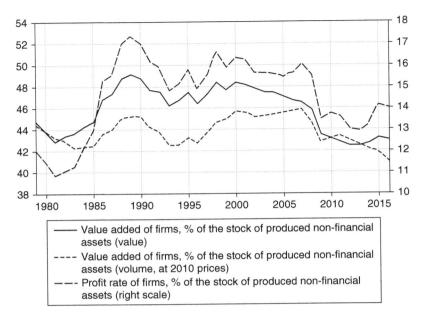

Figure 1.2 Profit rate (*Pro/pk K₋₁*) and productivity of capital★ at constant (*Y/K₋₁*) and current prices (*pY/pk K₋₁*) of non-financial firms, %.

★ capital = produced non-financial assets excluding changes in inventories

Source: Own calculations based on data from *INSEE*'s *Comptes d'agents détaillés* (operating surplus) and *INSEE*'s *Comptes de Patrimoine* (non-financial assets).

This evolution is well documented and reflects the new forms of the wage nexus which characterizes the growth regime since the late 1980s under the domination of shareholders and the pressure of the international competition (in a nutshell, more labour market flexibility).

Another measure of the profit rate for non-financial firms can be obtained using a broader concept of capital including land (*Ktot*, total capital, including non-produced capital in national accounts jargon). The results are significantly different (Figure 1.3). Unsurprisingly, the level is smaller as the definition of the capital is larger (*Pro/pkt Ktot₋₁*). Starting from a relatively low level in the early 1980s a recovery is observed by the end of the decade, although less important than with the profitability indicator mentioned above. The main difference stands out after the 2000 peak, when a sharp fall takes place that is not present in Figure 1.2. The origin of this decline is clearly the evolution of the relative prices (*p/pkt*), as it is shown by the fall in total capital productivity, measured at current prices (*pY/pkt Ktot₋₁*). As a consequence of this, the profit rate level in 2007 was already weak. This lacklustre profitability appears, beside the financial factors often mentioned, as a key determinant of the crisis that burst in 2008. After the euro zone crisis, the economic situation

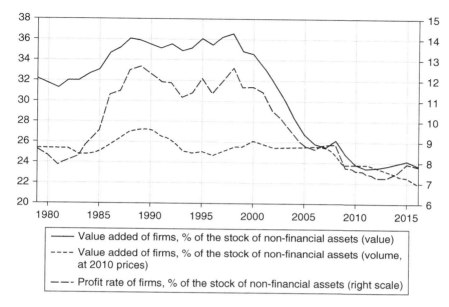

Figure 1.3 Profit rate (*Pro/pkt Ktot₋₁*) and productivity of total capital★ at constant ($Y/\ Ktot_{-1}$) and current prices (*pY/pkt Ktot₋₁*) of non-financial firms, %.

★ total capital = sum of produced and non-produced non-financial assets + changes in inventories

Source: Own calculations based on data from *INSEE's Comptes d'agents détaillés* (operating surplus) and *INSEE's Comptes de Patrimoine* (non-financial assets).

of non-financial firms was even worse than before, with a profit rate below the already low levels observed in the early 1980s. The dynamics of relative prices are in turn explained as a consequence of the boom in property prices (p_j) that started at the beginning of the 2000s and has been fuelled by the credit boom and financial liberalisation. From that perspective, the 2007 profitability crisis has a financial origin.

We now turn to the rate financial of return, which we consider a major driver of financial accumulation. The latter is defined as the sum of distributed dividends and capital gains divided by the stock of equities issued the previous period ($re = (Div + E_{-1}\ \Delta pe)/pe_{-1}E_{-1} = Div\ /\ pe_{-1}E_{-1} + \Delta pe/pe_{-1}$). In Figure 1.4, the rate of financial return is measured in real terms ($re - \Delta p/p_{-1}$), deflated by the GDP deflator, in order to provide a neater comparison with the economic profit rate previously examined. The series exhibit a cyclical pattern with large ups and downs. The peaks in 1986, 1999 and 2006 reached unusually high levels (around 40%, 60%, and 20% respectively). On average, the rate of financial return has been around 20% during the 1980–2007 period, far above the economic rate of profit. As is shown in Figure 1.4, the rate of growth of the equity price ($\Delta pe/pe_{-1}$) is the main determinant of the financial rate of return.

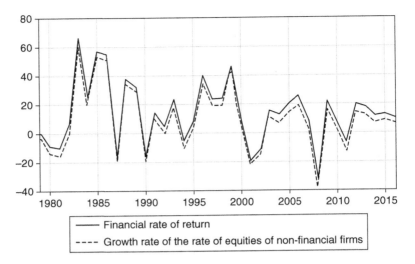

Figure 1.4 Financial rate of return in real terms ($re - \Delta p/p_{-1}$) and growth rate of the price of equities of non–financial firms ($\Delta pe/pe_{-1}$), %.

$re = Div \ / \ pe_{-1}E_{-1} + \Delta pe/pe_{-1}$

Source: Own calculations based on data from *Banque de France's Comptes Financiers*.

This is consistent with the great attention paid to the evolution of equity price by shareholders and the firms' management.

Financial markets are regulated by periodic financial crises which eliminate or reduce previous imbalances and eventually lead to a revival. This is illustrated in Figure 1.5, which shows the level of French equity price index (*pe*, base 100 in 2000). The cyclical pattern is visible with a growing scale of the fluctuations since the first (rather 'modest') stock market crashes of 1987 and 1991. The figure also exhibits the evolution of the Standard and Poor's stock price index for the main 500 firms based in the United States. The figure illustrates the strong interdependency that exists at the world level across financial markets. Rey (2018) highlighted the existence of '*a global financial cycle in capital flows, asset prices and credit growth*'. However, this question is debated and national specificities persist. For instance, it is clear from the graphs that the boom in the French stock market is lagging behind that of the United States since 2009, which in part reflects the effects of the euro zone crisis that explains a limited recovery. The Japanese case appears also very specific since the Nikkei index has only partially recovered since the crash of 1991.

Firms' indebtedness has played a major role in the financialization process. Nevertheless, a mixed assessment can be provided, depending on the definition used for the debt ratio. Measured as percentage of the fixed capital stock, the debt ratio (*L/pk K*) has increased in three waves at the end of the

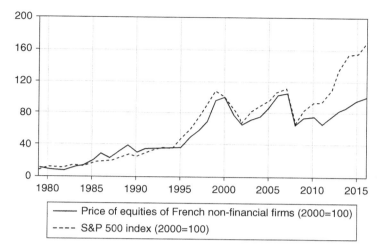

Figure 1.5 Price of equities of French non-financial firms (*pe*) and S&P 500 index, 2000 = 100.

Source: Own calculations based on data from *Banque de France's Comptes Financiers* (French equity prices) and Robert Shiller's 'Irrational Exuberance' (S&P 500).

1980s, 1990s and 2000s (Figure 1.6). This increase in leverage can be linked to the recovery of the accumulation rate during the first two periods and to the declining real interest rate since the mid-1990s. Financial liberalisation, coupled with a reduced cost of credit, has encouraged firms' indebtedness. Nevertheless, if we use a larger definition of capital, which includes land (i.e. non-produced capital), the result is quite different. Like the previous ratio, the debt ratio measured with total capital ($L/pkt\ Ktot$) increased significantly until 2001. Since then, however, with the property price boom fuelled by financial liberalisation and despite the credit cheapness, it has declined sharply. It is thus clear that over-indebtedness has been masked by the large valuation of total fixed capital.

An even stronger conclusion can be reached when the firms' debt ratio is expressed as a percentage of own funds ($L/\ peE + Ve$, with *peE* stands for issued equities, *Ve* for firms' net wealth and *peE + Ve* are own funds). This alternative debt ratio has fallen significantly in three successive waves, first in the second half of the 1980s (in the context of profit restoration), then at the end of the 1990s with the stock market boom, and last during the 2000s before 2008 crisis (dashed line with circles in Figure 1.6). The boom in the price of equity plays a major role in these reductions of leverage, which raises thanks to the valuation of own funds, which mechanically reduces the denominator of the debt ratio. Despite this fall in leverage, firms can be threatened by over-indebtedness in the case of a stock market's reversal, as it has been observed in 1991, 2001 and 2008.

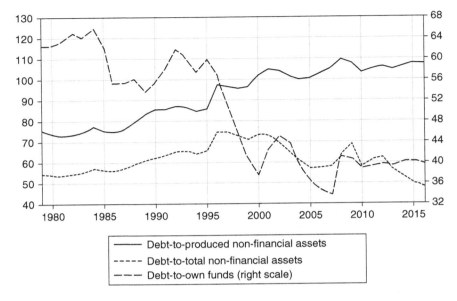

Figure 1.6 Debt ratios of non-financial firms (%).
Debt-to-produced non-financial assets (($L/pk\ K$).
Debt-to-total non-financial assets ($L/pkt\ Ktot$).
Debt-to-own funds ($L/\ peE + Ve$).
Source: Own calculations based on data from *INSEE*'s *Comptes de Patrimoine* (non-financial assets) and *Banque de France*'s *Comptes Financiers* (debt and own funds).

Koo (2008) explains that, following a bubble burst, firms' balance sheets are most likely underwater. Firms may not want banks to know this (because their credit ratings are in jeopardy), and banks may even want to pay a blind eye to the issue (because otherwise they will be exposed as conceding nonperforming loans). This dangerous combination (falling equity prices, falling credit demand, low interest rates, falling profit rates) may generate a balance sheet recession after the bubble burst.

Interest rates have met a major rupture in 1979 following the change in the orientation of monetary policy, and the financial authorities' will to ensure a better remuneration for lenders. In spite of the progressive fall in nominal interest rates, along with the taming of inflation, real interest rates remained high in France until the first half of the 1990s, in part because of existing tensions within the European Monetary System. The decline of real interest rates appeared only in the second half of the 1990s (Figure 1.7). Apart from observed long-term interest rates, the apparent (or implicit) interest rate (computed as interests paid divided by the stock of debt from the previous period) provides an alternative measure of the cost of debt for non-financial

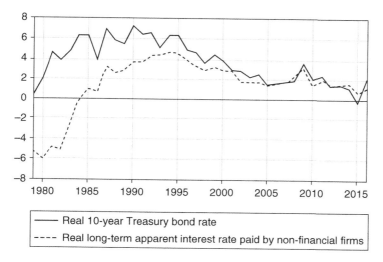

Figure 1.7 Real 10-year Treasury-bond rate and real long-term apparent interest rate paid by non-financial firms deflated by GDP price, %.

Source: Own calculations based on data from *Banque de France* (Treasury-bond rate), INSEE's *Comptes d'agents détaillés* (interest payments) and *Banque de France's Comptes Financiers* (stock of debt).

firms. Its evolution is slightly different. Its initial rise is more progressive, but the apparent rate remains persistently higher. This movement in the real cost of credit has had a significant impact on firms' financial behaviour, pushing them to limit their indebtedness during the first part of the period and to issue new equities in larger quantities.

To sum up, since the end of the 1980s the finance-led growth regime in France can be characterized by several specific features: a limited recovery of non-financial accumulation in spite of the restoration of the rate of profit, coupled with an important fall in the labour share during the 1980s; a less favourable evolution of profitability when a broader notion of total capital (which includes land) is used, with a sharp fall during the 2000s due to the boom of the property prices fuelled by the credit boom and financial liberal-isation; a more sustained growth of the rate of financial accumulation following financial cycles since the 1980s (with the financial rate of return as the main driver); an increasing indebtedness of the firms masked by revaluation effects (property price and equity price bubbles), which do not prevent the risk of over-indebtedness in case of a reversal in financial markets. In order to describe this regime where financial markets are regulated by periodic financial crisis, it seems appropriate to use an SFC model linking the real and financial sides of the economy with a thorough description of assets and liabilities.

SFC models and financial cycles

One of the first attempts to empirically deal with financial phenomena and their interaction with the real economy in a macroeconomic perspective, combining stocks and flows rather than dealing with one at the time, was that of Brainard and Tobin (1968), then extended by Tobin (1969). This approach did not make its way to current mainstream economics mainly because it lacked micro foundations, which explained the mechanism by which agents allocated their financial resources. Some years later, Godley and Cripps (1983) at the University of Cambridge took over SFC models. They highlighted the fact that monetary stocks and flows satisfy accounting identities provide a fundamental macroeconomic law. Thanks in part to the ease of access to computational techniques, they gave more realism to their models. Godley (1999) developed this approach at the Levy Institute during the 1990s and created the Levy Macroeconomic Model of the US economy based on the SFC approach. A fruitful collaboration with Lavoie led to more comprehensive models (Lavoie and Godley, 2001; Godley and Lavoie, 2007a, with their book *Monetary Economics*). Instead of a general equilibrium approach, these authors aimed at explaining endogenously created disequilibrium without optimizing behaviour from economic agents. SFC models consist of systems of simultaneous equations which combine stocks (of debt, capital or deposits) with flows (of production, income or assets) using a national accounting framework. Taking into account the fact that all forms of wealth, including capital gains and valuation effects, in an economy come from somewhere and go somewhere, these models have an advantage above other techniques and are well suited to study a finance-led growth regime.

Minsky's analysis can be partly integrated in this framework. Two attempts by Keen and Taylor are worth mentioning although they are rather unconvincing. Keen (1995) has enlarged Goodwin's (1967) model by introducing two stylised facts: an investment function depending of the rate of profit and an interest rate which varies with the debt-to-output ratio, reflecting an increasing risk premium. The model generates both cycles (with low interest rates) and a trend of rising debt, leading to a debt-induced crash. Keen presents his model as an illustration of Minsky's hypothesis. This is rather strange, given that the model is completely supply-side and the cycles are driven by capital accumulation with a fully constrained households' consumption. Thus, there is no demand analysis. This bizarre approach for a Minskyan model remains in recent works where a more complete banking sector is introduced (Keen, 2013) or where the national income identity is abandoned and replaced by a 'new relation' claiming that effective demand is equal to income plus the change in debt (Keen, 2014).

In the same vein, Taylor (2012) introduces asset prices and financial cycles in a Harrod-style growth model. A first attempt is based on a highly simplified hypothesis whereby there is a constant rate of return on equity, which allows a simple determination of the growth rate of the equity price, incorporating a positive feedback of the equity price itself. This basic assumption, however, is unrealistic, to say the least. In a second step, Taylor tried to formalize a Minsky-style model with an investment demand function and loan determined by the firms' flow of funds but asset prices are no longer studied in this new model.

By way of contrast, in the SFC approach, thanks to the complete description of the balance sheets of each agent and of the associated flows of funds, the most relevant macroeconomic relations can be incorporated in a consistent way for analysing financial and non-financial dynamics: relations between capital accumulation and income distribution, wealth effects (especially for rentiers), revaluation effects (due to capital gains or losses) and a debt-led growth regime. Godley and Lavoie (2007a) use computer simulations to study the macro-dynamics which seem more powerful in some respect than analytical tools used by Taylor (2004) in *Reconstructing Macroeconomics* and Dos Santos and Zezza (2008). Beyond this methodological divergence, the models differ in the way they deal with debt and equity issuing.

Godley, Lavoie, Dos Santos, and Zezza, as well as Taylor in some of his models, postulate an equation describing new issuance of equities as a share of investment demand. As a consequence, credit demand by firms is simply determined as a residual of the firms' flows of funds. Alternatively, Taylor (2004) in two other versions of his model, maintains an explicit credit demand by firms equation with new issuance of equities determined as a residual of the firms' budget constraint. The treatment of these items is not usually discussed in the SFC literature. However, the trade-off between debt, new issuance of equities and retained earnings (all of which finance investment), is important in the growth regime that has prevailed since the 1990s. The relation between new issuance of equities and investment seems rather unstable and has limited empirical foundations. In practice, the parameter linking these two variables is often negative, in part due to share buybacks. It seems more fruitful to keep a traditional firms' credit demand equation which can also be interpreted as an indebtedness norm.

Another important (and often ignored) issue is the place devoted to financial accumulation in SFC models. Despite the fact that equities held by firms have played an increasingly important role in the finance-led growth regime, they are seldom explicitly described in these models. In our view, it is necessary to analyse the existing arbitrage between financial and non-financial accumulation and the impact of the financial rate of return.

Under this perspective, and taking stock of the discussion, we propose a simplified SFC framework, outlined later in this chapter. The firms' balance sheet includes equities held on the asset side with an explicit financial accumulation behaviour related to the rate of return on equities. This financial rate of return also has a negative impact on investment as firms arbitrate in favour of financial accumulation. Credit demand is analysed separately as a specific relation with the usual negative effect of interest rate in it, but also with a positive impact of the rate of return on equities, as higher financial profitability induces firms to get more indebted. Lastly, new issuances of equity are obtained as a residual of the firms' flows of funds. Since this approach includes explicitly the firms' balance sheet and loan demand, it is of potential use to integrate the analysis made by Koo (2008, 2015) on balance sheet recession. The following section describes the model that we propose.

The model

We assume there are five sectors in the economy: households, non-financial firms, the government, private banks and a Central Bank. Some important elements (dwellings, households' debt, evolution of wages and prices) have been omitted for simplification. The price level (of production) is assumed to be constant across all periods. The approach is limited to a closed economy as the questions of trade openness and capital movements are examined in other chapters. There are no supply effects and the economy is driven by final demand (investment, consumption, public spending). The finance-led feature comes from the role played by the rate of return on equity and its impact on financial accumulation, debt and real investment. The price of equities is determined by a market-clearing mechanism between supply of equities (by firms) and demand for them (from firms and households).

Table 1.2 gives the structure of the balance sheet for the five sectors. The last row of the table is the net wealth of each institutional sector. As liabilities are presented with a minus sign and the total must be zero, each sector's net wealth is also shown with a minus sign. The net wealth held by households $(-Vh)$ is made up of cash (Hh), bank deposits (BD), bonds $(pb{\star}B$, where pb is their price) and equities $(pe{\star}Eh$, with pe their price and Eh the amount they hold). In the same vein firms contract debts $(-L)$ and issue equities $(-pe{\star}E$ with pe for equity price) in order to finance non-financial capital (K) and financial capital $(pe{\star}Ee$, equities held). They hold a net wealth $(-Ve)$.

The government issues bonds $(-pb{\star}B)$ held by households and Treasury bills $(-BT)$ held by private banks. The net wealth of the government $(-Vg)$

Table 1.2 A simplified balance sheet for a closed economy

	Households	Firms	Government	Banks	Central Bank
Capital		K			
Money	Hh			Hb	$-H$
Deposits	BD			$-BD$	
Loans		$-L$		L	
Bonds	$pb{\star}B$		$-pb{\star}B$		
Equities	$pe{\star}Eh$	$pe{\star}Ee$			
		$-pe{\star}E$			
Bills			$-BT$	BT	
Refinancing				$-RF$	RF
Net wealth	$-Vh$	$-Ve$	$-Vg$	$-Vb$	

Source: Authors' construction.

is the opposite of the total government debt which is the sum of the last two terms. Private banks make loans to firms ($-L$), buy Treasury bills (BT) and hold reserves at the Central bank (Hb). They receive deposits from the households (BD) and get refinanced by the Central Bank ($-RF$). Their net wealth is $-Vb$. Last, the Central Bank issues the cash ($-H$) and refinances the banks without restriction (RF). It holds no wealth.

Turning now to the real (i.e. non-financial) side of the economy, the first equation of the model is the equilibrium of goods and services. As we assume a closed economy, the gross domestic product (Y, which stands for GDP) is equal to the sum of consumption (C), investment (I) and government spending (G).

$$Y = C + I + G \tag{1}$$

Households' behaviour

Disposable income (YDh) is the sum of wages (W), interests on bank deposits ($id{\star}BD_{-1}$) and on bonds (B_{-1}) one period before, and dividends ($DIVh$) net of taxes (T). The Haig-Simons definition of income is the sum of disposable income and households' capital gains (CGh). Taxes are a proportion (θ) of gross disposable income. The consumption function (eq. (5)) depends on the Haig-Simons definition of income with a marginal propensity to consume a_1 and a lagged 'wealth effect' a_2. In the long run, the ratio wealth to income is constant and equal to $1 - a_1/a_2$.

$$Ydh = W + id{\star}BD_{-1} + B_{-1} + DIVh - T \tag{2}$$

$$YHSh = YDh + CGh \tag{3}$$

$$T = \theta{\star}(W + id{\star}BD - 1 + B - 1 + DIVh) \tag{4}$$

$$C = a_0 + a_1{\star}YHSh + a_2{\star}Vh_{-1} \tag{5}$$

Following Godley and Lavoie (2007a), households are supposed to share their wealth Vh between bonds ($pb{\star}B$), deposits (BD), and equities ($pe{\star}Eh$) in relation with the relative rate of return of the assets, the interest rate on bonds (rb), the interest rate on deposits (id) and the rate of return on issued equities (re) (eq. (6) and (7)). The cash held by households is a fixed proportion (λ_0) of consumption (eq. (8)). The change in the stock of bank deposits is calculated as a residual of other forms of incoming wealth (eq. (9)). Households' capital gains are defined as the revaluation effects of bonds and equities, respectively. Total households' wealth is the sum of assets.

$$pb{\star}B = Vh{\star}(v0 + v1{\star}rb - v2{\star}id - v3{\star}re) \tag{6}$$

$$pe{\star}Eh = Vh{\star}(w0 - w1{\star}rb - w2{\star}id + w3{\star}re) \tag{7}$$

$$Hh = \lambda_0 \star C \tag{8}$$

$$\Delta BD = YDh - C - pb \star \Delta B - pe \star \Delta Eh - \Delta Hh \tag{9}$$

$$CGh = B_{-1} \star \Delta pb + Eh_{-1} \star \Delta pe \tag{10}$$

$$Vh = BD + pb \star B + pe \star Eh + Hh \tag{11}$$

Firms' behaviour

Following a Kaleckian framework, the investment function (eq. (12)) is assumed to depend positively on the lagged profit rate $(UP/K_{-1})_{-1}$ and the growth rate of the economy $(\Delta Y/Y_{-1})$ with k_2 being the accelerator effect. This element might be replaced by a rate of capacity utilization. Capital accumulation depends negatively on the debt ratio $(L/K)_{-1}$, given the increasing risk effect as debt grows above the stock of capital. The interest rate on loans (rl) has also a traditional negative impact. δ is the depreciation rate of capital.

Finally, in order to take into account the finance-led regime, we introduce an indicator of financial profitability, the financial rate of return on equities held (ree), with a negative impact on accumulation, reflecting an arbitrage between real and financial accumulation. Higher financial profitability induces more financial investment at the expense of productive investment. This question is highly debated. Other authors have preferred to introduce a valuation ratio or Tobin's q ratio with a positive effect (Lavoie and Godley, 2001), but empirical results appeared fragile. Stockhammer (2004) proposed an investment function with a negative financialization effect captured by the ratio of interest and dividend income in the firms' value added. Von Treek (2008) estimated a long-run relationship of investment which included the net payments of dividends by firms, in percent of the capital stock, as a proxy of the degree of shareholder value orientation with a negative impact. Although interesting, these indicators ignore the capital gains (or losses) which play a major role in the finance-led regime. Nor do they take into account the problems of financial profitability and of financial assets. The introduction of the rate of return on equity as a direct determination of investment seems a more straightforward way. Some empirical results have been obtained in this direction (Clévenot et al., 2010).

$$g = k_0 + k_1 \star (UP/K - 1)_{-1} + k_2 \star (\Delta Y/Y - 1) - k_3 \star L/K)_{-1} - k_4 \star rl - k_5 \star ree \tag{12}$$

$$I = g \star K_{-1} \tag{13}$$

$$\Delta K = I - \delta K_{-1} \tag{14}$$

Financial accumulation, in spite of its importance, is little analysed in the literature. This is understandable because of the hybrid nature of financial assets, especially equities held by firms. The rise of financial assets reflects new behaviour by firms since the 1980s, crystallized around mergers and acquisitions, taking financial stakes in support of domestic or foreign activities and share buy backs to preserve control or increase share prices. At the macroeconomic level, financial accumulation might either be described via the share of the value of equities held by firms out of their total capital, real and financial ($pe{\star}Ee/(K + pe{\star}Ee)$, eq. (15)), or as the rate of financial accumulation ($pe\Delta Ee/(peEe)_{-1}$, eq. (15bis)). It is assumed a linear function of the rate of return on equities held (*ree*), as higher expectations of financial profitability induce greater accumulation of financial assets. Second, the profit rate (UP/K_{-1}), which reflects the firms' global performance, exerts a positive influence on their financial accumulation. The debt ratio (L/K) also has a positive influence on financial accumulation, given that leverage effects favour financial accumulation, in contrast with the negative impact of higher risk on real investment. Some empirical results can be found in Clévenot et al. (2010).

$$pe{\star}Ee = (K + pe{\star}Ee){\star}(f_0 + f_1{\star}ree + f_2{\star}(UP/K{-}1)) \tag{15}$$

$$pe\Delta Ee/(peEe)_{-1} = f_0 + f_1{\star}ree + f_2{\star}(UP/K{-}1) + f_3{\star}(L/K)_{-1} \tag{15bis}$$

The closure of the model is obtained by a loan demand by firms which works as an indebtedness norm. This approach seems the most appropriate way to analyse how firms finance their real and financial investment with an arbitrage between external funds (loan) and internal funds (undistributed profit and issuance of equities). The debt ratio (L/K) depends positively on the rate of profit (as higher profitability makes it easier to borrow from banks), on the rate of return on equities (as higher financial profitability induces firms to borrow more) and, lastly, as usual, negatively on the rate of interest (eq. (16)). The amount of new issue of equities ($pe{\star}\Delta E$) is simply deducted from the firms' flow of funds (eq. (17)).

$$L/K = g_0 + g_1{\star}(UP{-}1/K{-}1) + g_2{\star}re_{-1} - g_3{\star}rl \tag{16}$$

$$pe{\star}\Delta E = I + pe{\star}\Delta Ee - UP - \Delta L \tag{17}$$

The rest of the firms' behaviour is written in a traditional way. Undistributed profits (UP) are the difference between GDP (Y) and costs (wages, interest payments as well as dividends paid to households). Wages (W) are a constant (r_0) share of GDP. Dividends are calculated (as in Lavoie and Godley, 2001) as a proportion ($1 - sf$) (where sf is the firms' saving rate) of profits realized the previous period (eq. (22)). Dividends paid to firms ($DIVe$) are derived from the total dividends as the share of equities held by firms out of total equities issued in the previous period (Ee_{-1}/E_{-1}). Dividends paid to households are calculated as a residual, as well as the amount of equities they hold. The rate of return of equities issued (*re*), which is a key variable in the model, is equal to firms' capital gains (*CGe*) plus the distributed dividends out of total equities previously issued. The rate of return of equities held (*ree*) is calculated in the same way. The growth rate of the price of equities $(\Delta pe/pe_{-1})$ appears as the main driver of the rate of return on equities (see Figure 1.2). Firms' capital gains (*CGe* and *CGee*) come from changes in the price of equities multiplied by the stock of equities previously issued or held (revaluation effect). The outstanding amount of wealth held by firms is defined through the balance sheet.

$$UP = Y - W - rl \star L_{-1} - DIVh \tag{18}$$

$$W = r_0 \star Y \tag{19}$$

$$re = (CGe + DIV)/(pe \star E)_{-1} \tag{20}$$

$$ree = (CGee + DIVe)/(pe \star Ee)_{-1} \tag{21}$$

$$DIV = (1 - sf) \star (Y_{-1} - W_{-1} - rl\text{-}1 \star L_{-2}) \tag{22}$$

$$DIVe = DIV \star (Ee_{-1}/E_{-1}) \tag{23}$$

$$DIVh = DIV - DIVe \tag{24}$$

$$Eh = E - Ee \tag{25}$$

$$CGe = E_{-1} \star \Delta pe \tag{26}$$

$$CGee = Ee_{-1} \star \Delta pe \tag{27}$$

$$Ve = K + pe \star Ee - L - pe \star E \tag{28}$$

Government

Treasury bills (ΔBT) newly issued by the government are a residual of its expenditures, on current spending (*G*), interests on its long and short-term debt, and its revenues, from taxes on personal income (*T*), taxes on banks (*TB*) and taxes on the Central Bank (*TCB*) and from newly issued bonds ($pb \star \Delta B$). The price of bonds is assumed to vary inversely with respect to the interest rate paid, which is supposed to be equal to interest rate on bills (short-run). The total wealth held by the government is equal to its debt with a minus sign.

$$\Delta BT = G + r \star BT_{-1} + B_{-1} - T - TB - TCB - pb \star \Delta B \tag{29}$$

$$pb = 1/rb \tag{30}$$

$$Vg = -D = -BT - pb \star B \tag{31}$$

Banking sector

Private banks receive deposits from households (ΔBD). They grant loans to firms (ΔL) and buy Treasury bills (ΔBT) to the government without restriction. This hypothesis is made for the sake of simplification. A more elaborated model of the banking sector with credit rationing can be found in Le Heron and Mouakil (2008). Banks hold mandatory reserves (ΔHb) as a fixed proportion (λ) of bank deposits (eq. (35)). They make profits (BP) and pay taxes (TB) out of their income. The latter is made up of interests on loans to non-financial firms and to the government minus interest paid on deposits and refinancing from the Central Bank. θ_b is the tax rate they pay. Banks' refinancing (ΔRF) balances their flow of funds (eq. (34)). This refinancing is granted without restriction by the Central Bank. The change in the wealth held by banks (ΔVb) is equal to their profits.

$$BP = (1 - \theta b)\star(rl\star L_{-1} + r\star BT_{-1} - id\star BD_{-1} - ib\star RF_{-1}) \tag{32}$$

$$TB = \theta_b\star(rl\star L_{-1} + r\star BT_{-1} - id\star BD_{-1} - ib\star RF_{-1}) \tag{33}$$

$$\Delta RF = \Delta Hb + \Delta L + \Delta BT - BP - \Delta BD \tag{34}$$

$$Hb = \lambda\star BD \tag{35}$$

$$\Delta Vb = BP \tag{36}$$

The Central Bank receives interests from private banks out of previous refinancing and transfers them as taxes to the government (TCB). As a consequence, the Central Bank makes no profit and its net wealth remains constant, equal to zero. Total high-powered-money (H) is the sum of cash held by households and reserves made by commercial banks. The interest rate on loans (rl) is assumed higher than the short-term interest rate controlled by the Central Bank (ib) and supposed exogenous. Inversely, the interest rate on deposits (id) is supposed at a lower level that the latter, which is at the origin of banks' profit. The interest rate on Treasury bills (r) is assumed to be equal to the interest rate on loans (rl) and to the yield on long-term bonds (rb).

$$TCB = ib\star RF_{-1} \tag{37}$$

$$H = Hh + Hb \tag{38}$$

$$rl = ib + m_1b \tag{39}$$

$$id = ib - m_2b \tag{40}$$

$$r = rl \tag{41}$$

$$rb = r \tag{42}$$

On the whole, we have the same number of equations as unknowns, with two exogenous variables, *ib* the short-term interest rate controlled by the Central Bank and *G* the public expenditures. The Central Bank's equilibrium (*H= RF*) is the unwritten equation of the model which results from all the other accounting relations. It is used to check the accounting consistency of the model.

Last, the sum of all wealth held by all the economic agents equals the capital stock *K*. The economic interpretation is simple. Only fixed capital accumulation creates wealth. Financial accumulation creates no wealth as any financial asset has its counterpart in the liability side.

$$Vh + Ve + Vg + Vb = BD + pb \star B + pe \star Eh + Hh + K + pe \star Ee - L - pe \star$$
$$E - BT - pb \star B + Hb + L + BT - BD - RF$$

(43)

$$Vh + Ve + Vg + Vb = K \tag{44}$$

The operating mode of the model

The model is driven by final demand (consumption, investment, public expenditures) without supply effect. The finance-led nature of the growth regime comes from the role played by the rate of return on equities and its impact on financial accumulation, debt and fixed investment. In order to illustrate the causal mechanism of the model, let us begin by assuming a rise in the rate of financial return. This stimulates financial accumulation and equities' demand by households. On the other hand, higher financial profitability induces firms to borrow more, thus increasing their indebtedness. The latter further sustains financial accumulation through the leverage effect. By way of contrast, fixed capital accumulation suffers a slowdown via the negative impact of two factors: the rise in the rate of return on equities (as firms prefer financial accumulation) and the increasing debt ratio (which reflects increasing risk appetite). The contrast between booming financial accumulation and the half-baked recovery of fixed capital accumulation has been a common feature of the 1990s and 2000s in several industrialized countries.

In this ascending phase of the financial cycle, the main stabilizing mechanism is the likely issue of new equities ($pe \star \Delta E = I + pe \star \Delta E - UP - \Delta L$) induced by the constraints on firms' flow of funds and which contributes to limit the increase in, equity prices. In the model's solution, the price of equity is determined implicitly by the adjustment between equities' demand and supply ($pe = (peEh + peEe)/(E_{-1} + \Delta E)$). This leads to a fall in the financial rate of return, which in turn limits financial accumulation and reinforces the adjustment mechanism. In contrast, if no new equities are issued, the increase in the price of equity is further enhanced and the financial boom strengthened. Another feedback of the financial sphere on the real sector is via capital gains on households' income and consumption. Overall, depending on the circumstances, the model describes how the process can end with an endogenous reversal and generate a financial cycle. But it may not be always the case if the stabilizing mechanisms are insufficient, leading to a lasting financial bubble. Last, a restrictive monetary policy may contribute to stabilize the system. An increase in interest rates imposes a halt to financial accumulation as indebtedness is reduced. The overall effect on fixed investment and growth is negative due to the rising cost of credit, which also contributes to limit the dynamics of the financial sphere as the demand for equity is reduced.

The model focuses mainly on the relations between firms' behaviour and finance, which is a key link of a finance-led growth regime. It clearly provides only a simplified representation of households, since it ignores their debt and investment in housing, which has played an important role in the financial crisis of 2008 in several countries. Households' portfolio behaviour would also have to be adapted with two types of households, according to the level of their wealth and income. The behaviour of banks is also highly simplified and does not reflect their active role in the economy, neither in financial accumulation nor in financialization. Despite these simplifications, the model remains rather comprehensive and allows us to take into account some of the main features of the real and financial accumulation.

Simulations

A set of simulations of the model is proposed to provide a better understanding of how it works. Calibration has been loosely based on French national accounts in stock and flows for 2009. For firms' equations the corresponding parameters are taken from Clévenot et al. (2010, 2012). The value of the parameters is given in the appendix. A baseline scenario is built and we simulate four shocks which are representative of some of the main features of the finance-led regime of the 1990s and 2000s: a decrease in the labour share, an increase of the financial accumulation rate, an increase of the firms' debt ratio and an increase of the households' demand of equities. The effects of these shocks are analysed graphically, as compared to the baseline scenario, for the following variables: production (Y), non-financial accumulation rate (I/K_{-1}), price of equities (pe), rate of profit (UP/K_{-1}), rate of return on equities (re), debt ratio (L/K). Production and price of equities are presented as ratios of the baseline $(Y/Y^r$ for instance). The other variables, which are ratios, are presented as differences, with respect to the baseline $(L/K - L/K^r$ for instance).

A decrease of the wage share

The decline of the wage share has been observed in most industrialized countries since the 1980s. In this simulation it is assumed that the wage share (r_0) is 2% lower than in the baseline (Figure 1.8). This implies a higher rate of

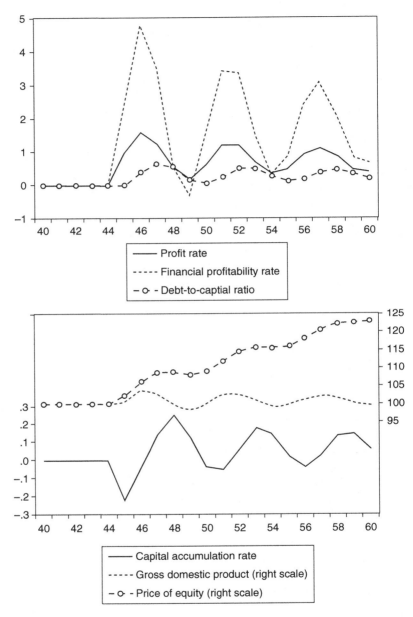

Figure 1.8 Decrease of 2% of the wage share (compared with the base line).

profit and an increase of investment and financial accumulation. In a better economic environment firms have a larger access to credit and their debt ratio rises.
With increasing profit and larger credit, firms issue less equity, which induces
a rise in its price in order to clear the market. The financial rate of return is
boosted and the financial boom is amplified. Consumption is preserved thanks
to the increase of dividends and of capital gains, in spite of the decline in
wages. Production is increased in the short term, but a turning point appears as
firms issue more equities in order to finance the real and financial investments.
The price of equity stabilizes and the financial rate of return decreases. With
reduced wages and less capital gains, households' consumption declines, inducing an economic slowdown. With falling demand, investment decreases and
firms reduce their issuance of equities, which in turn allows for a new upturn
in equities' price.

Overall, financial cycles can be observed in the stock market, with acceler-
ation and deceleration of growth in the price of equity and in the financial rate
of return. This is mainly explained by the variation of equities issued facing the
indebtedness norm and by the role played by the price of equity to clear the
market. The stock market bubble does not burst properly as the periodic price
falls are unable to compensate for previous increases. Stabilizing forces are insufficient. It may be recalled, however, that in the real world equity prices have
been growing in the long run in spite of periodic financial crises.

An increase in firms' financial accumulation

The increase in firms' financial accumulation has been another characteristic of
the finance-led regime of the 1990s and 2000s. In the simulation the increase
in firms' financial accumulation is represented by a 1% rise of the share of the
equities held out of their total wealth, compared to the baseline ($\Delta f_0 = 0.01$ in
eq. (15)). The financial shock on firms' demand for equities implies a cyclical
increase in output, thanks to a stock market boom which can be seen through
the rise in the price of equity and in the financial rate of return (Figure 1.9).
Capital gains stimulate households' demand. However, this is followed by a
gradual decline in financial profitability due to the new equities issued by firms.
This is a consequence of the indebtedness norm which makes investment more
dependent on own funds. Troughs are not as deep so as to compensate for the
initial gains achieved during peaks, and variations in the profit rate remain
above the variations of the accumulation rate. A financial cycle is observed on
the whole, as in the previous shock, with the price of equity clearing the market.

An increase in households' demand for equities

As mentioned above, one of the main features of a finance-led growth regime
is rising income inequality. This can be indirectly captured in the model by
a change in the households' portfolio behaviour with a larger share of their
wealth devoted to financial assets and, more precisely, to equities. The scenario

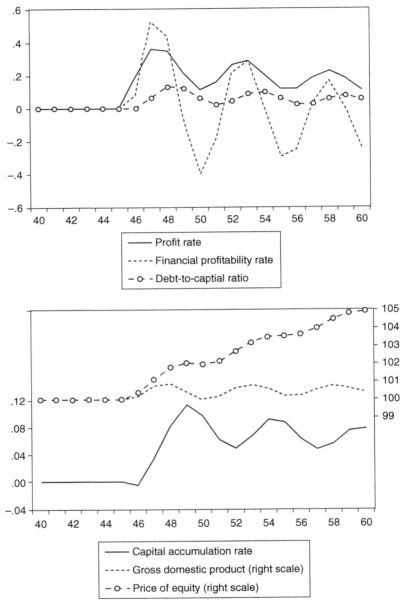

Figure 1.9 Increase of 1% of the firms' financial accumulation rate (compared with the base line).

assumes a 1% increase in the share of equities held by households out of their wealth, compared with the base line ($\Delta w_0 = 0.01$ in eq. (7)). Figure 1.10 shows graphically what happens under this scenario.

This shock generates large financial cycles with a strong impact on the real side of the economy. The price of equity is boosted by the stronger equity demand which increases the financial rate of return. Capital gains improve households' income and demand, while firms' investment is reduced for the benefit of financial accumulation. However, a reversal appears a few periods later. Loan demand works as an indebtedness norm and the issue of equities increases. This depresses the financial market and induces a decline of the price of equities and of the financial rate of return. This, in turn, has a negative impact on households' income and demand and, more broadly, on growth. Financial cycles follow as in the preceding scenarios, but in a more unstable way than in the previous cases. In the longer run, the increase in the price of equities is unsustainable and thus eventually tends to fall despite the peaks that take place every five periods. This happens because non-financial firms must issue more equities in order to finance investment, due to the indebtedness constraint they face. Broadly speaking, what we see is a succession of financial cycles with similar effects on the real side of the economy which appears unstable without any gain in terms of output growth in the medium- to long-run.

Increase of 2% of the firms' debt ratio

The increase of the firms' indebtedness has been used regularly since the 1980s to sustain capital accumulation in a context of financial liberalisation. In the simulation it is represented by a rise of 2% of the debt ratio, compared with the base line ($\Delta g_0 = 2\%$ in eq. (16)).

This rise in firms' debt reduces the issuance of equities which leads to an increase of the price of equity and of the financial rate of return. This higher profitability sustains financial accumulation by firms and households, which in turn reinforces the upward movement (see Figure 1.11). Capital gains improve households' income and demand. In a first step firms' investment is reduced for the benefit of financial accumulation. However, in a second step, the upswing of the profit rate stimulates the rate of capital accumulation which consolidates the recovery. But this is followed by a reversal in financial markets. With the boom of financial (and later on non-financial) accumulation, the issuance of equities increases, leading to a fall in the price of equity. Financial cycles continue afterwards without sustainable gains in terms of real economic growth.

On the whole, the simulations provide a better understanding of the workings of the model. Financial cycles can be generated with the price of equity clearing the market between equities issued and equities held by firms and households. Financial fluctuations, with ups and downs more or less pronounced in the price of equity and the rate of financial return, appear as the normal mode of regulation of this financial regime. The non-financial rate of accumulation also follows a cyclical pattern, without any lasting recovery, and real economic

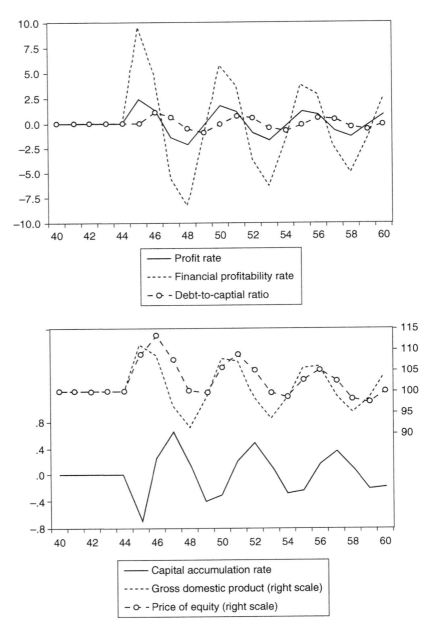

Figure 1.10 Increase of 1% of the households' demand of equities (compared with the base line).

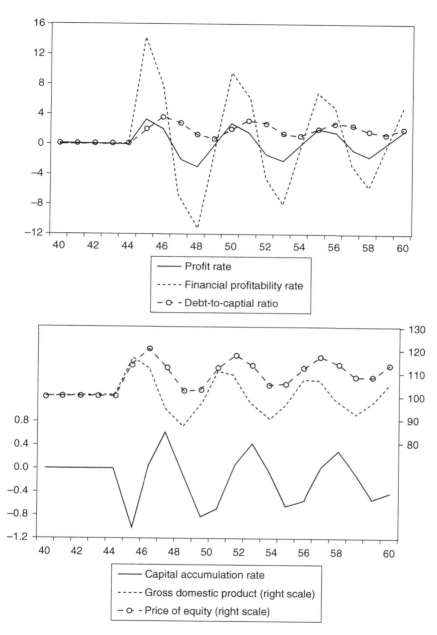

Figure 1.11 Increase in the firms' debt ratio by 2% (compared with the base line).

growth remains limited. Some of the main characteristics of the cycles of the 1990s and 2000s have been reproduced as a consequence of the four shocks: a decrease of the wage share, an increase of firms' financial accumulation, a rising demand of equities by households linked to the larger income inequality and an increasing indebtedness of firms.

Further developments

The financial crisis observed in 1992, 2001, and 2008 in the United States and in most European countries can be partly understood within this simple framework. But the adjustment mechanism by equities' prices clearing the market remains relatively simplistic. Other components of the financial regime, rising income inequality, the booming housing sector, the financialization of the economy and the global imbalances have played major roles in this process too. They have begun to be integrated in the SFC framework.

First, the increasing income inequality has boosted the indebtedness of the households at the bottom 90% of the distribution. It has contributed in the United States to the subprime crisis and in European countries such as Spain, Ireland and the United Kingdom to a large housing bubble. The question of income inequality can be introduced in the SFC approach with a more detailed treatment of the households sector and a distinction between capitalists and working class (i.e. white-collar and blue-collar) households. The rise in income inequality induces a decrease of the saving rate and an increase of the indebtedness of the poorest households (Nikiforos, 2016). Simultaneously, the demand for financial assets by households at the top of the distribution is increased, which strengthens the financial bubble. These two mechanisms have contributed to enlarge the imbalances before the burst of the crisis in 2001 and 2008.

Second, the housing bubble has been driven by the rising indebtedness of the households. It is another face of the imbalances which have been growing during the 2000s. The basic SFC model can be extended to include more than one real asset (Zezza, 2008). Residential capital is treated separately with an analysis of the dynamic of the real estate price which is simply related to the variation of the unsold houses. The model shed light on some aspects of the US economic growth during the 2000s with the increase of the housing price and the decline of the households' propensity to save. The increase in the stock of mortgages related to the disposable income has put the US economy into an unstable growth path.

Third, beyond residential capital, land capital must also be considered. It has been introduced in the national accounts as 'non-produced non-financial assets'. Its price has also increased greatly in many countries since the 1990s with strong speculative movements, inducing important capital gains. This trend has also been boosted by the increasing debt of both firms and households. It has contributed to enlarge the imbalances during the 2000s but has remained partly hidden. However, its impacts of the rate of profit are important, as has been shown in

Figure 1.2. In the case of France, during the 2000s before the crisis burst, the decline in the productivity of capital at current prices and of the rate of profit has been larger with respect to the total capital, including land, than with respect to fixed capital (machines and housing). This fall of the profit rate in a context of rising indebtedness has contributed to the severity of the crisis of 2008.

Fourth, the process of financialization could be more explicitly treated than in our highly simplified model where the banking sector is passive. The financial variables only describe how the difference between saving and investment of various sectors (financing capacity or need) is financed through the net variation of financial assets and liabilities. Gross financial flows of assets and liabilities are not described in full. This masks the role played by the financial sector and the deep changes that have occurred since the 1990s. Financialization has led to a considerable enlargement of the financial sector on both sides of the balance sheet (that is, considering gross financial instruments). The deposits of the non-financial sectors have not grown at a rate much higher than GDP growth has. As a consequence, the large relative increase of the size of the financial balance sheets has been mainly due to the high growth of wholesale lending between financial institutions. This wholesale lending has been facilitated by financial innovations (securitization, derivatives, etc).

The modelling of the financialization in an SFC framework has been limited until now. Sawyer and Passarella (2017) have proposed a simple model with a distinction between banks and other financial institutions where securitization is described through the transformation of household loans into derivatives. But the mechanism remains rather simple. The derivatives are only determined by the demand of rentier households without any specific behaviour of the financial institutions. The price of derivatives is exogenous with a random component. The results are consistent with the common belief that financialization is associated with a worsening in income distribution and an increase in the level of indebtedness by working households, but these findings seem to be preliminary. Nikolaidi (2015) puts forward a model of the securitization process limited to home mortgages owned by workers. The model is complex, with three categories of households and a distinction between commercial banks, special purpose vehicles underwriters (SPV) and institutional investors. The price of the mortgage-backed securities (MBS) clears the market between demand by institutional investors and supply by SPV underwriters. The simulations indicate that a rise in securitization practice can induce a debt-led expansion, a housing boom but with an increasing financial fragility and, ultimately, a reversal with a declining price of MBS and a volatility in home prices. Combined with an exogenous decline of the wage share, the debt burden of households increases more rapidly, and long-run negative effects are enhanced. The model is attractive but the consistency of all the mechanisms does not seem to be fully guaranteed, and it looks more like work in progress.

Fifth, the increasing global imbalances, both at the real and financial levels, have been another main characteristic of the 1990s and 2000s. They will be discussed in detail in the next two chapters.

Conclusion

The aim of this chapter was to present a simple SFC model in order to give a first glance at the finance-led regime that settled in most developed countries since the 1980s. Based on the French case, considered as representative of the main trends, four specific features have been highlighted: a limited recovery of the non-financial rate of accumulation despite the recovery of the profit rate; a less favourable evolution of profitability due to the boom in property prices fuelled by financial liberalisation, when a broader notion of total capital (which includes land) is used; a stronger growth of the financial accumulation, with the financial rate of return as the main driver and financial markets regulated by periodic crisis; an increasing indebtedness of the firms masked by revaluation effects (boom in property price and equity prices) with lasting risk of over-indebtedness in the case of a reversal in financial markets. A brief survey of the contribution of the SFC models to analyse the financial cycles has been made. The difficulties to provide a complete modelling of the Minsky's approach have been analysed.

We have presented a simple SFC model for a closed economy with constant prices. Compared to the usual ones, two functions for firms have been introduced for a better description of the finance-led regime: a financial accumulation related to the rate of financial return; a debt demand, which also depends (positively) on the financial rate of return and (negatively) on the interest rate. Simulations with shocks have reproduced some of the main characteristics of the cycles of the 1990s and 2000s. Financial cycles are generated by the price of equity clearing the market between issued and held equities. They appear as the normal mode of regulation of the finance-led regime. The financial crises observed in 1992, 2001, and 2008 can be partly understood within this simple framework. But the adjustment mechanisms remain rather simple. Other components of the finance-led regime have played important roles. Some have begun to be integrated in the SFC approach (rising income inequality and the housing bubble). Others are more work in progress (taking into account the rising property price and the process of financialization). And last but not least, the increasing global imbalances, which are examined in the following chapters.

Annex Values of parameters

Households' consumption
$a_0 = 0.5658628$ $\qquad a_1 = 0.83$ $\qquad a_2 = 0.04$

Firms' investment
$k_0 = 0.1086$ $\qquad k_1 = 0.35$ $\qquad k_2 = 0.025$ $\qquad k_3 = 0.1$ $\qquad k_4 = 0.5$
$\qquad k_5 = 0.1$ $\qquad \delta = 0.0625$

Households' portfolio
$v_0 = 0.2238$ $v_1 = 0.2$ $v_2 = 0.2$ $v_3 = 0.1$
$w_0 = 0.3897$ $w_1 = 0.01$ $w_2 = 0.02$ $w_3 = 0.02$
$\lambda_0 = 0.1591$

Firms' financial accumulation
$f_0 = 0.0982$ $f_1 = 0.2$ $f_2 = 0.6$

Firms' loan demand
$g_0 = 0.2352$ $g_1 = 0.3$ $g_2 = 0.04$ $g_3 = 0$

Firms' saving rate
$sf = 0.3410$

Wage share
$r_0 = 0.6765$

Tax rates
$\theta = 0.1$ $\theta_b = 0.2863$

Mandatory reserves ratio
$\lambda = 0.05$

Interest rates
$ib = 0.015$ $m_1 b = 0.005$ $m_2 b = 0.005$

2 Exchange rate misalignments and global imbalances

Jacques Mazier and Jamel Saadaoui

Introduction

World imbalances have been increasing since the end of the 1990s with a large US current account deficit facing Asian surpluses, mainly Chinese and Japanese ones (Figure 2.1). The European current account has remained close to equilibrium, until 2010, but with huge intra-European imbalances. These imbalances were far larger than what had been observed in the past and could hardly be regarded as sustainable. They reflected internal imbalances in each area, mainly the over-indebtedness of US households and declining US competitiveness, on the one hand, the insufficient Chinese consumption and wage share, on the other hand. These world imbalances have been lasting thanks to the financial liberalisation which made their financing easier. The financial crisis of 2008 has been partly the consequence of these imbalances, starting with the US subprime market and diffusing at the world level. Since 2007 adjustments have been achieved, mainly through the effects of the production decline which has reduced imports of the deficit countries and cut the exports of the surplus countries, but the euro area surplus has increased in a huge proportion.

Contrary to what was expected by some observers (Blanchard et al., 2005; Obstfeld and Rogoff, 2005), world imbalances in 2007 and, especially the US deficit, did not lead to large exchange rate adjustments with a dollar crisis. In the past exchange rate fluctuations have been important, as in the case of the fluctuations of the dollar against the European currencies in the 1980s or the sharp appreciation of the yen in the second half of the 1980s. After the nominal appreciation of the dollar between 1995 and 2002 against the euro and the yen, the dollar has depreciated from 2002 to 2008, significantly against the euro, but more moderately against the yen. The yuan has been pegged to the dollar from 1994 to 2005, with a limited appreciation later on. After the burst of the crisis in 2008 the dollar served as a safe haven and has been stronger against the euro and the yen until 2012 while the yuan has kept its moderate appreciation. In real effective terms the evolutions are slightly different, as it will be examined more in detail below. On the long run the evolution of the real effective exchange rate of the euro has been the mirror of the dollar's one.

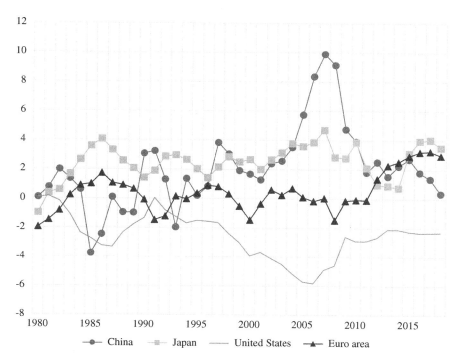

Figure 2.1 Current account balance (in % of GDP).
Source: World Economic Outlook, IMF, 2019.

These evolutions can be analysed in relation with the global imbalances according to various ways: standard international macroeconomic models with price and volume effects, general equilibrium models or simpler portfolio models which integrate financial flows and valuation effects, multi-country SFC models which give a comprehensive description of the real and financial flows and stocks at the world level. These questions will be examined in the next chapter. Before, it seems useful to give a more precise evaluation of the global imbalances, of their size and evolution. In this perspective the exchange rate equilibrium approach can give a synthetic view. Exchange rate equilibrium has been studied in the literature using two main approaches: the Behavioural Equilibrium Exchange Rate (BEER) and the Fundamental Equilibrium Exchange Rate (FEER). The chapter presents an estimation of the exchange rate misalignments since the 1980s for the main currencies, the dollar, the euro, the yuan, the yen and the pound sterling in bilateral nominal terms and in real effective terms, using a FEER approach. The FEER is defined as the level of exchange rate which allows the economy to reach the internal and external equilibrium at the same time (Williamson, 1983). The internal equilibrium is defined as the full utilization of productive resources of one country without generating inflation pressures. The external equilibrium corresponds to a sustainable current account.

The chapter, based on Jeong et al. (2010), is organized as follows. A second section summarizes the theoretical and methodological background and explains why we prefer the FEER approach. A third section presents the models used to estimate the FEERs with a two-step analysis: first, a multinational model of the world economy for the main countries: the United States, China, the euro area, Japan, the United Kingdom and the rest of the world; and second, a national model of foreign trade for smaller countries. A fourth section gives econometric estimates of the external and internal equilibrium. The notion of equilibrium current account will help visualize the global imbalances. A fifth section presents estimates of the FEER for the main currencies (dollar, euro, yen, yuan, and pound sterling). The case of the smaller countries is referred to Chapters 4 (euro zone countries) and 7 (East Asian countries). Lessons are drawn from these results. The relation between exchange rate misalignments and growth appears as another important issue.

Theoretical and methodological background

Exchange rate misalignment is defined as the gap, in percentage, between observed exchange rate and equilibrium exchange rate. Various methodologies can be used to estimate equilibrium exchange rate.

Equilibrium exchange rates methodology

The PPP (Purchasing Power Parity) is the oldest and simplest methodology to estimate equilibrium exchange rates. In order to explain the movements of equilibrium exchange rates, this simple approach only relies on the relative prices. It ignores, however, other structural factors and seems too schematic, even when completed by a Balassa-Samuelson effect. Beyond the PPP hypothesis, two main theories of equilibrium exchange rates can be distinguished: the Behavioural Equilibrium Exchange Rate which is an econometric approach (Clark and MacDonald, 1998); the Fundamental Equilibrium Exchange Rate (Williamson, 1983) and its more recent developments (Cline, 2008).

The BEER approach explains the exchange rate dynamic with some main variables (usually the net foreign assets, the terms of trade, the relative productivity, the oil prices) which influence the real exchange rate at long term. A long-term equation is first estimated by a co-integration method and then, using an error correction model, a short-term equation is estimated. The exchange rate misalignments are simply measured by the gap between the observed exchange rate and its long run value. This econometric approach is rather easy to manage and gives useful results. But the BEER methodology suffers from some drawbacks, such as the lack of theoretical basis and the sensitivity of the results to the variables retained. More importantly, the estimation can only be made country by country. When the estimation is done for a whole set of countries, there is no guarantee of the consistency of the equilibrium exchange rates across the different currencies, as it can be seen in recent estimations (Couharde et al., 2017). Last, due to the econometric method of estimation, the BEER approach requires that the exchange rate is on average in equilibrium over the sample period since the expected value of the residual of the long-term equation must equal to zero. The validity of such an assumption is not guaranteed a priori as a currency can be durably over or undervalued.

The FEER is defined as the exchange rate prevailing when the economy simultaneously reaches the external equilibrium (sustainable current account determined by structural parameters) and the internal equilibrium (full utilization of the productive potential). This approach is based on a structural model which mainly describes foreign trade relations and relates explicitly movements of exchange rates to internal and external imbalances. It has the advantage of focusing directly on structural parameters of each country (foreign trade elasticities, degree of openness). It allows for the estimation of equilibrium exchange rates of the different partners in a coherent manner by using a multinational trade model, which is rarely assured in other approaches. Its limited linkages with the inter-temporal optimizing literature have been criticized but the FEER does not claim to describe the modality of the return to the equilibrium. It searches only, for each period, to estimate the real misalignment induced by the internal and external imbalances in terms of comparative statics. Other critics concern the dependence of the FEER on the value of foreign trade elasticities and the weakness of the definition of the internal and external equilibrium. In spite of these limits, we prefer the FEER approach because it is more explicitly articulated with the structural characteristics of each country and it ensures greater consistency of estimates across countries.

The FEER approach and the SNIM

The objective is to assess the equilibrium exchange rates at the world level. A two-step analysis is implemented in order to estimate the exchange rate misalignments, first at the level of the main currencies (dollar, euro, yuan, yen, pound sterling), second at the level of smaller countries' currencies (euro zone countries, other OECD or emerging countries). For the main currencies, the methodology used (Jeong et al., 2010) is a synthesis of previous works on the FEER (Jeong and Mazier, 2003) and of the Symmetric Matrix Inversion Method (SMIM) proposed by Cline (2008). A multinational model describing the foreign trade of the main countries and of the rest of the world is used to calculate the main currencies' equilibrium exchange rates. It is well known that in a n-country model there are only n-1 independent bilateral exchange rates, because the first country's exchange rate (usually the dollar) is the numeraire against which the others are compared. Consequently, there is an overdetermination problem in the FEER approach, as there are more equations (current account targets) than unknowns (exchange rates). In our model we use the nth country as a residual in order to solve the overdetermination problem and to ensure the consistency of the world trade in volume and in value. Exports and imports of the residual country are calculated as residual of the world trade equilibrium in constant and current prices. But the equilibrium exchange rate of the residual currency, consistent with those of the other currencies, cannot allow the residual country to reach its equilibrium current account. In that respect the residual country is ignored in the estimation of the equilibrium exchange rates of the other currencies. In practice, in earlier works, it was generally the rest of the world which was the residual country.

To avoid such an asymmetric approach, the six countries (the United States, China, Japan, the United Kingdom, the euro area, and the rest of the world) are treated symmetrically by carrying out six sets of estimates with six multinational models where each country is treated successively as a residual. A simple average of the results could be obtained. However, there is a high degree of consistency in the alternative estimates of equilibrium exchange rates for any given country across the five solutions in which the current account target of the country in question is included (designated OCI for own country included). Conversely, there is sometimes a great difference between the average value and the value obtained in the resolution where the country or area target is not included (designated OCE for one country excluded). Consequently, the solution adopted is to use as the estimate the average of equilibrium exchange rates obtained from all the solutions, except the one for which the country in question is regarded as a residual (OCI).

For smaller countries an equilibrium exchange rate will be estimated using a simple national model of foreign trade. The equilibrium exchange rate will be defined, as previously, as the exchange rate compatible with the internal and external equilibrium of each country. It has been shown that, for a relatively small country like the European or the emerging ones, a national model gives results very close to the ones obtained with a multinational model where the studied country would be explicitly described (Jeong and Mazier, 2003).

This methodology improves previous works at several levels. Compared with approaches which ignore one area (the rest of the world in practice), our model gives a symmetric treatment of all the countries, like Cline's SMIM, as each country is successively treated as residual. Compared with Williamson's earlier works using large econometric models, the model is simpler and easier to manage. However, the foreign trade model takes fully account of the interdependencies among the main economies, including the one treated as a residual, which ensures consistency of worldwide results. Another advantage of the approach is the case of small countries which can be simply linked to the world model's results, as it will be explained more in detail later. This approach takes more consistently account of structural parameters of each economy and is more manageable than a model of 35 countries with a simple reduced equation between current account and real effective exchange rate for each country (Cline and Williamson, 2008). Moreover, our model incorporates the effects of the foreign debt service and of the oil prices on the current account but they are treated as exogenous.

Lastly, based on studies of the medium-term determinants of current accounts (Faruqee and Isard, 1998; Chinn and Prasad, 2003), the equilibrium current account are determined by estimating structural determinants of current account (the demographic features, the developmental stage, the public deficit, the net foreign assets, etc.) relying on panel regression techniques. It avoids using an ad hoc approach which is often the case, but seems less well founded. Sensitivity tests are conducted in order to assess the sensitivity of the results to adopted targets (current account target, internal equilibrium) and to values of parameters (price elasticities).

Macroeconomic modelling

The multinational model

The model describes the trade structure of the main countries or areas, namely, the United States, Japan, China, the euro area, the United Kingdom and the rest of the world using standard foreign trade equations: export volume eq. (1), import volume eq. (2), export price eq. (5), and import price eq. (6). Each country is successively treated as a residual and in that case export and import volumes are determined as residual of the equations of world trade equilibrium in value (3) and in volume (4) while their export and import prices are determined in the same manner as for other trading partners. This multinational specification gives a full account of interdependent effects in volume and prices of exports and imports of all countries. We incorporate a consumer prices eq. (7) to take into account the feedback effect between the consumer prices and the import prices. The real effective exchange rate is defined relatively to the consumption prices. Finally, the current account is defined as in eq. (9). For the residual country, its current account can be calculated (eq. (9.a)) but is not taken into account. With usual notations, the model is written as:

Export volume equation $\quad X_i = X_{0i} DM_i^{\eta xi} COMPX^{\varepsilon xi}$

$$DM_i = \prod_{j \neq i} M_j^{\alpha ij} \tag{1}$$

$$COMPX_i = \left(\frac{PMX_i}{PX_i} \right)$$

Import volume equation $\quad M_i = M_{0i} DI_i^{\eta mi} \left(\frac{PD_i}{PM_i} \right)^{\varepsilon mi} \tag{2}$

With i = 1 ~ 5 {among Japan, China, the United States, the euro area, the United Kingdom, the rest of the world} = {all the countries except the residual one}

World trade equilibrium in value and in volume

$$\frac{\sum_i PX_i X_i}{E_i} = \frac{\sum_i PM_i M_i}{E_i} \tag{3}$$

$$\sum_i X_i = \sum_i M_i \text{ with } i = 1 \sim 6 \tag{4}$$

Export price equation $PX_i = PMX_i^{\alpha xi} P_i^{1-\alpha xi}$ \hfill (5)

$$PMX_i = \prod_{j \neq i} \left(\frac{E_i PX_j}{E_j} \right)^{\lambda ij}$$

Import price equation $PM_i = PMM_i^{\alpha mi} PD_i^{1-\alpha mi}$ \hfill (6)

$$PMM_i = \prod_{j \neq i} \left(\frac{E_i PX_j}{E_j} \right)^{\mu ij}$$

Consumer price equation $PD_i = PM_i^{ai} PD_i^{1-ai}$ \hfill (7)

Real effective exchange rates $R_i = \prod_{j \neq i} \left[\left(\frac{PD_j}{E_j} \right)^{vij} \bigg/ \left(\frac{PD_i}{E_i} \right) \right]$ with i = 1 ~ 6

\hfill (8)

Current account $B_i = PX_i X_i - PM_i M_i - E_i P_{pet} M_{peti} - i_i E_i F_i$ \hfill (9)

$$B_{res} = -\sum_{i=1}^{5} B_i \tag{9.a}$$

With i = 1 ~ 5 {among Japan, China, the United States, the euro area, the United Kingdom, the rest of the world} = {all the countries except the residual one}

The multinational model variables are defined as follow: X, non-oil exports in volume; DM, world demand in volume; DI, internal demand in volume; $COMPX$, export prices competitiveness; PX, export prices; PMX, competitor export prices; M, non-oil imports in volume; PM, import prices; PMM, world import prices; PD, consumer prices; P, production prices; E, nominal bilateral exchange rates vis-à-vis the dollar; R, real effective exchange rates; B, current account; i, interest rates for external debt; F, net external debt; P_{pet}, oil price; M_{pet}, net oil import. The dollar plays the role of numeraire ($E_3 = 1$) and the bilateral exchange rates of other currencies against the dollar are written as 1 dollar = E_1 yens = E_2 yuans = E_4 euros = E_5 pounds = E_6 monetary unities of the rest of the world.

In this framework, FEERs are defined as the real effective exchange rates compatible with the simultaneous realization of the internal and external equilibrium at medium term of each trading partner. The internal equilibrium means that actual output follows the potential production and the external equilibrium means that actual current account corresponds to the sustainable current account at medium term. The model is written in logarithmic differential compared with the equilibrium, which directly calculates the extent of the misalignment. Variables in lower case correspond to the log differences of these variables, thus $e = dE / E = (E - E^e) / E^e$ for the bilateral exchange rate and $x = dX / X = (X - X^e) / X^e$ for other variables, except for current account $b = (B / PY) - (B / PY)^e$ where b represents the difference between the observed current account and the equilibrium current account as a percentage of GDP. The values of bilateral exchange rate misalignments (e) are given by solving the model in logarithmic differential (Annex 2.1).

On the whole, each multinational model comprises 35 endogenous variables (x, m, px, pm, pd for the six countries or areas and the five bilateral exchange rates e) for 35 equations (x, m, b for the five countries other than the residual one, px, pm, pd for the six countries and the two world trade equilibrium equations). The real effective exchange rates are calculated *ex post* using bilateral exchange rates and consumer prices. The production prices p are supposed to be at equilibrium, which means that we do not include a price-wage loop in our model. The two exogenous variables are the internal and the external equilibrium gap (di and b, respectively).

In logarithmic differential form, the degree by which the economy deviates from its internal and external equilibrium determines the degree of misalignments of its currency. On the one hand, the degree of deviation of internal demand is measured by $di = (DI - DI^e) / DI^e$ where DI^e is the equilibrium internal demand. This equilibrium internal demand is linked to the potential production. On the other hand, the gap between actual current account and equilibrium one, as a percentage of GDP, is given by $b = (B / PY) - (B / PY)^e$. This variable, which quantifies the deviation from the external equilibrium, is central in determining exchange rate misalignments. As mentioned before, each country is treated successively as residual, which gives six multinational models. The six countries are treated symmetrically, including the rest of the world, and six sets of estimates are done successively with each multinational model. In each case it permits to calculate an 'equilibrium exchange rate' of the residual currency (e_{res}) coherent with the equilibrium exchange rates of the five other countries, but not with its current account target. A simple average of the results could be obtained. But it is preferable to use as an estimate of the equilibrium exchange rates the average obtained for all the solutions, except the one for which the country in question is regarded as a residual (OCI).

The national model

For smaller countries, it is possible to estimate an equilibrium exchange rate using a foreign trade model in which the world demand and world trade prices are exogenous. The following equations specify the trade volume and price equations for a small country facing world economy.

$$X_i = X_{0i} D_i^{*\eta xi} \left(\frac{E_i P_i^*}{PX_i} \right)^{\varepsilon xi} = X_{0i} D_i^{*\eta xi} R_i^{(1-\alpha xi)\varepsilon xi} \tag{10}$$

$$M_i = M_{0i} DI_i^{\eta mi} \left(\frac{P_i}{PM_i} \right)^{\varepsilon mi} = M_{0i} DI^{\eta mi} R_i^{-\alpha mi \varepsilon mi} \tag{11}$$

$$PX_i = \left(E_i P_i^* \right)^{\alpha xi} P_i^{1-\alpha xi} = R_i^{\alpha xi} P_i \tag{12}$$

$$PM_i = \left(E_i P_i^* \right)^{\alpha mi} P_i^{1-\alpha mi} = R_i^{\alpha mi} P_i \tag{13}$$

$$B_i = PX_i X_i - PM_i M_i - E_i P_{pet} M_{peti} - i_i E_i F_i \tag{14}$$

$$R_i = \left(\frac{E_i P_i^*}{P_i} \right) \tag{15}$$

$$P_i^* = PX_i^* = \prod_{j \neq i} \left(\frac{PX_j}{E_j} \right)^{\lambda ij} \cong PM_i^* = \prod_{j \neq i} \left(\frac{PX_j}{E_j} \right)^{\mu ij} \tag{16}$$

With j = 1 ~ 6 {Japan, China, the United States, the euro area, the United Kingdom, the rest of the world}

The national model variables are the same as in the multinational model, except for R, real effective exchange rate based on production prices which is distinguished from RC based on consumer prices; D^*, world demand in volume; P^*, world prices. Solving this simplified model in logarithmic differential form (Annex 2.2) gives r, the misalignment in real effective terms ($r = dLogR = dR / R = (R - R^e) / R^e$):

$$r_i = \left[\frac{\left(\left(b_i / \mu_i T_i \left(1 - \sigma_{petxi} - \sigma_{xi} \right) \right) + \eta m_i di_i - \eta x_i d_i^* \right)}{\left(\left(1 - \alpha x_i \right) \varepsilon x_i + \varepsilon m_i \alpha m_i + \alpha x_i - \alpha m_i \right)} \right] \tag{17}$$

Where $\sigma petx = EP_{pet}M_{pet}/PXX$, ratio of net oil imports on non-oil exports and $\sigma x = iEF/PXX$, ratio of foreign debt service on non-oil exports.

The FEER approach focuses on real effective exchange rates. However, the nominal bilateral exchange rate against the dollar can be more intelligible. By using the equation (15), we can find out e, the degree of misalignment in bilateral nominal terms against the dollar. The partner countries' misalignments are given by the multinational model.

$$e_i = r_i - \sum_{j \neq i} \lambda_{ij} \left(px_j - e_j \right) \tag{18}$$

We can also compute the effective exchange rate misalignments based on consumer prices pd:

$$rc_i = \left(1 - \alpha m_i \mu_i \right) r_i + \sum_{j \neq i} v_{ij} \left(pd_j - e_j \right) - \sum_{j \neq i} \lambda_{ij} \left(px_j - e_j \right) \tag{19}$$

(pd_j, e_j, px_j obtained thanks to the multinational model)

Foreign trade elasticities

Without doing original econometric work, trade equations are taken from existing estimations realized with specifications close to the standard model presented before. We use especially long-term elasticities. Considering the uncertainties surrounding the estimations, sensibility tests to elasticities modifications are provided in annex.

The elasticities of the MIMOSA model for Japan, the United States and the United Kingdom (close to those of Wren-Lewis and Driver, 1998), those of Dées, 1999 for China and those of Hervé, 2000 for the euro area are taken for our simulation. The price elasticities are rather in accordance with the generally admitted hierarchical position of countries in the world trade. The relatively weak value for China could be surprising, but might be explained by the particular nature of the Chinese trade. The trade model of China was estimated for the period 1985–1998 and for the first half of the 1980s the role of exchange rates in exports and imports is considered as little significant. Japanese and American exporters turn out to be largely price maker. The price elasticities are weaker in the OECD model (Pain et al., 2005) as they concern the total trade of good and services. For the rest of the world ad hoc values have been used, but are close to estimations of elasticities made using data from CHELEM and OECD. The elasticities of the trading partners of the multinational model are presented in Annex 2.3 (Table 2.4). Those of the European and emerging countries are given in Chapters 4 and 7.

External and internal equilibrium at medium term

Estimation of equilibrium current account

As the current account equals the difference between domestic saving and investment, current account developments are examined from the perspective of the medium and long run determinants of saving and investment behaviours (Faruqee and Isard, 1998; Chinn and Prasad, 2003). According to these authors, the main determinants of the current account at medium term are: the demographic characteristics, such as the dependency ratios of dependent populations relative to the working age population, which is expected to exert a negative influence, with a higher dependency ratio leading to more spending; the net foreign asset, which is expected to have a positive effect, due to the capital income resulting from it; the government budget balance, with a public deficit having a negative effect on the current account, but this effect may be regarded as a simple accounting one which should not to be introduced. Finally, we introduce a short-term effect, the output gap, since a higher utilization of production capacity leads to a deterioration of the current account. Yet, this last variable will be eliminated in the simulation of the equilibrium current account. The equations of current account are estimated with panel data for the 1980–2003 period and for two groups of countries. In a medium-term perspective, we use non-overlapping four years average of annual data.

$$CA_{it} = \alpha_i + \alpha_t + \beta_0 + \beta_1 ISNFA_{it} + \beta_2 CDR_{it} + \beta_3 ODR_{it} + \beta_4 OG_{it} + \varepsilon_{it} \ (20)$$

The variables of eq. (20) are defined as follows: CA, current account as percentage of GDP (World Economic Outlook, IMF); $ISNFA$, initial stock of net foreign assets at the beginning of each period of 4 years as percentage of GDP (Lane and Milesi-Ferretti, 2007 Data Base); CDR, child dependency ratio, population under the age of 15 years as percentage of population aged 15 to 64; *ODR*, old dependency ratio, population over the age of 65 years as percentage of population aged 15 to 64 (World Population Prospect, ONU, 2012); *OG*, output gap in percentage of the potential production (Economic Outlook, OECD, 2016).

Two groups of countries are considered. The first one is composed of 19 industrial countries (Australia, Austria, Canada, Denmark, Finland, France, Germany, Ireland, Italy, Japan, the Netherlands, New Zealand, Norway, Portugal, South Korea, Spain, Sweden, the United Kingdom, and the United States) and will be used for determining the current account targets of the United States, Japan, the euro area and the United Kingdom. The other group, composed of 20 emerging economies (Argentina, Brazil, Chile, China, Colombia, Ecuador, Egypt, India, Indonesia, Malaysia, Mexico, Morocco, Pakistan, Peru, Philippines, South Africa, Sri Lanka, Thailand, Tunisia, and Turkey), will be used for determining the current account target of China and other emerging countries (see Chapter 7). According to the results of unit root tests, the null hypothesis of non-stationarity is rejected in all the series (Jeong et al., 2010).

For industrialised countries, the estimated coefficients of equation (20) are on the whole significant with the predicted signs (Table 2.1) in different specifications. The dependency ratios are not highly significant, although they are the best theoretically justified variables. Output gap turns out to have negative effects on current account. Country effects raise the determination ratio. On the whole, the cross-section specification with country fixed effects seems the most relevant and is adopted in order to calculate the equilibrium current account.

Results for emerging countries are less conclusive than those for industrial countries, as in the case of other empirical studies (Chinn and Prasad, 2003). As

Table 2.1 Determinants of the current account for industrialised countries

	OLS Pooled	Individual Fixed Effects	Temporal Fixed Effects
Constant	6.69	11.27	0.69
	(2.14)	(3.29)	(0.29)
ISNFA	0.06	0.02	0.07
	(10.87)	(2.22)	(8.51)
CDR	-0.16	-0.26	0.00
	(-2.23)	(-4.18)	(0.02)
ODR	-0.09	-0.19	-0.03
	(-1.32)	(-2.28)	(-0.51)
OG	-0.31	-0.47	-0.51
	(-2.82)	(-5.77)	(-4.09)
Adjusted R^2	0.47	0.89	0.56

Source: Authors' estimates.

Note

() = T statistics.

Table 2.2 Determinants of current account for developing countries

	OLS Pooled	Individual Fixed Effects	Temporal Fixed Effects
Constant	6.46	-4.22	-0.28
	(3.50)	(-1.13)	(-0.12)
ISNFA	0.02	-0.01	0.04
	(6.46)	(-1.66)	(4.22)
CDR	-0.09	-0.08	0.00
	(-3.97)	(-2.85)	(0.15)
ODR	-0.21	0.86	-0.51
	(-2.89)	(3.53)	(-0.61)
OG	-0.44	-0.39	-0.38
	(-4.46)	(-11.43)	(-5.35)
Adjusted R^2	0.40	0.61	0.46

Source: Authors' estimates.

Note
() = T statistics.

previously, the coefficients are on the whole significant with predicted signs in the different specifications, with some exceptions (Table 2.2). Comparing cross-section specification with the fixed effects and the pooled OLS, the former has a higher determination ratio, but the net foreign asset has a negative sign and the old dependency ratio a positive one, which can hardly be explained. A possible explanation is that the NFA are more dispersed in the case of emerging countries and they might capture individual fixe effects. Consequently, panel OLS specification is adopted to estimate equilibrium current accounts for emerging countries.

The simulated equilibrium current balances

In simulating equilibrium current balances, we use the value of initial stocks of net foreign asset at the beginning of each four years period's and four years average values of dependency ratios and exclude output gap in order to remove short-term effects. Figure 2.2 shows the observed and equilibrium values of the current account for the main countries analysed in the multinational model. Two corrections should be specified. First, the observed current accounts of the main trade partners have been corrected from the global discrepancy that exists at the world level in the international data basis, proportionally to theirs weights in the world trade. Second, in the FEER theoretical framework, the whole difference between observed current balance and equilibrium one must not be interpreted entirely as an external disequilibrium. This difference is partly due to delayed effects of exchange rates variations that have not yet occurred entirely, but should be taking into account in the estimation. This correction is made using the dynamic structure of the external trade equations. The figures show observed and adjusted current accounts with equilibrium ones.

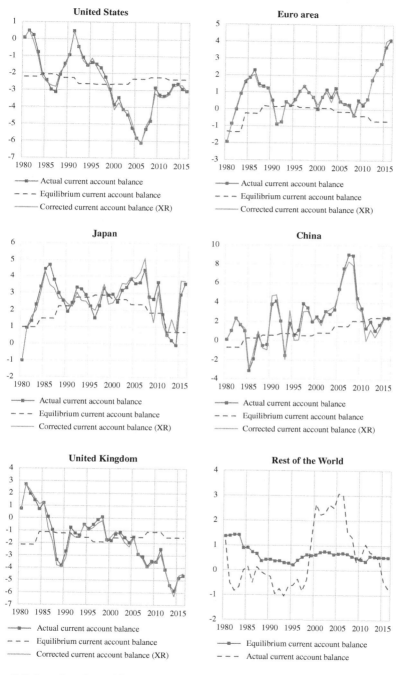

Figure 2.2 Actual and equilibrium current accounts of the main trade partners (in % of GDP).

Sources: Authors' calculations; IMF, World Economic Outlook, 2019.

The US current account target is between −2 and −3% of GDP over the period, which is consistent with several approaches on international imbalances where the target of −3% of GDP is selected for the US current account deficit in the medium term (Ahearne et al., 2007). Until the end of the 1990s the US current account declined but remained above its equilibrium value. The continuation of this evolution during the 2000s led to larger deficits which reflected huge internal imbalances, such as the decline of US competitiveness and the over-indebtedness of US households. With the crisis of 2008 and the fall of economic activity, the US deficit has been reduced and remained close to its equilibrium value since 2009.

On the other hand, since the mid-1990s, the euro area's equilibrium current account has been close to zero with a slight improvement over the early 1980s, thanks to a growing external position. The amplitude of current imbalances in the euro area (as a whole) has been weak until 2008, compared to those observed in other major world economies. But, since then, the euro area surplus has increased a lot, up to more than 4% of GDP, which constitutes one of the main global imbalances. As it will be argued later, this evolution results mainly of the inconsistency of the euro zone construction.

Japan has experienced contrasting trends. Its equilibrium current account balance has increased until the mid-1990s under the effect of its improving net external position due to surpluses' accumulation. Then the Japanese equilibrium current account balance deteriorated due, mainly, to a sharp increase in the old dependency ratio (ODR) which reduced national savings since it increased the share of inactive with low saving ratio. In this context the Japanese current surplus has been important three times (2–3% of GDP above the equilibrium value), at the beginning of the 1980s, during the first part of the 2000s and since 2014. These surplus periods have been followed by sharp adjustments.

China had an equilibrium current account close to 0% of GDP during the 1980s and the first years of 1990s, which seems coherent with the policy adopted by Chinese authorities that wanted to avoid the resort to large external debt. Since the mid-1990s, the equilibrium current account has increased to reach 2% of GDP in 2008. In this evolution the improvement of net external position and the decreasing of the child dependency ratio (CDR) played a positive role. The Chinese current surplus became huge and lasting from the second part of the 1990s and reached 9% of GDP in 2008. But the decline has been large with the crisis and since 2011 the Chinese current account is close its equilibrium value.

The United Kingdom is a smaller economy, but closely connected to the euro zone. Like the United States, its equilibrium current account has been stable and negative (−1.5 % of GDP) over the period. The actual current account has suffered large fluctuations since the beginning of 1980s when the United Kingdom benefited of the oil boom. But the trend has been declining with large deficits (−4% of GDP) in 1989, 2007, and 2014.

The current account of the rest of the world is equal to the opposite of the sum of the other main countries' current accounts in dollars, as the global discrepancy at the world level has been eliminated. The rest of the world's current account target is calculated, in the same way, as the opposite of the sum of the other countries' current account targets in dollars. This treatment guarantees the consistency of the current account targets at the world level, which is crucial in the FEER approach. In percentage of GDP, the rest of the world's current account target has remained rather stable around 0.5% of GDP during the whole period, which is close to the target (0%) generally used in the ad hoc approach. The actual current account of the rest of the world, in percentage of GDP, has fluctuated around 0% in the 1980–1990s, not far from the equilibrium value. But it has increased to 2–3 % in the first half of the 2000s, with huge surpluses of many emerging countries and oil producers. These surpluses were another illustration of the global imbalances which prevailed at the eve of the crisis of 2008.

The estimation of internal equilibrium

The internal equilibrium is defined as the state of full utilization of productive resources, without inflation pressures. For sake of simplification, a restrictive approach, limited to the measure of the potential output, is adopted. This approach of internal equilibrium seems less suited for emerging countries like China, where the concepts of potential output and full employment raise many problems, particularly because of the extent of regional imbalances and hidden underemployment in rural areas. This estimation of output gap is simply taken as representative of the degree of deviation of the internal demand (*di*). It must be regarded as a first step, which seems, however, sufficient at this stage. Indeed, as we shall see, results are only slightly sensitive to output gap's estimates. Different methods can be employed in calculating potential production and the corresponding output gap. For industrialised countries, we take the values estimated with production function by the OECD. This approach relies on estimated production functions and a measure of the available production factors in the country.

For developing countries, this kind of estimates is not available. So we calculate output gap by using the Hodrick-Prescott filter on real GDP over the period 1970–2013. As it is well known, this filter has certain disadvantages. It does not define well the output gap at the beginning and at the end of samples. It tends to neglect the structural breaks and the regime shifts. For prolonged slowdowns it deviates too much from a production function gap. In spite of these limits, we use these estimations of output gap as a first approximation which can be regarded as sufficient. A study in depth on this issue found that output gaps of East Asian countries estimated by several methods are similar for the period 1975–2000 (Gerlach and Yiu, 2004). In addition, our sensitivity tests show that errors in output gap estimation do not disrupt the whole conclusion. In the case of China, an increase of 1% in output gap leads to less than 1% of undervaluation.

Equilibrium exchange rates and misalignments

Computation

With the internal and external equilibrium previously estimated, the multinational model for the main economic partners is used six times to produce misalignments in terms of real effective exchange rates ($r = dLogR = dR / R = (R - R^e) / R^e$) and nominal exchange rate against the dollar ($e = dLogE = dE / E = (E - E^e) / E^e$), each country playing successively the role of residual country without its own current account target. The final solution is obtained by making an average of the five runs in which the current account target of each country is included (designated OCI for own country included). This allows determining undervaluations ($e > 0$ and $r > 0$) or overvaluations ($e < 0$ and $r < 0$) for the dollar, the euro, the yen, the yuan, the pound sterling, and the rest of the world's currency over the period 1980–2016. The results are presented in Table 2.3. Figure 2.3 shows the evolution of the observed and equilibrium exchange rate in real effective terms of the dollar over the period. Figures 2.4 and 2.5 show the same exchange rates in nominal bilateral terms against the dollar and in real effective terms for the other currencies.

Some more technical issues are sent back to annex. First, the ex ante and ex post current account targets are equal for all the countries of the world model, except the one treated as a residual. In the methodology used all the countries or areas are treated successively as a residual. When the average is calculated, the ex ante and ex post current account targets can be slightly different. But the average deviation remains inferior to 0.3 % of GDP (in absolute value) for the period 2004–2009 (Jeong et al., 2010). Second, the impact of the uncertainties in the estimation of external and internal equilibrium and in the measure of trade elasticities can be assessed by making sensitivity tests on the different parameters. The results are given in annex of Chapter 4. The sensitivity of the results to the potential production, to the current account target and to the export and import price elasticities turns out to be rather limited, which assures that the FEER approach provides rather robust results. Last, a comparison with Cline and Williamson's estimates is possible in spite of some differences in the FEER methodology. The results are rather close for the dollar, the yen and the yuan. For the euro and the pound sterling a larger undervaluation of the euro and overvaluation of the pound sterling is found in our simulations in the recent period due to differences in the choice of the current account target (Annex 2.4).

Dollar

The exchange rate misalignments enlighten the global imbalances which have increased since the 1990s. During the 1980s the dollar has experienced contrasted evolutions. The nominal appreciation of the dollar at the beginning of the 1980s, due to a highly restrictive monetary policy combined with

Table 2.3 Undervaluation (e > 0 and r > 0) or overvaluation (e < 0 and r < 0) for Japan, China, the United States, the euro area, the United Kingdom and the rest of the world (in %)

	Real effective						Bilateral nominal				
	RJP	RUK	RCH	REU	RUS	RROW	EJP	EUK	ECH	EEU	EROW
1982	4.9	2.3	33.7	8.0	13.8	-5.1	-3.0	-0.4	29.9	2.8	-11.4
1983	5.2	-2.6	25.4	15.2	7.4	-5.5	1.2	1.7	25.6	14.1	-6.0
1984	5.5	-4.6	5.7	12.2	-3.9	-2.5	10.3	6.1	12.9	18.2	5.2
1985	14.1	-6.1	-48.7	19.1	-7.4	-3.6	18.9	9.4	-42.6	27.4	8.0
1986	11.0	-11.6	-15.2	21.0	-7.8	-2.5	21.0	9.0	-1.1	33.2	13.4
1987	6.9	-7.7	13.0	11.0	-9.3	-0.3	17.3	7.2	27.2	21.6	11.7
1988	1.9	-6.4	-8.2	9.5	5.3	-4.8	-2.0	-6.6	-12.3	5.3	-6.4
1989	4.1	-6.7	-18.6	11.7	9.6	-6.3	-2.7	-8.6	-26.0	5.1	-9.9
1990	4.3	-0.7	27.3	1.2	15.1	-3.3	0.2	-4.8	25.2	-3.4	-8.4
1991	6.1	8.1	24.9	-10.6	23.6	-3.2	-4.9	-7.6	15.0	-22.1	-16.9
1992	6.5	5.3	7.4	-10.0	19.2	-4.6	-5.6	-11.8	-5.3	-23.6	-18.8
1993	1.8	-4.2	-21.0	4.5	11.1	-6.8	-8.8	-13.4	-33.7	-7.1	-15.2
1994	-0.8	2.0	18.6	-3.4	7.1	0.1	-2.5	-1.6	17.3	-5.5	-3.4
1995	-3.4	0.0	0.8	1.2	8.5	-4.1	-10.6	-7.2	-7.4	-6.6	-10.6
1996	-4.7	-0.1	0.7	4.2	3.7	-5.4	-14.7	-8.2	-9.9	-5.6	-13.5
1997	-2.7	0.7	14.5	3.5	0.0	-3.7	-10.2	-5.3	7.1	-3.4	-10.3
1998	-2.8	3.4	16.0	0.6	-1.5	-3.0	-10.7	-4.4	7.4	-6.7	-10.7
1999	-8.9	-0.5	8.5	2.0	-4.3	-2.4	-14.3	-5.6	1.8	-3.8	-7.5
2000	-5.0	0.6	6.1	0.1	-13.0	3.1	-2.1	3.7	8.8	3.6	5.3
2001	-1.4	-2.6	1.0	6.8	-11.0	2.7	2.3	4.5	5.2	11.8	7.9
2002	2.4	-3.9	7.1	6.6	-16.3	4.8	9.7	6.5	16.4	15.2	13.6
2003	4.0	-3.9	8.4	2.2	-17.7	8.8	15.9	9.2	23.0	15.1	20.8
2004	8.2	-5.5	6.0	7.2	-21.9	4.9	20.9	10.3	20.6	20.8	17.8
2005	7.8	-1.7	11.0	1.9	-29.1	9.4	25.0	16.8	30.3	20.7	25.0
2006	8.5	-2.9	16.7	1.6	-31.0	8.7	26.5	15.6	36.7	20.5	24.6
2007	9.0	-0.4	20.7	-0.2	-20.7	3.8	17.2	7.0	29.3	8.1	10.2
2008	2.5	-6.0	17.6	0.9	-18.9	3.5	15.6	5.8	31.5	12.4	14.4
2009	-4.6	-13.0	6.4	6.6	-11.1	0.6	9.4	1.4	21.6	17.6	13.7
2010	4.7	-9.6	4.5	4.9	-11.7	0.5	19.3	4.8	21.0	16.9	14.2
2011	-2.3	-11.9	-3.4	8.6	-12.9	3.1	13.2	6.4	14.4	23.1	18.8
2012	-1.0	-17.2	-2.6	16.3	-9.9	-1.7	10.3	-0.6	10.5	25.8	11.9
2013	3.4	-18.6	-5.9	18.0	-5.4	-4.7	14.2	-2.5	6.9	26.0	8.9
2014	-0.4	-21.0	-3.7	20.1	-4.0	-6.1	8.3	-6.2	6.5	25.8	6.0
2015	7.0	-19.4	-0.6	26.1	-4.9	-9.0	5.7	-10.9	-1.1	23.9	-4.3
2016	7.0	-20.8	-0.6	28.6	-6.8	-9.2	4.9	-11.5	-1.8	26.1	-4.6

Source: Authors' calculations.

an expansionary fiscal policy, has led to a real appreciation and to a large US current account deficit, but with limited exchange rate misalignments. However a coordinated intervention of the central banks was decided with the Plazza agreements of 1985 to stop the rise of the dollar and avoid the building of unsustainable imbalances (McKinnon, 1993). In the second half of the 1980s

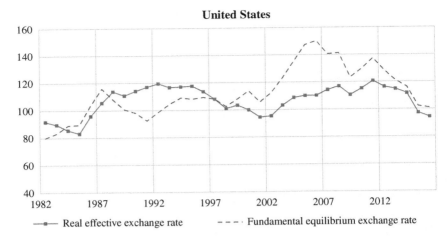

Figure 2.3 Actual and equilibrium real effective exchange rate of the dollar (basis 100 in 2000).

Source: Authors' calculation.

the appreciation of the European currencies and of the yen against the dollar allowed a large real depreciation of the dollar and an important improvement of the US current account. A new international intervention, the Louvre agreements of 1987, authorised a stabilisation of the dollar. The US current account continued to improve and the dollar became increasingly undervalued in real terms (20% in 1991–1992).

But, from the beginning of the 1990s, a complete reversal has been at work. A progressive real depreciation of the equilibrium value of the dollar has reflected the structural loss of US competitiveness due to the effects of the globalisation, of the increasing offshoring and of the debt-led growth regime. The undervaluation of the dollar has decreased and the US currency became overvalued (−11% in 2001). Since then, in spite of a new real depreciation, the dollar has appeared more and more overvalued (reaching −30% in real effective terms in 2005–2006). This real overvaluation of the dollar was an illustration of the structural imbalances of the US economy at the eve of the crisis of 2008. Another side of these imbalances were the huge current deficit (−6% of the GDP in 2006) and the net borrowing and, consequently, the indebtedness of the private sector. Such process was hardly sustainable.

After the crisis erupted, the real depreciation of the dollar has been small. Even more, after 2011, the dollar has appreciated in real effective terms, mainly due to the difficulties of the European and Japanese economies. However the overvaluation of the dollar has been progressively reduced. This evolution appeared as the consequence of the real appreciation of the equilibrium value of the dollar which has been induced by the fall of the activity and the cuts of

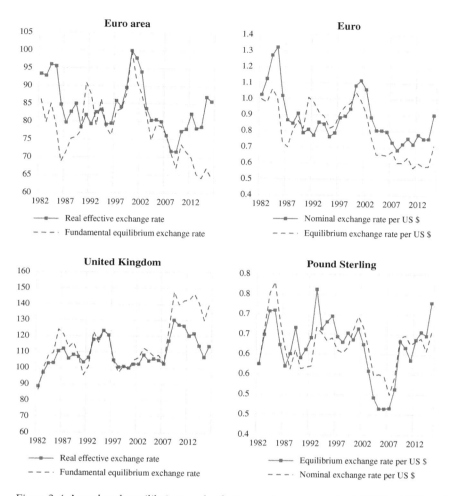

Figure 2.4 Actual and equilibrium real effective exchange rates (basis 100 in 2000) and bilateral exchange rates against the dollar of the euro and the pound sterling.

Source: Authors' calculation.

the imports. The current deficit has been brought back to a level close to its equilibrium value and the overvaluation of the dollar appeared limited.

Euro and pound sterling

The story of the European currencies and of the euro is quite different. Figure 2.4 represents a weighted average of the national European currencies that existed before 1999. During the first half of the 1980s the euro has depreciated in nominal terms against the dollar, reflecting the European inflationist drift which contrasted with the US stabilisation. As a result, the euro was largely undervalued against the dollar in 1985 (30%), but less in real effective terms (18%). After the Plazza and Louvre agreements, the second part of the 1980s was marked by a rebalancing with a large nominal appreciation against the dollar and a more moderate real effective one. In 1990 the euro was close to its equilibrium value. A stabilised parity, both in nominal and real terms, prevailed until the middle of the 1990s. The FEER of the euro depreciated in the second part of the 1990s as a consequence of the costs of the reunification for the German economy. This didn't lead to exchange rate misalignments as the actual euro also depreciated. From 2000 the euro became undervalued, slightly in real effective terms, more clearly in nominal terms against the dollar, in spite of its appreciation. This undervaluation resulted from painful adjustments, especially in Germany with the Shroeder plan, which led to a real appreciation of the euro FEER. In 2007, just before the financial crisis, the imbalances were less marked at the level of the whole euro zone than in the United States. The euro zone current account was close to its equilibrium value and the real exchange rate close to the FEER.

Since the burst of the crisis in 2008, things have changed a lot. Due to the institutional crisis of the euro zone and the fragility of the monetary union (see Chapter 4), the euro has depreciated in nominal and real terms and has became massively undervalued (28% in real terms, 26% in nominal terms against the dollar in 2016). The euro zone current surplus has exceeded 4% of GDP, mainly at the benefit of Germany. As it will be explained later in this chapter, this is due to the inconsistency of the European monetary union. The euro zone has became one of the main sources of the global imbalances.

Before turning to the two main East Asian currencies, a quick look can be thrown at the pound sterling case. From the beginning of the 1980s to the middle of the 1990s the trend of real depreciation has been sustained (around 30%) and has allowed the disappearance of the real overvaluation with the restoration of a current surplus. Since the end of the 1990s a reversal has appeared with a new real appreciation and an increasing current deficit. However the exchange rate misalignment remained limited before the burst of the financial crisis of 2008, in contrast with the US case. The pound sterling was even undervalued compared with the dollar. Afterwards the financial crisis has strongly hit the British economy. A large real overvaluation (around −20% from 2012 to 2016) has appeared in spite of a real and nominal depreciation of the pound sterling. This was due to the even larger depreciation of the real exchange rate equilibrium which reflected the deep imbalances of the British economy. A new worsening of the current account appeared in 2014–2016 and was at the opposite of the increasing current surplus of the euro zone.

Yen and yuan

The yen has followed a specific path since the 1980s (Figure 2.5). After the Plazza agreements a sharp nominal revaluation of the yen (the "endaka"), beginning in 1986 and continuing until 1995, has removed progressively the structural undervaluation of the yen which was a major component of the Japanese strategy of industrialisation since the 1960s. This revaluation could be endured thanks to the efficiency of the Japanese productive system which authorised a large revaluation of the equilibrium exchange rate of the yen. The "toyotism" was triumphing at the world level during the 1980s and appeared as the successor of the "fordism". The real overvaluation of the yen remained limited until the middle of the 1990s (−3% in 1995) and the yen was close to its equilibrium parity, both in nominal and real terms.

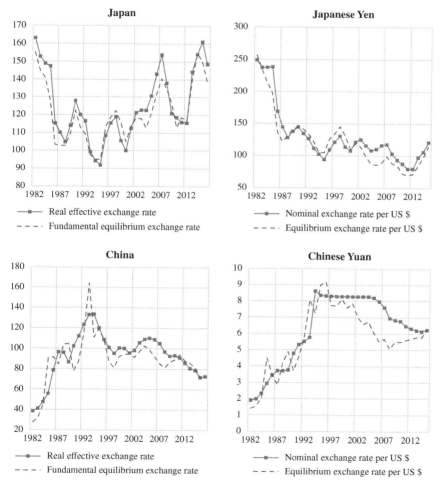

Figure 2.5 Actual and equilibrium real effective exchange rates (basis 100 in 2000) and bilateral exchange rates against the dollar of the yen and the yuan.

Source: Authors' calculation.

However a turning point took place in 1995. The Japanese economic situation has been deteriorated a lot since 1991 with the burst of a housing and financial crisis due to an uncontrolled liberalisation. The Japan faced a large slowdown, the balance sheet recession (Koo, 20081), which was only mitigated by an active fiscal policy. From 1995 the exchange rate policy changed with a depreciation of the yen compared to the dollar (25% between 1995 and 1998). A flexible policy, anchored to the dollar, continued until 2007, leading to a large real depreciation (55% between 1995 and 2007) due to the Japanese deflation. The undervaluation of the yen has been re-established, although relatively limited (17% in nominal terms, 9% in real effective terms in 2007). This moderate undervaluation of the yen is explained by the simultaneous depreciation of the FEER linked to the decline of the Japanese competitiveness during this period (limits of the offshoring strategy, lesser performances in the new technologies). In spite of these drawbacks, the export-led strategy was used to help the Japanese economy to partly recover from the long stagnation of the 1990s. Moreover, the increasing Japanese current surplus contributed to the global imbalances.

The financial crisis of 2008 badly hit the Japanese economy. The yen appreciated sharply against the dollar and the undervaluation disappeared once again, which penalized more the Japanese growth. The current surplus shrunk. Since 2012 a new change, the Abenomics, occurred with another wave of quantitative easing and the aim of sustaining the inflation. It induced a new depreciation in nominal and real terms, leading to a return of a moderate undervaluation of the yen (7% in real terms in 2015–2016) and an upswing of the current account, but without solving the long-term problems of the Japanese economy.

China is the country where the structural changes have been the deepest since the launching of the transition period in 1979. The evolution of the exchange rate of the yuan at the beginning of the 1980s is difficult to interpret due to the mode of regulation of the external trade that prevailed at that time. However, the yuan seemed to be strikingly overvalued in the middle of the 1980s (20% in nominal terms compared to dollar, 30% in real terms) with a massive current account deficit. The introduction of an exchange rate determined by the swap centres led to de facto devaluation that permitted to reverse this situation until the stabilisation of 1990 when the yuan was close to its equilibrium parity, with significant current surplus contrasting with the slowing down of the economic activity. Renewed devaluations and the increasing usage of the swap exchange rate allowed to follow the nominal and real depreciation of the equilibrium exchange rate in a context of degradation of the current account and of considerable inflation, so that in 1994, the year of the unification of the exchange rate system, the yuan was always close to its equilibrium parity in nominal and real terms.

The second half of the 1990s marked a turning point. The economic boom and the return of current surplus, while the FDI inflows allowed a reduction of the current account target, led to a revaluation of the equilibrium level of the yuan which illustrated the important progress of the Chinese competitiveness. The maintenance of the nominal parity of the yuan meant then an increasing, and afterwards persistent, undervaluation of the Chinese currency in nominal (around 60%) and in real terms (around 33%). This framework helps to explain the resistance of the yuan facing the Asian crisis. The undervaluation has been only temporarily reduced in 1999 after the large devaluations of most of the East Asian competitors. After the Asian crisis the yuan has been stable against the dollar until 2005 and has after moderately appreciated until 2008. It remained largely undervalued, in spite of a real effective appreciation. This apparent paradox is simply explained by the larger revaluation of the equilibrium exchange rate of the yuan due to the remarkable improvement of the Chinese productive system's efficiency. This exchange rate policy can be easily understood from the Chinese point of view as it boosted the manufacturing sector but it contributed to the persistency of global imbalances.

The impact of the financial crisis of 2008 on East Asia has been more limited, although significant at short term and unequal according to the countries. The undervaluation of the yuan has been preserved and then progressively reduced. Combined with the huge Chinese recovery plan of 2008, it has allowed China to preserve a high growth and to escape to the crisis. The undervaluation has come to an end in 2011 in real terms, in 2015 in bilateral term against the dollar. Large capital flights happened since 2014, leading to a period of tensions during the summer 2015 which have been overcome rather efficiently. Chinese authorities faced new challenges and had to consolidate a new growth regime, more turned towards the domestic market and consumption. Exchange rate policy is a key component of this new growth regime. Three options have been considered. The first one was to accept a progressive and moderate depreciation against the dollar to limit the increase of the Chinese labour cost. The risk would have been to perpetuate the capital flights and create some insecurity. The second option was a larger devaluation to recreate more important cost advantages based on an undervaluation of the yuan. It would have been a shock treatment with a major impact at world level. It would also have been in contradiction with the strategy of progressive upgrading of the production, which has been reaffirmed many times. The third option was a stabilisation of the yuan with the continuation of some forms of capital controls. It was coherent with the industrial strategy followed but it was more in contradiction with the desire of a progressive financial liberalisation. It is the choice which has been made in 2016 and confirmed in 2017. The yuan has remained close to its equilibrium parity and, in this sense, China is no more a source of global imbalances, as it is illustrated by the stabilisation of its current surplus around 2% of GDP, also close to its equilibrium value. But China is still a source of concern in matter of foreign trade for a lot of subjects (the role of state-owned enterprises with opaque subsidies, the controls on foreign firms operating in China, the problems of intellectual property rights).

Exchange rate misalignments and growth

Exchange rate misalignments reflect internal and external disequilibria. The question of their impact on economic activity is another issue which has been highly debated. Traditionally a lasting undervaluation sustains exports and reduces imports thanks to a better price competitiveness. It leads to transfers in favour of the tradable sector that can improve its profit and its investment and generates a virtuous circle. Growth is led by the net exports. Higher investment in the sectors exposed to the international competition can improve the productivity and the quality of the products that enhances the non-price competitiveness. This favourable dynamics can allow a progressive revaluation of the currency and an extinction of the initial undervaluation. However, this virtuous circle is not secured. It assumes that the firms don't take advantage of the undervaluation to increase more their prices, inducing a higher inflation and a loss of the original advantage of price competitiveness. It assumes also that firms are not content with their initial favourable position and make effort to upgrade their products and the quality of their specialization.

Conversely, a lasting overvaluation has the opposite effects. It reduces exports and fosters imports at the detriment of domestic producers. The export sectors suffer from negative transfers and reduced profits that limit their investments. A vicious circle follows with deterioration of productivity and of non-price competitiveness that strengthens the initial overvaluation, unless a devaluation interrupts this sequence. However, this vicious circle can be mitigated or even reversed. The overvaluation reduces the imported inflation, which improves the price competitiveness. A stronger competition from foreign producers encourages firms to increase their productivity and to enhance their non-price competitiveness. Bresser-Pereira, among others, has emphasized the need for a competitive exchange rate to sustain the development of the manufacturing sector (Bresser-Pereira, 2010; Bresser-Pereira et al., 2014). He has underlined that the overvaluation often occur in developing countries due to the Dutch disease (associated to abundant natural resources) and excessive capital inflows.

Furthermore, this relation between exchange rate misalignments and growth is non-linear. For many reasons exchange rate misalignments may have a decreasing impact on growth and foreign trade. There are limits to the improvement of foreign trade due to undervaluation. Exports cannot increase without limits due to supply-side and many imports cannot be reduced due to problems of non-substitutability. The international division of labour with the global value chains holds trade in tight constraints. Perverse effects can appear with induced inflation and change in the relative prices. High undervaluation may even have negative effects on growth. Symmetrically, there are limits to the imports' increase due to overvaluation. Exports can become less sensible to larger loss of competitiveness. This non-linearity depends of the structural characteristics of each country, especially in terms of specialization, and can be studied in more details.

Without pretending to treat this question in its entirety, an illustration can be given. A non-linear relation between exchange rate misalignments and growth has been estimated, based on the previous exchange rate misalignments and on panel data for developed and emerging countries (Aflouk and Mazier, 2013). A Panel Smooth Transition Regression associated to the real exchange rate misalignments with a threshold effect has been used in complement to traditional explanatory variables used in the literature on growth (lagged income per capita, human capital stock, investment rate, government expenditures, degree of openness, foreign direct investment). An overvaluation has a negative impact on growth while an undervaluation sustains growth until an estimated threshold (15.5% for the emerging countries and 9% for the developed ones). This can be explained by the fact that misalignments are generally higher in emerging countries than in the developed ones. The coefficient linking growth and misalignment is weaker for emerging countries (0.02) than for developed countries (0.08). Due to non-linearity and coefficients' value an undervaluation has a positive effect on growth even beyond the estimated threshold for the developed countries. For the emerging countries the impact of misalignments on growth is positive only in the case of small undervaluation.

The results will be discussed more in detail for the European countries in the Chapter 4 and for the emerging countries in the Chapter 7. Regarding the main economic partners examined in this chapter, several points are worth highlighting. The undervaluation of the dollar has significantly supported the US growth at the end of the 1980s and the beginning of the 1990s (up to 1% of GDP growth more in 1990) while the dollar overvaluation in the first half of the 2000s has been a drag on the US growth. Similarly, the Japanese growth has been supported by the undervaluation of the yen in the 1980s (up to 0.75% of GDP growth more in 1985) and this was a permanent development strategy for the Japanese industry since the 1970s. On the opposite after the yen revaluation the overvaluation has contributed to the blocking of the growth in the 1990s before undervaluation was used again in the 2000s to help fight stagnation. For the euro zone as a whole, the exchange rate misalignments have been too limited to have a significant impact but, as we will see in the Chapters 4 and 5, the results are quite different for each European country. Last, for China the results are less convincing and would need further investigation. The support of the yuan undervaluation for the growth exists, especially from 1994 to 2010, but seems rather limited. It is a general result for the emerging countries. The coefficient linking growth and misalignment is weaker and undervaluation has a negative effect on growth above a threshold of 15%.

Conclusion

The aim of this chapter was to give an evaluation of the global imbalances using the notion of FEER. The FEER is defined as the level of exchange rate which allows the economy to reach simultaneously the internal and external equilibrium. This approach has been preferred to the BEER, mainly because with the BEER there is no guarantee of the consistency of the estimation of the different equilibrium exchange rates at the world level and because the econometric method imposes that the exchange rate misalignments have an average value equal to zero over the sample period, which is a strong hypothesis. A FEER approach has been followed, combining both previous methodology and recent improvements in order to solve the problem raised by the treatment of the residual country. Equilibrium current accounts have been estimated for the main countries. Using a model of world trade, a FEER has been estimated for the main currencies.

A first wave of global imbalances has emerged during the beginning of the 1980s with an increasing US current account deficit contrasting with Japanese and European surplus. The dollar has appreciated in nominal and real terms, but the movement has been stopped by the international cooperation of central banks in 1985–1987, leading to a devaluation, then a stabilisation of the dollar. In return the European and Japanese currencies have appreciated and reduced their undervaluations. International cooperation has played an important role at that time with a rather precocious intervention and an outstanding contribution of Japan which has accepted a sharp revaluation of the yen.

During the 1990s and 2000s the European economies, marked by the transition to the single currency and the launching of the euro, have not been at the source of global imbalances. Germany faced a major shock with the reunification which deeply affected its external performances and more broadly those of the whole Europe during the 1990s. European current surplus vanished and the euro depreciated. During the 2000s, on the contrary, German adjustments led to a reversal with the return to current surplus and a moderate undervaluation of the euro. During these two decades the international imbalances were limited at the European level but large intra-European imbalances existed, as it will be analysed below.

In Japan facing long-term stagnation, a turning point appeared in 1995 with a depreciation of the yen which induced a new real undervaluation and rising current surplus. Accordingly, during the 2000s Japan contributed to the rise of new global imbalances.

China became progressively a major player at the world level with the success of the transition period toward market economy during the 1980s. The unification of the exchange rate regime in 1994 marked the end of a long period of nominal and real devaluation of the yuan. A new regime settled from the second half of the 1990s with a structural undervaluation of the yuan which represented a strong support to the manufacturing sector. A virtuous circle combined improvement of the efficiency of the export sector, revaluation of the exchange rate equilibrium, increasing undervaluation of the yuan, implicit transfer to the export sector. But with increasing current surplus, China also contributed massively to global imbalances.

These global imbalances, coming from Japan and China but also from many emerging countries which wanted to constitute international reserves after the shock of the Asian crisis in 1998, concentrated in the United States. The US deficits enlarged with an increasing overvaluation of the dollar and rising indebtedness of the private sector, leading to hardly sustainable imbalances.

With the financial crisis of 2008 large adjustments occurred through the fall of activity and the cut of imports. US current deficits shrunk, the real overvaluation of the dollar was progressively reduced in spite of the real dollar appreciation. The dollar acted as a safe haven currency facing the crisis of the euro area and the lasting blockage of the Japanese economy.

The post-crisis period has been characterized by new configurations. To a large extent China managed to escape to the crisis. A new growth regime, more turned towards the domestic market, settled progressively. The current surplus has been reduced while the undervaluation of the yuan has vanished since 2011–2015, both in real and nominal terms against the dollar. To a certain extent, from a macroeconomic point of view, China is no more a source of global imbalances, although many subjects of concern subsist at the world level in matter of intellectual property rights, transfer of technology or control of foreign investments. China didn't accept to play a role equivalent to Japan in the second half of the 1980s or Germany in the 1970s. The yuan has been brought back to its equilibrium value but China has avoided a too large revalorisation and managed to preserve an equilibrium position.

Japan is in a less favourable position. The Japanese current surplus has been cut by the fall of exports. Firstly, the yen has appreciated and the undervaluation disappeared. But secondly a new wave of quantitative easing led to a yen depreciation in real and nominal terms. The undervaluation of the yen and the current surpluses have reappeared. The difficulty of the Japanese economy to define a new growth regime contributes to perpetuate international imbalances. A wage–led strategy would be more appropriate in the case of Japan to sustain both domestic demand and inflation.

The European case is more worrying. Due to the inability to reform the euro area governance, the status quo has been maintained with a weak growth, a real and nominal depreciation of the euro and a rising current surplus. Intra-European imbalances have contributed to maintain international imbalances far larger than the Chinese ones. The question of these intra-European imbalances will be examined in detail in Chapter 4.

On the whole, in 2016 the yuan was close to its equilibrium parity while the dollar was only moderately overvalued. It was not at this level that the potential conflict between the United States and China had to focus. Exchange rate misalignments remained however with, on the one hand, the yen and, mostly, the euro undervalued and, on the other hand, the pound sterling largely overvalued. In this respect the depreciation of the pound sterling after the Brexit was welcome. The currency of the rest of the world was also overvalued, reflecting the difficulties of many emerging countries after the end of the boom of the raw materials. Global imbalances were more diffuse than in 2007.

In a long-term perspective, the role played by the exchange rate policy to sustain the manufacturing sector and an export-led strategy has been discussed. A non-linear relation between exchange rate misalignments and growth could be highlighted. The relation appeared significant in the case of the US and Japan. Structural undervaluation of the yen has been a key component of the

Japanese industrial strategy from the 1960s to 1985. Conversely, the sharp revaluation of the yen after the second half of the 1980s has been a handicap and has contributed, beside other factors, to the long-term stagnation. The impact of exchange rate misalignments was also marked in the United States in the second half of the 1980s (positively) and in the first half of the 2000s (negatively). More surprisingly, the role of the long-term undervaluation of the yuan from the middle of the 1990s to 2010 seemed more limited. Further investigation would be needed.

This analysis of exchange rate misalignments has shed some light on the nature of the global imbalances which appeared since the 1990s. The world macroeconomic adjustments have now to be analysed more explicitly to understand how exchange rates, production, price, and capital flows interact.

Annex 2.1 Multinational model in differential logarithmic

Multinational model in logarithmic differential ($x = dX / X = (X - X^e) / X^e$) is transformed into:

$$x_i = \eta x_i \sum_{j \neq i} \alpha_{ij} m_j + \varepsilon x_i \left(pmx_i - px_i \right) \tag{1'}$$

$$pmx_i = \sum_{j \neq i} \lambda_{ij} \left(px_j - e_j \right) + e_i$$

$$m_i = \eta m_i di_i + \varepsilon m_i \left(pd_i - pm_i \right) \tag{2'}$$

$$pmm_i = \sum_{j \neq i} \mu_{ij} \left(px_j - e_j \right) + e_i$$

$$\sum_i vx_i \left(x_i + px_i - e_i \right) = \sum_i vm_i \left(m_i + pm_i - e_i \right) \tag{3'}$$

$$\sum_i wx_i x_i = \sum_i wm_i m_i \tag{4'}$$

$$px_i = \alpha x_i pmx_i + \left(1 - \alpha x_i \right) p_i \tag{5'}$$

$$pm_i = \alpha m_i pmm_i + \left(1 - \alpha m_i \right) pd_i \tag{6'}$$

$$pd_i = a_i pm_i + \left(1 - a_i \right) p_i \tag{7'}$$

$$r_i = e_i - pd_i + \sum_{j \neq i} \left(pd_j - e_j \right) \qquad (8')$$

$$b_i = \mu_i T_i \left(1 - \sigma_{petx_i} - \sigma_{x_i} \right) \left(px_i + x_i - pm_i - m_i \right) \qquad (9')$$

With *wx, wm, vx, vm* = the shares of each country in the world exports in volume, the world imports in volume, the world exports in value and the world imports in value, respectively; $T = PXX / PMM$ = ratio of exportation to importation; $\mu = PMM/PY$ = openness ratio; F = net external position in dollars; i = interest rates; $\sigma_x = iEF/PXX$ = ratio of external debt services to exports; $\sigma_{petx} = EP_{pet}M_{pet}/PXX$, ratio of net oil imports on non-oil exports;

$$\lambda_{ij} = \frac{X_{i \rightarrow j}}{X_i}; \mu_{ij} = \frac{M_{i \leftarrow j}}{M_i}; \alpha_{ij} = \frac{X_{i \rightarrow j}}{M_j}; v_{ij} = \left(\frac{X_{i \rightarrow j} + M_{i \leftarrow j}}{X_i + M_j} \right); \text{Source: CHELEM,}$$

CEPII database.

Annex 2.2 National model in differential logarithmic

National model in logarithmic differentials ($x = dX / X = (X - X^e) / X^e$) is transformed into:

$$x_i = \eta x_i d_i^* + \left(1 - \alpha x_i \right) \varepsilon x_i r_i \qquad (10')$$

$$m_i = \eta m_i di_i - \left(\alpha m_i \varepsilon m_i \right) r_i \qquad (11')$$

$$px_i = \alpha x_i r_i + p_i \qquad (12')$$

$$pm_i = \alpha m_i r_i + p_i \qquad (13')$$

$$b_i = \mu_i T_i \left(1 - \sigma_{petxi} - \sigma_{xi} \right) \left(px_i + x_i - pm_i - m_i \right) \qquad (14')$$

We can compute *r*, the misalignment of "national euro" in real effective terms ($r = dLogR = dR / R = (R - R^e) / R^e$):

$$\frac{dT_i}{T_i} = px_i x_i - pm_i m_i$$

$$\frac{dT_i}{T_i} = \left(\eta x_i d_i^* - \eta m_i di_i \right) + \left[\left(1 - \alpha x_i \varepsilon x_i \right) + \varepsilon m_i \alpha m_i + \alpha x_i - \alpha m_i \right] r_i$$

$$b_i = \mu_i dT_i \left(1 - \sigma_{petxi} - \sigma_{xi} \right)$$

$$\frac{dT_i}{T_i} = \frac{b_i}{\mu_i T_i \left(1 - \sigma_{petxi} - \sigma_{xi} \right)}$$

$$r_i = \left[\frac{\left(\left(b_i / \mu_i T_i \left(1 - \sigma_{petxi} - \sigma_{xi} \right) \right) + \eta m_i di_i - \eta x_i d_i^* \right)}{\left(\left(1 - \alpha x_i \right) \varepsilon x_i + \varepsilon m_i \alpha m_i + \alpha x_i - \alpha m_i \right)} \right] \tag{17}$$

By using the equation (4), we can find out e, the degree of misalignment in bilateral nominal terms. The partner countries' misalignments are given by the multinational model.

$$r_i = e_i + px_i^* - p_i \tag{15'}$$

Like in the multinational model, we suppose that $p_i = \dfrac{\left(P_i - P_i^e \right)}{P_i^e} = 0$

$$e_i = r_i - \sum_{j \neq i} \lambda_{ij} \left(px_j - e_j \right) \tag{18}$$

We can also compute the effective exchange rate misalignments based on consumer prices.

$$RC_i = \frac{E_i PD_i^*}{PD_i}$$

$$rc_i = e_i + pd_i^* - pd_i$$

$$pd_i^* = \sum_{j \neq i} v_{ij} \left(pd_j - e_j \right)$$

$$pd_i = \mu_i pm_i + \left(1 - \mu_i \right) p_i$$

$$pm_i = \alpha m_i \left(e_i + pm_i^* \right) + \left(1 - \alpha m_i \right) p_i$$

$$pd_i = \alpha m_i \mu_i \left(e_i + pm_i^* \right)$$

$$rc_i = \left(1 - \alpha m_i \mu_i \right) r_i + pd_i^* - px_i^*$$

$$rc_i = \left(1 - \alpha m_i \mu_i \right) r_i + \sum_{j \neq i} v_{ij} \left(pd_j - e_j \right) - \sum_{j \neq i} \lambda_{ij} \left(px_j - e_j \right) \tag{19}$$

(pd_j, e_j, px_j obtained thanks to the multinational model)

Annex 2.3

Table 2.4 Foreign trade elasticities

Country	Source	ε_x	ε_m	α_x	α_m	η_x	η_m
Japan	MIMOSA	1.26	1.47	0.19	0.56	1.01	1.50
	NIGEM	1.19	0.61	0.24	1.00	1.00	1.69
	Wren-Lewis	1.36	1.16	0.16	0.78	0.91	1.20
	OECD	1.05	0.40	0.28	0.51	1.00	1.00
China	Dées	0.71	1.02	0.56	0.66	0.75	1.04
	Brillet	0.66	0.46	0.85	0.60	1.00	0.98
	OECD	1.50	0.50*	1.00	1.00	1.00	1.57*
United States	MIMOSA	0.91	1.44	0.09	0.50	1.04	1.56
	NIGEM	0.52	0.61	0.00	1.00	1.00	2.52
	Wren-Lewis	0.96	1.35	0.19	0.55	1.12	2.00
	OECD	0.60	0.33	0.07	0.36	1.00	1.00
United Kingdom	MIMOSA	0.70	1.33	0.07	0.59	0.87	1.82
	Wren-Lewis	1.26	0.22	0.71	0.75	0.91	2.00
	OECD	0.60	0.28	0.47	0.79	1.00	1.00
Euro area	ECB	0.50	0.81	0.50	0.51	1.00	0.51**
	Hervé	1.39	0.30	0.75	0.64	1.05	1.06
RoW	Ad hoc	1.00	1.00	0.50	1.00	1.00	1.00
	Our estimates	0.58	1.66	0.65	1.02	1.00	1.35

Notes
*Kwack et al (2007).
** Non-oil import in volume.

Annex 2.4 Comparison with Cline and Williamson's estimates

In spite of some differences in the methodology, a comparison with Cline and Williamson's estimates is possible (Table 2.5). If, in both cases, the FEER framework is used, Cline's model has 35 countries, a simpler analysis of the foreign trade for each country with only one reduced equation to explain the current account and no structural approach of the current account equilibrium. Instead, it is simply supposed that external imbalances should not exceed 3% of GDP (in absolute value) in the medium term, which allows building a scenario of current account targets for the 30 non-oil exporting countries.

The results are close for the dollar, the yen, and the yuan. For the euro and the pound sterling a larger undervaluation of the euro and overvaluation of the pound sterling is found in our simulations in the recent period due to differences in the choice of the current account target (larger EU surplus and larger UK deficit compared with the target).

Table 2.5 Comparison with Cline and Williamson's estimates (in %)

REER		USA	EU	CHN	JPN	UK
2008	Our results	-18.9	0.9	17.6	2.5	-6.0
	Cline	-7.8	-4.3	12.6	4.2	-4.2
2014	Our results	-4.0	20.1	-3.7	-0.4	-21.0
	Cline	-1.0	-1.2	-0.9	-0.8	-0.7
BILATERAL		USA	EU	CHN	JPN	UK
2008	Our results	–	12.4	31.5	15.6	5.8
	Cline	–	2.7	23.4	15.1	1.0
2014	Our results	–	25.8	6.5	8.3	-6.2
	Cline	–	10.9	8.9	11.9	8.7

Sources: Cline, 2014; Williamson and Cline, 2008; authors' calculations.

3 Global imbalances and macroeconomic adjustments

A three-country SFC model

Jacques Mazier

Introduction

Beyond exchange rate misalignments, global imbalances must be analysed in a broader perspective. World macroeconomic adjustments are usually studied with the help of a general equilibrium model or with simpler portfolio models. These models provide an interesting analysis of the impact of exchange rates adjustments, the rates of return differential or the valuation effects. However, most of the time they consider that adjustments are carried out through relative prices with production and income remaining constant, which is rather unrealistic when a large depreciation occurs. This hypothesis is incompatible with the sharp decline in real production that has been observed during the crisis of 2008. Multi-country SFC models, along the lines of Godley and Lavoie, are more appropriate to deal with these events because they give a comprehensive description of the real and financial flows and stocks at the world level, can include most of ingredients of the previous models and do not presuppose that adjustments are limited to relative prices. They appear as an extension at the world level of the simple SFC model for a closed economy presented in Chapter 1 but without the description of the equities' market and of the financial cycles, which is an important simplification.

The chapter, based on Mazier and Tiou-Tagba Aliti (2012), is organized as follows. A second section summarizes the theoretical background. A third section presents a three-country SFC model with the United States, China, and the euro zone. Three versions will be considered. The first one, with fixed dollar–yuan parity, includes an active policy of the Chinese central bank regarding the diversification of its reserves. It is directly inspired by Lavoie and Zhao (2010). The second version is based on a flexible dollar–yuan parity, which can either be freely floating or the result of a policy target of the People's Bank of China, using the desired level of either the current account or the foreign reserves. This version emphasises the role that a more flexible dollar–yuan parity could play to reduce world imbalances. The third version generalises the previous results with a flexible-price model instead of a fixed-price one. The last section concludes.

Theoretical background

Applied forecasting macroeconomic models often pay little attention to the financial sector, due to the difficulty of accurately modelling financial variables. At a more theoretical level, world macroeconomic adjustments are usually analysed with two kinds of models. General equilibrium models (Obstfeld and Rogoff, 2005) give a representation of the world economy with a distinction between home and foreign produced traded goods and between traded and non-traded goods, using two or three countries. The general pattern of these models is based on traditional consumer choice theory, where the role of relative prices is formalized in great detail. In each market, supply and demand adjust via relative prices, with production assumed constant. Using net foreign assets, current accounts can be computed for each country. Given the structure of gross assets and liabilities denominated in each of the currencies involved, valuation effects can be introduced, while at the same time it is also possible to analyse the effects of changing interest rates. The model is used to evaluate different scenarios describing how the US current account could have returned to equilibrium thanks to exchange rate adjustments of the dollar, euro, and yuan.

The model is rather powerful, as it can incorporate a whole set of effects (valuation effects, differentials in interest rates, traded and non-traded goods). One of the main results is the importance of the terms of trade between traded and non-traded goods, which are often underestimated in this kind of analysis. Conversely, the valuation effect seems less important than in other studies (Gourinchas and Rey, 2005). However, the model suffers from several weaknesses. First, production levels are assumed given, which seems rather unrealistic considering the amplitude of exchange rate adjustments (around 30% in real terms, or even more) and the size of actual declines in production after the crisis of 2008. Second, the model is focused on the real sphere. The link with the financial side is realised only through a rigid matrix that describes the structure of assets and liabilities in each currency, without a consistent analysis of the stock-flow dynamics. Third, as it is usual in this kind of models, there is no analysis of firms' investment. Last, the model is simulated only in real terms. Inflation is introduced in a very simplified way, through the assumption that central banks have control over inflation rates.

A simpler portfolio model of exchange rate and current account (Blanchard et al., 2005) is only focused on the imbalances between the United States and the rest of world. Two equations are considered, one describing the portfolio balance, the second the current account balance, with two main variables: US net debt and the dollar exchange rate. The model incorporates valuation effects and, exogenously, the difference between US and foreign rates of return. The dollar devaluation necessary to return to a balanced US current account is evaluated (at around 40%) and alternative scenarios are built in. The model is more elegant and easier to manage than the previous one, but it suffers from the same weaknesses. Production is assumed constant and all the adjustments take place via relative prices. The description of financial variables is highly simplified with only one asset, the supply of which is taken as exogenous. As in Obstfeld and Rogoff's model, there is no real capital accumulation. With constant production and assets, international macroeconomic adjustments are analysed in an overly restrictive way. The integration between real and financial variables, although central in the core of the model, appears to be limited.

SFC models along the lines of Godley and Lavoie (2005) and Lavoie and Zhao (2010) are more appropriate for these purposes. They provide a consistent analysis of the real and financial flows and stocks at the world level, with a whole description of the main institutional sectors: households, firms, banks, and the government. Starting with two countries, the United States and the rest of the world, they have been enlarged to three countries in order to analyse US, European, and Chinese imbalances. They can include most of the ingredients of the previous models, such as valuation effects and differences across rates of return. They do not assume that adjustments are limited to relative prices, since production is determined by aggregate demand, as in the Keynesian tradition. Exchange rates result from an explicit confrontation between the supply of and the demand for assets, although exchange rates require adjustments operating throughout the whole model. Fixed exchange rates can also be introduced. These SFC models look like Taylor's (2004) approach, but they do not include an additional exchange rate expectation equation. This is an important difference.

A three-country SFC model is considered in this chapter. A comparison of two exchange rate regimes with fixed or adjustable dollar–yuan parity shows its key role for global rebalancing. Other mechanisms, such as reducing US demand or increasing Chinese domestic demand, could be studied with this model but are not presented due to lack of space. The introduction of flexible prices attempts at considering the constraints induced by the yuan revaluation and the risk of deflation.

A three-country model with fixed dollar–yuan parity

The world economy is divided into three blocks: the United States, the euro area, and China. The dollar and the euro are floating while the dollar–yuan parity is fixed. Two kinds of assets are considered in each country, banking deposits and Treasury bills, issued by each government and held by households and the banking sector of each country. Firms accumulate fixed capital and finance their investments by profit and credit. The wage share and prices are assumed constant. World adjustments take place both through income and exchange rates. The impact of a change in the foreign reserves' behaviour of the Chinese central bank is also studied.

The structure of the model

Each bloc is made up of four institutional sectors (households, firms, government, and banks, the latter sector including the central bank). Exchange rates are defined as 1 dollar = xr_1 euro = xr_2 yuan and 1euro = $1/xr_1$ dollar = xr_3 yuan. Table 3.1 describes the balance sheet of each sector. In the following paragraphs equations are written for a generic country, with indications in case of national specificities. The three countries are assumed quite similar, except with regards to exchange rate policy and central bank behaviour. More details with the whole set of equations, list of variables, calibration and sensitivity tests are available at Mazier and Tiou-Tagba Aliti (2009).

Equilibrium of goods and services

$$Y^{\mathfrak{E}} = C^{\mathfrak{E}} + G + I^{\mathfrak{E}} + X^{\mathfrak{E}} - IM^{\mathfrak{E}} \tag{1}$$

Exports

$$X^{\mathfrak{E}} = X_{\$}^{\mathfrak{E}} + X_{¥}^{\mathfrak{E}} \tag{2}$$

$$X_{\$}^{\mathfrak{E}} = IM_{\mathfrak{E}}^{\$}.xr1 \tag{3}$$

$$X_{¥}^{\mathfrak{E}} = IM_{\mathfrak{E}}^{¥} / xr3 \tag{4}$$

Imports

$$IM^{\mathfrak{E}} = IM_{\$}^{\mathfrak{E}} + IM_{¥}^{\mathfrak{E}} \tag{5}$$

$$logIM_{\$}^{\mathfrak{E}} = \mu m_{1}^{\mathfrak{E}} + \mu m_{2}^{\mathfrak{E}} * logS_{t-1}^{\mathfrak{E}} - \mu m_{3}^{\mathfrak{E}} log(xr1_{t-1}) \tag{6}$$

$$logIM_{¥}^{\mathfrak{E}} = \mu m_{4}^{\mathfrak{E}} + \mu m_{5}^{\mathfrak{E}} * logS_{t-1}^{\mathfrak{E}} + \mu m_{6}^{\mathfrak{E}} log(xr3_{t-1}) \tag{7}$$

Sales equal domestic and foreign demand in each country

$$S^{\mathfrak{E}} = C^{\mathfrak{E}} + G^{\mathfrak{E}} + I^{\mathfrak{E}} + X^{\mathfrak{E}} \tag{8}$$

Households

Disposable income

$$Y^{d,\mathfrak{E}} = W^{\mathfrak{E}} + r_{t-1}^{\mathfrak{E}} B_{\mathfrak{E},d,t-1}^{\mathfrak{E}} + r_{t-1}^{\$} B_{\mathfrak{E},d,t-1}^{\$} + r_{t-1}^{¥} B_{\mathfrak{E},d,t-1}^{¥} + r_{d,t-1}^{\mathfrak{E}} M_{t-1}^{\mathfrak{E}} - T^{\mathfrak{E}} \tag{9}$$

Table 3.1 Balance sheet of the three blocs

	Euro area				United States				China			
	H	F	Gov	CB	H	F	Gov	CB	H	F	Gov	CB
Capital		$K^€$				$K^\$$				$K^¥$		
Money	$M^€$			$-M^€$	$M^\$$			$-M^\$$	$M^¥$			$-M^¥$
Bills €	$B_€^€$		$-\boldsymbol{B}^€$	$B_{€,CB}^€$	$B_\$^€ / xr1$			$B_{\$,CB}^€ / xr1$	$B_¥^€.xr3$			$B_{¥,CB}^€.xr3$
Bills $	$B_€^\$.xr1$			$B_{€,CB}^\$.xr1$	$B_\$^\$$		$-\boldsymbol{B}^\$$	$B_{\$,CB}^\$$	$B_¥^\$.xr2$			$B_{¥,CB}^\$.xr2$
Bills ¥	$B_€^¥ / xr3$				$B_\$^¥ / xr2$				$B_¥^¥$		$-\boldsymbol{B}^¥$	$B_{¥,CB}^¥$
Loan		$-L^€$		$L^€$		$-L^\$$		$L^\$$		$-L^¥$		$L^¥$
Wealth	$-V_h^€$	$-V_f^€$	$\boldsymbol{B}^€$	$-V_{CB}^€$	$-V_h^\$$	$-V_f^\$$	$\boldsymbol{B}^\$$	$-V_{CB}^\$$	$-V_h^¥$	$-V_f^¥$	$\boldsymbol{B}^¥$	$-V_{CB}^¥$

Source: Authors' construction.

Haig-Simons disposable income including capital gains

$$Y_{hs}^{d,\epsilon} = Y^{d,\epsilon} + \Delta\left(xr1\right)B_{\epsilon,s,t-1}^{\$} + \Delta\frac{1}{xr3})B_{\epsilon,s,t-1}^{¥} \tag{10}$$

Taxes

$$T^{\epsilon} = \theta^{\epsilon} \star (W^{\epsilon} + r_{t-1}^{\epsilon}B_{\epsilon,d,t-1}^{\epsilon} + r_{t-1}^{\$}B_{\epsilon,d,t-1}^{\$} + r_{t-1}^{¥}B_{\epsilon,d,t-1}^{¥} + r_{d,t-1}^{\epsilon}M_{t-1}^{\epsilon}) \tag{11}$$

Households' consumption with wealth effect

$$C^{\epsilon} = \alpha_1^{\epsilon}Y_{hs}^{d,\epsilon} + \alpha_2^{\epsilon}V_{h,t-1}^{\epsilon} \tag{12}$$

Households' wealth accumulation

$$\Delta V_h^{\epsilon} = Y_{hs}^{d,\epsilon} - C^{\epsilon} \tag{13}$$

Households' demand for bills

According to Godley–Tobin's approach, the demand for assets depends on the rates of return of a basket of assets. For foreign assets, expected exchange rate variations would have to be included for a better understanding of exchange rate determination. However, this question has been examined by Lavoie and Daigle (2011) in a simple two-country model. They introduced fundamentalist and chartist expectations based on some assessed conventional value and past trends respectively. They found that, as long as the proportion of chartist actors relative to fundamentalist agents is not too large, the main conclusions of the model without exchange rate expectation hold, although the introduction of exchange rate expectations has a significant impact on the actual exchange rate. When chartists dominate over fundamentalists, the model becomes more unstable and there is no convergence when a shock occurs. This unstable case will not be considered here, and fundamentalists will be assumed to be dominant. Since it does not change results fundamentally, it will also be assumed, following Godley and Lavoie's previous works, that the expected exchange rate variation is constant (positive or negative) and equal to zero on average.

$$B_{\epsilon,d}^{\epsilon} = V_h^{\epsilon}\left(\gamma_{10}^{\epsilon} + \gamma_{11}^{\epsilon}r^{\epsilon} + \gamma_{12}^{\epsilon}r^{\$} + \gamma_{13}^{\epsilon}r^{¥} + \gamma_{14}^{\epsilon}r_d^{\epsilon}\right) \tag{14}$$

$$B_{\epsilon,d}^{\$} = V_h^{\epsilon}\left(\gamma_{20}^{\epsilon} + \gamma_{21}^{\epsilon}r^{\epsilon} + \gamma_{22}^{\epsilon}r^{\$} + \gamma_{23}^{\epsilon}r^{¥} + \gamma_{24}^{\epsilon}r_d^{\epsilon}\right) \tag{15}$$

$$B_{€,d}^{¥} = V_h^{€} \left(\gamma_{30}^{€} + \gamma_{31}^{€} r^{€} + \gamma_{32}^{€} r^{\$} + \gamma_{33}^{€} r^{¥} + \gamma_{34}^{€} r_d^{€} \right) \tag{16}$$

$$M_d^{€} = V_h^{€} \left(\gamma_{40}^{€} + \gamma_{41}^{€} r^{€} + \gamma_{42}^{€} r^{\$} + \gamma_{43}^{€} r^{¥} + \gamma_{44}^{€} r_d^{€} \right) \tag{17 bis}$$

Coefficients must respect some constraints according to Godley and Tobin's approach (Godley and Lavoie, 2007a). Given the accountable constraint on households' wealth, only three asset demand equations are independent. The equation describing the demand for deposits (17 bis) will not be written.

$$M_d^{€} = V_h^{€} - B_{€,d}^{€} - B_{€,d}^{\$} - B_{€,d}^{¥} \tag{17}$$

Government

The public deficit is financed by issuing Treasury bills. Public expenditures G are exogenous. Banks' profit is transferred to government as taxes. Consequently, banks' saving is nil.

$$\Delta B_s^{€} = G^{€} - T^{€} + r_{t-1}^{€} B_{s,t-1}^{€} - P_{CB}^{€} \tag{18}$$

$$P_{CB}^{€} = r_{t-1}^{€} B_{€,CB,s,t-1}^{€} + r_{t-1}^{\$} B_{€,CB,s,t-1}^{\$} \star xr1 + r_{l,t-1}^{€} L_{t-1}^{€} - r_{d,t-1}^{€} M_{t-1}^{€} \tag{19}$$

American and European Treasury bills are bought by households and banks of the three areas. On the contrary Chinese bills are bought only by Chinese banks and households of the three areas.

$$B_s^{€} = B_{€,s}^{€} + B_{€,CB,s}^{€} + B_{\$,s}^{€} + B_{\$,CB,s}^{€} + B_{¥,s}^{€} + B_{¥,CB,s}^{€} \tag{20}$$

$$B_s^{\$} = B_{\$,s}^{\$} + B_{\$,CB,s}^{\$} + B_{€,s}^{\$} + B_{€,CB,s}^{\$} + B_{¥,s}^{\$} + B_{¥,CB,s}^{\$} \tag{21}$$

$$B_s^{¥} = B_{¥,s}^{¥} + B_{¥,CB,s}^{¥} + B_{€,s}^{¥} + B_{\$,s}^{¥} \tag{22}$$

The equilibrium between the supply of and the demand for assets by households is given by:

$$B_{€,s}^{¥} = B_{€,d}^{¥} \star xr_3 \tag{23}$$

$$B^\$_{\text{€},s} = B^\$_{\text{€},d}/xr_1 \tag{24}$$

$$B^{\text{€}}_{\text{€},s} = B^{\text{€}}_{\text{€},d} \tag{25}$$

Firms

The wage share is assumed constant. Profit is determined as a residual.

$$W^{\text{€}} = \lambda^{\text{€}} \star Y^{\text{€}} \tag{26}$$

$$P^{\text{€}} = Y^{\text{€}} - W^{\text{€}} - r^{\text{€}}_{l,t-1} L^{\text{€}}_{t-1} \tag{27}$$

Non-financial investment is determined following an accelerator principle, with a desired capital stock K^T and a constant capital productivity in the long run. The influence of the rate of profit and of the credit cost could be added as in Chapter 1. Investment is financed by retained earnings and debt. Firms can obtain all the credit demanded, without rationing. The wealth of firms is given by the balance sheet equilibrium.

$$I^{\text{€}} = \gamma^{\text{€}}\left(K^{T,\text{€}}_{t-1} - K^{\text{€}}_{t-1}\right) + \delta^{\text{€}} K^{\text{€}}_{t-1} \tag{28}$$

$$K^{\text{€}} = \left(1 - \delta^{\text{€}}\right)K^{\text{€}}_{t-1} + I^{\text{€}} \tag{29}$$

$$K^{T,\text{€}} = k^{\text{€}} Y^{\text{€}}_{t-1} \tag{30}$$

$$\Delta L^{\text{€}}_d = I^{\text{€}} - P^{\text{€}} \tag{31}$$

$$V^{\text{€}}_{ff} = K^{\text{€}} - L^{\text{€}} \qquad or \qquad \Delta V = P^{\text{€}} - \delta^{\text{€}} K^{\text{€}} \tag{32}$$

Banks

We consider an aggregated banking system with both commercial banks and a central bank. We suppose that the Fed does not hold foreign bills, due to the international status of the dollar ($B^{\text{€}}_{\$,CB} = 0$). By contrast, the European and Chinese central banks do hold foreign bills: US bills for the European central bank (ECB), US and European bills for the People's Bank of China. There are valuation effects due to exchange rate variations and European and Chinese banks accumulate net wealth despite lack of saving. Foreign reserves are described in a simplified way without a specific line like 'gold and currencies' or 'foreign reserves'. Banks supply all the credit demanded by firms, and money supply is endogenous.

$$M_s^{\epsilon} = L_s^{\epsilon} + B_{\epsilon,CB,s}^{\epsilon} + B_{\epsilon,CB,s}^{\$} \star xr_1 - V_{CB}^{\epsilon} \tag{33}$$

$$M_s^{\epsilon} = M_d^{\epsilon} \tag{34}$$

$$L_s^{\epsilon} = L_d^{\epsilon} \tag{35}$$

Banks' bills supply and demand are balanced, and the Fed holds no reserves.

$$B_{\epsilon,CB,d}^{\epsilon} = B_{\epsilon,CB,s}^{\epsilon} \tag{36}$$

$$B_{\yen,CB,d}^{\epsilon} = B_{\yen,CB,s}^{\epsilon} \star xr_3 \tag{37}$$

$$B_{\$,CB,d}^{\epsilon} = B_{\$,CB,s}^{\epsilon} / xr_1 \tag{38}$$

$$B_{\epsilon,CB,d}^{\$} = B_{\epsilon,CB,s}^{\$} \star xr_1 \tag{39}$$

$$B_{\yen,CB,d}^{\$} = B_{\yen,CB,s}^{\$} \star xr_2 \tag{40}$$

$$B_{\$,CB,s}^{\epsilon} = 0 \tag{41}$$

The wealth of banks increases as a result of valuation effects.

$$\Delta V_{CB}^{\epsilon} = B_{\epsilon,CB,s,t-1}^{\$} \star \Delta xr_1 \tag{42}$$

$$\Delta V_{CB}^{\$} = B_{\$,CB,s,t-1}^{\epsilon} \star \Delta\left(\frac{1}{xr_1}\right) = 0 \tag{43}$$

$$\Delta V_{CB}^{\yen} = B_{\yen,CB,s,t-1}^{\epsilon} \star \Delta xr_3 + B_{\yen,CB,s,t-1}^{\$} \star \Delta xr_2 \tag{44}$$

Interest rates are exogenous in each country without margin behaviour.

$$r^{\text{€}} = r_d^{\text{€}} = r_l^{\text{€}}$$

Exchange rate determination

Equation (24) describing the supply of and demand for US bills by European households serves to determine the euro–dollar exchange rate xr_1 implicitly. As the euro–dollar exchange rate is floating, we suppose that foreign reserves held by the ECB are constant.

$$xr_1 = B_{\text{€},d}^{\$} / B_{\text{€},s}^{\$} \qquad\qquad (24\text{ bis})$$

$$B_{\text{€},CB,s}^{\$} = constant \qquad\qquad (45)$$

The Chinese currency is anchored to the dollar and the dollar–yuan exchange rate (xr_2) is constant. The euro–yuan exchange rate (xr_3) is floating and the foreign reserves of the Chinese central bank in euros are supposed constant.

$$xr_3 = xr_2 / xr_1 \qquad\qquad (46)$$

$$B_{\text{¥},CB,s}^{\text{€}} = constant \qquad\qquad (47)$$

All the accounting equations are written down, except one. Equation (20) describing the equilibrium between the supply of and the demand for

Table 3.2 Alternative closure of the exchange rate regimes

	Variables determined in bills market		Variables determined by central banks		
	$B^{\$}$	$B^{\text{¥}}$	$CB^{\$}$	$CB^{\text{€}}$	$CB^{\text{¥}}$
€/$ (xr_1) floating ¥/$ (xr_2) fixed	xr_1	$B_{\text{¥},CB,s}^{\text{¥}}$	$B_{\$,CB,s}^{\$}$	$B_{\text{€},CB,s}^{\text{€}}$	$B_{\text{¥},CB,d}^{\$}$
€/$ (xr_1) floating ¥/$ (xr_2) floating	xr_1	$B_{\text{¥},CB,s}^{\text{¥}}$	$B_{\$,CB,s}^{\$}$	$B_{\text{€},CB,s}^{\text{€}}$	$xr2$
€/$ (xr_1) floating CH target $B_{\text{¥},CB,d}^{\$}$	xr_1	$B_{\text{¥},CB,s}^{\text{¥}}$	$B_{\$,CB,s}^{\$}$	$B_{\text{€},CB,s}^{\text{€}}$	$B_{\text{¥},CB,d}^{\$}$ and $xr2$
€/$ (xr_1) floating CH target $CAB^{\text{¥}}$	xr_1	$B_{\text{¥},CB,s}^{\text{¥}}$	$B_{\$,CB,s}^{\$}$	$B_{\text{€},CB,s}^{\text{€}}$	$B_{\text{¥},CB,d}^{\$}$

Source: Author's construction.

European bills is not written and is used to check the accounting consistency of the model. Table 3.2 summarizes the closure of the exchange rate regime. The first two columns refer to variables that ensure equilibrium with respect to each country's bills market. The last three columns indicate the variables which ensure the equilibrium of each central bank's balance sheet.

Equation (24bis), which gives the euro–dollar exchange rate, seems to suggest that this exchange rate is only determined by the confrontation between the demand for and the supply of US bills by European households. This is not the case. All the other parts of the model, including the trade balance, are playing a role. Another more intuitive presentation of the determination of the exchange rate may be given based on the identity in equation (50) between the current account balance (CAB) and the capital account balance (KAB).

$$CAB^{\in} = X^{\in} - IM^{\in} + r_{t-1}^{\$} B_{\in,d,t-1}^{\$} + r_{t-1}^{\yen} B_{\in,d,t-1}^{\yen} + r_{t-1}^{\$} B_{\in,CB,d,t-1}^{\$}$$
$$- r_{t-1}^{\in} (B_{\$,t-1}^{\in} - B_{\in,s,t-1}^{\in} - B_{\in,CB,s,t-1}^{\in}) \tag{48}$$

$$KAB^{\in} = \left(\Delta B_{\$,s}^{\in} + \Delta B_{\yen,s}^{\in} + \Delta B_{\yen,CB,s}^{\in} \right) - \left(\Delta B_{\in,d}^{\$} + \Delta B_{\in,d}^{\yen} + \Delta B_{\in,CB,d}^{\$} \right) \tag{49}$$
$$= capital\ inflows - capital\ outflows$$

$$CAB^{\in} + KAB^{\in} = 0 \tag{50}$$

This result can surprise as it seems to mean that the increase in foreign currency reserves would always be nil, the current account balance being equal to the capital account balance. This result only reflects the way we treat the reserves of central banks, which in our model are only made up of foreign bills (US or European) held by the Chinese or European central banks. This result holds if international monetary assets held by banks ($M_{\in,CB}^{\in}$ and $M_{\in,CB}^{\$}$) or international credit are introduced. This equation can be used in the model instead of equation (24). By solving equation (50), combined with equations (41), (45), and (47), to determine xr_1, we obtain the following formula where the exchange rate xr_1 is determined both by the real and financial flows (xr_2 is exogenous).

$$IM^{\$}\in xr_1 + IM^{\yen}\in xr_1/xr_2 - IM^{\in} + r_{t-1}^{\$} B_{\in st-1}^{\$} xr_1 + r_{t-1}^{\yen} B_{\in st-1}^{\yen} xr_1/xr_2$$
$$+ r_{t-1}^{\$} B_{\in CBst-1}^{\$} xr_1 - r_{t-1}^{\in} (B_{st-1}^{\in} - B_{\in st-1}^{\in} - B_{\in CBst-1}^{\in})$$
$$+ (\Delta B_{\$s}^{\in} + \Delta B_{\yen s}^{\in}) - (\Delta B_{\in s}^{\$} xr1 + \Delta B_{\in s}^{\yen} xr_1/xr_2) = 0 \tag{51}$$

$$xr_1(IM^{\$}\in + IM^{\yen}\in /xr_2 + r_{t-1}^{\$} B_{\in st-1}^{\$} + r_{t-1}^{\yen} B_{\in st-1}^{\yen} /xr_2 + r_{t-1}^{\$} B_{\in CBst-1}^{\$}$$
$$-(\Delta B_{\in s}^{\$} + \Delta B_{\in s}^{\yen} xr_2) = IM\in + r_{t-1}^{\in} (B_{st-1}^{\in} - B_{\in st-1}^{\in} - B_{\in CBst-1}^{\in})$$
$$-(\Delta B_{\$s}^{\in} + \Delta B_{\yen s}^{\in}) \tag{52}$$

$$xr_1 = \frac{IM\mathit{\euro} + r\mathit{\euro}t - 1\,(B\mathit{\euro}st - 1 - B\mathit{\euro\euro}st - 1 - B\mathit{\euro\euro}CBst - 1) - (\Delta B\mathit{\euro}\$s + \Delta B\mathit{\euro}\yen s)}{(IM\$\mathit{\euro} + IM\yen\mathit{\euro}/xr_2 + r\$t - 1\,B\$\mathit{\euro}st - 1 + r\yen t - 1\,B\yen\mathit{\euro}st - 1/xr_2 + r\$t - 1}$$
$$B\$\mathit{\euro}CBst - 1 \; -(\Delta B\$\mathit{\euro}s + \Delta B\yen\mathit{\euro}s\,xr_2)$$

$$\text{(53)}$$

$$xr_1 = \frac{\left(imports \; \mathit{\euro} + interests\,paid\,by\;\mathit{\euro} - capital\,inflows\,in\;\mathit{\euro}\right)}{\left(exports\;\mathit{\euro} + interests\,received\,by\;\mathit{\euro} - capital\,outflows\,outside\;\mathit{\euro}\right)} \qquad \text{(53bis)}$$

In other words, the euro exchange rate depreciates against the dollar (xr_1 increases or the dollar appreciates) when European imports increase, the flow of interests paid outside the euro area rises and capital inflows inside the euro area decrease or, alternatively, when the European exports decrease, the flow of interests received by the euro area falls and the capital outflows increase. This familiar way of interpreting the variations of the exchange rates is included in our model. When exchange rate expectations are introduced in the asset demands, as is done in Lavoie and Daigle (2011), these expectations also play a role in the determination of exchange rates. This implicit determination is more synthetic than an explicit equation focusing on a limited number of determinants. This approach differs from Taylor (2004) who claims that the exchange rate is indeterminate in portfolio models or in macroeconomic models 'based on fundamentals'. Consequently, according to the author, it would be necessary to introduce a supplementary equation describing explicitly exchange rates expectations with uncertainty. This point of view is odd as his analysis is based on a two-country SFC model close to the one we use.

The world's net wealth equals the total amount of accumulated fixed capital (eq. (54) with $V_g = -B$). On the whole, the model contains 112 equations for 112 endogenous variables. The value of the parameters of the equations is given in Annex 3.1.

$$\left(V_h^{\mathit{\euro}} + V_f^{\mathit{\euro}} + V_g^{\mathit{\euro}} + V_{CB}^{\mathit{\euro}}\right) + \left(V_h^{\$} + V_f^{\$} + V_g^{\$} + V_{CB}^{\$}\right)xr_1 + \frac{\left(V_h^{\yen} + V_f^{\yen} + V_g^{\yen} + V_{CB}^{\yen}\right)}{xr_3}$$

$$= (K^{\mathit{\euro}} + xr_1.K^{\$} + \frac{K^{\yen}}{xr_3})$$

$$\text{(54)}$$

Adjustments with a fixed dollar–yuan parity

Simulations will be conducted by assuming a single kind of supply shock, a loss of competitiveness of the United States with respect to either China or the EU. These supply shocks are described through an increase in the relevant propensity to import. In all the forthcoming tables and figures, GDP and exchange rates are relative deviations with respect to the baseline, in percentage $((X - X_b) / X_b)$; for the current account, measured in percentage of GDP, the absolute deviation is given $(CAB - CAB_b)$.

A loss of US competitiveness with respect to China induces, unsurprisingly, a large decline of US production (Table 3.3 and Figure 3.1). China benefits from the decline in US competitiveness and, consequently, Chinese production is strongly stimulated. The US public deficit and current account deficit increase widely, in contrast to the rising Chinese surpluses. European production hardly changes, because the gains arising from exports to the Chinese market are being compensated by losses in the US market.

The evolution of exchange rates is more surprising. The dollar ends up with a slight appreciation against the euro, while the yuan depreciates against the euro. This evolution is all the more striking since the rising US public deficit induces a large issuance of US Treasury bills while the US demand for these declines due to the slowdown in activity. This should lead to a dollar depreciation against the euro. However, there is a countervailing force arising from the strong demand for US bills by the Chinese central bank, in its efforts to keep the dollar–yuan parity fixed. Consequently, the amount of US bills being supplied to European households declines slightly, while the European demand for US bills hardly changes. This explains the slight dollar appreciation against the euro, despite the decline in US competitiveness. This result enlightens the evolution of the late 1990s and early 2000s when the dollar was appreciating relative to the euro despite rising US current account deficits. This configuration began to change later on, due to the progressive modification of the behaviour of the Chinese central bank, as will be discussed below. Overall, in the case of a loss of US competitiveness with respect to China, the rigidity of the dollar–yuan parity limits adjustments at the world level. US production declines but the US current account deficit holds and the dollar can appreciate somewhat against the euro.

A loss of US competitiveness with respect to the EU has very different effects (Table 3.3 and Figure 3.1). US production is also negatively affected, but due to rising US current account and public deficits, the dollar depreciates against the euro (−9%). Consequently, the European increase in GDP does not last, and the gains in European output all get nearly wiped out in the medium run, due to the impact of the euro appreciation, the US slowdown and the Chinese gains in competitiveness arising from the yuan depreciation relative to the euro. The European current account surplus is reduced to almost zero in the medium run. The US trade deficit is also reduced in the medium run, but the US current account remains in deficit because of interest payments. China appears once again as the winner with an increased GDP (+9% in the medium run) and a surplus current account, thanks to the impact of the yuan depreciation. On the whole, the decline in US production remains, but the US trade deficit is smaller than in the case of a loss of competitiveness with respect

Table 3.3 Loss of US competitiveness with fixed dollar–yuan parity (in %)

	Loss of US competitiveness								Towards China with diversification of Chinese foreign reserves			
	Towards China				Towards EU							
	$\mu m^{\$}_{¥} = 0.4$ to 0.5				$\mu m^{\$}_{e} = 0.6$ to 0.7				$\mu m^{\$}_{¥} = 0.4$ to 0.5			
	T = 1	T = 5	T = 10	T = 20	T = 1	T = 5	T = 10	T = 20	T = 1	T = 5	T = 10	T = 20
US GDP	-3.5	-7.1	-7.8	-8.8	-8.2	-10.0	-11.0	-12.6	-3.4	-5.7	-6.2	-6.9
China GDP	3.1	6.3	6.9	7.7	1.1	7.9	9.0	10.4	3.3	7.8	8.7	9.9
EU GDP	0.0	-0.0	0.0	0.0	6.3	1.3	1.0	0.9	-0.3	-2.9	-3.5	-4.1
Dollar/euro	0.1	0.5	0.6	0.7	-7.2	-9.1	-9.3	-9.6	-1.2	-2.1	-2.2	-2.4
US CAB	-3.7	-2.9	-3.1	-3.3	-9.1	-4.3	-4.5	-5.0	-3.6	-2.3	-2.2	-2.4
China CAB	3.0	2.1	2.0	2.1	1.0	2.6	2.7	2.8	3.1	2.5	2.5	2.6
EU CAB	0.0	-0.0	0	0	5.9	0.3	0.3	0.3	-0.3	-1.2	-1.3	-1.5

Source: Authors' calculation.

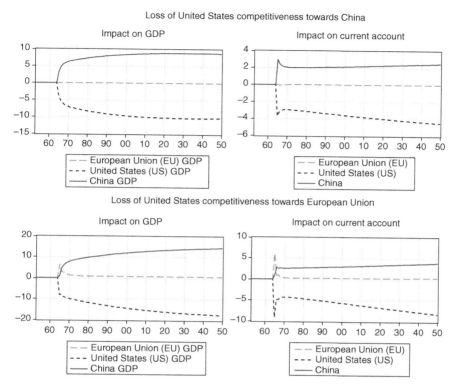

Figure 3.1 Loss of US competitiveness towards China or the EU with fixed dollar–yuan parity.

Source: Mazier and Tiou-Tagba Aliti (2012).

to China, thanks to the dollar depreciation against the euro. The fixity of the dollar–yuan parity reduces the amplitude of possible adjustments, at the benefit of China and at the expense of the EU.

Sensitivity tests have been made for different sets of coefficients of the main equations. The results are given in Annex 3.2. They show that the coefficients of dispersion of relative deviations with regards to the baseline appear small. It illustrates the stability of the model regarding the value of the different parameters.

Introduction of a diversification of Chinese foreign reserves

Instead of having Chinese foreign reserves mainly composed of US bills with constant reserves in euros, the People's Bank of China could have, and actually has, pursued a more diversified strategy, especially in the context of large

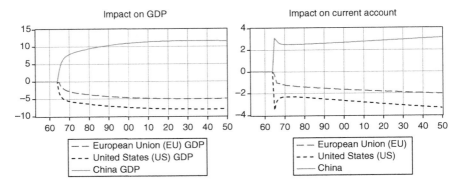

Figure 3.2 Loss of US competitiveness towards China with diversification of Chinese foreign reserves.

Source: Mazier and Tiou-Tagba Aliti (2012).

US deficits and uncertainty regarding future value of the dollar. Different scenarios could be considered with increasing foreign reserves held in euros by the Chinese central bank, but we will limit ourselves to one, already proposed by Lavoie and Zhao (2010). As soon as current account surpluses appear, the Chinese central bank decides to diversify its foreign reserves gradually, with a target structure of foreign reserves in dollar and euro bills and a partial adjustment mechanism. This behaviour is rather close to what has been observed since 2008, but the dollar–yuan parity is assumed constant at this stage.

$$B^{\epsilon}_{\yen,CB,d} = \beta B^{\$}_{\yen,CB,d} \tag{55}$$

$$\beta = \beta_{t-1} + \theta(\beta^{e} - \beta_{t-1}) \tag{56}$$

β^{e} is the target share of reserves held by the Chinese central bank in euros, in percentage of the reserves in dollars. θ is an adjustment coefficient reflecting a more or less pronounced inertia in the Chinese behaviour. β^{e} is equal to 0.7 in the simulation, which means that the foreign reserves are composed of 59% (1/1.7) of US bills and 41% of bills issued in euros. The operating mode of the model remains the same as in the previous case with constant Chinese reserves although the results are particularly contrasted. The distinction is not made in Table 3.2. The case of the loss of US competitiveness with respect to China will only be considered (see Table 3.3 and Figure 3.2). As before, US production declines and Chinese output increases. But with a diversification of foreign reserves, the dollar depreciates against the euro, because of the reduced demand for dollars coming from the Chinese central bank. Consequently, while US production is less badly affected than without diversification, EU output now decreases instead of remaining roughly constant. The structure of international imbalances is modified by the decision of the Chinese monetary authorities to diversify their foreign reserves, but these imbalances remain important. Although the US current account deficit as a percentage of GDP is smaller than without diversification, the EU current account deficit now deteriorates significantly and the Chinese current surplus increases. The EU now carries the burden of the adjustment.

Sensitivity tests can be carried out to appreciate how the value of the target share of reserves held in euros (β^e) influences growth paths, exchange rates, and external imbalances (see Annex 3.3). In the case of a loss of US competitiveness towards China, β^e varies from 0 (the basic model without diversification) to 1 (foreign reserves equally shared between US and European bills). Unsurprisingly, the simulations show that the more the Chinese reserves are diversified, the more the dollar depreciates against the euro due to a declining demand for US bills. European output is more and more negatively affected, at the benefit of Chinese output and at the benefit of US output which declines less. World imbalances increase, with larger external Chinese surpluses and European external deficits, while the US current account deficit gets reduced thanks to the dollar depreciation.

These conclusions are similar to those obtained by Lavoie and Zhao (2010). However, they are obtained under the hypothesis of a fixed dollar–yuan parity, an assumption which is rather restrictive. Since 2005 the Chinese central bank has managed a progressive appreciation of the yuan with regard to the dollar, although this experience has been (temporarily) suspended from the beginning of 2009 to the middle of 2010, as a consequence of the 2008 crisis. We now analyse global adjustments assuming flexible dollar–yuan parity, either of the freely floating or managed float type.

A three-country model with floating or managed dollar–yuan parity

New versions of the model

In order to analyse what could be the adjustments at the world level in the future when the Chinese exchange rate policy would be progressively liberalised, new versions of the previous model can be written with different modes of determination of the dollar–yuan parity. A first version corresponds to a pure mechanism of floating exchange rates which cannot pretend to be a realistic description of the Chinese exchange rate regime in the near future, due to the still very incomplete financial liberalisation in China. But, as it will be shown, this theoretical regime can represent a useful reference to understand the adjustment mechanisms prevailing in more plausible exchange rate regimes.

In this configuration the Chinese foreign reserves in US bills are constant ($B^\$_{\yen,CB,s} = constant$). Equation (40) is replaced by (40bis) which determines the dollar–yuan parity xr_2 (1 dollar = xr_2 yuans).

$$xr_2 = B^\$_{\yen,CB,d} / B^\$_{\yen,CB,s} \tag{40bis}$$

A second version corresponds to an impure mechanism of floating exchange rates with inertia due to interventions of the Chinese central bank which are not explicitly described. The Chinese foreign reserves in US bills are always constant ($B^\$_{\yen,CB,s} = constant$). Equation (40) is replaced by (40★) where xr_2^* represents an equilibrium exchange rate. The actual exchange rate is determined with inertia by equation (40ter).

$$xr_2^* = B^\$_{\yen,CB,d} / B^\$_{\yen,CB,s} \tag{40★}$$

$$xr_2 = xr_{2t-1} + \varepsilon(xr_2^* - xr_{2t-1}) \tag{40ter}$$

A third version corresponds to a managed exchange rate regime with a target fixed by the PBOC, either in terms of foreign reserves in dollars or in terms of a current account surplus. The Chinese foreign reserves in US bills are once again endogenous and equation (40) of the initial version of the model is kept. The dollar–yuan parity xr_2 can be managed by the Chinese central bank with a target, either on the reserves in US bills ($R^{e\yen}$ is a percentage of GDP beyond which the yuan is revaluated) or on the current account, also in percentage of GDP ($CAB^\yen / Y^\yen)^e$.

$$B^\$_{\yen,CB,d} = B^\$_{\yen,CB,s} \star xr_2 \tag{40}$$

$$xr_2 = xr_{2t-1} + \gamma_1 (B^\$_{\yen,CB,d} / Y^\yen - R^{e\yen}) \tag{57}$$

or

$$xr_2 = xr_{2t-1} + \gamma_2(CAB^\yen / Y^\yen - (CAB^\yen / Y^\yen)^e) \tag{57bis}$$

γ_1 and γ_2 are negative adjustment parameters of the exchange rate which can be considered as controlled by the Chinese central bank.

Table 3.2 summarizes the alternative closures of the exchange rate regime. The case of the impure floating of the yuan which is very close to the pure floating (not shown). These new versions of the model are used in the same way as in the previous section to analyse the adjustment mechanisms facing shocks. Comparisons with the results of the previous section will show the new adjustment possibilities arising from a more flexible yuan.

The different flexible exchange rate regimes of the yuan

The three flexible exchange rate regimes previously defined can be simply compared by examining the consequences of the same shock, the loss of US competitiveness towards China (simulated through an increase in the propensity to import of the same magnitude than in the initial case). In the case of a freely floating yuan, there is still a short-run reduction in US production and a short-run rise in Chinese production, accompanied by a deteriorating US current account and an improving Chinese current account (Table 3.4 and Figure 3.3). However, the floating exchange rates and the depreciation of the dollar lead to a substantial reduction of these imbalances (the dollar moves by −7% against the yuan and −3.6% against the euro). The US production recovers while Chinese growth slows down. The US current deficit and Chinese surplus offset each other. The main difference with the case of the fixed dollar–yuan parity (Table 3.3 and Figure 3.1) is that global imbalances can now be reduced by exchange rate adjustments thanks to the floating yuan. By contrast, in the fixed yuan regime, changes in output levels were the main adjustment tool, but this tool was unable to reduce the external imbalances between the United States and China. In the case of an impure floating yuan with inertia in adjustments, results are very similar to the freely floating regime. They are slightly affected by the value of the adjustment coefficient ε. The smaller the adjustment coefficient, the slower the exchange rate adjustment is and the larger the adjustments on production are. But the differences remain very small (figures are not shown to gain space).

In the case of a managed exchange rate regime with a target fixed by the PBOC for the level of foreign reserves in dollars, the impact of a loss of US competitiveness towards China also closely resembles the impact observed in a freely floating regime where foreign reserves in dollars are assumed constant (Table 3.4). In the managed regime these reserves are not constant, but the Chinese central bank tries to reach a foreign reserve target as a percentage of Chinese GDP. External imbalances are reduced within a few years. The proximity of the two scenarios can be easily understood as the closure of the model is the same (see Table 2.2). Chinese foreign reserves are constant in a pure floating scenario while they are brought back to a target in the managed regime thanks to the variation of the exchange rate (eq. (57)). The two exchange rate regimes, the managed one with a target on foreign reserves in dollars and the freely floating one, are very similar. Indeed, visually, this regime is no different from the free-floating regime described in Figure 3.3, and hence it will not be shown here to save space.

Table 3.4 Loss of US competitiveness towards China with various regimes of floating yuan (in %)

	Loss of US competitiveness towards China											
	A pure floating dollar–yuan				A yuan managed regime with target on foreign reserves				A yuan managed regime with target on current account			
	$\mu m^\$_¥ = 0.4$ to 0.5				$\mu m^\$_¥ = 0.4$ to 0.5				$\mu m^\$_¥ = 0.4$ to 0.5			
	$T=1$	$T=5$	$T=10$	$T=20$	$T=1$	$T=5$	$T=10$	$T=20$	$T=1$	$T=5$	$T=10$	$T=20$
US GDP	-2.6	-0.6	-0.3	-0.3	-2.7	-0.5	-0.3	-0.3	-2.2	-0.3	-0.5	-0.6
China GDP	2.4	0.7	0.5	0.4	2.5	0.6	0.4	0.3	1.8	0.1	0.2	0.2
EU GDP	-0.0	0.1	0.1	0.0	-0.0	0.2	0.1	0.1	-0.1	0.1	0.0	0.0
Dollar/euro	-1.9	-3.4	-3.6	-3.8	-1.5	-3.4	-3.6	-3.8	-4.1	-3.7	-3.7	-3.8
Dollar:yuan	-4.0	-6.8	-7.2	-7.4	-3.4	-7.0	-7.2	-7.4	-8.5	-7.4	-7.5	-7.6
Euro/yuan	-2.2	-3.5	-3.7	-3.8	-1.9	-3.7	-3.7	-3.8	-4.6	-3.8	-3.9	-4.0
US CAB	-2.6	-0.2	-0.1	-0.1	-2.7	-0.2	-0.1	-0.1	-2.2	-0.1	-0.2	-0.2
China CAB	2.3	0.2	0.1	0.1	2.4	0.1	0.1	0.1	1.7	60.0	0	0
EU CAB	-0.0	0	0	0	-0.0	0.1	0	0	-0.1	0	0	0

Source: Authors' calculation.

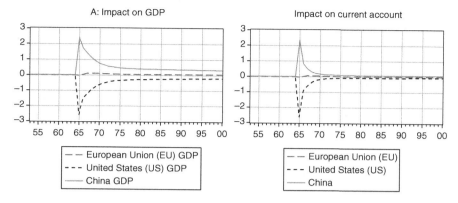

Figure 3.3 Loss of US competitiveness towards China in case of a pure floating yuan.
Source: Mazier and Tiou-Tagba Aliti (2012).

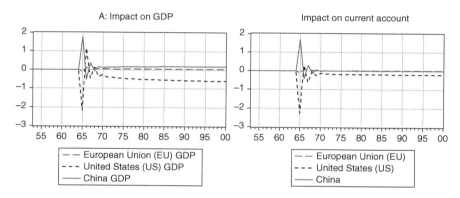

Figure 3.4 Loss of US competitiveness towards China with a yuan managed regime and
a target set on the current account balance.
Source: Mazier and Tiou-Tagba Aliti (2012).

Lastly, a managed exchange rate regime based on a target on the current account surplus set by the Chinese central bank yields similar results but with some unstable trajectories (Table 3.4 and Figure 3.4). The closure of the model is different as the dollar/yuan exchange rate xr_2 is now determined by the Chinese current account balance relatively to the target (eq. (57bis)) and only more indirectly by the foreign reserves ($B_{¥,CB,d}^{\$}$). A loss of US competitiveness towards China induces, as before, a decline of US production, a depreciation of the dollar against the yuan and the euro, and an increase in Chinese production.

Exchange rate adjustments lead to a progressive reduction of external imbalances in this case also. The smaller the adjustment parameters, the slower the exchange rate adjustments and the larger the production adjustments. The value taken by the adjustment parameter plays a larger role than it was the case previously, but this role remains limited, as can be shown by sensitivity tests.

To conclude, two points can be highlighted. First, a floating dollar–yuan exchange rate is a powerful adjustment mechanism to reduce world imbalances characterised by US deficits and Chinese surpluses. The contrast appears clearly when the model based on a fixed dollar–yuan parity is compared to the model with a freely floating dollar–yuan parity. Second, such a freely floating yuan is unrealistic under current circumstances. But a managed float for the dollar–yuan parity, where the Chinese central bank intervenes to achieve a target, either on foreign reserves in dollars or on its current account balance, yields similar adjustment mechanisms. They can reduce world imbalances in the same proportions as a pure floating regime, especially in the case where the target is on the level of foreign reserves. The adjustment is more unstable in the case of a target on the current account balance. This approach does not detail the institutional forms that such exchange rates regimes would take, nor does it describe the internal consequences for the Chinese economy of a yuan revaluation. It is limited to general considerations at the world level.

A three-country SFC model with flexible prices

New version of the model with flexible prices

The previous model can be enlarged with a simple modelling of prices and wages. The structure of the model remains unchanged. A price-wage loop is introduced to determine the GDP price (*py*) and the nominal wage per capita (*w*). The GDP price depends on unit wage costs and import prices, with an adjustment to the desired level and a short-term effect of the rate of capacity utilization (TUC). The wage per capita is determined by a simplified Philips curve with an effect of the capacity rate of utilization, an indexation formula based on internal demand prices (*pdi*) and on labour productivity (*PR*). The internal demand price (*pdi*) is given by an accounting equation relating internal demand in constant and current prices.

$$W^{\epsilon} = w^{\epsilon} \star N^{\epsilon} \tag{58}$$

$$logpy_{des}^{\epsilon} = \mu_1^{\epsilon} \star logpm^{\epsilon} + \left(1 - \mu_1^{\epsilon}\right) \star log\left(w^{\epsilon} / PR^{\epsilon}\right) \tag{59}$$

$$logpy^{\epsilon} = \pi_1^{\epsilon} \star log\left(py_{des}^{\epsilon}\right) + \left(1 - \pi_1^{\epsilon}\right)log\left(py_{t-1}^{\epsilon}\right) + \pi_2^{\epsilon} log\left(TUC^{\epsilon}\right) \tag{60}$$

$$log\,w^{\epsilon} = \lambda_1^{\epsilon} log\left(w_{des}^{\epsilon}\right) + \left(1 - \lambda_1^{\epsilon}\right)logw_{t-1}^{\epsilon} \tag{61}$$

$$logw_{des}^{\epsilon} = \lambda_2^{\epsilon} logpdi^{\epsilon} + \lambda_3^{\epsilon} logTUC^{\epsilon} + \lambda_4^{\epsilon} logPR^{\epsilon} \qquad (62)$$

$$TUC^{\epsilon} = Y^{\epsilon} / K^{\epsilon} \qquad (63)$$

$$logPR^{\epsilon} = \varphi_0^{\epsilon} + \varphi_1^{\epsilon} \quad logY^{\epsilon} \qquad (64)$$

$$N^{\epsilon} = Y^{\epsilon} / PR^{\epsilon} \qquad (65)$$

Foreign trade equations are enlarged to include a price competitiveness effect and a simple analysis of foreign trade prices.
Exports

$$logX_{\$}^{\epsilon} = \mu x_1^{\epsilon} + \mu x_2^{\epsilon} \star logY^{\$} - \mu x_3^{\epsilon} log\left(px_{\$}^{\epsilon} / (py^{\$} \star xr1)\right) \qquad (66)$$

$$logX_{¥}^{\epsilon} = \mu x_4^{\epsilon} + \mu x_5^{\epsilon} \star logY^{¥} - \mu x_6^{\epsilon} log\left((px_{¥}^{\epsilon} \star xr3) / py^{¥}\right) \qquad (67)$$

Export price

$$logpx_{\$}^{\epsilon} = \rho_1^{\epsilon} + \rho_2^{\epsilon} logpy^{\$} \star xr1 + \left(1 - \rho_2^{\epsilon}\right)log\left(py^{\epsilon}\right) \qquad (68)$$

$$logpx_{¥}^{\epsilon} = \rho_3^{\epsilon} + \rho_4^{\epsilon} \frac{logpy^{¥}}{xr3} + \left(1 - \rho_4^{\epsilon}\right) log\left(py^{\epsilon}\right) \qquad (69)$$

Usual equations relating variables in constant and current prices are added. The determination of household real Haig-Simons disposal income ($Y_{hs}^{d,\epsilon}$)€and wealth (V_h^{ϵ})can be explained, as it is less straightforward.

$$\Delta V_{v,h}^{\epsilon} = \Delta Y_{v,hs}^{d,\epsilon} - C_v^{\epsilon} \qquad (70)$$

$$Y_{hs}^{d,\epsilon} = \frac{Y_{v,hs}^{d,\epsilon}}{PDI^{\epsilon}} - V_{v,h,t-1}^{\epsilon} \left(\frac{\Delta PDI^{\epsilon}}{PDI^{\epsilon}}\right) \qquad (71)$$

$$V_h^{\epsilon} \qquad (72)$$

Finally, a kind of simple Taylor rule, only dependent on the rate of inflation, has been added to avoid an incoherent evolution of the real rate of interest.

$$rt^{\in} = r\star^{\in} + 0.8\left(\Delta logpdi^{\in} - 0.02\right) \tag{73}$$

On the whole, the model has now 176 endogenous variables, public expenditures being exogenous. This new version of the model is used in the same way as in previous sections to analyse adjustment mechanisms towards global imbalances with, alternatively, fixed or flexible dollar–yuan parity.

Complementary results with flexible prices

The results obtained with the flexible prices model broadly confirm those obtained with fixed prices. The different configurations of the model will be successively considered.

Fixed dollar–yuan parity

A supply shock with a loss of US competitiveness towards China gives results rather close to those obtained in the fixed-price case, at least in qualitative terms (Table 3.5 and Figure 3.5). The results cannot be compared directly as the shock is smaller in the case of flexible prices with an increase of the propensity to import from 0.5 to 0.52 (instead of 0.4 to 0.5 in the constant prices case). The US production declines and the current account is unbalanced at the benefit of China. The dollar slightly appreciates in nominal terms due to increasing demand for US bills by the Chinese central bank in order to maintain the dollar–yuan parity. But the dollar depreciates moderately in real terms due to a decline in US prices, in contrast to the constant-price case. However, as in this case, the rigidity of the dollar–yuan parity limits the adjustments at the world level.

As in the fixed-price case, a loss of US competitiveness with respect to the European Union yields a more contrasted impact (Table 3.5 and Figure 3.5). US production is negatively affected in the short run, at the benefit of the EU, and the dollar depreciates in nominal and real terms due to current account and public deficits, despite rising US prices. Actually, the dollar depreciation is larger than in the case of constant prices and US production recovers in the medium run, at the expense of European production which declines, while China appears once again as the winner thanks to the depreciation of the yuan versus the euro.

Fixed dollar–yuan parity with diversification of Chinese foreign reserves

A supply shock with a loss of US competitiveness towards China gives contrasted results by comparison with the case without foreign reserves diversification, as was the case with the fixed prices model (Table 3.5 and Figure 3.6). Chinese production increases and US output declines in the short run. Due to the declining demand for US bills by the Chinese central bank, the dollar

Table 3.5 A loss of US competitiveness with fixed dollar–yuan parity and flexible prices (in %)

	Loss of US competitiveness											
	Towards China				Towards EU				Towards China with diversification of Chinese foreign reserves			
	$\mu x_5^{¥} = 0.5$ to 0.52				$\mu x_5^{€} = 0.5$ to 0.52				$\mu x_5^{¥} = 0.5$ to 0.52			
	$T=1$	$T=5$	$T=10$	$T=20$	$T=1$	$T=5$	$T=10$	$T=20$	$T=1$	$T=5$	$T=10$	$T=20$
US GDP	-1.0	-1.7	-1.9	-2.2	-1.0	-0.7	-0.1	0.4	-1.0	-0.8	-0.2	0.7
China GDP	1.0	1.7	1.9	2.2	0	0.9	1.8	2.7	1.0	2.6	3.7	5.3
EU GDP	0	0	0	0	1.0	-0.1	-1.6	-3.2	0	-1.9	-3.9	-6.9
US PDI	-0.1	-0.1	-0.2	-0.2	0	0.5	1.1	2.4	0	0.4	1	2.4
China PDI	0.1	0.1	0.1	0.1	0.1	0.5	1.1	2.3	0.2	0.7	1.2	2.5
EU PDI	0	0	0	0	-0.1	-1.1	-2.3	-4.7	-0.2	-1.3	-2.9	-6.3
Dollar/euro	0.1	0.1	0.1	0.1	-0.7	-4.2	-7.2	-12.1	-0.8	-4.3	-7.8	-14.5
Real dollar/euro	-0.0	-0.1	-0.1	-0.1	-0.6	-2.6	-3.9	-5.5	-0.6	-2.3	-3.8	-6.1
US CAB	-1.0	-0.7	-0.7	-0.8	-1.1	-0.7	-0.7	-0.6	-1.1	-0.7	-0.6	-0.6
China CAB	1.0	0.7	0.7	0.7	-0.1	0.1	0.1	0.2	0.9	0.7	0.7	0.7
EU CAB	-0.0	0	0	0	1.2	0.6	0.5	0.4	0.2	0	-0.1	-0.2

Source: Authors' calculation.

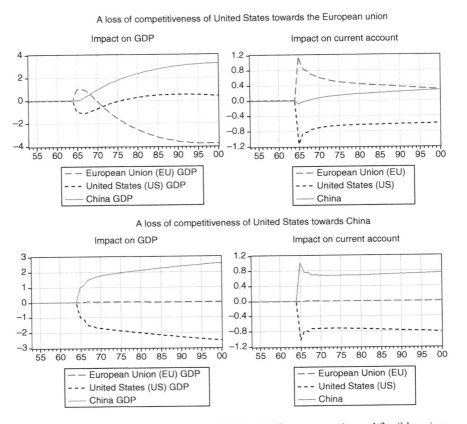

Figure 3.5 Loss of US competitiveness with fixed dollar–yuan parity and flexible prices.
Source: Mazier and Tiou-Tagba Aliti (2012).

depreciates relative to the euro in nominal and real terms. As a consequence, Chinese output remains stimulated by competitiveness gains while US production recovers with the dollar depreciation. In contrast, the euro appreciation induces a decline in European production. The Chinese current surplus remains high and stable. The initial US current deficit is reduced but does not disappear while the European deficit increases. Compared with the fixed prices model the main difference is that the real depreciation of the dollar relative to the euro is more marked than the nominal depreciation of the dollar. This larger devaluation allows a moderate US recovery.

Floating yuan

With a floating yuan, adjustments through real dollar depreciation are larger. In the short run, a loss of US competitiveness towards China induces a fall

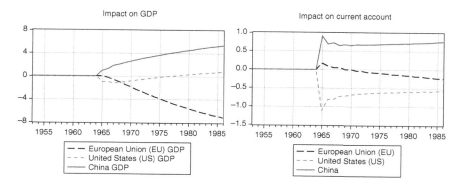

Figure 3.6 A loss of US competitiveness towards China with fixed dollar–yuan parity, diversification of Chinese foreign reserves and flexible prices.
Source: Mazier and Tiou-Tagba Aliti (2012).

in US production and an increase of Chinese production (Table 3.6 and Figure 3.7). The US current account deteriorates while the Chinese one improves. But the dollar depreciates strongly against the yuan and less strongly against the euro. This dollar depreciation is linked to a larger supply of US bills abroad while the Chinese foreign reserves in US bills are held constant. The nominal dollar depreciation holds in real terms despite US price increases. Consequently, US production recovers and Chinese growth slows down. The Chinese current surplus and the US current deficit are reduced. EU production is preserved as the appreciation of the euro against the dollar is compensated by the depreciation of the euro against the yuan. Compared to the fixed dollar–yuan parity regime without Chinese foreign reserves diversification (Table 3.5 and Figure 3.5), the main difference is that the dollar depreciation allows an important recovery in US production and a reduction of the US current account deficit, while China is penalised by the yuan appreciation. Global imbalances are reduced more by relative prices than by production. Compared to the case of Chinese foreign reserves diversification (Table 3.5 and Figure 3.6), two differences can be underlined. EU production is now less adversely hit, thanks to the euro depreciation against the yuan. Furthermore, current account imbalances, especially the Chinese surplus, are further reduced. Also, Chinese GDP is more negatively affected due to the adverse consequences of the yuan revaluation.

These conclusions are qualitatively similar to those that were observed with the fixed-price models, as a floating dollar–yuan exchange rate allows a reduction of global imbalances. However, this reduction is less marked than in the previous case and more important reversals of the production are induced by the exchange rates' adjustments in favour of the US production and at the detriment of Chinese production. The negative impact on Chinese growth of the

Table 3.6 A loss of US competitiveness towards China with various regimes of floating yuan and flexible prices

Loss of US competitiveness towards China

	A pure floating dollar–yuan				A yuan managed regime with a target on Chinese foreign reserves				A yuan managed regime with a target on current account			
	$\mu x_5^{¥} = 0.5$ to 0.52				$\mu x_5^{¥} = 0.5$ to 0.52				$\mu x_5^{¥} = 0.5$ to 0.52			
	$T=1$	$T=5$	$T=10$	$T=20$	$T=1$	$T=5$	$T=10$	$T=20$	$T=1$	$T=5$	$T=10$	$T=20$
US GDP	-0.9	0.1	1.6	3.4	-0.9	0.1	1.7	3.4	-1.6	4.5	4	16.9
China GDP	1.0	0.2	-1.4	-3.5	1	0.15	-1.6	-3.9	1	-1	-2.7	-1.8
EU GDP	0	-0.2	-0.4	-0.5	0	-0.3	-0.4	-0.5	0	0.4	0.2	1.5
US PDI	0.1	1.3	2.6	5.7	0.2	1.3	2.7	5.9	0	3.1	5.1	11.1
China PDI	-0.1	-1	-2.3	-5.3	-0.0	-1.1	-2.5	-5.6	-0.4	-1.7	-3	-4.6
EU PDI	0	-0.1	-0.3	-0.5	0	-0.2	-0.3	-0.6	-0.2	0.3	0.4	1.3
Dollar/euro	-0.5	-3.4	-5.9	-10.3	-0.3	-3.6	-6.2	-10.7	-2.5	-5.8	-8.8	-9.6
Dollar/yuan	-0.9	-5.7	-10.3	-18.0	-0.7	-5.9	-10.7	-18.8	-3.7	-11.3	-16.1	-19.2
Real dollar/euro	-0.3	-1.9	-3.1	-4.6	-0.2	-2.0	-3.1	-4.7	-2.7	-3.7	-5.2	-0.9
Real dollar/yuan	-0.7	-3.4	-5.4	-8.1	-0.4	-3.3	-5.5	-8.3	-4.5	-9.8	-13.0	-7.9
US CAB	-1.2	-0.7	-0.6	-0.5	-1.2	-0.7	-0.6	-0.5	-1.8	-0.1	-1.3	5.2
China CAB	1.2	0.7	0.6	0.5	1.2	0.7	0.6	0.5	1.5	0.3	0.9	-2.5
EU CAB	0	0	0	0	-0.0	0	0	-0.0	0.2	-0.2	0.2	-1.3

Source: Authors' calculation.

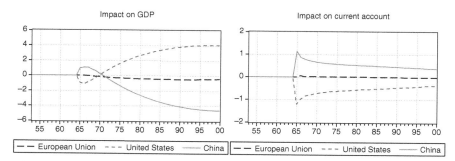

Figure 3.7 A loss of US competitiveness towards China with a floating yuan and flexible prices.
Source: Mazier and Tiou-Tagba Aliti (2012).

yuan revaluation is mainly induced by the loss of competitiveness and is more marked in case of flexible prices. However, the risk of deflation cannot be studied in more details with the present model as there is no impact of the debt ratio on firms' behaviour. Conversely, the wealth effect on households plays positively in case of deflation.

Comparison of different floating exchange rate regimes for the yuan

An impure floating yuan with inertia in adjustments or a managed exchange rate regime with a target on the level of Chinese foreign reserves in dollars gives results very similar to the freely floating regime, as could be seen from Table 3.6. Finally, a managed exchange rate regime with a target on the Chinese current account balance also gives rather similar results, but once again with more unstable trajectories in the long run (Table 3.6 and Figure 3.8).

Conclusion

The aim of this chapter was to analyse macroeconomic adjustments at the world level using a three-country SFC model and to shed more light on the rising global imbalances since the 1990s and their partial reduction after the financial crisis of 2008.

Lessons from SFC modelling

Three kinds of SFC three-country models have been considered. The first model was inspired by Lavoie and Zhao (2010), with fixed dollar–yuan parity, including a version where the Chinese central bank proceeds to reserves

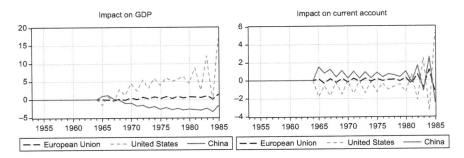

Figure 3.8 A loss of US competitiveness towards China with a yuan managed regime and a target on the current account balance and with flexible prices.

Source: Mazier and Tiou-Tagba Aliti (2012).

diversification. The second model introduced a flexible dollar–yuan parity which can be freely floating or managed by the Chinese central bank on the basis of external targets. The third model dropped the hypothesis of constant prices and combined a simple modelling of prices and wages with the two previous versions. This SFC approach seems better adapted than the traditional general equilibrium models as it gives a complete description of the real and financial flows and stocks at the world level and is based on adjustments both by relative prices and by the level of activity.

Supply shocks, mainly a loss of US competitiveness, have been used to analyse macroeconomic adjustments at the world level. With a fixed dollar–yuan parity, a loss of US competitiveness is partly compensated thanks to the euro–dollar variations, but the fixity of the dollar–yuan parity limits the adjustments at the benefit of China and at the expense of the US. The dollar appreciation against the euro at the end of the 1990s and beginning of the 2000s, despite of the rising US current deficits, has been rather well explained by the model. It was due to the strong demand of US bills by the Chinese central bank to keep the yuan-dollar parity fixed. However, the diversification of the Chinese reserves since the end of the first decade of the 2000s has contributed to a dollar depreciation against the euro and to a reduction of the US deficit. But this has been more than offset by the dollar appreciation, given that the dollar appeared as a safe haven currency following the crisis of 2008.

From 2005 to 2008 and from 2010 on, after a short pause during the financial crisis, the People's Bank of China has allowed a limited appreciation of the yuan relative to the dollar. This new configuration has been examined with another version of the model. Two points can be highlighted. First, a floating dollar–yuan exchange rate appears as an efficient mechanism to reduce world imbalances characterised by a US deficit and a Chinese surplus. Second, although a freely floating yuan is unrealistic with the current Chinese monetary and financial regime, a managed float, where the Chinese central bank intervenes to reach a target expressed as a percentage of GDP, either based on the amount of foreign reserves in dollars or on a current account balance, gives adjustment mechanisms that are roughly similar. However, the targets used are not equivalent. A target based on foreign reserves gives results very close to a free-floating regime, as it can be easily understood. A target based on current account balance gives results broadly similar, but more unstable. The pure floating yuan regime can thus be used as a reference to examine what could occur if the Chinese monetary authorities were to turn towards a more managed floating regime.

Lastly, the previous models with fixed prices have been enlarged by introducing flexible prices. Using the same shocks as before, the main results obtained with fixed prices have been confirmed in the case of flexible prices, although some differences appeared. In case of a floating dollar–yuan parity, the reduction of world imbalances is less marked than in the case of fixed prices and Chinese production is more reduced by a yuan appreciation.

The global imbalances in practice

The actual evolution of global imbalances can only be partially understood with these theoretical results. The increase of the international imbalances at the beginning of the 1980s has been contained thanks to international cooperation of the central banks of the main countries in 1985–1987 (the Plaza–Louvre agreements), leading to a devaluation of the dollar and an appreciation of the European and Japanese currencies. Exchange rate adjustments have played a role but, far from free-floating, internationally coordinated intervention has been necessary. Since the second half of the 1990s, world imbalances rose once again, with increasing US deficit and Asian surpluses. As it has been seen, the fixity of the dollar–yuan parity has contributed to these rising imbalances, which is also coherent with the increasing undervaluation of the yuan. From 2005 to 2008, the appreciation of the yuan against the dollar has been too limited to have a significant impact on these imbalances. Exchange rate misalignments were important on the eve of the financial crisis of 2008. Exchange rate adjustments could have contributed to reduce the imbalances and they were expected by some observers. Nonetheless, among the main currencies, only the yen has appreciated against the dollar, which helped to reduce the Japanese surplus. On the contrary, the yuan was briefly pegged to the dollar between 2008 and 2010 before returning to a moderate revaluation with an anchor on basket of currencies. Exchange rate adjustment of the yuan did occur but remained limited and could not explain the important reduction of the Chinese imbalances. This reduction is linked to the depreciation of the equilibrium exchange rate of the yuan since 2008 due the reduction of the external markets induced by the crisis and to the progressive settlement of a new growth regime turned more towards the domestic market. For the future, a pragmatic Chinese exchange rate policy based, for example, on a target of the current account or of the foreign reserves could help to preserve a more balanced growth regime but the issue is far larger, as it will be discussed more in detail further.

The euro is another story. It was close to its equilibrium value in 2008 and the global European current imbalance was limited. Floating exchange rate between the euro and the dollar could have led to a further revaluation of the euro against the dollar due to the large US imbalances. It did not happen due to the fragility of the euro area and to the huge intra-European imbalances. The euro crisis led on the opposite to a depreciation against the dollar which paved the way to further imbalances. These observations are an incentive to examine more deeply in the second part of the book the EU imbalances.

Annex 3.1 Value of the parameters

α_1 = propensity to consume income = 0.8
α_2 = wealth effect coefficient = 0.0182 (USA), 0.0243 (EU), 0.0235 (China)
κ = capital income ratio = 2.5
λ = wage share = 0.75
γ_1 et γ_2 = adjustment parameters of the dollar–yuan parity = −5
d = depreciation rate of capital = 0.1
q = tax rates = 0.0964 (USA), 0.1067 (EU), 0.0942 (China)
ε = adjustment parameter of the dollar–yuan parity = 0.5

Households' portfolio choice

China	European Union	United States
$\gamma_{10}^{\yen} = 0.08$	$\gamma_{10}^{\euro} = 0.142857$	$\gamma_{10}^{\$} = 0.13794$
$\gamma_{11}^{\yen} = -0.2$	$\gamma_{11}^{\euro} = -0.2$	$\gamma_{11}^{\$} = 0.6$
$\gamma_{12}^{\yen} = -0.2$	$\gamma_{12}^{\euro} = 0.6$	$\gamma_{12}^{\$} = -0.2$
$\gamma_{13}^{\yen} = 0.6$	$\gamma_{13}^{\euro} = -0.2$	$\gamma_{13}^{\$} = -0.2$
$\gamma_{14}^{\yen} = -0.2$	$\gamma_{14}^{\euro} = -0.2$	$\gamma_{14}^{\$} = -0.2$
$\gamma_{20}^{\yen} = 0.04$	$\gamma_{20}^{\euro} = 0.071429$	$\gamma_{20}^{\$} = 0.10345$
$\gamma_{21}^{\yen} = 0.6$	$\gamma_{21}^{\euro} = 0.6$	$\gamma_{21}^{\$} = -0.2$
$\gamma_{22}^{\yen} = -0.2$	$\gamma_{22}^{\euro} = -0.2$	$\gamma_{22}^{\$} = 0.6$
$\gamma_{23}^{\yen} = -0.2$	$\gamma_{23}^{\euro} = -0.2$	$\gamma_{23}^{\$} = -0.2$
$\gamma_{24}^{\yen} = -0.2$	$\gamma_{24}^{\euro} = -0.2$	$\gamma_{24}^{\$} = -0.2$
$\gamma_{30}^{\yen} = 0.08$	$\gamma_{30}^{\euro} = 0.07143$	$\gamma_{30}^{\$} = 0.0690$
$\gamma_{31}^{\yen} = -0.2$	$\gamma_{31}^{\euro} = -0.2$	$\gamma_{31}^{\$} = -0.2$
$\gamma_{32}^{\yen} = 0.6$	$\gamma_{32}^{\euro} = -0.2$	$\gamma_{32}^{\$} = -0.2$
$\gamma_{33}^{\yen} = -0.2$	$\gamma_{33}^{\euro} = 0.6$	$\gamma_{33}^{\$} = 0.6$
$\gamma_{34}^{\yen} = -0.2$	$\gamma_{34}^{\euro} = -0.2$	$\gamma_{34}^{\$} = -0.2$

Imports elasticity

China	European Union	United States
$\mu m_0^Y = -1$	$\mu m_0^\epsilon = -1$	$\mu m_0^\$ = -1$
$\mu m_1^Y = 0.5$	$\mu m_1^\epsilon = 0.5$	$\mu m_1^\$ = 0.5$
$\mu m_2^Y = 0.8$	$\mu m_2^\epsilon = 0.8$	$\mu m_2^\$ = 1$
$\mu m_3^Y = -1$	$\mu m_3^\epsilon = -1$	$\mu m_3^\$ = -1$
$\mu m_4^Y = 0.5$	$\mu m_4^\epsilon = 0.5$	$\mu m_4^\$ = 0.5$
$\mu m_5^Y = 0.8$	$\mu m_5^\epsilon = 1$	$\mu m_5^\$ = 0.8$

Parameters of the model with flexible prices

Export prices $\quad \rho_2^\epsilon = \rho_4^\epsilon = 0$ (price maker)

GDP price $\quad \mu^\epsilon = 0 \quad \mu_1^\epsilon = 0.15 \quad \mu_2^\epsilon = 0.12 \star \log 2$

Wage equations $\quad \lambda_1^\epsilon = 0.5 \quad \lambda_2^\epsilon = 1 \; \lambda_3^\epsilon = 0.1 \star \log 2 \quad \lambda_4^\epsilon = 1$

Labour productivity $\quad \varphi_0 = 0.02 \quad \varphi_1 = 0$

Exogenous variables $\quad r = 0.01 \quad \Delta \log G = 0.02$

Annex 3.2 Coefficient of dispersion

Table 3.7 gives the coefficient of dispersion of relative deviations with regard to the base line (b) for different sets of coefficients in the case of a shock of loss

Table 3.7 Coefficient of dispersion of relative deviations with regard to the base line (in %)

			Y^Y	Y^ϵ	$Y^\$$	$xr1$	CAB^Y	CAB^ϵ	$CAB^\$$
$\alpha_1^\epsilon = 0.8$	0.7	1970	0.10	0.01	0.08	0.02	0.03	0.02	0.02
		2000	0.08	0	0.08	0.01	0.02	0	0.01
	0.9	1970	0.20	0.25	0.05	0.36	0.05	0.08	0.08
		2000	0.17	0.19	0.04	0.29	0.04	0.05	0.03
$\lambda^\epsilon = 0.75$	0.7	1970	0.18	0.07	0.11	0.04	0.05	0.02	0
		2000	0.21	0.09	0.09	0.09	0.05	0.02	0.02
	0.8	1970	0.24	0.10	0.11	0.02	0.06	0.03	0
		2000	0.33	0.11	0.11	0.04	0.08	0.04	0.02
$\gamma_{20}^\epsilon = 0.07$	0.10	1970	0	0	0.01	0.01	0.01	0	0.02
		2000	0.01	0	0.01	0	0.02	0	0.03
	0.14	1970	0	0	0.02	0.03	0.04	0.01	0.05
		2000	0.03	0	0.03	0	0.04	0	0.07

Source: Authors' calculation.

Notes

α_1^ϵ = European propensity to consume

λ^ϵ = wage share in Europe

γ_{20}^ϵ = share of US bills in the European households' assets of US competitiveness facing China. For example, in the case of propensity to consume equal to 0.8 in the basic model or 0.9 in the sensitivity test, we obtain for the relative deviation of European GDP (y^{ϵ}) the following coefficient of dispersion measured in absolute value:

$$\left[\frac{Y^{\epsilon} - Y_b^{\epsilon}}{Y_b^{\epsilon}} \right] \text{with } \alpha_1^{\epsilon} = 0.9 - \left[\frac{Y^{\epsilon} - Y_b^{\epsilon}}{Y_b^{\epsilon}} \right] \text{with } \alpha_1^{\epsilon} = 0.8$$

For the current account balance in percentage of GDP (CAB) the coefficient of dispersion is measured with the simple deviation:

$$[CAB^{\epsilon} - CAB_b^{\epsilon}] \text{ with } \alpha_1^{\epsilon} = 0.9 - [CAB^{\epsilon} - CAB_b^{\epsilon}] \text{ with } \alpha_1^{\epsilon} = 0.8$$

On the whole, the coefficients of dispersion of relative deviations with regard to the base line (measured in %) appear small. It illustrates the relative stability of the model regarding the value of the different parameters.

Annex 3.3 Sensitivity tests regarding the structure of China's foreign reserves: loss of US competitiveness facing China

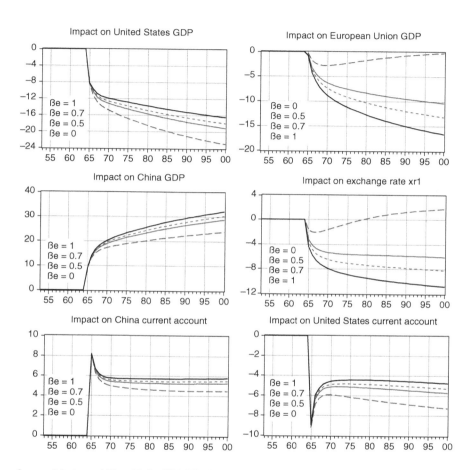

Source: Mazier and Tiou-Tagba Aliti (2009).

Part II
European challenges

4 From the European Monetary System to the single currency trap

Jacques Mazier, Vincent Duwicquet, and Jamel Saadaoui

Introduction

The failure of the European construction is a long story. A major turning point happened in the mid-1980s with the launching of the Single Market. Since this period, the mismanagement of the European economic policy has appeared as one of the main causes of the poor economic performances of the EU. The European Monetary System (EMS) was functioning asymmetrically and the countries with weak currencies beard the adjustment costs burden. In 1985, instead of bringing solutions to the identified blocking factors, it was decided to use market forces to re-launch Europe with the Single Market programme. According to the already prevailing liberal approach, growth and innovation were to be encouraged by both the completion of a large domestic market and the reinforcement of competition. At the end of the 1980s, financial liberalisation and the increasingly rigid EMS mechanisms made a change of the monetary regime necessary. The single currency prevailed without the obvious consequences in terms of economic policy organisation being ever envisaged. The project was shaky from the very beginning. However, the benefits of the single currency were thought to be determining and its costs largely underestimated. Furthermore, the transitory measures towards the single currency adopted in Maastricht in December 1991, added to the aftermath of the German reunification, contributed to the halt of European growth during the long 1992–1998 transition period. After the brief 1998–2000 recovery, the blocking factors were fully at play again and the economic slide reappeared. The welfare systems which were specific to each country and appeared as one of the pillars of European societies have since then been gradually questioned. The EU was all the more up against the wall as its enlargement to Eastern Europe represented an additional challenge. The European Constitution project in 2005 was a tentative of answer, largely open to criticism, which explained its rejection. The 'simplified' treaty of Lisbon was mainly a new version of the same text. The EU was still suffering from persistent paralysis and was locked into a slow growth process. A monetary union among heterogeneous countries with no adjustment mechanism except wage deflation can only lead to divergent developments.

On the eve of the crisis of 2008 the disequilibria were still hidden but were characterised by an undervalued euro for the countries of the German block and an overvalued euro for the countries in the South of the euro zone. The financial crisis revealed these disequilibria. Exchange rate changes being impossible, the financial markets finally realised that the debts of the South were not equivalent to those of the North and interest rates exploded in the South. Faced with the crisis of the euro, the European governments in general adopted austerity policies to bring about internal devaluation and reduce public sector deficits. They established new European rules and institutions in order to provide the necessary financing. But the monetary and financial federalism guided by the ECB, together with the rules of the Fiscal Treaty did not make it possible to overcome the euro zone crisis in spite of a transitory recovery in 2016–2018.

The chapter is organised as follows. A second section is dedicated to the exchange rate misalignments within the EU which have been a key issue since the beginning of the ESM in the late 1970s. The FEER methodology presented in the Chapter 2 is used for each European country. A third section covers the whole period since the Single Market programme in the 1980s to the launching of the monetary union. It underlines the main drawbacks and the failures of the European economic policy until the rising imbalances during the 2000s. A fourth section analyses the trap of the single currency since the burst of the financial crisis in 2008 and the reforms undertaken under the pressure of events. Finally, with the incoherence of the euro zone regime the question of its sustainability is raised.

Exchange rate misalignments within the European Union

Intra-European exchange rate misalignments have been a key issue since the launch of the EMS in 1979. This question remains crucial even in the euro zone. It can be examined with the FEER approach already proposed in the Chapter 2. For each country of the euro area, an equilibrium exchange rate can be estimated using a simple national model of foreign trade. The foreign trade elasticities are those of the MIMOSA (1996) model for France, Germany, and Italy. For other European countries, the elasticities are derived from a previous contribution on interdependencies and adjustments in the European Union (Mazier and Saglio, 2008). These elasticities are presented in Annex 4.1 (Table 4.8). Equilibrium current balances and internal equilibrium are estimated in the same way as previously.

External and internal equilibrium at medium term

Figure 4.1 shows the observed and equilibrium values of the current account for the main euro area's members. In simulating equilibrium current balances, we use the equations estimated in Chapter 2 for the industrialised countries with the value of initial stocks of net foreign asset at the beginning of each four years period's and the four years average values of dependency ratios but we exclude output gap in order to remove short-term effects. Since the mid-1990s, the euro area's equilibrium current account has been close to zero with a slight improvement over the early 1980s, thanks to a growing external position. The amplitude of current imbalances in the euro area (as a whole) has been weak until the end of the 2000s compared to those observed in other major world economies (see Figure 2.2). However, this 'balanced' situation in the euro area masked a great heterogeneity for each euro area's member.

The Spanish, French, and Italian current account have been alternatively in surplus and deficit. They were in deficit before the crisis of the EMS in 1992, then in surplus between 1992 and 2002 in contrast with the unusual German current deficit due to the effect of the reunification. Since the launching of the euro deficits have reappeared in southern European countries in the 2000s while huge German current surpluses reemerged. After the financial crisis of 2008 Italian, Spanish, and even later French deficits have disappeared and the German surplus reached summits hardly sustainable (more than 8% of GDP). The current account's targets were more stable. Since the mid-1990s, the equilibrium current account of France has even improved, thanks to more favourable demographic evolutions. By contrast, the German equilibrium current account has returned to 0% of GDP as a result of the aging German population. The equilibrium current account of Italy and Spain have increased in the 1980s thanks to net external position improvement but they have deteriorated around – 2% of GDP, again due to a substantial aging of the population.

As at the world level, the internal equilibrium is defined as the state of full utilisation of productive resources, without inflation pressures. For sake of simplification, a restrictive approach, limited to the measure of the potential output, is adopted using the OECD estimations.

European disparities and exchange rate misalignments

At the level of the whole euro area exchange rate misalignments have remained relatively limited, as we have seen in the Chapter 2, especially during the 2000s before the financial crisis. Beyond these estimations, intra-European disparities must be examined in more details. The misalignments are not of the same magnitude at the level of each European country due to a structural heterogeneity. The two most obvious sources of heterogeneity regarding exchange rates are the foreign trade structure, which differs largely among European country, and the inequality between national rates of inflation, which is less important, but not negligible. These two sources of heterogeneity explain the dispersion of effective exchange rates in nominal and real terms, as shown in Figure 4.2.

The effective exchange rates are more stable at the level of each national country than at the level of the whole euro area because the importance of intra-European trade with fixed exchange rates stabilises the effective exchange rate. Between 2001 and 2008 the euro appreciation has been more limited at each national level than at the whole euro area level. This function of stabilisation of the euro is an important argument in favour of monetary unification.

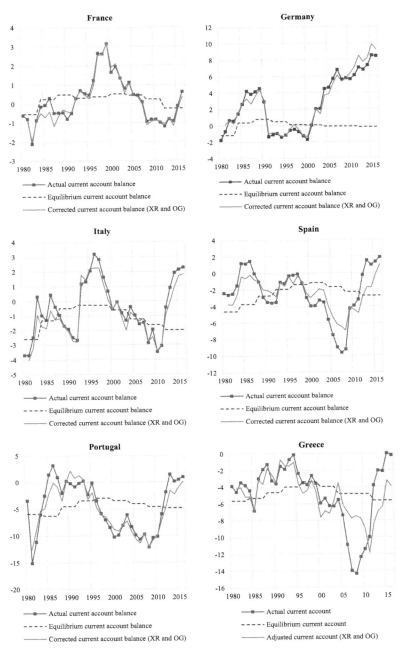

Figure 4.1 Actual and equilibrium current accounts of the main euro area's members (in % of GDP).

Source: International Monetary Fund (World Economic Outlook, April 2016; authors' calculation).

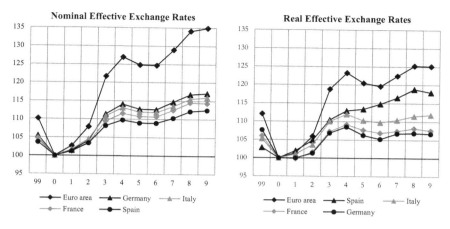

Figure 4.2 Nominal and real effective exchange rates (2000 = 100).
Source: Bank for International Settlements; 2009.

But the dispersion between countries is significant. In nominal terms, Germany has suffered of the strongest appreciation since 2001, due to the importance of the extra-European trade for this country, while, on the contrary, the euro appreciation was more limited in Spain where intra-European trade occupies a larger share. For real effective exchange rates, which are more crucial for competitiveness, it is the opposite. The dispersion is more noticeable between countries, due to the divergence between rates of inflation. In this case, Germany suffered of the smallest appreciation, thanks to its low relative rate of inflation, while Spain has faced a stronger real appreciation.

Like in the case of the main currencies, the following tables present the overvaluation ($r < 0, e < 0$) or undervaluation ($r > 0, e > 0$) for each 'national euro' for the period 1982–2016 in real effective terms (Table 4.1) and bilateral terms against the dollar (Table 4.2). Two preliminary remarks can be done. First, sensitivity tests are given in Annex 4.2 to appreciate the dependency on the estimates of external and internal equilibrium and on the parameters of the trade model. They show that the results are rather robust in spite of the uncertainties in estimating the internal and external equiilibrium and the parameters of the trade elasticities. Second, the weighted sum (by the GDP) of the intra-European misalignments is equal to the euro misalignment. Our estimates of intra-European misalignments are derived from the national models. The weighted sum of these misalignments is close to the euro misalignment derived from the world model. When there was a discrepancy (small in all the cases), the difference (between misalignments of the euro and the weighted sum of intra-European misalignments) has been distributed proportionately to the weight of the country in the euro area GDP.

Table 4.1 Undervaluation (rc > 0) or overvaluation (rc < 0) for each 'national euro' in real effective terms (in %)

rc	EUR	FRA	GER	ITA	SPA	AUT	FIN	IRL	NLD	PRT	GRC
1982	8.0	-23.5	3.9	-8.4	11.9	23.8	-19.8	-9.3	-9.2		4.8
1983	15.2	-13.9	-1.3	0.3	34.4	21.4	-23.5	-5.4	-11.7	6.5	-5.7
1984	12.2	-7.6	5.4	-2.5	44.5	9.5	-9.8	-3.3	-1.1	2.2	-5.6
1985	19.1	-23.0	0.3	-11.9	24.6	-4.2	-21.5	-3.4	-9.1	20.4	-38.8
1986	21.0	-20.3	2.5	-7.1	22.9	-4.5	-17.7	-1.5	-18.8	23.3	3.2
1987	11.0	-25.9	1.4	-6.7	23.5		-19.2	0.2	-18.1	20.5	-2.2
1988	9.5	-13.1	8.1	-1.7	25.5	1.2	-14.8	4.0	-12.8	8.7	9.1
1989	11.7	-9.0	9.7	-7.6	9.4	6.5	-24.6	-1.4	-8.2	19.2	10.2
1990	1.2	-5.2	12.1	-6.4	14.5	17.0	-32.9	0.9	-5.1	39.2	8.4
1991	-10.6	-2.8	-0.4	-5.6	16.2	22.5	-55.6	8.8	-2.9	40.8	33.6
1992	-10.0	6.7	1.2	-5.4	10.2	20.7	-45.2	8.2	-3.9	45.5	25.0
1993	4.5	6.2	-4.0	10.1	7.2	10.4	-13.2	9.2	-6.7	26.5	16.4
1994	-3.4	2.4	-7.4	6.9	1.4	4.8	-5.8	-0.7	-5.3	0.9	15.1
1995	1.2	-0.7	-7.5	8.2	9.6	-1.5	5.1	-1.7	-7.5	3.8	-0.1
1996	4.2	3.2	-4.8	6.7	-0.1	-4.1	8.3	-0.8	-7.2	-10.4	-11.3
1997	3.5	12.9	-1.6	5.4	1.1	-6.1	20.1	-1.5	-3.5	-18.5	-8.2
1998	0.6	14.0	-4.3	2.1	0.5	0.6	22.9	-2.6	-6.6	-16.8	-1.7
1999	2.0	19.2	-7.3	-1.5	-5.0	-2.0	21.6	-0.3	-3.3	-21.4	-7.2
2000	0.1	8.7	-8.1	-3.8	-7.6	1.4	24.9	-0.6	-6.7	-29.3	-16.8
2001	6.8	6.8	-2.9	-3.1	-7.9	-7.1	25.3	-4.0	-9.5	-36.1	-17.4
2002	6.6	2.5	3.8	-6.3	-4.8	5.7	25.6	-4.8	-13.4	-30.1	-19.0
2003	2.2	-2.9	1.3	-8.5	-3.2	-0.4	15.2	-3.6	-7.7	-26.1	-9.1
2004	7.2	-0.1	5.6	-5.4	-15.4	-4.0	19.6	-3.8	-5.2	-40.1	5.0
2005	1.9	-4.6	5.3	-4.1	-20.3	-2.2	7.8	-4.8	-5.7	-46.1	-7.6
2006	1.6	-4.8	9.1	-3.8	-24.6	4.0	9.7	-2.0	-1.6	-47.9	-6.3
2007	-0.2	-6.0	13.1	-0.7	-26.4	11.3	15.5	-0.9	-1.5	-34.5	-5.2
2008	0.9	-13.3	13.0	-4.5	-33.3	13.7	11.7	-4.7	-3.1	-46.3	-3.7
2009	6.6	-8.3	13.9	-2.9	-10.2	3.0	0.2	-0.7	-2.7	-34.4	-8.5
2010	4.9	-6.9	16.8	-4.2	-14.6	5.0	2.5	-0.9	0.0	-28.1	-21.1
2011	8.6	-10.1	16.8	-5.8	-22.9	2.6	-5.9	-2.5	-1.2	-19.6	-53.1
2012	16.3	-12.6	19.3	-2.5	-14.1	1.5	-8.9	-7.9	-2.1	-12.2	-30.9
2013	18.0	-5.0	18.7	1.5	-3.6	2.2	-7.2	1.4	-0.9	6.8	-20.3
2014	20.1	-10.1	19.4	3.8	-2.7	-0.9	-7.4	5.9	-0.8	4.4	-15.4
2015	26.1	-8.2	18.7	2.4	6.1	-2.3	-6.7	12.8	-3.9	8.6	1.9
2016	28.6	-5.2	15.8	2.0	14.3	-4.1	-8.6	11.7	-5.2	14.1	-5.2

Source: Authors' calculations, forecasts for 2016.

It appears that misalignments for each 'national euro' are important and quite different from what is observed for the euro itself. Consequently, the constraints exerted on each European country are very different. The relative position of each 'national euro', in terms of misalignments, is not permanent and can vary in the medium to long run according to structural adjustments which affect each economy. The cases of Germany and France are interesting to examine first in that perspective. In the mid-1990s, the 'euro-mark', which was in fact the deutschmark at that time, was overvalued (nearly 7% in real effective terms,

Table 4.2 Undervaluation (e > 0) or overvaluation (e < 0) for each 'national euro' in nominal terms against the dollar (in %)

e	EUR	FRA	GER	ITA	SPA	AUT	FIN	IRL	NLD	PRT	GRC
1982	2.8	−29.2	1.5	−12.9	9.6	25.3	−28.7	−11.4	−12.9	0.0	3.0
1983	14.1	−10.4	3.2	4.5	42.8	31.2	−26.6	−1.2	−7.9	14.2	−1.3
1984	18.2	2.9	17.2	8.0	61.1	23.5	−2.6	5.4	12.0	14.2	5.4
1985	27.4	−8.9	16.6	2.5	43.1	14.4	−11.7	10.5	7.7	43.6	−29.2
1986	33.2	0.6	24.3	14.4	47.5	20.6	−1.5	15.2	0.6	52.8	28.9
1987	21.6	−12.5	17.2	8.7	42.9	0.0	−7.8	12.8	−6.2	44.0	15.0
1988	5.3	−13.9	9.3	−1.3	29.9	3.4	−18.5	2.6	−15.8	13.0	12.1
1989	5.1	−10.6	9.7	−9.2	10.5	8.8	−31.5	−5.6	−10.9	26.5	12.6
1990	−3.4	−10.0	9.4	−11.3	12.5	17.3	−42.0	−3.4	−11.5	47.7	5.8
1991	−22.1	−20.2	−17.1	−23.5	0.9	8.5	−77.6	−2.1	−23.1	33.1	21.9
1992	−23.6	−11.5	−17.1	−25.1	−7.9	4.3	−68.7	−5.9	−26.3	36.6	9.5
1993	−7.1	−2.4	−14.2	1.5	−1.1	3.5	−25.7	1.1	−18.4	24.8	10.0
1994	−5.5	−1.1	−11.7	3.8	−2.4	1.5	−10.1	−4.0	−11.3	−3.5	13.5
1995	−6.6	−8.0	−15.8	1.9	4.1	−9.4	−2.0	−9.5	−17.4	−2.4	−7.5
1996	−5.6	−3.9	−13.5	−0.5	−7.4	−12.6	0.8	−8.6	−17.1	−20.5	−21.3
1997	−3.4	9.8	−7.4	0.7	−3.4	−12.2	17.5	−6.5	−9.2	−28.9	−14.9
1998	−6.7	9.3	−11.9	−4.7	−6.1	−6.2	19.6	−8.8	−15.5	−29.0	−9.1
1999	−3.8	17.4	−13.2	−6.5	−10.7	−6.9	20.0	−5.0	−9.1	−33.4	−13.4
2000	3.6	14.0	−5.6	−0.6	−5.5	5.8	34.1	3.2	−5.1	−36.4	−16.8
2001	11.8	16.9	5.0	5.2	0.3	1.5	38.2	2.2	−3.2	−38.2	−11.9
2002	15.2	15.6	16.7	5.6	7.9	21.1	42.6	3.9	−4.4	−25.3	−9.7
2003	15.1	11.8	17.0	5.8	11.8	15.8	34.2	7.8	5.2	−18.7	5.0
2004	20.8	17.8	23.8	11.5	−0.2	14.4	40.8	9.9	11.7	−33.5	24.6
2005	20.7	15.1	26.7	16.0	−4.0	18.9	31.0	11.9	13.6	−41.1	12.2
2006	20.5	14.8	31.6	16.5	−10.0	27.9	33.9	15.4	19.1	−45.2	13.8
2007	8.1	1.9	25.0	8.2	−24.4	25.4	28.5	7.0	7.4	−36.9	3.0
2008	12.4	−3.7	27.9	7.2	−30.0	31.9	26.8	3.9	7.8	−47.4	8.5
2009	17.6	4.0	30.2	10.8	1.3	19.5	13.8	8.6	9.7	−29.3	4.8
2010	16.9	6.0	33.9	9.5	−4.2	22.0	17.0	9.3	13.5	−21.4	−10.2
2011	23.1	6.5	37.9	12.0	−9.9	24.5	10.8	10.6	16.7	−4.9	−43.8
2012	25.8	2.5	39.0	14.3	0.5	23.0	4.3	1.8	14.6	4.7	−18.7
2013	26.0	10.5	37.2	17.9	12.9	23.0	4.9	11.9	15.0	28.2	−7.2
2014	25.8	3.2	36.6	19.2	12.8	17.6	2.9	15.5	13.9	24.2	−2.8
2015	23.9	1.3	30.8	12.5	20.2	12.5	−2.3	20.2	6.4	26.4	12.8
2016	26.1	5.9	28.2	12.8	31.9	11.6	−4.2	19.4	6.0	35.0	5.4

Source: Authors' calculations, forecasts for 2016.

around 15% against the dollar) because of the consequences of the German reunification. It required a substantial transfer of resources from West to East Germany, induced a drift of unit costs and significantly reduced the German external surplus. At the official launching of the euro in 1999 the 'euro–mark' was still slightly overvalued. This contrasted with the position of the global euro which, at that time, was close to equilibrium. Since the late 1990s, the German economy has realised a painful adjustment process by cost reducing and industrial restructuring with delocalization of activities. This strategy has significantly slowed down economic growth in Europe during this period but helped to rebuild new foundations for German competitiveness. As a consequence, since the mid-2000s, the 'euro-mark' has become undervalued (around 18% in real effective terms, around 35% against the dollar) while the euro, for the whole area, but pushed by the German surpluses, also became undervalued in the 2010s.

France is, for a large part, in an opposite situation. In the second half of the 1990s, the 'euro-franc' was undervalued (around 15% in real effective terms and against the dollar). France took advantage of the German economic difficulties and of its long run strategy of competitive disinflation. This situation did not last. Since the mid-2000s, the 'euro-franc' became overvalued in real effective terms in contrast with a global euro close to its equilibrium value. This induced strong constraints on the French economy during this period and reflected structural problems of competitiveness which had remained unsolved since the 1990s. These problems had only been mitigated by the German transitory difficulties following the reunification and by the disinflation strategy, which turned to be only a short-term solution, without solving more structural handicaps.

Spain and Italy are other interesting cases to examine. Following the devaluations that took place during the EMS crisis, the peseta and the lira were undervalued during the mid-1990s. But, like for the French franc, its did not last. After the launching of the euro, we observed an overvaluation of the 'euro-peseta' and, to a lesser extent, of the 'euro-lira', which has strengthened. This overvaluation reflected large inequalities of competitiveness inside the euro area. Actually constraints were less important in the case of Italy than in the case of Spain, with the housing bubble during the first half of the 2000s. The large overvaluation of the 'euro-peseta' (33% in 2008, in real effective terms) was largely related to insufficient productivity and weaknesses in R&D in a context of unsustainable economic growth (see Tables 4.3 and 4.4). Portugal and Greece are another cases of southern European economies affected by the overvaluation of their currency since the second half of the 1990s. With a weak productivity, a peripheral localization and a specialisation in low costs products, the Portuguese and Greek economies have had huge difficulties to invert this situation within the constraints of the euro area.

Table 4.3 R&D in % of GDP and number of patents registered (per millions of inhabitants)

	R&D		Patents	
	North	*South*	*North*	*South*
1998	2.17	1.40	64.16	19.44
2009	2.65	1.64	67.26	20.90

Source: OECD, 2010.

Table 4.4 Structure of the working age population by level of education

In %	North		South	
	Below the second cycle of secondary school	Superior education	Below the second cycle of secondary school	Superior education
1999	26	23	52	17
2008	18	27	40	23

Source: OECD, 2010.

On the opposite, Ireland is an illustration of a catch up strategy which has been more successful, at least until the beginning of the 2000s. Until this period, the exchange rate has remained close to its equilibrium. But, since 2002, the Irish economic growth has become more unbalanced with the housing bubble, although the overvaluation of the 'Irish euro' remained rather limited. This illustrates the fact that small opened economies generally suffer less of exchange rate misalignments, as it can be understood with the equation (17) of Chapter 2, where the openness ratio plays a key role. However, the Portuguese economy, small but less opened, shows that this general rule may suffer of exception in cases of larger unbalances due to structural weaknesses. After the financial crisis Ireland has realised painful adjustments through wage deflation and the Irish euro has become again undervalued.

Netherlands, Austria, and Finland, three small opened northern and alpine European economies are the last cases to be examined. Netherlands and Austria have kept their exchange rates close to equilibrium during most of the period, although the Austrian and Dutch currencies were slightly overvalued during the second half of the 1990s and the beginning of the 2000s, due to stronger connections with Germany. On the contrary, the Finnish mark was more undervalued during the second half of the 1990s (around 20% in real effective terms), thanks to a large devaluation after the crisis of 1991–1992. This under-valuation has been progressively reduced and has disappeared in the 2010s, facing the difficulties of Nokia and of the Russian crisis. But the overvaluation remained limited thanks to structural adjustments and increasing R&D effort.

To sum up, beyond estimates of exchange rate misalignments of the euro, important disparities are observed between 'national euros'. The euro misalignments do not represent a pertinent indicator for each national euro. The misalignments are often more important for each individual euro area member than for the whole euro area. These exchange rates misalignments reflect structural heterogeneity between the north (Germany, Netherlands, Belgium, Austria, Finland) and the south (France, Italy, Spain, Portugal, Greece) of Europe. First, the northern Europe is more specialised in manufacturing (around 20% of total value added) while the southern Europe is increasingly specialised in non-tradable goods (housing, trade, tourism) with a decreasing share of manufacturing sector (from 16% in 2000 to 13% of total value added in 2010). Second, the rate of innovation is significantly smaller in the south than in the north. The share of R&D in GDP is 1.5% instead of 2.6% in the north. Similarly, the number of patents registered by inhabitants is three times smaller in the south than in the north (Table 4.3). Last, the active population is clearly less qualified in the south (Table 4.4). This approach in terms of intra-European exchange rate misalignments and of structural heterogeneity between European countries will be a useful reference in the assessment of the European integration process since the early 1980s.

From the Single Market to the single currency

In 1982 an international conference 'Out of crisis' was held in Paris trying to propose an issue at the crisis which was lasting since 1974 with rising mass unemployment and high inflation rates. The solution proposed was rather simple: a coordinated demand policy at the European level was able to impulse a recovery thanks to intra-European feedbacks and created the basis of a sustained growth at medium term. In spite of the participation of the French ministry of Finance, Jacques Delors, and of many European social-democrat leaders, nothing happened. Since 1980 Germany was engaged in a stabilisation policy and the United Kingdom has adopted since 1979 a new liberal policy with Mrs Thatcher. In 1983 Jacques Delors launched its competitive disinflation policy in France which was progressively generalised in all the European countries during the 1980s. It must be recalled that, at the same time, rather different economic policies were followed in the USA and Japan. Beyond the 'supply side policy', the USA were giving more attention to demand with large fiscal cuts and increasing public expenditures, especially in the military sector. Japan was experimenting since 1978 a strong recovery thanks to a yen devaluation and an export led strategy.

The Single Market programme

In 1985, instead of bringing solutions to the identified blocking factors, Jacques Delors, new president of the European Commission, decided to launch the Single Market programme which was regarded as the only feasible strategy at the European level in the liberal environment which was already dominant. According to the Single Market logic, non-tariff barriers were to be suppressed up to 1992. The completion of a large domestic market, scale economies' effects and the reinforcement of competition might lead to costs reduction, improve European competitiveness and stimulate growth and innovation. Financial liberalisation was supposed to induce a decrease of interest rates and improve investments financing. Very optimistic evaluations of the impact of this Single Market programme were published. According to the Cecchini report (European Commission, 1988), a GDP increase of 7.5% and the creation of 6 million jobs were expected between 1988 and 1994 (Table 4.5).

Table 4.5 Macroeconomic effects of the achievement of the Single Market 1988–1994: relative (%) or absolute deviations in 1994 with regard to the central account

Ex ante evaluation UE 12

	Suppression of border controls	Public procurement openness	Liberalisation of financial services	Supply effects	Total	Total with demand policy
PIB (%)	0.4	0.6	1.5	2.1	4.5	6.5/7.5
Employment (thousands)	210	360	440	860	1900	4500/5700

Ex post evaluation UE 15

	GEM–E3 model	QUEST model
PIB (%)	1.1	1.5
Employment (thousands)	300	900

Source: Authors' construction from European Commission (1988; 1996).

This report was highly questionable, especially because the estimation included a strong demand policy, around 2% of GDP, which was never mentioned in the official discourses on the Single Market. In practice, the impact of the Single Market achievement was far more limited, as the European Commission (1996) itself did recognise. This project, which was presented as the 'European supply side policy' in response to the US one, failed to give the basis to a sustained growth. But it marked a turning point with the increasing weight of the European competition policy and the end of any temptation to impulse industrial policies at the European level.

The EMS: the first stage (1979–1992)

At the monetary level, the EMS, settled in 1979, was an exchange rate mechanism aimed at giving more monetary stability among European currencies. The EMS was in itself attractive since it meant fixed, but adjustable exchange rates, by mutual agreement, according to the economic situation of each member country. It obviously reduced the exchange rate volatility of participating currencies, but one of its main flaws was its asymmetrical functioning. Theoretically speaking, responsibilities were shared between member countries and any given participant was supposed to intervene as soon as its currency became under- or overvalued against the divergence threshold. But, in practice, the Bundesbank never intervened to stop the mark's appreciation, and the EMS became pegged to the German currency. The weight of alignments was always borne by the countries whose currencies were weaker. Given the belatedness of devaluations that never corresponded to the required amount, the weaker currencies (the French franc and the Italian lira) have always tended to be overvalued and the mark undervalued (Tables 4.1 and 4.2).

Two rather contrasted periods can, in fact, be distinguished. From 1979 to 1987, the EMS operated rather flexibly, with numerous monetary realignments, especially for the franc and the lira. The preservation of the control of capital flows by many countries also meant the opportunity for monetary authorities to intervene whenever necessary. However, the competitiveness of the Italian industry deteriorated dramatically against Germany's (by nearly 30%), thus stressing a strong 'EMS effect'. From 1987 to 1992, the EMS became much more rigid. A 'new EMS' was then envisaged, which was supposed to work without resorting to regular devaluations whose efficiency was much questioned. The set back of inflation and the early stages of nominal convergence between European countries contributed to a more rigid functioning. Following the 1987 Nyborg Agreements, the Bundesbank was also supposed to participate in the coordinated interventions on interest rates and increase its short-term loans whenever weak currencies were attacked. The peseta integrated the EMS in 1989, followed by the sterling in 1990. In 1990–1991, the peseta and the lira, as well as the pound, even if in lesser proportions, tended to appreciate despite major current deficits and the persistence of strong inflation differentials compared with the European average. Those evolutions, encouraged by very high interest rates in the three countries, were wrongly interpreted as the positive consequences of the credibility of the 'new EMS'. Such optimistic interpretation was harboured by the single currency project, which had already largely begun to take shape at that time. The liberalisation of capital flows, which was initiated in the United Kingdom in the early 1980s and then extended to the rest of Europe in the late 1990s, made capital inflows and the financing of current deficits easier.

But such a situation could not last very long. The drift of Italian, and then Spanish and British unit costs was extremely strong in the early 1990s. Such a pattern led to the repeated crises of the EMS in 1992 and 1993. The United Kingdom and Italy withdrew from the EMS, Spain adopted wider fluctuation bands, and the three countries resorted to major devaluations. The franc was under severe speculative attacks with the main one in July 1993. However, thanks to the French Central Bank's massive interventions which led to the total exhaustion of its reserves, to persistent high interest rates and to the Bundesbank's support, the franc was not devalued. Keeping the franc/mark parity, which was wrongly defended as a necessary condition to the success of the single currency project, proved particularly costly as it hampered growth in the early 1990s.

Taking into account of equilibrium exchange rates allows a detailed approach (see Table 2.3 for the pound sterling, the dollar, and the yen). Older estimations can also be found in Couharde and Mazier (2001). The most striking exchange rates misalignments appeared between the early 1980s and the early 1990s with a turning point when the dollar started to soar at the beginning of the 1980s. In 1985, its overvaluation was balanced by the undervaluation of the yen and the mark, corresponding to those two countries' big current surpluses. On the contrary the franc, the lira and the pound were overvalued. The misalignments that characterised the EMS in its early stages clearly played in favour of Germany. Following the Plazza and Louvre agreements, the fall of the dollar and the yen's appreciation reversed the situation. The dollar became undervalued in 1990 but the mark remained undervalued. The other European currencies, particularly the lira and the franc, appeared overvalued. Those imbalances being unbearable, the EMS was hit by the 1992–1993 crises. This particular configuration of exchange rates bore serious consequences for the countries whose currencies were overvalued and helped Germany's economic growth, to the detriment of its partners'. As the German Minister for the Economy, Otto Graf Lambsdorff, then admitted, 'The EMS was operating as a way to subsidize German exports'.

The German reunification, the 1992–1993 EMS crises and the depth of the Japanese crisis contributed to the reduction of misalignments in the early 1990s. European currencies, including the mark, appeared slightly overvalued in 1995. In Germany's case, the new conditions resulting from the reunification, implying rising unemployment and the end of current surpluses, erased the factors that previously used to be at the origin of the undervaluation of the mark. In other words, the real equilibrium exchange rate of the mark was devalued, putting an end to the undervaluation of the German currency, which had been one of the main causes of imbalances within the EMS. The yen, for its part, remained near its equilibrium real exchange rate. The dollar continued to be undervalued. These conclusions are also illustrated by the non-linear relation between exchange rate misalignments and growth, already presented in Chapter 2 (Aflouk and Mazier, 2013). Using this relation it can be shown that in the second half of the 1980s the impact of the misalignments on the GDP rate of growth has been negative around −1% in France and positive in Germany, at around 0.5%. This was reversed after the EMS crises of 1992–1993 and the economic consequences of the German reunification. At the end of the 1990s, the impact was positive in France and negative in Germany.

The transition towards the single currency (1992–1998)

A new step appeared necessary in the European monetary integration process in the late 1980s. Indeed, it had become impossible to conciliate the stability of exchange rates (as sought in 'the new EMS'), the free circulation of capital (which had become widespread in the late 1980s) and the autonomy of national monetary policies. The 1992–1993 crises were the most striking manifestation of the situation. Several solutions could then be envisaged:

- the submission to the German monetary policy within the framework of an enlarged mark area. Such a solution was possible for a limited number of economies around Germany (Austria, Netherlands) but meant hardly surmountable political problems for others, especially in the case of France.

- a step backwards consisting in the reintroduction of controlled capital flows. This solution was technically possible and proposals were made in that direction, that is an anti-speculative mechanism installing compulsory reserves on financial intermediaries' exchange rate positions, the introduction of 'sand in the wheels' so as to limit capital flows, with a Tobin tax. But such a prospect implied the persistence of elements of instability within the framework of a strengthened EMS. It was also too much in opposition with the financial liberalisation process which was actually ruling the system.
- the adoption of a single currency which was supposed to eliminate every financial instability factor at an intra-European level, but this hypothesis revealed itself largely erroneous.
- two other solutions were put forward, but never really explored. The first one was the setting up of a common currency which would have been used in parallel with national currencies and let competition play its role. This solution was once defended by the United Kingdom. The second one was the creation of a single currency solely to be used in foreign exchanges, while national currencies would have still been used for intra-European exchanges. Though attractive from a theoretical point of view, this solution was deemed too complex.

The single currency project prevailed, partly as a consequence of a Franco-German compromise. Germany, which was at first very reluctant, gave its preference to an enlarged mark area. It eventually joined the single currency in exchange for France's promise to accept its reunification. Indeed, France had always been very sceptical about Germany's reunification, but much preferred the single currency project to the idea of a mere enlargement of the mark area. In its instigators' minds, the single currency was initially meant to apply to a small core of countries only, around the Franco-German couple, and left the other European countries inside a 'parallel EMS', at least at first.

The credibility of the project, which was officially approved in Maastricht in December 1991, was only very slowly acquired. The strategy that was finally adopted consisted in a long transition period, from 1992 to 1998, so that the nominal convergence criteria should be abided by (convergence of inflation and interest rates, public deficit limited to 3% of national GDP and public debt to 60% of GDP, exchange rates' stability, Central Banks' independence). In order to abide by those criteria, all European economies simultaneously enforced adjustment policies of their public finances, with devastating effects in terms of growth and employment. Simulations made with macroeconomic international models of the EU clearly show the high costs of these Maastricht criteria. Simultaneous stabilisation policies contributed to block European growth during most of the 1990s while, at the same time, the United States and East Asia (at the exception of Japan) were booming (Table 4.6).

The European Commission was fully aware of these negative impacts on growth. To compensate these effects, Jacques Delors presented in December 1992 at Edinburgh a very modest European Growth Initiative (0.15% of GDP

Table 4.6 Macroeconomic consequences of Maastricht criteria

	Reduction of public expenditures (in % of GDP) necessary each year to:	
	Fulfil 3% of public deficit in 1999	*Fulfil 60% of public debt*
Germany	-0.2	-0.6
Belgium		-5.0
Denmark	-0.4	-1.4
Spain	-1.6	-2.0
France	-0.6	-1.4
Greece	-0.9	-3.0
Ireland		-0.3
Italy	-1.0	-5.2
Netherlands		-1.0
United Kingdom	-0.9	-0.9
UE	-0.65	-1.95

	Impact on the whole EU of a reduction of public expenditures of 1% of GDP					
	1994	*1995*	*1996*	*1997*	*1998*	*1999*
GDP (%)	-1.0	-1.1	-1.1	-1.2	-1.3	-1.5
Inflation (%)	0.2	-0.2	-0.7	-1.4	-2.1	-2.9
Public surplus (% GDP)	0.7	0.6	0.7	0.5	0.4	0.4

Source: Authors' construction from CEPII-OFCE-MIMOSA (1994).

for new investments) which was adopted, but never applied. In 1993 the White Book on 'Growth, Competitiveness and Employment' also contained proposals of large infrastructures investments in transports, telecommunications and energy at the European level. Although accepted by the European Council, they were never implemented and were progressively opposed by the Council of Ministers of Finance in order to fulfil the restrictive fiscal policy. Only 14 projects of trans-European transport were decided in Essen in 1994. Out of these 14 projects, only three have been completed ten years after. This illustrates the difficulty to implement a reflation policy at the European level. Public investments are not well suited to impulse a short-term recovery. Coordinated actions are extremely difficult, if not impossible, to manage in the present institutional context.

At the monetary and financial level, the years 1992–1993 were particularly unstable, which led to a very flexible EMS, with broad fluctuation bands. This instability was generally expected to last and even liberal oriented economists suggested the adoption of anti-speculative mechanisms (Eichengreen and Wyplosz, 1994). However, this instability did not last and exchange rates soon stabilised within narrow bands against their central rates. This stabilisation is often attributed to the credibility of the programmes implemented, the governments' determination and the merits of an exchange rate policy, referred to as an 'elastic policy', which consisted in accepting a certain degree of flexibility in the defence of reference parities, without subsequent unbearable hikes in interest rates, but admitting the existence of a risk premium (Davanne, 1998).

Another factor seems to lie in more fundamental determinants. Most of the imbalances which affected European parities until the early 1990s and opposed an undervalued mark to overvalued southern European currencies had disappeared (see Tables 4.1 and 4.2). This result shows that the central rates which prevailed when the euro was set up proved rather satisfactory. Several factors account for this. The successive devaluations of 1992–1993, followed by a control of inflation by the countries concerned, had permitted to correct the overvaluation of the lira, the peseta, and the pound. France had reached the same goal by cutting unit wage costs within the framework of a competitive disinflation policy. In Germany, the shock caused by the reunification had put an end to current surpluses and caused unemployment to soar, and that trend manifested itself in the depreciation of the mark's real equilibrium exchange rate and the end of the undervaluation trend of the German currency.

These results suggest that the market mechanisms, and notably the realignments that followed the 1992–1993 EMS crises, worked well and allowed European currencies exchange rates to converge towards their equilibrium values. It is the reason why the launching of the euro was a success. The European currencies' conversion rates which had been announced long in advance did not cause any speculative attack because they corresponded relatively well to their equilibrium values. This result was all the more surprising as the Asian crisis was then at the origin of a general feeling of greater instability. It also enables us to understand why southern European countries could join the euro area, contrary to what was initially expected by the instigators of the project. In addition to the efforts that were made in order to restore the situation of public finance and to control inflation, the fact that exchange rates almost reached their equilibrium values also constituted a major element. However, Portugal and Greece were in less favourable situation with currencies still overvalued.

The transition to the euro in 1999 marked the culmination of 20 years of efforts to move towards monetary integration. It represented a major and unique institutional change in the history of industrialised countries and could only be carried out thanks to strong political determination. Its costs in terms of growth slowdown have been high in the 1980s, considering the functioning of the EMS, and even higher in the 1990s, because of the criteria adopted in Maastricht in order to achieve the transition to the euro. But those costs have been accepted on account of the gains that were expected from the Monetary Union and of the absence of any credible alternative. A rapid assessment can be made of the expected advantages of the single currency, but also of its limits which have been largely underestimated at the beginning of the 1990s (European Commission, 1990).

The expected gains of the single currency

The expected advantages of the single currency, as they were put forward, appeared many:

- a significant reduction of transaction costs, which would represent an additional GDP growth of 0.5% on average, with a higher gain for smaller countries;
- a lesser external constraint in the case of current deficits linked to intra-European trade, since they can be financed in euros. A major element of the growth slowdown of the 1970s and 1980s would thus disappear, more particularly for countries like France or Italy, which had been under severe constraint. This argument, often underlined during the 1980s and 1990s, appeared fallacious, as it will be explained below and as it has been illustrated by the Spanish case;
- the end of speculative attacks between European currencies and of the resulting factors of instability; the end of the risk premium in many countries, which in fact allowed a significant decrease of interest rates in the 2000s. Here also the argument didn't resist to the facts, as it has been shown by the crisis of the euro area and the soaring of interest rates in southern European countries in 2010. The speculative attacks did not disappear but have changed of nature;
- an incentive for trade exchanges and investments thanks to lesser uncertainty, at least theoretically, and to higher competition due to increased price comparison;
- the setting up, within a very integrated economic area, of a drastic coordination of monetary policies, thanks to the enforcement of a single monetary policy, which notably avoid 'unfair' policies consisting in exporting unemployment by devaluating. The EMS had unsuccessfully tried to solve this problem. But, as it will be shown later, competitive devaluations have been largely replaced by very painful competitive disinflation policies;
- a stabilisation of the effective exchange rate since a large share of foreign trade (around 50%) is intra-Euro area trade which is now at fixed exchange rates. This was illustrated earlier (see Figure 4.2);
- the advent of the euro as an international currency which could challenge in the future the domination of the dollar. The euro has actually become the second international currency, especially in terms of international reserves but it has not been able to reverse, or even compete, the hegemonic position of the dollar in the international financial system, largely because of the structural weaknesses of the euro area.

The underestimated costs of the single currency

Beside those expected advantages of the single currency, the Monetary Union presented important limits which have been largely underestimated during the launching of the euro. The first one concerned the weakness of the adjustment mechanisms after the end of the intra-European exchange rate adjustments. The second was linked to the very particular status of the European Central Bank (ECB). The third was due to the rules imposed to the national fiscal policies by the Stability Pact.

The weakness of the adjustment mechanisms

With the elimination of intra-European exchange rates, adjustment mechanisms, in case of asymmetrical evolutions, are weak. The flexibility of relative prices, i.e. wage and employment flexibility, was for a long time the answer given by the single currency advocates. However, several reports have shown that it could only allow a very slow and partial realignment (Cadiou et alii, 1999; Mazier and Saglio, 2008; Blanchard and Katz, 1992). The contrasting ways various countries react to a similar (i.e. symmetrical) shock should also be taken into account because of structural differences. These divergences are a source of asymmetries, even in case of shocks affecting all countries similarly. The problems of asymmetrical evolutions are more important than it was initially considered.

Labour force interstate mobility has sometimes been suggested as a possible adjustment mechanism, playing a significant role in the case of the United States. However, its adjustment function seems to remain limited even in the United States, where people's migrations are higher than in the EU. These interstate migrations essentially correspond to structural determinants (decline of some old manufacturing areas, climatic factors, level of the infrastructures). It was, and it is still, therefore illusory to hope that a wider intra-European mobility would provide a satisfactory answer in the long run (Mazier et al., 2002). We will come back on this issue later, as this intra-European mobility did increase since the 2010s.

Federal budgets might play a readjustment function in the case of a negative shock affecting one state, since the latter would pay fewer federal taxes and could get increased transfers. Such a mechanism actually operates in the United States and the stabilisation ratio is about 15–20% (Melitz and Zumer, 2000), but it could not be the case in Europe because of the absence of a federal budget. The creation of a cheap 'budget insurance' mechanism, which would play a stabilising role for a country affected by a negative shock, has been proposed since the beginning of the 1990s (Italianer and Pisani-Ferry, 1992) but has never been adopted for fear of lenient behaviours or of the redistributive biases it could generate.

Well integrated capital markets with portfolio diversification and intra-zone credit were supposed to have powerful adjustment mechanism by the 'international risk sharing' approach. Intra-zone credit and capital income from international portfolio would have stabilisation coefficients quite important, around 25% each in the case of the United States, which was above the stabilising and redistributive role of a federal budget (around 15–20%), according to indirect econometric methods (Asdrubali et alii, 1996; Asdrubali and Kim, 2004). These results have been used during the 2000s by advocates of liberal economic policies in the case of the EU to promote a deeper monetary and financial integration without having to develop a federal budget (European Commission, 2007; Trichet, 2007). However the econometric methodology used can be criticised. It gives only an indirect estimation of the stabilisation coefficient with hypothesis that cannot be regarded as realistic, especially for the role of external financing (Clévenot and Duwicquet, 2011). An alternative approach of this question based on a SFC model of the Monetary Union will re-examine this question in the next chapter.

National budgets could also be used to reach stabilisation, but mainly in case of a negative demand shock and within the limits set by the Stability Pact which reduces a lot the room for manoeuvre and tends to favour pro-cyclical policies.

The Monetary Union is thus helpless when faced with shocks or asymmetrical evolutions. The nature of the shocks likely to hit the European Union was much debated upon. Several elements pleaded for the persistence, even the reinforcement, of asymmetrical factors. Regional inequalities tended to become stronger in the 1980s and 1990s, which constituted an element of asymmetry, despite the convergence of national economies. The concentration of activities per country measured by Krugman's specialisation index for the whole of the European Union rose in most cases (Midelfart-Knarvik et al., 2000). The concentration of activities in America, though declining since the 1950s, was stronger than within the European Union. The increasing specialisation of economies in terms of technological contents and product quality (development of quality intra-sector trade) was a cause of asymmetry, but was compensated by the decline of inter-sector trade (Fontagné et al., 1998). The institutional differences existing between European countries were still important and could account for differentiated answers from each country faced with a shock that hit all of them similarly. The importance of those asymmetries clearly appeared when the euro was launched and surprised some of the analysts who had been too much confident in the unifying virtues of monetary integration and nominal convergence.

The particular status of the ECB

In this context, the choice of an ECB independent from political power and whose main goal was to reach price stability (with an inflation rate close but inferior to 2%) posed several problems. It was, first, a worrying choice with regard to democratic principles because supranational authority had no legitimacy whatsoever in Europe. In the absence of an unattainable 'economic government' or European federal authority, the ECB's autonomy in terms of internal monetary policy and exchange policy was larger than that of the Fed in the United States or the Bundesbank in Germany.

Unlike in the United States, no reference was made to the goal to preserve growth and employment.

The efficiency of monetary policies varied from one country to another. A common monetary policy was inadequate vis-à-vis countries having to deal with contrasted economic situations. It was too restrictive for the countries going through an economic slowdown, and too flexible for those which were submitted to inflationary pressures, as shown by the economic situation during the 2000s. The different ways of financing housing in European countries, with fixed or variable interest rates, have also been a source of divergence during the 2000s.

The end of a lender in last resort for the national States has been another major change. Before the creation of the euro the national Central Banks played a role of lender not only in the last resort for the banks but also for the national States. The ECB being independent of any political power, as well as the national Central Banks of the euro-system, could no more finance directly the national States. They were only authorized to buy public bonds on the secondary market by refinancing the banks. The ECB was no more acting as a lender in last resort for each national State. The euro was a single currency but appeared as a foreign currency for each national country.

The national fiscal policies under constraint

The fear that larger financing facilities within the European Union might lead to some countries' lax behaviours has explained the setting up of the Growth and Stability Pact in 1997, limiting public deficit to 3% of GDP and public debt to 60% of GDP. In actual fact, an even more drastic goal was pursued, that is, a medium-term budget balance. In theory, the Stability Pact had two functions. On the one hand, it was supposed to avoid a member country's insolvency as the no bail out rule for States in difficulty was a key component of the monetary union. On the other hand, it was also supposed to prevent a country's budgetary laxity from resulting in higher interest rates.

These functions were badly carried out by the Stability Pact. Its rules did not take into account the positive effects on growth of public investments or education and research spending which were eroded by the Stability Pact constraints. For the effects on interest rates, the public deficit criterion was also ill-adapted. These effects only appeared in case of a higher rate of inflation or a significant reduction of the area's saving. A more adequate ratio to appreciate these effects would have been the current account balance in percentage of GDP which integrated both adjustments of public and private savings and investment. A country like Germany which faced in the early 2000s simultaneously a significant public deficit and a big trade surplus would not have been concerned. On the opposite, Spain enjoyed balanced finance public in the second half of the 2000s but faced increasing current account deficits. This reflected huge structural imbalances which were ignored by the rules of the Stability Pact. Maintaining these rules in their current form was little justified but, for a long time, reform proposals, despite their interest, have been of a very academic nature. It was only since 2004, facing the blocking with France and Germany, that some limited flexibility has begun to be introduced by the European Commission.

The euro: an unfinished construction

More broadly, the euro appeared as an unfinished construction which was badly armed to face the growing imbalances of the 2000s. The euro zone lacked of an appropriate framework for the economic policy. The independence of the ECB, the constraints weighing on the fiscal policy with the Stability Pact and the weakness of adjustment mechanisms have made it very difficult to coordinate the monetary policy and the national fiscal policies in order to find an appropriate solution to divergent evolutions. The various studies undertaken for several years to try to improve coordination have led to very few operational results (Boyer, 1999; Jacquet and Pisani-Ferry, 2000). The Broad Economic Policy Guidelines that were presented each year by the Commission, represented a very conventional exercise which repeated the traditional liberal scheme adapted to each country, without any major practical impact. Each government went on, making its decisions without cooperation and exchange of information with its partners. Improvements brought to the functioning of the Eurogroup, an informal group gathering the ministers of finance of the euro area, have been modest.

Another factor contributed to the difficulty. The exchange policy actually came under the ECB's sole competence and evolutions of the euro have been hardly controlled since 1999. The problem of the external representation of the euro zone has not been solved yet. Following the positive effects of the initial depreciation of the euro, the cost of the appreciation during the second half of the 2000s has been unequally shared between the countries according to their international specialisation and their degree of openness.

The areas of employment and social policies were subjected to mere non-constraining 'open coordination methods', based on the exchange of information and best practices. No provision has been made in terms of wage policy, which would however represent a major stake within the framework of an enlarged conception of policy mix. The 'macroeconomic dialogue', introduced in the Köln process in 1999 and gathering the ECB, national governments and European trade unions has been deprived of all its substance, with the ECB solely announcing its orientations without any prior dialogue.

A Social Europe was theoretically one of the goals of the European construction, which resulted in the implementation of Social and Structural Funds or the adoption of the Charter of Fundamental Rights. However, social policy came under the sole competence of national States. Notwithstanding each country's strong specificities, it was at the heart of the European model but was threatened with decline in many respects. First of all, social welfare was increasingly analysed in public debates under the sole aspect of its costs. 'Social costs' must be lowered in order to preserve employment and develop competitiveness. The analysis of budgetary constraints, linked to increasing health care and pension costs, was biased. Social welfare was increasingly controlled by European authorities because of its impact on public finance. Secondly, welfare expenditures provided a new field for private capital accumulation in such areas as pensions or health care. A new, increasingly non-egalitarian and costly model has been taking shape, based on privatisation. The calling into question of social welfare was used to discipline the workforce. It was a matter of 'workfare' versus 'welfare'. Lastly, the directive concerning services on domestic markets directly threatened social welfare and public services and encouraged social dumping.

Competition rules repeatedly referred to principles of an open market economy and non-biased competition. State subsidies, which had been widely used in many European countries in the past, were narrowly controlled by the European authorities. Conversely, the interventions likely to be made at European level to stimulate supply in such areas as R&D, education as well as subsidies to the industrial sector and to large infrastructure programmes remained extremely modest and difficult to manage. Given the constraints exerted on national policies and the limited interventions at the European level, structural policies were unable to overcome accumulated backwardness and support a long-term growth strategy.

The enlargement to Eastern European countries raised new challenges. Although in reduction compared with the previous enlargements, the EU–15's support has been significant in terms of net transfers. For 2004–2006, it accounted for a yearly amount of 2 to 4% of the new members' GDP, when combining common agricultural policy and cohesion policy. This cohesion policy appeared as a survival of the more interventionist policies which existed in the 1970s at the EU level. Although its conditions of implementation can be discussed, it remained as a positive point which has to be underlined. It has contributed to the catch up of the Eastern European countries with the recovery in the second half of the 1990s. But unemployment remained high in some countries. Regional and income inequalities have increased. With the privatisation, especially in the public utilities, and the restructuration in the productive sector, the foreign direct investments have been booming. In counterpart the flows of repatriated profits have increased and have overcome the level of the EU net transfers. Liberalisation, increasing competition and flexibility of the labour market have become generalised with a risk of fiscal and social dumping.

On the whole, the construction of a liberal Europe has been going ahead. Problems of its functioning remained unsolved, particularly within the euro zone. The easy financing in euros of intra-European deficits represented a growth asset in the euro zone which has been largely used in the 2000s by southern European countries, fuelling huge structural imbalances. However, given the disappearance of exchange rates as adjustment variables in a context of asymmetrical evolutions, the pressure on prices and costs remained one of the main answers. Competitive devaluations have disappeared, but competitive disinflation policies could become generalised. More broadly, fiscal competition has been also largely used with declining capital income taxation, cuts in the employers' social contribution and increase in value added tax, as it has been done in 2007 in Germany.

The single currency trap

The proponents of the single currency hoped that a process of economic convergence would take place through more sustained growth promoted by lower interest rates, a reduction in transactions costs, the stimulation of competition, the expansion of intra-European trade and deeper financial integration. Right from the start, on the other hand, numerous economists considered that a monetary union among countries displaying great structural heterogeneity and with no adjustment mechanism except internal devaluation through wage deflation could only lead to divergent development and a polarisation of economic activity on the most competitive bloc.

Divergent developments in heterogeneous economies

In fact, a convergence of inflation rates and interest rates did take place. At the beginning of the 2000s the debt securities of Greece, Spain, or Portugal appeared to be equivalent to German debt securities. This led to an investment boom, with capital flowing in from northern Europe, including massive speculation in Spanish and Irish real estate. Growth was slower in Germany, held back by wage adjustments under the Schröder reforms of the early 2000s. This apparent convergence disguised important imbalances. There was a wide divergence in unit labour costs with, in relative terms, big increases in Spain, Ireland, Greece, and Italy and falls in Austria, Finland and, above all, Germany (Figure 4.3). Current account imbalances widened enormously, with deficits in the South in contrast to surpluses in the North (see Figure 4.1). But these current account disequilibria were regarded as a secondary matter in the monetary union where the overall current account was close to balance (see Chapter 2, Figure 2.3). Rather, the key issue for governance in the eurozone was seen as public finance. Here things seemed to be going well: European countries had reduced their public sector deficits; Germany returned to balance in 2007 while Spain, Portugal, and Ireland were regarded as models of budgetary rigour in complete conformity to the Maastricht norms.

On the eve of the financial crisis of 2008 the wide disequilibria due to heterogeneity appeared to be hidden. They were characterised by an undervalued euro for countries in the German block and an overvalued euro for the countries of southern Europe (including France) while for the eurozone as a whole the euro was close to its equilibrium value (see Tables 4.1 and 4.2). The case of Italy is less clear, as there is no evidence of overvaluation. This can be related to the strong divide between north Italy (with rather competitive small and medium firms) and south Italy (clearly less developed). These exchange rate misalignments are meaningful at the intra-European level if we recognise the existence of an equilibrium current account related to structural specificities of each member of

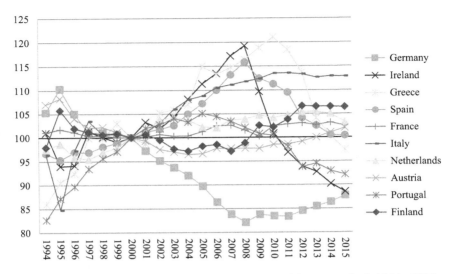

Figure 4.3 Real effective exchange rates based on unit labour cost, basis 100 in 2000.
Source: Authors' calculations, European Commission data (AMECO).

the Euro Area. This kind of concept has been considered in discussions on the extended Stability Pact which included other criteria than the public deficit and debt. These maladjusted exchange rates reflected the structural heterogeneity between northern and southern Europe with France in several respects in an intermediate position. The north of Europe is more specialised in manufacturing while the south of Europe is increasingly specialised in non-tradable goods. The size of industrial firms is clearly smaller in Greece, Portugal, Spain and Italy than in the rest of Europe. In general, small firms have lower productivity. Innovation efforts are significantly weaker in the south than in the north and the active population is clearly less qualified (see Tables 4.3 and 4.4).

These misalignments of real exchange rates among the countries of the euro zone generated a gain or a loss in terms of cost competitiveness. They were the source of important transfers at the expense of the export sector and of the domestic firms competing with imported products in case of an overvalued exchange rate and to the advantage of the same sector in case of an undervaluation. In a monetary union, an equivalent transfer associated to the exchange rate misalignment can be computed. We present only the case of a bilateral exchange rate. A more complex model with a monetary union with two countries and the rest of the world can be found in Duwicquet et al. (2012).

$$\frac{Ep^*}{p} = (1+e).\frac{E_e p^*}{p} \tag{1}$$

With E observed bilateral exchange rate, E_e equilibrium bilateral nominal exchange rate, e bilateral misalignment, p domestic prices, p^* foreign prices. In case of overvaluation ($e < 0$), we observe a lower price competitiveness and in case of undervaluation ($e > 0$), we observe a higher price competitiveness. The equivalent transfer T, associated to the misalignment and which is, in fact, an additional unit cost, positive or negative, can be obtained by equalizing the actual level of competitiveness, Ep^*/p, and the equilibrium level of competitiveness, corrected by the unit transfer T, $Ep^*/p = E_e p^*/p(1+T)$. We obtain:

$$E_e p^*/p(1 + T) = Ep^*/p = (1 + e)E_e p^*/p \tag{2}$$

$$1 + T = 1/1 + e \tag{3}$$

In case of overvaluation ($e < 0$), we have a transfer which corresponds to an additional unit cost. The country suffers of a loss of competitiveness. In case of undervaluation ($e > 0$), we have a transfer which corresponds to a reduction of the unit cost. This reduction improves the competitiveness of the country. In level, *ex ante*, in a case of overvaluation, the transfers represent an additional cost for exports ($T.pxX$) and, in a symmetric way, an additional cost for local producers in competition with imported products ($T.pmM$). For the overvalued country, the total transfer in percent of GDP is equal to $T^*(pxX + pmM)/pY$. In practice, an important share of imports corresponds to products which are not in competition with domestic products (raw materials, goods not locally produced). This share depends of the characteristics of the international specialisation of each country. For simplicity, we suppose in the evaluation of these implicit transfers that only half of the imports is in competition with domestic products. This gives a total transfer in percent of GDP equal to $T^*(pxX + 0.5pmM)/pY$. In

Table 4.7 Implicit transfers due to exchange rate misalignments (in % of GDP)

Average variations of the costs linked to exchange rate misalignments (in % of GDP) for each period (when >0 additional costs, <0 reduction of costs)

	2000–2004	2005–2008	2009–2011
Germany	-4.2	-11.2	-12.1
Netherlands	-3.7	-8.0	-9.3
Austria	-6.8	-10.1	-8.7
Ireland	-3.7	5.7	-6.3
Finland	-12.0	-7.5	-2.0
Italy	-2.0	-1.4	-0.6
France	-3.6	4.3	5.1
Spain	4.1	31.9	5.7
Greece	2.6	12.9	9.2
Portugal	14.6	29.8	13.9

Source: Authors' calculation.

order to give a numeric illustration, an overvaluation de 10% (e = -0.1 and T = 1/9) combined with a degree of openness de 30% (*(pxX + 0.5pmM)/pY* = 0.3) gives a transfer (an additional cost) of 3.3% of GDP (1/9* 0.3 = 0.033).

Taking into account the exchange rate misalignments previously estimated for each European country and their degree of openness, the implicit transfers generated by these misalignments can be computed for the whole period (Table 4.7). The undervaluation of the euro for the northern European countries has led ex ante to important reductions of costs (around 10% of GDP in average at the middle of the 2000s). The southern European countries on the contrary have suffered of large increases of costs due to the overvaluation of the euro for them. Although less touched, France has also endured increased costs (around 5% of GDP in average at the middle of the 2000s). It must be recall that these transfers generated by the exchange rate misalignments are ex ante transfers. In order to appreciate the ex post impact, a model describing explicitly the intra and extra-European exchanges would be necessary. The non-linear relation between exchange rate misalignments and growth, estimated in Aflouk and Mazier (2013) and already mentioned in Chapter 2, gives another illustration of the significance of these effects. According to this relation, the negative impact of the overvaluation of the 'euro-franc' on the French rate of growth was around −1% at the end of the 2000s while the positive impact on the German growth of the undervaluation of the German euro was around 1%.

From the financial crisis to the crisis of the euro

The financial crisis of 2008 worked to reveal these disequilibria. Economic activity declined and the banks were shaken, especially in countries where a real estate bubble was bursting, such as Spain and Ireland. Current account deficits were reduced because of the fall in imports brought about by the recession. Public sector deficits widened in order to support economic activity and rescue the banks. Exchange rate adjustments being impossible, the markets realised that the debts of southern Europe were not equivalent to those of Germany. Interest rates exploded in the South leading to the crisis of the euro and of public debt. The measures adopted in a series of steps since 2010 in the face of this crisis have been partial responses to the threat of immediate breakdown. They have gained some time without providing a solution for the structural imbalances of the euro zone. The strategy of European governments has been in two directions: the general adoption of austerity policies to implement internal devaluations (that is, reductions in wages, employment, and prices); and, in a series of steps, the introduction of new European rules and institutions in order to provide finance to the countries in difficulty.

Wage deflation and budgetary austerity

Mechanisms of adjustment by relative prices are only effective in the long term and in the short term they lead to a brake on growth and an increase in unemployment. They are not equally effective across different countries. They are more effective in small countries with a big sector exposed to international competition, such as Ireland or the Baltic Republics. They are less effective in countries less open to the outside, even when they are small (the case of Greece and of Portugal). The effectiveness is even more limited when the same policy is implemented generally across a large number of interdependent countries as was the case in the euro zone. Budgetary cuts made in an indiscriminate way amplified the decline in economic activity. This policy was imposed throughout the EU and especially in the countries of southern Europe. The results are not surprising: a decline in production and a rise in unemployment while the reduction in budgetary imbalances and deficits could only be partial, or indeed non-existent because of the collapse of production and tax receipts. At the same time, southern current imbalances have been progressively reduced thanks to declining imports induced by the slowdown of activity (Figure 4.1). The sharp decrease of relative unit costs in Ireland, Spain, Portugal, and Greece as a result of wage deflation policy has also played a role (Figure 4.3). It can be noticed that relative unit cost has remained stable in France while it did not decline in Italy and remained rather high. To a large extent, cost adjustments did not happen in these two countries.

The surveillance of budgetary policies was reinforced in the framework of the reform of European governance known as the 'six-pack', which established new rules for budgetary and economic supervision and which came into force in December 2011 (taking into account new indicators, current account deficit in particular, and the 'European semester' procedure intended to structure national budgetary policies). In 2012 the Treaty on Coordination, Stability and Governance (TCSG) went further in the same direction but focussing solely on the issue of budgetary discipline and giving the 'golden rule' a constitutional dimension. The 'fiscal pact,' included in the treaty, sets as a medium-term objective a structural deficit of no more than 0.5% of GDP and a level of public sector debt below 60% of GDP. There is no serious economic justification for this quasi-equilibrium in the public finances. The true 'golden rule' for public finance would rather be that public investments (around 3% to 4% of GDP) can be financed by debt because they give rise to wealth in the future. There is however some methodological difficulty. Public investments now include public spending on R&D (more than 1% of GDP) but in all logic it would be necessary to include some part of educational expenditures which are wrongly considered as current expenditures when they in fact lead to the production of human capital and are therefore an investment. The notion of a structural deficit is also debatable because, to allow for the phases of the business cycle, it requires a measure of potential GDP, and there is no consensus about how to estimate that magnitude. Thus it becomes very contestable to impose very restrictive budgetary rules on such a fragile basis.

With regard to coordination, the TCSG did not bring any real advance. Many studies carried out over several years to try to make progress on coordination have led to very few operational results in the multiplication of packets, pacts, procedures and reports, mostly of little practical significance. There is nothing to encourage surplus countries, even those with massive surpluses, especially Germany, to expand their economies. The European semester, supposed to reinforce the coordination of economic policies, is a very conventional exercise where liberal guidelines are reaffirmed in a somewhat repetitive manner. The Fiscal Pact imposes a path of rapid convergence and return to balanced budgets on deficit countries, together with a programme of 'structural reforms'. This is certainly the real motive behind the TCSG. Its economic justification is weak but, as has been shown in practice, it is an effective instrument to pressurise European governments to implement liberal policies, the liberalisation of labour, output, and capital markets. In particular, the social protection systems which, in different ways in each country, are one of the foundations of European societies, are increasingly called into question under budgetary pressure.

In France, after the assessment of the competitiveness constraints faced by the French manufacturing sector, the policy followed since 2013 has been a tax credit given to firms without any counterpart and any target (as it was given to all firms, exposed or not to international competition). The amount was initially already high (20 billion euros, around 1% of GDP) and has been doubled later on. The wage deflation has been avoided, as it has been noticed above, but the cost for the public finance was considerable and limited any action in the other fields. While trying to improve competitiveness and to preserve at the same time the employment, the policy didn't succeed to reach any target. The result appears poor for a prohibitive cost.

Accommodating monetary policy and financial federalism

Tensions increased in 2011 with attacks on Spanish and Italian government bonds and on the banks with big holdings of those bonds. Measures adopted in the last quarter of 2011 made it possible to gain some time.

Firstly, the ECB experimented with a new policy, offering three-year credit at 1% to European banks on two occasions, December 2011 and January 2012, for the substantial sum of 1,000 billion euros (*Very Long-Term Refinancing Operation*, VLTRO). This policy aimed to restore confidence in the banking sector, which had been shaken by the reappearance of the debt crisis, to encourage the take-up of credit by the non-financial private sector and to reduce pressure on government debt prices by encouraging banks to purchase bonds in order to exploit the difference between the high yields on government debt and the low rate at which they were borrowing from the ECB. It was no miracle cure but time had been gained. Confidence was partly restored. Significant quantities of Spanish and Italian bonds had been purchased, which brought down the interest rates paid on government borrowing, but at the risk of putting banks in trouble if bond prices fell back again. But there could be no new take-up of credit by the private sector because of the deep recession. With a similar approach the key interest rate of the ECB was brought down to 0.75% in 2012, 0.05% in 2014, then 0% in 2016. The interest rate paid to banks on their deposits with the ECB was brought down to 0% in 2013, then to negative figures of −0.3% in 2014 and −0.4% in 2016, to encourage banks to lend more or to buy foreign and domestic assets.

The European Stability Mechanism (ESM), created in 2010, in the midst of the Greek crisis, and starting operations in 2012 replaced the European Financial Stability Fund and the European Financial Stability Mechanism, which were temporary structures. It offers loans to countries in difficulty or buys their government bonds, with, in return, strict control of their budgetary policies in the framework of the Fiscal Pact. Its main limitations are the low total of available funds (700 billion euros) relative to the potential risks, the budgetary tutelage imposed on countries who borrow and the fact that they face continuing constraints in seeking other credit because the loans from the ESM have priority over other debts and thus increase the risks in holding the latter.

In July 2012 the president of the ECB broke new ground in undertaking to do 'whatever it takes' to save the eurozone. With this perspective the procedure of *Outright Monetary Transactions* (OMT), that is the purchase on the secondary market, with no limit, of the government bonds of countries in difficulty was put in place in September 2012. Purchase on the secondary bond market rather than direct purchase from the issuing government is a concession to the formal rules of the ECB but does not change anything fundamental. However, the procedure only applies, in a restrictive way, to governments which have concluded a recovery plan with the ESM. Although the procedure has not yet been put into practice, its introduction helped to reduce interest rate spreads substantially on the interbank market.

The Banking Union, also launched in 2012 despite German reluctance and coming into effect in 2014, was a further stage in the move towards more supportive monetary conditions. It aims to overcome the fragmentation of regulatory authorities in banking and finance, which proved to be paralysing in the first phase of the crisis. Countries not in the eurozone are free to participate or not as they choose. The Banking Union makes possible direct aids from the ESM to banks in trouble without going through member state government budgets. This is an important step forward but there are three problematic points.

Only the 123 largest banks are involved. The smaller ones are not subject to direct central control and relate rather to national regulators. This is understandable from an operational point of view but small accidents can have big consequences.

More seriously, because of the reluctance of member states the other two functions needed for bank regulation have not been fully established. The rules of a single resolution mechanism in the case of a bank failure have been in force since January 2016. Shareholders and creditors will have to pay. This mechanism, which aims to bail in private sector actors may work in the case of a small bank but becomes destabilising if a big bank is affected. The dilemma of 'too big to fail' is still there. It can only be dealt with effectively by a strict regulation of financial actors. But so far the regulatory framework is inadequate because of international competition and the inability of States either to establish a global regulatory regime or to call into question the supposed benefits of international capital flows. Furthermore, the resolution fund, supposed to assist financial institutions in difficulty will only be provided with 50 billion euros between now and 2024, which is too little, too late.

Finally, the guarantee of deposits up to 100,000 euro remains a member state responsibility. In other words, the Germans don't want to guarantee Greek deposits, which may reflect the actual situation in Europe but which could well destabilise the whole European structure in the event of a banking crisis.

To sum up, there has been progress with the architecture of banking and financial regulation but the situation is still complex, mixing member state competence, eurozone competence and competence of the EU as a whole. A certain centralisation has taken place for banks, but not for other financial corporations and insurance companies in particular.

A final step was taken in January 2015 with the launch of Quantitative Easing (QE) intended, in principle, to combat the risk of deflation. This programme consists of the purchase, with newly created central bank money, of asset-backed securities and private and public bonds for an initial sum of 60 billion euros a month, which rose in March 2016 to 80 billion. By adding to liquidity, the programme was meant to reinforce the low interest rates and to encourage the banks to increase their loans or to buy financial assets. It has had only a limited impact on real growth and inflation. Most of the liquidity created by the ECB has gone towards financial markets, both in the eurozone, pushing up the price of assets, and outside, with a corresponding outflow of capital and a decline in the euro exchange rate. In spite of the very low interest rates little stimulus has been imparted to productive investment because of the low level of demand and a climate of uncertainty which favoured the holding of financial assets. The two main channels through which QE has affected the economy are the boom on financial markets which can give rise to wealth effects on expenditure but also lead to asset price bubbles in the future, and the depreciation of the euro which can advantage sectors producing tradable goods and services. All in all, limited effects. The ECB has helped to put out the fire but not to relaunch economic growth.

In 2015, the Commission opened up a new field, the Capital Markets Union, which is to be brought about by 2019. The aim is to integrate capital markets in order to direct capital towards enterprises, including SMEs, and towards infrastructure projects. It promotes increased use of market-based finance, in particular through the securitisation of loans to SMEs, with the aim of facilitating the free movement of capital and providing more finance for investment. All it will do is expand the financial market-linked activities of banks with increased risks for the new securitised assets.

The incoherence of the euro zone regime

Monetary and financial measures combined with the Fiscal Treaty could only find partial solution to the crisis of the euro zone. These successive reforms have given some room for manoeuvre but without changing the basic finding. The euro zone members have the same currency but their national public debts are not equivalent. There is no political agreement to allow the ECB to guarantee the national public debts, nor a fortiori for permanent transfers between countries. The crisis resulted from structural imbalances linked to the heterogeneity of the countries in the zone and from the inadequacy of the mechanisms to deal with these problems.

The current deficits of the southern European countries have been replaced by current surpluses and overvaluation of their currencies (the euro) has disappeared at the cost of painful deflation policies. France has followed as a more balanced strategy and the adjustment has been more limited. Consequently, the euro remained overvalued for France in 2016 in real effective terms (Tables 4.1 and 4.2). More embarrassing, the surplus countries did not contribute to any rebalancing. The German surplus has reached a summit in 2015 at 8% of GDP and the German relative unit cost has only moderately increased since 2008 (Figure 4.3). The euro remained undervalued in real effective terms for Germany (around 15 to 20% from 2010 to 2016). The other northern countries (Netherlands, Austria) have also increased their current surpluses, but in a lesser proportion. The euro was closer to the equilibrium for them. Finland appeared specific as it has faced a double shock, the crisis of Nokia and the economic difficulties of Russia. At the level of the whole euro zone, current surplus has increased up to 4% of the GDP, fuelled by the German surplus and reflecting a large undervaluation of the euro (around 25% in real effective terms). The inadequacy of the euro mechanisms to deal with this heterogeneity of the zone has led both to persistent intra-zone disequilibrium and to world imbalances.

The 'monetary federalism' of the ECB and 'financial federalism' suffered from other weaknesses. The non-conventional monetary policy of the ECB is more limited than it seems. QE is not allowed to absorb more than one third of the debt of any issuer of bonds and bond purchases have to be in proportion to the economic weight of the country concerned. This limits the assistance which can be given to countries in difficulty and makes it difficult over time to keep the promise of *'whatever it takes'*. The limits on purchases of German bonds are close to being reached – it is the largest economy, but with a declining amount of debt – while it would be easy to buy more Italian bonds but that would exceed the Italian quota. Moderation of the rules would be necessary (raise the fraction of debt that can be bought to 50% for example, and permit bond purchases above the economic weight of the country concerned) but this would be difficult to negotiate. The provision of Emergency Liquidity Assistance (ELA) to banks which are solvent but under pressure raises a further problem: the decision is taken by the central bank of the country concerned and not, as would be logical, the EU-level authority responsible for banking supervision. Here again we see the incomplete nature of the federal project and the different levels of confidence in different countries.

ECB policy poses a further problem. The ECB has helped to put out the fire or, at least, to stop it spreading. QE has only been effective to a limited extent, as we have seen, and works to feed the boom on financial markets. Given the weak state of the economy, equity prices seem very high with the possible development of a financial bubble. The risk of a bubble on bond markets is even more worrying. European banks and central banks have bought enormous quantities of bonds. If bond prices should fall because of a political crisis, because of financial problems in one country or because interest rates rise in the rest of the world there could be significant losses on bond holdings which, in the last resort, would impact on the central bank. The central bank would have to recognise the losses in its accounts and this would require it to be recapitalised. In itself this can be a difficult operation. It would be all the more difficult in the eurozone because, unlike the Fed in the United States, the ECB is not backed by a single State but by 17. Recapitalisation of the European system of central banks would be financed by all member states in proportion to their share in its capital while it might be only one country, or a limited number of them, which was involved in the losses on bonds. This could make the operation even more complex.

Finally, even though current account imbalances have been reduced, overall payments imbalances are still widening. The ECB plays the role of a clearing house and records in its TARGET2 system (Trans-European Automated Real-time Gross settlement Express Transfer) the deficits of the South and the surpluses of the North, that is for each country the sum of its current account and net inflows of capital. Until 2008 the current account deficits of the South were matched by capital inflows, so that the TARGET2 system as a whole was close to balance. Since 2009 this has no longer been the case. The deficits and surpluses now being registered in TARGET2 reflect net outflows of capital from South to North which cannot be sustained indefinitely because they arise from a loss of confidence by investors in the countries concerned. These deficits rose even further in 2016 and reached very high sums for Italy and Spain because of the size of the two countries. In the American case, where *Fedwire* is the equivalent of TARGET2, supervisory mechanisms exist at the level of the regional central banks. Balances are brought back close to equilibrium every year through incentives for local banks to help finance intra-regional imbalances and, above all, by asset transfers among the regional central banks. Such mechanisms do not exist at the level of the eurozone and, in present circumstances, it is hard to envisage them, given the incomplete character of European integration.

In spite of everything, a sustainable regime?

In a context of continuing tension, some modifications can be seen since 2015. Wages have risen more in Germany under pressure from IG Metall and infrastructure investment (becoming in any case increasingly necessary) has been re-launched. Although these changes are much less than Germany could achieve, they head in the right direction. At the EU level, the Juncker Plan, launched in 2015, contains some very impressive numbers, but one should not be mistaken. In theory 315 billion euros of additional investment are expected by the end of 2018, that is 0.8% of EU GDP and an increase in investment of 4% per year. In practice, the Juncker Plan is to be managed by the European Investment Bank (EIB) where a special fund has been set up but endowed with only 21 billion euros (of which 16 are being raised from an existing line of credit). The EIB can lend up to 60 billion by borrowing. The rest must come from the participation in the plan of other public or private investors. Overall, although the size of the plan has been increased to 500 billion and its period of operation extended to 2020, the value added by the plan is very small. Its implementation is also open to question (few genuinely new projects, not enough effort being made to reinforce cohesion through the investments, a risk of dissipating the effect of the funds directed towards SMEs). These difficulties remind us of the problems faced by European-level plans to re-launch investment since the 1980s.

Macroeconomic conditions in several European countries have improved somewhat from 2015 to 2017, sustained by depreciation of the euro, the fall in petroleum prices and a slight relaxation of the severe budgetary constraints imposed the Commission. In the Netherlands, characterised by a very high level of household debt and by banks affected by doubtful assets, recovery has been drawn by a more expansionary budgetary policy (reduction in income tax and measures to receive refugees) but also by liberal measures, labour market reforms (easier dismissals, reduction in the duration of unemployment indemnities, raising the retirement age to 67) and by a recovery in the real estate sector resulting from low interest rates and higher prices. Since 2015, Spain has begun to harvest some of the fruits of its policy of wage deflation but unemployment, precarious employment, and inequality remain at high levels. Small, very open countries, such as Slovakia and the Baltic states, after deep adjustments, are experiencing a rapid recovery, based on automobiles in the former country but also on investment in infrastructures financed on a large scale by European funds. France is still on a knife-edge, with a limited recovery and persistent unemployment. In 2016 constraints on the Portuguese economy were modestly relaxed. A successful modification of budgetary policy was compatible with a reduction in the public sector deficit (−2.1% of GDP) but the fragility of the banking sector and the high level of public debt (131% of GDP) continue to pose significant risks. Italy remains locked into slow growth with high public debt also and banks undermined by their bad or doubtful loans. The arrival in 2018 of a populist coalition trying to implement a policy based, first on restrictive immigration policy, but also on tax cuts and social transfers, raised new challenges as it did not respect the European fiscal rules. Waiting for the next restructuring of its debt, Greece, in spite of a small improvement, is mired in endless austerity.

One should not build false hopes on this slightly sunnier interval, and this for two reasons. Firstly, although a real recovery has been taking place in the eurozone in 2016–2017, unemployment remained very high in the south of the zone and income inequalities very wide. All this led to persistent social tensions. Secondly, destabilising factors remained, with high levels of both public and private debt, fragile banks and the threat of higher interest rates to come. There continue to be serious misalignments of real exchange rates among the countries of the zone, mainly at the advantage of Germany. For countries where the real exchange rate did not adjust, this means the slow asphyxiation illustrated by the French and Italian cases. The sustainability of the euro zone growth regime in the absence of thoroughgoing reforms remains an open question.

Conclusion

The aim of this chapter was to assess the European integration process from the early blocking of the EMS at the beginning of the 1980s. Intra-European exchange rate misalignments have first been estimated with a FEER approach since these misalignments have been a key issue at the time of the EMS, but also within the monetary union. On the whole the performance of the EU in terms of growth and employment has been poor since the 1980s, compared with the United States of other OECD countries. Only Japan has done worst due to the long stagnation since the 1990s. Some European countries have done better, especially the German block around which the manufacturing activities have been more and more concentrated, but also many Eastern countries which have been catching up since the 1990s.

In the 1980s the EMS was functioning asymmetrically and the countries with weak currencies suffered of overvaluation periodically and were forced to adjust. The Single Market programme launched in 1985 appeared as a major turning point with an increasing use of the market forces in most of the fields and the abandonment of any active polices at the EU level in the R&D or infrastructures. The positive effects of the Single Market have been roughly overestimated. At the end of the 1980s the more and more rigid EMS and the financial liberalisation made a change of a monetary regime necessary. The single currency prevailed mainly as a French-German political compromise but the project remained shaky and unfinished. The benefits of the single currency have been overestimated and the costs largely underestimated: weakness of the adjustment mechanisms, absence of a federal State, status of the ECB no more acting as a lender in last resort for the national States, fiscal policy under strong constraint. With the monetary adjustments following the crises of the EMS in 1992–1993, the exchange rate misalignments were limited during the rest of the 1990s but the transitory measures towards the single currency, based on the Maastricht criteria, were too restrictive and contributed to a persistent slowdown.

After a brief recovery in 1998–2000 and a successful launching of the euro, disequilibrium factors reappeared with speculative boom in many southern

European countries contrasting with a slowdown and wage adjustment in Germany. This led to large current account imbalances and increasing exchange rate misalignments with undervalued euro in the northern European countries and overvalued euro in the southern ones. The financial crisis revealed these disequilibria and the lack of appropriate adjustment mechanisms to compensate them. After a public support to sustain the activity and rescue the banks, interest rates on the public bonds exploded in southern countries as the ECB could not act as a lender in last resort for the national States. The euro, although a single currency, appeared as a foreign currency for each national State. The European authorities followed then two directions: wage deflation and fiscal austerity in order to adjust and the introduction of new rules and institutions in order to provide finance for countries in difficulty.

The TCSG reinforced the restrictive fiscal policies already at work since the 1990s and condemned countries with higher public debt to a permanent austerity. Other institutions on the financial side remained incomplete. The ESM has limited funds and imposes strict budgetary controls. The Banking Union suffers of a limited Resolution Fund and of the absence of agreement on a European guarantee of deposits. The QE has stopped the fire but has mainly favoured the financial markets and the capital outflows. The current account imbalances have been reduced but the TARGET2 system at the ECB has recorded huge deficits for the southern countries and surplus for Germany. In spite of the achieved adjustments, the euro remained undervalued for Germany and overvalued for France (the case of Italy being less clear).

In this context the recovery which took place in 2016–2017 in the euro zone must not be overestimated. Underemployment remains high in the southern European countries, even if it has decreased. The wage share is at a historical low level and income inequalities very large with social tensions and destabilising factors. Persistence with a growth regime which performs so badly may seem surprising. There are many losers, but also winners. Some countries have been catching up, especially the Eastern European countries. Others have faced the new challenge with success. Financial incomes have reached summits. High income share has improved. Some large European firms are doing well. This contrasted assessment can explain the European apparent paralysis which is profitable to some.

More precisely, the winners are composed of two groups, on the one hand the countries of northern Europe, on the other the 'European elite'. The first, grouped around Germany, benefit from an undervalued currency and do reasonably well even if they are affected by the weakness of the southern countries. The small, very open economies can also adapt more easily. The second, the 'European elite', consisting of the dominant strata in industry and finance and the European technocracy, uses the crisis to deepen and extend neo-liberal policies: increased flexibility on the labour market; reduction in social expenditures leading households to resort increasingly to private insurance; tighter budgetary frameworks to reduce the role of the State and re-launch the process of privatisation; refusal to increase taxes on financial revenues, high incomes or big wealth holdings, which have all seen considerable tax reductions; failure to impose adequate constraints on the financial sector. This is also coherent with the relative indifference to developments in the internal market of the big European corporations which are more global than European.

In front, the losers are numerous, but heterogeneous and less organised. With durable high unemployment and slow growth, France and Italy appeared as the main losers, but also the other southern European countries, Spain and Portugal, where the recovery must be relativised, and Greece where the costs of the adjustment have been dramatic. At the individual level the losers are many with unemployed persons, especially the non-qualified ones, the precarious jobs which have increased, even in the northern countries, the low wage earners and the pensioners which have suffered from loss of purchasing power in a context of lasting inequalities. Although numerous, the losers are not well organised at the European level and are split between specific national configurations with little political outlet, except rejection through populist movements, whose Italy is the clearest example. Therefore, the status quo might last with limited modifications. The dangers of disaster inherent in such a scenario, however, are so great as to have led to the emergence of many proposed alternatives which will be examined in the next chapter.

Annex 4.1

Table 4.8 Trade elasticities for European countries

Country	Source	ε_x	ε_m	α_x	α_m	η_x	η_m
France	MIMOSA	**0.66**	**0.63**	**0.41**	**0.63**	**0.88**	**1.07**
	NIGEM	0.63	0.59	–	–	1.00	1.51
	OECD	0.60	0.28	0.28	0.51	1.00	1.00
Germany	MIMOSA	**0.94**	**0.82**	**0.14**	**0.55**	**0.99**	**0.86**
	NIGEM	0.55	0.28	–	–	1.00	1.84
	OECD	0.47	0.30	0.18	0.64	1.00	1.00
Italy	MIMOSA	**1.26**	**1.53**	**0.57**	**0.65**	**0.87**	**1.42**
	NIGEM	0.49	0.73	–	–	1.00	1.50
	OECD	0.60	0.37	0.41	0.55	1.00	1.00
Spain	Hervé	1.11	0.45	–	–	**1.00**	**2.14**
	NIGEM	0.31	0.82	–	–	1.00	1.00
	Saglio★	**1.50**	**0.80**	–	–	–	–
	Aglietta★★	–	–	**0.52**	**0.80**	–	–
	OECD	1.05	0.60	0.28	0.82	1.00	1.00
Austria	NIGEM	1.25	0.31	–	–	**1.00**	**1.56**
	Saglio★	**0.80**	**0.80**	–	–	–	–
	Ad hoc	–	–	**0.40**	**0.60**	–	–
	OECD	0.60	0.16	0.18	0.51	1.00	1.00
Finland	NIGEM	1.20	0.36	–	–	**1.00**	**1.17**
	Saglio★	**0.80**	**1.00**	–	–	–	–
	Ad hoc	–	–	**0.40**	**0.60**	–	–
	OECD	0.60	0.31	0.57	0.79	1.00	1.00

Table 4.8 Cont.

Country	Source	ε_x	ε_m	α_x	α_m	η_x	η_m
Ireland	NIGEM	4.28	0.12	–	–	**1.00**	**1.08**
	Saglio*	**2.30**	**0.80**	–	–	–	–
	Ad hoc	–	–	0.40	0.60	–	–
	OECD	0.60	0.32	0.28	0.51	1.00	1.00
Netherlands	NIGEM	0.40	0.37	–	–	**1.00**	**1.75**
	Saglio*	**1.88**	**0.76**	–	–	–	–
	Ad hoc	–	–	0.40	0.60	–	–
	OECD	0.60	0.28	0.41	0.36	1.00	1.00
Portugal	NIGEM	2.43	0.25	–	–	**1.00**	**1.85**
	Saglio*	**1.10**	**0.80**	–	–	–	–
	Ad hoc	–	–	0.60	0.80	–	–
	OECD	0.47	0.56	0.77	0.79	1.00	1.00

Notes
*Mazier and Saglio, 2008.
**Couharde and Mazier, 2000.

The selected elasticities are those of the MIMOSA model for France, Germany and Italy. For the others European countries, we used the elasticities in bold.

Annex 4.2 Sensitivity tests on the parameters of the FEER model

Considering the existing uncertainties in the estimation of external and internal equilibrium and in the measure of trade elasticities, four kinds of sensibility tests (see Table 4.9) have been performed: an increase of the target current balance of 1% of GDP (*bc*); an increase of the potential production of 1% (y^e); an increase of the export price elasticity of 20% (ε_x); an increase of the import price elasticity of 20% (ε_m).

The sensitivity to the potential production is limited. A higher potential production and consequently an increased under-utilisation of production capacities lead to a more significant real overvaluation of the currency. The elasticity is between −0.1 and −0.5 meaning that an additional under-utilisation of 1% results in an increased overvaluation between −0.1% and −0.5%. The sensitivity to the current account target is moderate. An increase in the current account target that is a reduction of the gap *b* leads to an overvaluation of the concerned currency. The effect weakens as the GDP share of exports and the elasticity of current account to real exchange rate increase. The sensitivity to the export and import price elasticities also turns out to be small. On the whole higher export price elasticity leads to smaller changes in exchange rates to absorb the same amount of current account imbalances. Absolute average of results means the degree of lesser misalignments of exchange rates under higher price elasticity. This result is reassuring considering the existing uncertainties in

Table 4.9 Sensitivity tests on real effective exchange rates (*rc*) (Absolute average of changes from the base simulation results)

	bc	γ^{ϵ}	ϵ_x	ϵ_m
FRA	0.0242	0.0049	0.0047	0.0048
GER	0.0116	0.0026	0.0051	0.0031
ITA	0.0101	0.0025	0.0011	0.0020
SPA	0.0176	0.0051	0.0101	0.0091
AUT	0.0107	0.0011	0.0022	0.0022
FIN	0.0100	0.0034	0.0061	0.0074
IRL	0.0038	0.0017	0.0021	0.0008
NLD	0.0044	0.0033	0.0014	0.0006
PRT	0.0184	0.0054	0.0079	0.0110

Source: Authors' calculation.

the estimation of these parameters. These sensitivity tests assure that the FEER approach provides rather robust results in spite of uncertainties in estimating the internal and external equilibrium and the parameters of trade equations.

5   Alternative economic policies in the euro zone

Jacques Mazier and Vincent Duwicquet

Introduction

Macroeconomic conditions have improved in the euro area in 2016–2017 but unemployment remained high in the South and income inequalities very wide. All this led to persistent social tensions. In spite of financial fragility, the reforms have not been brought to an end. The Banking Union remained unfinished with two pieces missing: the Single Resolution fund was too limited to be able to stabilise the European financial system; no compromise has been found for the European Deposit Insurance Scheme. The necessity of a deep reform of the European institutional framework has been reaffirmed. Several typical alternative structures have been suggested: a reaffirmation of the no bail-out clause for member state governments; the fiscal federalism; the model of European budgetary integration with public debt centralised at European level; the creation of a Euro Treasury. These alternatives will be presented in a first section. They raise serious problems and/or are hardly realistic in political terms. It reflects the lack of solidarity and trust between European countries. The euro zone members have the same currency, but their national public debts are not equivalent. There is no political agreement to allow the ECB to guarantee the national public debts, nor for permanent transfers between countries. The better economic conditions and the large political divergences between European countries add up in favour of the status quo.

Facing this risk, more hybrid proposals have been put forward and will be presented in a second section. The first one by the CEPR (Benassy-Quéré et al., 2018), rather technocratic, is based on new rules and institutions: a simple public expenditure rule, the possibility of sovereign debt restructuring and a more credible no-bail-out rule, a euro area fund to help countries facing large shocks, the creation of a synthetic euro area safe asset, a reform of the governance. Analysed in detail these proposals are not convincing. The second proposal by IMK (Watt and Waztka, 2018) is an attempt to find a pragmatic compromise between unconditional support by ECB and national fiscal policy and strict conditionality on risk-sharing measures. It implies to have symmetrical and counter-cyclical policies in all member states and to increase mutual trust between all the actors. However, the difficulty of implementation of the

IMK proposal cannot be ignored. A third scenario could be considered, a 'New Political Union' gathering the countries ready to accept political and fiscal union (Piketty et al., 2018), which would be also rather unlikely. Last the proposal of a complementary currency has always partisans. In this context the minimalist compromise remains the more likely scenario, as it is illustrated by the project of European budget presented in May 2008 by the European Commission.

In a third section, a two-country SFC model of a monetary union will be used to evaluate some of these alternative economic policies (federal budget with transfers, intra-European financing, implementation of eurobonds with or without large European projects) and compare them with the current configuration of the euro area. A last section will conclude and underline the narrowness of the room of manoeuvre.

Unconvincing or unlikely alternatives

Four alternative architectures have been proposed for the euro zone: a return to the no bail-out clause; the model of fiscal federalism; the model of European budgetary integration based on a partial mutualisation of the national public debts; last the creation of a Euro Treasury.

A return to the no bail-out clause

In this regime the original principles of the monetary union are restored and completed. States preserve or recover their budgetary sovereignty at the national level but reassert the no bail-out clause. States are no longer constrained by inappropriate rules such as the limit of 3% of GDP for the deficit or 60% of GDP for the debt but are subjected to the discipline of the markets. There is no solidarity between states. In the event of over-indebtedness and default on the debt of a state the investors (that is, essentially, the banks) suffer a loss. In theory this is made easier because states are protected from bank failures by the Banking Union. To reduce the risk of crisis, the banks have to cover their purchases of government debt with more of their own capital. Government bonds are no longer regarded as risk-free from the point of view of prudential supervision. Experience shows, however, that investors do not always assess accurately the solidity of states. To avoid large-scale panics, the ESM could be activated and the debt rescheduled by means of a strictly controlled adjustment plan.

This model has resonated to some extent in Germany (Fuest et al., 2016). In theory it gives autonomy back to the states while retaining the possibility of a stabilisation role for the EU in the event of an asymmetric shock, at least while the state concerned was regarded as solvent. It avoids both the ex ante and ex post co-ordinations and controls which function very badly.

But there are many difficulties. The possibility of a crisis of over-indebtedness leading to debt restructuring inhibits a state's capacity to use budgetary policy to respond to an asymmetric shock. We come up against the basic problem posed by the functioning of the euro zone. To avoid costly, difficult to control, dislocations, general patterns of convergence in tax regimes and public expenditure would be necessary. The budgetary autonomy which is supposedly recovered would be a trap. Government bonds would lose their status as risk-free asset which is one of the pillars of the financial system and the functioning of the financial system would be impaired. There is a risk that crises in the public finances could be amplified. This regime rests partly on the Banking Union which is unfinished. The failure of a very big bank would be difficult to manage and the Resolution fund does not have sufficient resources. Lastly, in the event of a restructuring of its debt the size of the state concerned could raise a problem. The limits of market-based regulation would appear if a large state such as Italy were affected.

The model of fiscal federalism

In this model a stabilisation function is introduced at the level of the euro zone by establishing a federal budget financed by new taxes (a tax on financial transactions, a carbon tax) or by moving some taxes from national to euro zone level in order to avoid a ruinous race to the bottom (taxes on interest on savings and on dividends, taxes on corporate profits). In the very probable case of difficulties in establishing such a fiscal base, a simple borrowing capacity would be introduced for crisis periods. In both cases transfers or investments could be undertaken to assist states affected by negative shocks.

As for the previous regime budgetary sovereignty would be restored to member states with no constraining European rules but this would be matched by a reassertion of the no bail-out principle. Consequently, there is a possibility of debt restructuring in cases of over-indebtedness. This is what can be observed in the United States, where the states of the union and cities are responsible for their own debts and where the federal government does not impose rules. Chapter 9 of the bankruptcy code provides the framework for debt restructuring of cities, counties, townships and school districts, and of public agencies (case of Jefferson County, Alabama in 2011, Detroit in 2013). But states cannot access Chapter 9. In the event of a negative shock, as well as the stabilisation effects linked to the working of the federal budget, there may be transfers or loans from the federal budget, accompanied by sanctions and direct budgetary control (New York in 1975, District of Columbia in 1996). More recently, however, a debt restructuring procedure has been carried out in Puerto Rico together with controls over its budget.

Transposing this American model into the European context would involve several problems which would be difficult to overcome. The size of the federal system is large in the United States, which contributes to explain its efficiency. In 2015 the federal expenditures represented around 25% of the US GDP, which were split between 25% for health care, 24% for social security, 16% for defence, 16% for non-defence discretionary expenditures (like education, justice or research), 13% for non-mandatory expenditures (like food coupons) and 6% for the interests paid. The establishment of such a federal budget is hardly probable in the euro zone because of the absence of any spirit of solidarity among euro zone countries and the scale of the changes which it would require. A less ambitious solution would involve opting for a mechanism where there were no permanent transfers across states (states being net contributors or net beneficiaries according to the changing circumstances) and where, over the long run, accumulated transfers would be close to zero. Several studies, of which the first go back to the early 1990s (Italianner and Pisani-Ferry, 1992) have shown that a common system of unemployment insurance at the European level would meet this objective and achieve a certain macro-economic stabilisation at a limited cost (Benassy-Quéré et al., 2016). It would be limited to periods of crisis and based on changes in the unemployment rate rather than its level. To illustrate the possible order of magnitude one can point to the American unemployment insurance system which supported some 0.4% of GDP each year between 2008 and 2011. But the successful introduction of even such a relatively modest mechanism would presuppose that a minimal harmonisation of labour markets had been achieved in order to avoid the same shock having opposite effects in different countries. Now the labour markets are very heterogeneous and even a minimal harmonisation would take time. And the more successful countries fear having to contribute more than the countries with a weaker performance.

Finally, the no bail-out principle would raise the same problems as in the previous regime. The American model, combining a federal budget with a no bail-out principle cannot be transposed to the euro zone. In the United States the federal debt represents 100% of GDP, that of the states and municipalities about 30%. In the euro zone there is neither a federal budget nor European debt and all public debt is at the national level. To reassert the no bail-out principle for member states would be a destabilising factor and a constraint on national budgetary policies.

A model of European budgetary integration

This model draws lessons from the problems raised by the two models considered above. It starts from the observation that the principle that each state is individually responsible for its debt leads to an increased risk of crises of public debt even for countries regarded to begin with as solvent. To make it possible for the euro zone to function a mutualisation of at least part of the debt would be introduced. Mutualisation could take different forms.

The most natural form would be a European fund for the redemption of public debt, issuing long-term debt instruments (eurobonds) and mutualising national debts above the threshold of 60% of GDP. Debts below that threshold would remain the responsibility of the member states because it would be too costly to mutualise the whole of the debt. However, the market value of the public debt which would not be covered by the eurobonds could decline or, even, collapse. The banks would therefore be unable to use it as collateral for refinancing at the ECB which could be at the source of a financial crisis.

Another solution which is sometimes put forward, to mutualise debts below the 60% threshold and leave debts above that level to the member states, seems to be less realistic because it would leave the most indebted states under market pressure. The ESM could play the role of redemption fund and organise the exchange of national debt for the European debt it would issue. This would require a substantial increase in its capital to allow it to carry out operations not in its original mandate.

However that may be, the mutualisation of debts would help to bring down the cost of the debt and to reduce the risk of default by the most indebted countries. There would be a transfer to the disadvantage of the less indebted countries linked to the difference in interest rates and the collective management of risks. With the diffusion of eurobonds as substitutes for national ones, the banks which hold the bulk of national bonds would be protected against the tensions which could come from the most fragile countries.

But to counterbalance the mutualisation of debts there would have to be substantial control over national budgets to avoid the risks of slippage in countries which are insufficiently disciplined in their public finances. Two contrasting methods can be envisaged. The first would rely on the greater budgetary discipline imposed by some independent body such as the European Fiscal Board, created by the Commission in 2005, whose role might be extended. On the basis of its diagnosis (favourable periods permitting budgetary surpluses, unfavourable ones allowing wider deficits) it would fix binding limits to the overall position of national budgets. The second method would be based on democratic progress with the establishment of a parliament of the euro zone which would determine broad budgetary guidelines for the euro zone as a whole and the allocation of corresponding targets to individual countries. The comparative strength of different countries within this euro zone parliament (23% for Germany, 50% for France, Italy, and Spain if they formed a bloc, 27% for the others) allows some commentators to hope that a majority less inclined towards austerity might emerge. It is far from obvious that this would happen. In any case, whether the procedure is technocratic or more democratic, it would establish tutelary supervision over the broad structure of national budgetary policy. The importance of that problem should not be underestimated. Further, there is the reluctance (or even the straight refusal) of the Germans to accept the largest part of the costs of this mutualisation. All this explains why nothing has come of this idea which was put forward at the beginning of the 2010s, in spite of the way it could make the monetary union more viable.

Beyond these observations, two basic problems would remain unresolved: macroeconomic stabilisation and the heterogeneity and unequal competitiveness of member states or, in other words, the persistence of misaligned real exchange rates.

The problem of stabilisation would arise since, because of the budgetary rules to be introduced, the highly indebted countries would have no more room for manoeuvre in the case of a negative shock. In theory the solution would involve a federal budget. This would be difficult unless it took the form, as discussed above, of a small budget making temporary transfers to stabilise economic activity but required to balance these out over the cycle, or the form of a European unemployment indemnity which, as we have seen would be equally difficult to organise. Another mechanism which has been suggested is the creation of national adjustment accounts to smooth out public expenditure over the cycle (Benassy-Quéré et al., 2016). In a period of crisis certain expenditures could be taken out of the calculation of the deficit and transferred to the adjustment account. They would be taken back into the budget calculation when things had returned to normal. The ECB would play a central role in the functioning of this technocratic arrangement in order to avoid it becoming a basis for excessive budgetary autonomy at member state level.

The persistence of misaligned intra-European real exchange rates, illustrated by current account surpluses in Germany and deficits in France, is more problematic, even though they have been reduced. In 2016 the euro remained under-valued for Germany and over-valued for France. In the framework of a monetary union there is no mechanism which can respond in a satisfactory way. If wage deflation in the South of Europe is rejected and wage increases in Germany are difficult to bring about then there only remain reductions in taxes and other charges such as the CICE (Crédit d'impôt pour la compétitivité et l'emploi; tax credit for competitiveness and employment) which have a high budgetary cost and thus cannot deal with the problem. Industrial policies aimed at improving non-price competitiveness could also contribute to the response to the problem. They ought to be used but are difficult to design and to implement and only make a difference in the long term.

European budgetary integration would amount to a considerable leap forward. The mutualisation of national debts might be used to avoid the need for a federal budget. Member states would no longer be threatened by the no-bail-out principle but the counterpart for this would be a loss of autonomy in national budgetary policies which would be controlled by an independent European institution or a euro zone parliament. This would be a difficult hurdle to clear and beyond it two problems would remain. For stabilisation purposes, some substitute for a federal budget would have to be introduced and it is not obvious how this could be done. Nor would a mutualisation of debts resolve the problem of misaligned real exchange rates among European countries and the structural imbalances linked to the heterogeneity of the euro zone.

The creation of a Euro Treasury

The creation of a Euro Treasury (Bibow, 2016) is based on the distinction between current expenditures and investment expenditures. In the national budgets the current expenditures should be balanced. The investment expenditures (around 3–4% of GDP) would be financed by indebtedness through a specific account managed by the Euro Treasury. This one would get into debt and would issue euro bonds. It would reverse investment grants to national governments in line with member states' GDP shares (or with the ECB's capital key). The same structure would be used to calculate their interest payment bonds. The Euro Treasury would raise taxes to meet the interest service on the common debt. The national debts in percentage of GDP would decrease tendentiously while the common European debt would rise and could cap at 60% of GDP at the medium to long term.

The idea of the Euro Treasury is attractive. It allows the funding of the public investment expenditures which have suffered long lasting erosion in the past and a progressive increase of a genuine European debt without mutualising the existent national public debts and without intra-European transfers. It creates a counterpart at the fiscal level to the ECB which, in case of crisis, would have with this European debt the possibility to act as a lender of last resort in a less controversial manner than with the current national public debts.

But it raises several difficulties which make the project not very operational. First, it is based on a fiscal rule, the 'true golden rule for public finance': current expenditures in equilibrium, public investment expenditures financed by government debt, as they can improve the productive potential and the future fiscal income. This rule has an objective basis in spite of the difficulty of definition of the notion of public investment. In practice it is far from being accepted at the European level, especially in Germany. It would lead to a permanent public deficit around 3–4% of GDP.

Second, the public investment expenditures would be financed by a European debt but would always be managed at the national level, which is well adapted for practical reasons. The problem of the control of these expenditures would none the less exist, as in the case of mutualisation of the national debt. Which institution would be in charge of this control beyond the national governments, a technocratic institution as a European Fiscal Council or a parliament of the euro zone?

Looking for operational compromises

The alternative architectures for the euro zone considered above raise a multiplicity of problems and/or are hardly realistic in political terms. More pragmatic proposals of varying kinds have been put forward. The first comes from a group of 14 economists from Germany and France, close to policy makers; the second was made by IMK is an attempt to find a pragmatic compromise; the third was advanced by Piketty in favour of a 'New Political Union'; and the last was the proposal of a complementary currency.

Reconcile market discipline and a limited solidarity

The proposal coming from the 14 French and German economists (Benassy-Quéré et al., 2018) wants to be constructive and tries to reconcile risk-sharing and market discipline with a very limited form of solidarity (Sterdyniak, 2018). First, the current fiscal rules are too complex and would be replaced by a simple one: the growth of public expenditures must not exceed long-term

GDP growth and must allow a reduction of the public debt. This rule would be in practice imprecise and would be very controversial. More worrying, if the public expenditures are considered as excessive (we will see later in this chapter by whom), the surplus of expenditures would be financed at a higher cost by the markets and the associate bonds would be downgraded.

Second, the public debts would be risky and could be restructured according to the principle of no-bail-out. Banks would take variable risks according to the countries. In this framework the Banking Union would be completed to make a firewall between bank risks and public debts. A system of deposit insurance would be created but the banks' assets would be diversified according to the public bonds of the different states. The insurance premium paid by the banks would depend on the specific country risks. Restructuring of public debts would be possible in case of necessity under the control of the European Stability Mechanism (ESM). This would encourage the financial markets to impose risk premium and would favoured the speculation on public securities.

Third, a fund would be created to help euro zone's countries in the event of crisis with the usual strict conditionality (fiscal rules, European semester). Transfers would be temporary. The contributions of the member states to the funds would be so much higher than the country is more instable and has been using the funds. In other words, it would be the countries the most in difficulty in the past which would more contribute to the funds and finance the countries now in difficulty. The countries in better economic situation would less contribute. A strange conception of the solidarity.

Fourth, a synthetic safe asset without risk would be proposed to investors as an alternative to national public debts considered as potentially risky. It would be a basket of the most secured public debts of the different States. In practice, the German bonds would occupy a central place in this synthetic asset. Such a framework would only accentuate the financial disparity of the euro zone and would offer a new field for the speculation.

Last, the supervision of the national fiscal policies would be ensured by an independent European commissioner. The president of the Euro-group, Finance minister of the euro zone, would have the decision-making power.

On the whole, this CEPR proposal is a new flight forward with the reaffirmation of the principle of no-bail-out, a strengthening of the financial markets, a risk of more financial instability and insufficient accompanying measures (the European fund). The technocratic control would be reinforced.

A coherent and practical framework

The second proposal, made by IMK (Watt and Watzka, 2018), is an attempt to find a pragmatic compromise between unconditional support by ECB and national fiscal policy (which stabilises but may favour moral hazard) and strict conditionality on risk-sharing measures (which limits moral hazard but may be destabilising through financial markets). It implies to have symmetrical and counter-cyclical policies in all member states and to increase mutual trust between all the actors. Unconditional and unbureaucratic support can be given for small interventions to avoid self-fuelling crisis. More conditionality would be introduced in case of greatest support, but intervention would also be exerted on surplus countries. Based on these principles, three levels of action can be distinguished.

First, the Banking Union must be completed. Beside the Single Supervision Mechanism and the Single Resolution Mechanism, an area-wide deposit insurance mechanism must be created, irrespectively of which member state the bank is located in. This lack of any national compartment is crucial. It would require a fiscal back-stop to support unconditionally the Deposit Insurance fund and this could be done through the ESM.

The lender of last resort function of the ECB needs to be strengthened. Instead of only accepting government debt of sufficient rating according to private agencies, ECB could accept all government debt considered as sustainable in a fundamentals-based analysis. In order to reduce the risk of abuse, a preventive approach should be implemented. Conditionality could be introduced on the basis of politically legitimated decision.

Second, symmetric macroeconomic policies should be implemented to prevent imbalances and insure against macroeconomic risk. The CEPR proposal based on an expenditure rule with a debt target is supported in spite of its limits. Collective support measures are also needed in the prolongation of the Juncker Plan and the European Investment Stabilisation Function but the amounts remain too limited and the procedure too complex. Cross border automatic stabilisation would be necessary but technical and political obstacles are numerous. Among the set of proposals, the European unemployment insurance system is the most well-known working as a reinsurance scheme for national systems but concrete implementation remains an open question. More broadly the necessity to move to the euro area level with an enlarged budget and a borrowing capacity is underlined but the political obstacles are huge.

Third, institutional reforms should help to improve coordination mechanisms in order to promote convergence and more symmetric evolutions. The emphasis is put on soft coordination mechanisms: creation of an Advisory board for macroeconomic convergence at the national levels; enlargement of the Macroeconomic dialogue and of the Macroeconomic Imbalance Procedure at the European level; elaboration, within the framework of the single monetary policy, of a broad macroeconomic policy mix including fiscal, wage, and price developments.

On the whole, the IMK proposal is an elaborated attempt to find a compromise between all the constraints which exist within the European monetary union. However, the difficulties of implementation of the IMK proposal itself cannot be ignored in most of the fields. The euro area deposit insurance mechanism and the new form of lender of last resort function would face political obstacles. The soft coordination would be requisite but appears hardly manageable.

The temptation of a 'New Political Union'

The recent appeal of Piketty et al. (2018) for a new democratic Treaty is in the federalist perspective, but with some specificity. He is in favour of a European budget of around 4% of the GDP which would be discussed and voted by an assembly gathering the countries ready to participate and composed for 80% of members of the national parliaments. The resources of this budget would be based on some new taxes on large companies, on the higher incomes and wealth, and on CO_2 emission. Half of the resources would be reversed to the national states to finance public investments, 25% would be devoted to education and the other 25% to environment and migration policies. Last, in order to make the project more 'acceptable' by the public opinion, transfers between member states could not be above 0.1% of GDP.

This project seems attractive but suffers from weaknesses. An increased taxation of financial assets and of profit, although desirable, could lead to capital flights and outsourcing in the European countries staying outside this new Union. Retaliation could be necessary in case of too large capital flights. If there is no transfer between members of the new Union, the project would lose relevance. Disparities between countries would remain, especially in terms of exchange rate misalignments (at the advantage of Germany currently). In this Union divergent evolutions would remain due to the structural heterogeneity. The adjustments would only be possible through real devaluations (in practice through wage deflation, as the coordination of the wage policies, although preferable, is difficult to implement) or through labour mobility (which has a more limited impact and raise other problems). Structural change with an improvement of the non-price competitiveness of the southern European countries would be a better track but is a long-term and complex strategy. Last, within the new Union the relations between the central bank of the union (to be created) and the national public debts would not be fundamentally different from what they are within the euro zone. The Italian public bonds could hardly be considered as equivalent to German ones. The existence of a majority in favour of such a project is far from being evident.

An ultimate spare wheel, a complementary currency

The previous assessment has underlined how difficult it is to find a practicable answer to the current weaknesses of the euro zone. An ultimate spare wheel, the creation of a fiscal complementary currency, has always some partisans (Théret and Coutrot, 2018). The idea is simple and has been defended since a long time, especially in the Greek case (Papadimitriou et al., 2014, 2016). The euro would be kept as a common currency but would be completed by a national parallel currency under the form of Treasury bills of a small amount (5 to 50 euros), with a limited duration, but renewable. This mean of payment, designated as euro-peseta or euro-lira, would be backed as other public debt by the future tax revenues. It would be kept at parity with the euro, without being freely convertible on an exchange market. In that sense it would not be a true currency. But it could be used by the state to pay civil servants' wages, social transfers, and public procurement. Reciprocally the state would accept these bills in payment of taxes at the same parity and without restriction. This guarantee is a key issue to allow the social acceptance of this complementary currency. According to its advocates, it would reduce the austerity policy and help to implement recovery policy by stimulating the demand side. Due to the non-convertibility of this complementary currency, the producers of local goods would be advantaged by comparing with the foreign producers which would be reticent to accept this new currency. A self-centred recovery could be developed. All this would help to reduce the public debt, directly because the state would become less dependent from the financial markets to finance its expenditures, indirectly as the recovery would increase the GDP and reduce the debt ratio.

In practice, the positive effects seem to be overestimated by the advocates of the complementary currency. The self-centred recovery could be limited as it would be quite difficult to favour the producers of local goods. The firms would be reluctant to accept to be paid in this parallel currency as it would be difficult to use it after for other purchases. The positive loop stimulating the activity would exist but could be limited and reduced to the simple return effect on the taxes which would be paid with the complementary currency. The question of the social acceptability of this new (but non-convertible) currency is not sufficiently discussed by its advocates.

A minimalist compromise

To conclude, the solution of a minimalist compromise at the European level seems the most likely. A budget of the euro zone has been accepted but is reduced to a simple line in the EU budget which would itself suffer of strong constraints. The achievement of the Banking Union is considered as a priority but the system of insurance deposit would only be managed at the national level, for lack of sufficient solidarity. Likewise, the Resolution funds would remain with an insufficient endowment, but the possibility of a complementary support by the ESM remains in discussion. The transformation of the ESM in a European Monetary fund able to intervene in case of crisis of some countries, including in a preventive way or in managing debt restructuring, is more unlikely. The competition policy would remain the core of the EU with a race to the bottom in matter of taxation and the retention of the unanimity rule which is paralytic. Progress could be considered in some more limited fields, a harmonised definition of the consolidated tax base for the corporate income tax, some progress in the taxation of the GAFA, a European fund for investments in the breaking technologies and some forms of control of foreign investments in the EU. This compromise would be fragile in case of economic turnaround.

The Multiannual Financial Framework for the EU for 2021–2027 presented by the Commission (2018) is revealing the existing constraints. 'Do more with less' is the master word. The targets have been multiplied with less resource. New fields of intervention have appeared (border management, defence, migration policy, neighbourhood cooperation) with limited institutional basis. Debates on the euro zone governance don't appear. Without surprise the common agricultural policy and the cohesion policy which represent each around 36% of the total of the budget are the main potential sources of budget savings to finance the redeployment of the expenditures. On the whole, the budget amount is 1194 billion € for 7 years, 1.11% of National Income (instead of 1.13% during the previous period).

SFC modelling of alternative economic policies in a monetary union

These alternative economic policies will be studied and compared with the current configuration using a two-country SFC model of a monetary union inspired by Godley and Lavoie (2007a, 2007b). Each national model of the two countries will follow the structure of the model of Chapter 1 in this volume and will not be presented in too much detail. These models describe assets and liabilities of all the agents and are well adapted to analyse the European monetary and financial integration in a consistent manner. We will first focus on the current configuration of the monetary union and assess the stabilisation effects due to portfolio diversification and intra-zone credit, as it is advocated by the 'international risk-sharing' approach. The weakness of these stabilisation effects will be underlined as well as the risk of increasing interest rates in case of credit rationing. In a second step, the stabilising effects of a federal budget at the level of the euro zone with federal transfers, federal public expenditures, and eurobonds will be analysed in a simple case where the rates of interest are supposed exogenous. In a third step, we will return to a more general model with endogenous rates of interest and examine how alternative economic policies based on eurobonds or other intra-European financing could contribute to providing an answer to the crisis of the euro area.

A two-country SFC model of the monetary union

The monetary union is composed of two countries (N and S) with an asymmetry of size. The country N is five times larger than the country S. This configuration facilitates analysing the adjustment mechanisms of the country S facing the rest of the monetary union. The model is based on Duwicquet and Mazier (2010, 2011) and Duwicquet et al. (2013). The prices are fixed. Firms can accumulate both real (K) and financial capital ($p_e E_e$). They can finance their investments by non-distributed profits (UP), bank loans (L), or equities ($p_e E$). Commercial banks supply credit and the single central bank (ECB) refinances the commercial banks (RF). Households hold cash (H), banking

Table 5.1 Balance sheet of the monetary union

	Households N	Firms N	Govt N	Banks N	Federal budget	ECB	Households S	Firms S	Govt S	Banks S
Capital		K^N						K^S		
Deposits	BD^N			$-BD^N$			BD^S			$-BD^S$
Cash	H^N_h			H^N		$-H$	H^S_h			H^S
Credit		$-L^N$		L^N_N						L^N_S
				L^S_N				$-L^S$		L^S_S
Refinancing				$-RF^N$		$RF^N +$				$-RF^S$
						RF^S				
Bonds	$p^N_b B^N_N$		$-p^N_b$				$p^N_b B^N_S$			
			B^N							
	$p^S_b B^S_N$						$p^S_b B^S_S$		$-p^S_b B^S$	
Euro bonds	BT^E_{Nh}			BT^E_{Nb}		$-BT^E$	BT^E_{Sh}			BT^E_{Sb}
Bills			$-BT^N$	BT^N_N						BT^N_S
				BT^S_N					$-BT^S$	BT^S_S
Equities	$p^N_e E^N_{Nh}$	$p^N_e E^N_{Ne}$					$p^N_e E^N_{Sh}$	$p^N_e E^N_{Se}$		
		$-p^N_e E^N$								
	$p^S_e E^S_{Nh}$	$p^S_e E^S_{Ne}$					$p^S_e E^S_{Sh}$	$p^S_e E^S_{Se}$		
								$-p^S_e E^S$		
Wealth	$-VH^N$	$-V^N$	$-D^N$	$-VB^N$	$-D^E$		$-VH^S$	$-V^S$	$-D^S$	$-VB^S$

Source: Authors' construction.

deposits (BD), domestic and foreign bonds equities ($p_e E_h$). The two national governments issue bonds ($p_b B$) and Treasury bills (BT). Taxes on households (T_h), firms (T_f), and banks (TB) finance the budget of each government. In Table 5.1, we describe the balance sheet in terms of assets (written with a positive sign) and liabilities (written with a negative sign) of each sector. When there are two symbols (N and S), the subscript denotes the country where the asset is held, the superscript the country where the asset is issued. For example, BT_N^S represents the amount of Treasury bills held by the country N and issued by the country S.

Households

Consumption

$$C^N = a0^N + a1 \cdot YHS^N_h + a2 \cdot VH^N_{-1} \qquad (1)$$

$$YD^N_h = W^N + i_d \cdot BD^N_{-1} + B^N_{N-1} + B^S_{N-1} + DIV^N_{hN} + DIV^S_{hN} - T^N \qquad (2)$$

$$YHS^N_h = YD^N_h + CG^N_h \qquad (3)$$

(*YD* = *disposable income*, YHS^N_h = *disposable income with capital gains*, *W* = *wages*, $i_d \cdot BD_{-1}$ = *interests on bank deposits*, B^N_{N-1} *and* B^S_{N-1} = *interest on domestic and foreign bonds*, DIV^N_{hN} *and* DIV^S_{hN} = *received dividends on domestic and foreign equities*, T_h = *taxes*, CG_h = *households' capital gains*)

Taxes paid by households

$$T_h^N = \theta \ (W^N + id \ BD_{-1}^N + B_{N-1}^N + B_{N-1}^S + DIV_{hN}^N + DIV_{hN}^S) \tag{4}$$

Households' bonds demand

$$\frac{p_b^N . B_N^N}{VH^N} = v0 + v1 . r_b^N - v2 . r_b^S - v3 . i_d - v4 . r_e^N - v5 . r_e^S \tag{5}$$

$$\frac{p_b^S . B_N^S}{VH^N} = v0 + v1 . r_b^S - v2 . r_b^N - v3 . i_d - v4 . r_e^N - v5 . r_e^S \tag{6}$$

(r_b = interest rate on bonds, i_d = interest rate on bank deposits, r_e = rate of return on equities)

Households' equities demand

$$\frac{p_e^N . E_{hN}^N}{VH^N} = v0 \ - v1 . r_b^N - v2 . r_b^S - v3 . i_d + v4 . r_e^N - v5 . r_e^S \tag{7}$$

$$\frac{p_e^S . E_{hN}^S}{VH^N} = v0 - v1 . r_b^N - v2 . r_b^S - v3 . i_d - v4 . r_e^N + v5 . r_e^S \tag{8}$$

Cash demand

$$H_h^N = \lambda0 . C^N \tag{9}$$

Households' transaction equilibrium (*BD* = *bank deposits*)

$$\Delta BD^N = YD_h^N - C^N - p_b^N . \Delta B_N^N - p_b^S . \Delta B_N^S - p_e^N$$
$$. \Delta E_{hN}^N - p_e^S . \Delta E_{hN}^S - \Delta H_h^N \tag{10}$$

Households' balance sheet (*VH* = *households' net wealth*)

$$VH^N = BD^N + p_b^N . B_N^N + p_b^S . B_N^S + p_e^N . E_{hN}^N + p_e^S . E_{hN}^S + H_h^N \tag{11}$$

Households' capital gains on equities and bonds held

$$CG_h^N = \Delta p_b^N . B_{N-1}^N + \Delta p_b^S . B_{N-1}^S + \Delta p_e^N . E_{hN-1}^N + \Delta p_e^S . E_{hN-1}^S \tag{12}$$

Firms

Firms have both real and financial accumulation following a post-Keynesian theoretical framework (Clévenot et al., 2010, 2012 for more development). Their desired fixed investment (I^d) depends positively on the profit rate (r_f = UP/K_{-1}) and negatively on the debt structure (L/K_{-1}) and the cost of credit (r_l), with a possible positive demand effect. Their financial accumulation, that is, firms' demand for equities ($p_e . E_e$), is mainly related to the rate of return on equities held (r_e) with an arbitrage between domestic and foreign assets and a positive effect of the rate of profit reflecting the global environment. Firms can finance their investments through undistributed profit (UP), bank credit, or by issuing equities. New equities issued by firms ($p_e . \Delta E$) are determined as a percentage of the total real and financial investment, with positive effects of both credit cost and the debt ratio whose respective increases lead firms to issue more equities. The rate of return on equities r_e is determined by dividends and capital gains. Lastly, income distribution is analysed in a simple way with a con stant share of wages. Undistributed profit is determined by a constant rate of saving by firms (s_f). Distributed dividends between shareholders (households and firms of both countries) are related to the structure of the shares held.

Fixed investment

$$\frac{I^{dN}}{K_{-1}^N} = k_0{}^N + k_1 . r_{f-1}^N + k_2 . \frac{\Delta Y^N}{Y_{-1}^N} - k_3 . \frac{L^N}{K_{-1}^N} - k_4 . r_l \tag{13}$$

(I^d = *desired investment, K = fixed capital stock; Y = GDP; r_f = rate of profit* = $\frac{UP}{K_{-1}}$, *UP = undistributed profit, L = loans, r_l = interest rate on loans*)

$$K^N = K_{-1}^N (1 - \delta) + I^N \tag{14}$$

Financial accumulation (firms' equities demand)

$$\frac{p_e^N . E_{eN}^N}{(K^N + p_e^N . E_{eN}^N + p_e^S . E_{eN}^S)} = f0 + f1.r_e^N - f2.r_e^S + f3.r_f^N \tag{15}$$

$$\frac{p_e^S . E_{eN}^S}{(K^N + p_e^N . E_{eN}^N + p_e^S . E_{eN}^S)} = f0 + f1.r_e^S - f2.r_e^N + f3.r_f^N \tag{16}$$

($K^N + p_e^N . E_{eN}^N + p_e^S . E_{eN}^S = $ *total real and financial assets held by country N firms,*

$p_e = $ *equities' price, E = number of equities*)
New equities issued ($p_e . \Delta E$)

$$\frac{p_e^N . \Delta E^N}{(I^N + p_e^N . \Delta E_{eN}^N + p_e^S . \Delta E_{eN}^S)} = g_1 . r_1 + g_2 . \left(\frac{L^N}{L^N + p_e^N . E^N + V^N}\right)_{-1} + g_3 \quad (17)$$

$= (I^N + p_e^N . \Delta E_{eN}^N + p_e^S . \Delta E_{eN}^S = $ *real and financial investment,* $\dfrac{L}{L + p_e . E + V}$
debt ratio)

$$I'^N + p_e^N . \Delta E_{eN}^N + p_e^S . \Delta E_{eN}^S = \Delta L^{sN} + UP^N + p_e^N . \Delta E^N \qquad (18)$$

$$I = Min\left(I^d, I^r\right) \qquad (19)$$

(*I = effective investment, I' = restricted investment, ΔL^s = credit supply*)

$$K^N + p_e^N . E_{eN}^N + p_e^S . E_{eN}^S = L^N + p_e^N . E^N + V^N \qquad (20)$$

Wages and income distribution

$$W^N = \rho . Y^N \qquad (21)$$

$$UP^N = \left(Y^N - W^N - rl.L_{-1}^N - DIV^N + DIV_{eN}^N + DIV_{eN}^S - T_f^N\right) \qquad (22)$$

$$T_f^N = \theta_f^N . \left(Y_{-1}^N - W_{-1}^N - rl.L_{-2}^N - DIV^N + DIV_{eN}^N + DIV_{eN}^S\right) \qquad (23)$$

$$DIV^N = \left(1 - s_f\right).\left(Y_{-1}^N - W_{-1}^N - r_1.L_{-2}^N\right) \qquad (24)$$

$$DIV_{eN}^N = DIV^N.\left(\frac{E_{eN}^N}{E^N}\right)_{-1} \qquad (25)$$

Banks

Four different models can be considered. In the first one the firms can get from banks all the credits demanded without restriction. Credit demand is determined by the balance of the firms' flow of funds. Investment is equal to the desired investment (model 1). In the second model with credit rationing the credit supply of banks depends on the financial fragility of firms represented by two parameters: the rate of profit (r_f) describing the ability of firms to face debt commitments and the debt ratio as a proxy of firms' financial soundness. Credit rationing occurs when credit demand is larger than credit supply. The restricted investment (I') is then determined by the different sources of founding: profit, equities, and credit rationed from banks (L^s) (model 2).

The share between domestic and foreign banks' loans is simply related to the degree of openness of the economy. Reserve requirements in high powered money (H) represent a fixed share of bank deposits and do not provide interest payments. A simplified model of interest rates is retained. The interest rate on loans (r_l) is assumed to be equal to the key interest rate of the central bank (i_b) plus a constant mark-up. To make profits, banks apply a spread between the key rate and the rate on deposits (i_d). The central bank provides advances (RF) to commercial banks according to their needs. These advances are made at the key rate of interest (i_b). They are determined as banks' balance. The central bank pays taxes, equal to its profit, which are shared between the two national governments in relation with each country's size.

Credit supply (ΔL^s), credit demand (ΔL^d)

$$\Delta L^{sN} = \alpha_{n1}.r_f - \alpha_{n2}.\left(\frac{L^N}{K^N}\right)_{-1} + \alpha_{n3} \tag{26}$$

$$\Delta L^{dN} = I^{dN} - UP^N - p_e^N.\Delta E^N + p_e^N.\Delta E_{eN}^N + p_e^S.\Delta E_{eN}^S \tag{27}$$

$$\Delta L^N = min\left(\Delta L^{dN}, \Delta L^{sN}\right) \tag{28}$$

$$\Delta L^N = \Delta L_N^N + \Delta L_S^N \tag{29}$$

$$L_S^N = \left(\frac{X^N}{Y^N}\right).L^N \tag{30}$$

(L_S^N = *credit supplied by country S banks to country N firms*, $\dfrac{X}{Y}$ = *rate of openness*)

$$H^N = \varepsilon . BD^N \tag{31}$$

Taxes paid by commercial banks

$$TB^N = \theta_b . (r_l.L_{N-1}^N + r_l.L_{N-1}^S + r.BT_{N-1}^N + r.BT_{N-1}^S - i_d.BD_{-1}^N - i_b.RF_{-1}^N) \tag{32}$$

Banks' profit

$$PB^N = (1 - \theta_b) . (r_l.L_{N-1}^N + r_l.L_{N-1}^S + r.BT_{N-1}^N + r.BT_{N-1}^S - i_d.BD_{-1}^N - i_b.RF_{-1}^N) \tag{33}$$

$$\Delta VB^N = PB^N \tag{34}$$

$$\Delta RF^N = \Delta H^N + \Delta L_N^N + \Delta L_N^S + \Delta BT_N^N + \Delta BT_N^S - \Delta BD^N - PB^N \tag{35}$$

Central bank tax

$$T\epsilon B = i_b . \left(RF_{-1}^N + RF_{-1}^S \right) \tag{36}$$

$$T\epsilon B^N = T\epsilon B. \left(\frac{Y^N}{Y^N + Y^S} \right) \tag{37}$$

Central bank money

$$H = H_h^N + H_h^S + H^N + H^S \tag{38}$$

$$\Delta H = \Delta RF^N + \Delta RF^S \quad \left(\text{\textit{this equation is derived from others}} \right) \tag{39}$$

Interest rates

$$r_l = i_b + m1_b \tag{40}$$

$$i_d = i_b - m2_b \tag{41}$$

$$r = r_1 = r_b^N = r_b^S \tag{42}$$

$$p_b^N = \frac{1}{r_b^N} \tag{43}$$

In another model, resident and non-resident banks have specific behaviours. Credit rationing may come from banks of the small country S facing economic constraints while banks of the rest of the union provide credit without restriction (model 3). The corresponding equations will be given later on. Finally, in a last version, banks may ration the Treasury bills and tighten the financial conditions with rising interest rates. In this version interest rates will become endogenous (model 4). Equations will also be given later.

Government

Public finance is described in a simple way with exogenous expenditures and income taxes paid by households (T_h), firms (T_f), commercial banks (TB), and central bank $(T€B)$. Treasury bills (BT) are purchased by commercial banks without restriction, with the distribution between foreign and domestic bills related to the degree of openness. Public bonds are held by households $(p_b B)$. Interest rates on Treasury bills (r) and on bonds (r_b) are supposed to be equal to interest rates on loans (r_l). In the model 4 version banks are reluctant to purchase Treasury bills without restriction and variable interest rates are introduced. The corresponding equations are given later on.

$$\Delta BT^N = G^N + r_{r_1} BT_{-1}^N + B_{-1}^N - T_h^N - T_f^N - TB^N - T€B^N - p_b^N \Delta B^N \tag{44}$$

$$\Delta BT^N = \Delta BT_N^N + \Delta BT_S^N \tag{45}$$

$$BT_S^N = \left(\frac{X^N}{Y^N}\right).BT^N \tag{45}$$

$$\Delta B^N = \Delta B_N^N + \Delta B_S^N \tag{46}$$

Foreign trade and current account

Imports (IM) and exports (X) inside the monetary union depend only on the volume effect, since prices and exchange rates are fixed. The current balance (CUR) is composed of the trade balance, the balance of capital incomes received and paid to the rest of the monetary union, and the exchanges inside the banking system. Commercial banks pay interest to the central bank for their refinancing. But the central bank pays taxes to each government. In case of a deficit incurred by country S, the current balance is financed through three channels: the holding of more assets of country S (bonds, Treasury bills, equities) by country N than the opposite (holding of assets of country N by country S); the channel of credit by banks of country N to firms of country S; the refinancing by the central bank which plays a key role as lender of last resort.

$$\log\left(IM^{N}\right) = \mu_{0} + \mu_{1n} \cdot \log\left(Y^{N}\right) \tag{47}$$

$$X^{N} = IM^{S} \tag{48}$$

$$CUR^{N} = \left(X^{N} - IM^{N}\right) + \left(B_{N-1}^{S} + r.BT_{N-1}^{S} + r_{l}.L_{N-1}^{S} + DIV_{hN}^{S} + DIV_{eN}^{S} + TCB^{N}\right)$$
$$- \left(B_{S-1}^{N} + r.BT_{S-1}^{N} + rl.L_{S-1}^{N} + DIV_{hS}^{N} + DIV_{eS}^{N} + i_{b}.RE_{1}^{N}\right)$$
$$\tag{49}$$

$$Y^{N} = C^{N} + I^{N} + G^{N} + X^{N} - IM^{N} \tag{50}$$

On the whole, the model has 107 equations for 107 endogenous variables. G^{N}, G^{S} (public expenditures), and i_{b} (key interest rate fixed by the central bank) are exogenous.

Calibration

The model is calibrated using balance sheets and national accounts in flows from Eurostat for the European countries. Two sets of calibration have been used, the first one with an important share of equities (400% of GDP as in France in 2006) which reflects a high degree of financialization. Dividends are larger than interests. The second calibration retains a smaller share of equities (172% of GDP) and a greater role played by credit. The capital- income ratio is also smaller ($\frac{K}{Y}$ = 2 instead of 4), and equities are more held by firms than by households. Lastly, the share of foreign dividends in the total dividends received is kept constant instead of being determined by the structure of equities held. This assumption is more in line with the relative weakness of the capital income received from abroad. The second calibration can be regarded as more realistic.

But, as will be shown, the results of the two calibrations are rather close. The elasticities in the equations are close to usual estimations. The basic scenario follows a rate of growth of GDP of 2%, a gross rate of accumulation of 7% and a rate of accumulation net of depreciation of 2%. Annex 5.1 gives the values of the main parameters for calibration.

Adjustments inside the monetary union and stabilisation effects

Methodology

Adjustment mechanisms within the monetary union can be analysed thanks to supply or demand shocks. It allows a measure of stabilisation coefficients, especially for capital incomes coming from the rest of the union and intra-zone finance. In order to identify the stabilisation effects specific to each factor, three successive financial regimes will be considered:

- The basic regime corresponding to financial autarky (regime 1) is without foreign assets and without intra-zone credit; there is no capital income from abroad; the current account is then financed only through refinancing by the central bank to the commercial banks;
- The second regime is the most complete case of financial integration with foreign assets and intra-zone credit. Two calibrations are distinguished. In regime 2-a, residents hold 25% of foreign equities in their portfolio which is close to the observed value; in regime 2-b, the share of foreign equities is supposed to be higher (80% of the total) which corresponds to a rather unrealistic value, but gives an upper evaluation of the stabilisation effects through capital income;
- The third regime includes intra-zone credit and Treasury bills, but excludes foreign equities and bonds (regime 3). Capital incomes from abroad are consequently missing. This version allows an estimation of the stabilisation effect of intra-zone credit solely, by comparison with the basic regime 1 of financial autarky.

These three regimes will be combined with the four model versions which have been presented in the previous section, model 1 without global credit rationing, model 2 with global credit rationing, model 3 with credit rationing only by domestic banks, and model 4 with Treasury bills rationing and variable rate of interest on Treasury bills. Table 5.2 sums up the whole set of configurations which will be considered. Results are given with a simplified version of the model where the rate of growth of equities' prices is exogenous. Consequently, equation (17) is withdrawn. A single shock will be examined in each case, a loss of competitiveness in country S facing the rest of the union reflecting the overvaluation of the euro for the southern European countries. In the foreign trade equations, we introduce an exogenous effect of higher unit

Table 5.2 Adjustments in a monetary union: the different configurations

Model	Regime				
	Financial autarky	*Normal financial integration*	*High financial integration*	*Intra-zone credit alone*	*Intra-zone credit alone*
Model 1: without global credit rationing	Model 1.1	Model 1.2a	Model 1.2b	Model 1.3	
Model 2: with global credit rationing	Model 2.1	Model 2.2a	Model 2.2b	Model 2.3	
Model 3: with credit rationing by domestic banks	Model 3.1			Model 3.3a	Model 3.3b
Model 4: Treasury bills rationing with variables interest rates	Model 4.1			Model 4.3	

Source: Authors' construction.

labour costs in southern countries relative to the North. The term *TI* is equal to 0 in the baseline and to 10 between periods 10 and 50 in order to illustrate the loss of country S competitiveness.

$$\log\left(IM^{N}\right) = \mu 0n + \mu 1n.\log\left(Y^{N}\right) + \mu 2.log\left(\frac{W^{N} - TI}{Y^{N}}\right) - \mu 2.log\left(\frac{W^{S} + TI}{Y^{S}}\right)$$

(51)

$$\log\left(IM^{S}\right) = \mu 0s + \mu 1s.\log\left(Y^{S}\right) + \mu 2.log\left(\frac{W^{S} + TI}{Y^{S}}\right) - \mu 2.log\left(\frac{W^{N} - TI}{Y^{N}}\right)$$

(52)

Adjustments without credit rationing (model 1)

In the first model there is no credit rationing and firms can get from banks all the demanded credit. Similarly Treasury bills are purchased by commercial banks without restriction. The loss of competitiveness of country *S* due to an over-valuation of its currency induces a decrease of country *S* GDP to the benefit of the rest of the union (country *N*). The trade deficit and current account

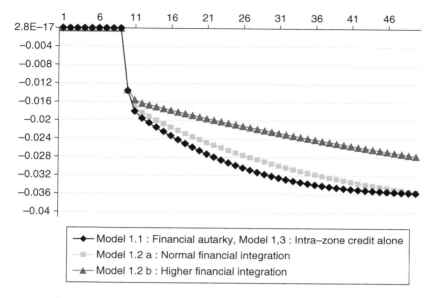

Figure 5.1 Effects on the GDP of a loss of competitiveness in country *S* without credit rationing.

Source: Authors' computation.

deficit of country *S* increase, inducing a larger foreign debt and payment of interest and dividends to country *N*. Due to their income's reduction, country *S* households consume less and demand fewer assets. Country *S* firms adjust in the same way and pay less dividends, which decreases the equities rate of return of country *S* and makes equities of country *N* more attractive. Thanks to the holding of country *N* assets, capital income of country S households and firms improves with rising dividends distributed by country *N* firms whose profit are increasing. This contributes to sustain the demand and reduces the country *S* decline, which leads to a stabilising effect. The loss of competitiveness and the foreign debt deteriorate the trade and current balances of country *S*. After an initial decline the current balance improves slightly more than the trade balance, thanks to the distribution of dividends of country *N* to country *S*. But this effect does not last and is quickly compensated by the rise of capital incomes paid to country *N* in the wake of growing foreign debt. These adjustment mechanisms through capital incomes and through external finance from country *N* can be analysed with the different versions of the model. Figure 5.1 compares the respective declines of GDP in country *S* after the loss of competitiveness in each of the four versions of the model 1.

The first result is the identity between financial autarky (model 1.1 without foreign assets and without intra-zone finance) and the case where there is only foreign finance with intra-zone credit and Treasury bills (model 1.3). This means that intra-zone credit or Treasury bills have no specific stabilisation effect. As the central bank refinances already the commercial banks, the development of intra-zone credit or Treasury bills has no additional stabilising effect. In a monetary union there is no difference of nature between domestic credit and intra-zone credit. The refinancing by the central bank plays in the same way.

The comparison between financial autarky (model 1.1) and the two cases of complete financial integration (model 1.2-a and 1.2-b) with foreign assets and capital income is interesting. The decline of the GDP is clearly less pronounced in model 1.2-b where the share of foreign assets in total assets is high. This means that capital incomes indeed have a stabilisation effect. However, in model 1.2-a, where the share of foreign assets is more limited (and more realistic), the dampening of the shock is reduced, but significant in the short to medium term. In the long run there is a reversal, characterised by a stabilisation that becomes more important in the basic model without foreign assets. This is explained by the more sustained growth which can be obtained in country N when capital income is kept at home instead of being distributed to country S. This stronger growth of country N is sufficient in the long run to sustain the country S growth through more exports from country S to country N. But this is only a long-term effect.

The stabilising effects within the monetary union after a loss of competitiveness in the country S can be summarised by the computation of a stabilisation coefficient. This stabilisation coefficient is obtained by comparing the relative variation of the GDP compared with the baseline in the model with financial integration and in the model with financial autarky (Table 5.3). The stabilisation by capital incomes (according to the model 1.2-a) would be 6.6%, which is small. For the model 1.2-b, the stabilisation would be around 19% for the period 13. This is obviously higher, but corresponds to an unrealistic hypothesis as already indicated. The underlying idea is simple: the more country S agents hold country N assets, the higher the adjustment effect will be thanks to capital incomes from country N to country S, since the country N benefits of a recovery due to its gain of competitiveness and distributes more dividends. Last, without surprise, in a monetary union with only intra-zone credit (model 1.3) the stabilisation coefficient is zero.

Adjustment with global credit rationing (model 2)

In model 2, there is a global credit rationing and country S firms cannot obtain from banks all the demanded credit. Therefore their investment is constrained by the total flow of available finance which depends especially of the credit supplied by banks. Like previously, adjustment mechanisms are analysed through a loss of competitiveness in country S facing the rest of the union. The loss of competitiveness induces an increase of country S imports and a decline of its production and profit. Firms demand more credit but are rationed by banks of both countries. Results are different according to the various versions of

Table 5.3 Stabilisation coefficients after a loss of competitiveness in country S due to an overvaluation in a monetary union without or with credit rationing (%)

Stabilisation coefficient $= 1 - (\Delta YS/YS')_{Fin\ int} / (\Delta YS/YS')_{Autarky\ 1}$
$(\Delta YS/YS') = (YS - YS')/YS' = (YS$ after the shock $- YS$ before the shock$) /$ YS before the shock

	$t = 13$	$t = 15$	$t = 20$
Without credit rationing			
Model 1.2a Normal financial integration	6.6%	7.5%	9.0%
Model 1.2b High financial integration	19.0%	22.5%	27.8%
Model 1.3 Intra-zone credit alone	0.0%	0.0%	0.0%
With global credit rationing			
Model 2.2a Normal financial integration	−0.9%	23.7%	9.8%
Model 2.2b High financial integration	29.0%	41.4%	33.2%
Model 2.3 Intra-zone credit alone	0.0%	0.0%	0.0%
With credit rationing by domestic banks			
Model 3.3a Intra-zone credit alone	8.6%	6.7%	2.9%
Model 3.3b High intra-zone credit	22.1%	16.8%	16.6%

Source: Authors' calculation.

the model (Table 5.3). As previously, there is no stabilising effect by the intra-zone credit. Model 2.1 (financial autarky) and model 2.3 (with only intra-zone credit) give the same results. By contrast, financial integration, via the stock market, has a stabilising effect. But, as in the case without credit rationing, this stabilisation effect remains limited when the degree of financial integration is close to the observed value.

Adjustment with credit rationing by domestic banks (model 3)

We now assume that only domestic banks ration credit. Banks from the rest of the union do not ration and a smoothing effect of asymmetric shocks may be obtained through this channel. In order to measure this stabilisation effect, version 3 of the model (with only intra-zone credit and without other foreign assets) is slightly modified. We first assume that domestic banks of country S ration credit of country S firms (eq. (53)) and do not finance the rest of the union (eq. (54)). The variation of the credit supply of domestic banks of country S is supposed constant.

$$\Delta CRED^S = \Delta CRED^{sS} = \Delta CRED_S^{sS} = \eta 0 \tag{53}$$

$$\Delta CRED_N^S = 0 \tag{54}$$

Banks of the rest of the union (country N) supply credit without rationing firms of country N ($CRED_N^{dN}$) and of country S ($CRED_S^{dN}$). Consequently, they supply credits requested by country S firms for financing their investments

(ΔL^{dS}). Country S firms are financed both by domestic credit ($CRED_S^{dS}$) and credit from the rest of the union ($CRED_S^{dN}$). The share of foreign credit is simply linked to the degree of openness.

$$CRED^{dN} = CRED_N^{dN} + CRED_S^{dN} \tag{55}$$

$$\Delta L^{dS} = I^{dS} - UP^S - p_e^S \, \Delta E^S + p_e^S \Delta E_{eS}^S + p_e^N \Delta E_{eS}^N \tag{56}$$

$$\Delta L^{dS} = \Delta CRED_S^{dS} + \Delta CRED_S^{dN} \tag{57}$$

$$\Delta L^{dS} = \eta 0 + \Delta CRED_S^{dN} \tag{58}$$

$$CRED_S^{dN} = (X^S / Y^S) L^{dS} \tag{59}$$

In the standard version of the model (model 3.3a), this share of foreign credit is stable around 25%, close to the observed data. In another version (model 3.3b), a higher level of intra-zone credit (75%) is introduced in order to appreciate the effect of a deeper integration. Finally, in model 3 with credit rationing by domestic banks, firms are constrained at domestic level, but not vis-à-vis the rest of the union. Banks of the rest of the union (country N) do not ration country S firms, which may constitute an adjustment mechanism facing asymmetric shocks. The identity between model 3.1 (financial autarky) and model 3.3 (with intra-zone credit), which was observed in the previous cases, does not prevail.

Adjustment mechanisms are analysed once again in case of a loss of competitiveness in country S. The increase of country S imports has a negative impact on production. The situation in autarky (model 3.1) is similar to the one studied in case of overall rationing on country S firms (model 2.1). Firms of country S have domestic credit as the sole source of bank financing. Credit rationing by domestic banks leads to a stronger recession than in the case where companies can underwrite loans abroad from the rest of the union (model 3.3a and 3.3b). In the short term, the stabilisation by external borrowing is around 9% in case of a moderate, but realistic, degree of intra-zone credit (model 3.3-a). In model 3.3-b (with a higher degree of intra-zone credit), stabilisation of production via the intra-zone credit is 22% (Table 5.3).

Adjustment with Treasury bills rationing and variable rates of interest (model 4)

The Greek and Irish crises of 2010 have highlighted the importance of external financing in a monetary union. The increase of public and external debt has led to a sharp rise of the interest rates of the southern European securities. In standard SFC models, the issuance of government securities is not constrained. State can finance its deficit without restriction. In order to take into account the constraints of financing public deficit, we modify the standard model and introduce rationing on government securities with endogenous interest rates. In country S facing a negative competitiveness shock due to an overvaluation we assume that banks of country S and N (the rest of the union) will finance part of the rising public deficit, but with higher rate of interest. The increase of interest rate on government securities is determined by confrontation of the supply of Treasury bills issued by government of country S to finance the remaining part of its public deficit (ΔBT^S, always determined by eq. (43)) and the demand of these Treasury bills by domestic banks (BT^S_S) and by banks from the rest of the union (BT^S_N). For sake of simplification, the demands of these bills by domestic and foreign banks are simple increasing linear functions of the rate of interest r_s.

$$BT^S_S = \beta_{1S}{}^{\star}r_s + \beta_{0S} \tag{60}$$

$$BT^S_N = \beta_{1N}{}^{\star}r_s + \beta_{0N} \tag{61}$$

$$\Delta BT^S = \Delta BT^S_S + \Delta BT^S_N \tag{62}$$

Fiscal policy takes into account the interest burden related to external financing and public expenditures of country S are cut (model 4.1a) or taxes increased (model 4.1b).

$$G^S = G^S_{baseline} - r_S\, BT^S_{-1} \tag{63}$$

Interest rates on bonds and loans (respectively rb_s and rl_s) are modelled in the same manner as the rates on Treasury bills (r_s). As bond prices represent the inverse of interest rates, the effect of a change in the interest rate of the bonds (r_{bs}) will lead to capital gains/losses. In order not to overestimate this effect on GDP, we introduce a lag vis-à-vis the interest rate of government securities (r_s). Interest rates on loans (rl_s) will be simply supposed equal to the rate on Treasury bills.

$$r_{bs} = (1 - a)\, rb_{s\text{-}1} + a\, r_{s\text{-}1} \tag{64}$$

$$rl_s = r_s \tag{65}$$

As previously, we compare the effect of a loss of competitiveness in country S in the case of financial autarky with endogenous interest rates and restrictive fiscal policy through expenditures cut or increasing taxes (model 4.1a or 4.1b) and in the case of intra-zone finance (model 4.3). The evolution of GDP after

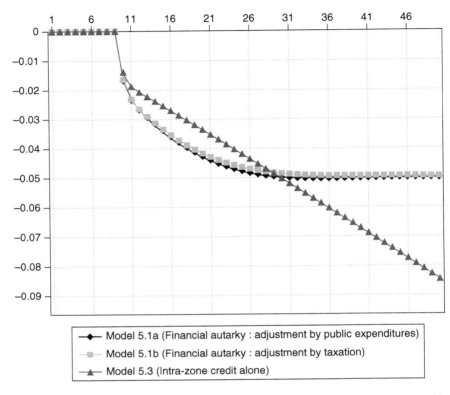

Figure 5.2 Impact on the GDP of a loss of country *S* competitiveness with variable
interest rates.

Source: Authors' computation.

the shock of competitiveness is illustrated by Figure 5.2. Stabilisation coefficients
are given in Table 5.4. At short term, in financial autarky domestic banks finance
a part of the public deficit, but with higher interest rates which increases the
deficit. The government is forced to adopt a restrictive policy which accentuates
the slow down. By contrast, at short term, external financing can cushion the
recession thanks to larger funds which authorizes a less restrictive policy and
mitigates the slow down. But at medium–long run, a reversal appears. Without
external financing the state pursues a restrictive fiscal policy which reduces the
public deficit and makes the state less dependent on financial markets. With
intra-zone finance, foreign resident banks contribute to finance a larger deficit
of country S. But public debt increases continuously and interest rates reach
high levels, generating a cumulative process. The slowdown is accentuated by
expenditures cut and the fall of investment which is more marked in model 4.3.
In financial autarky, the relative decline of GDP is stabilised at −5% in the long
term. GDP does not dive as in the model with external financing. The shock

Table 5.4 Stabilisation coefficients in case of a loss of country *S* competitiveness with variable interest rates

Stabilisation coefficient = $1 - (\Delta YS/YS') / (\Delta YS/YS')_{Autarky\ 1a}$
$(\Delta YS/YS') = (YS - YS')/YS' = (YS$ after the shock $- YS$ before the shock$) /$
    YS before the shock

	$t = 13$	$t = 15$	$t = 20$	$t = 30$	$t = 50$
Model 4.3 Intra-zone credit alone	24.2%	25.0%	21.4%	−0.7%	−68.8%
Model 4.1b Financial autarky: adjustment by tax	0.8%	1.1%	2.3%	2.5%	0.9%

Source: Authors' computation.

of competitiveness shows that a crisis may appear because of excessive leverage vis-à-vis the financial markets. Maintaining a funding too costly plunges the economy into a cumulative recession that could lead to payment default.

On the whole, with this first set of simulations, several results can be underlined. Foreign asset holdings have a stabilising role but the capital income stabilising coefficient seems smaller than the one obtained by the 'international risk-sharing' approach. By contrast, foreign loans (intra-zone credit) have no specific stabilisation effects. This is due to the credit mechanism in a monetary union and to the key role played by refinancing by the central bank. Inside a monetary union, domestic credit and foreign credit from another member of the union are of the same type. There is no increase of the stabilisation coefficient to expect from development of intra-euro zone credit. This is true without credit rationing or with global credit rationing by domestic and non-resident banks. However, when non-resident banks, contrary to domestic ones, do not ration credit and buy Treasury bills without restriction, intra-zone credit have a stabilisation effect but this stabilisation remains rather weak with realistic degree of intra-zone credit.

Furthermore, when interest rates increase due to banks' reluctance to finance more issuance of Treasury bills, intra-zone credit from the rest of the union has no more stabilising effect due to its increasing cost and can contribute to a cumulative slowdown, as it has been the case with the last Greek crisis. This leads us to examine alternative economic policies, first the fiscal federalism in a simple case with constant rates of interest, second the eurobonds and other intra-European financing with endogenous interest rates, and a more general model.

Adjustments inside the monetary union with a federal budget

The revised model with federal budget

The model has to be slightly modified to introduce a federal budget. The federal budget receives federal taxes paid by the households (T_{Nh}^{E}), the firms (T_{Nf}^{E}), the banks (T_{Nb}^{E}), and the *ECB* (*T*€B) on their capital income. These federal taxes have been calibrated to represent around 3% of the Euro zone GDP. In addition to national social transfers (ST) financed by national social contributions (CL), households receive federal social transfers (FT). These federal transfers are financed by the federal taxes (TE). The current federal budget before the payment of interests is equilibrated.

$$TE = T_{Nh}^E + T_{Sh}^E + T_{Nf}^E + T_{Sf}^E + T_{Nb}^E + T_{Sb}^E + T€B \tag{66}$$

$$T_{Nh}^E = \theta_{Nh}^E \cdot \left(B_{N-1}^N + B_{N-1}^S + id \cdot BD_{-1}^N + DIV_{hN}^N + DIV_{hN}^S \right) \tag{67}$$

$$T_{Nf}^E = \theta_{Nf}^E \cdot \left(Y_{-1}^N - W_{-1}^N - rl.L_{-2}^N - DIV^N + DIV_{eN}^N + DIV_{eN}^S \right) \tag{68}$$

$$T_{Nb}^E = \theta b.\left(r_l.L_{N_{-1}}^N + r_l.L_{N_{-1}}^S + r.BT_{N_{-1}}^N + r.BT_{N_{-1}}^S + r_e.BT_{Nb}^E - i_d.BD_{-1}^N - i_b.RF_{-1}^N \right) \tag{69}$$

$$T€B = i_b \cdot \left(RF_{-1}^N + RF_{-1}^S \right) \tag{70}$$

$$FT = TE \tag{71}$$

The allocation of transfers between North and South is made according to GDP differences (FT^S = Federal transfers received by South households, FT^N = Federal transfers received by North households).

$$FT^S = \frac{1}{5} \cdot FT + \beta \left[\frac{Y^N}{Y_{baseline}^N} - \frac{Y^S}{Y_{baseline}^S} \right] \tag{72}$$

$$FT^N = FT - FT^S \tag{73}$$

The federal authority also finances European investments (GE) split between the two countries and issues eurobonds (BT^E) to finance them. These eurobonds are held by households (BT_{Nh}^E) and the banks (BT_{Nb}^E) of the two countries with the balance entirely bought by the banks. The distribution of the federal debt between North and South banks depends on the GDP share. Equation (35) that gives the banks' refinancing (RF) is completed by adding the eurobonds held by the banks.

$$\Delta BT^E = FT + GE^N + GE^S + r_e.BT_{-1}^E - TE \tag{74}$$

$$\frac{BT_{Nh}^{E}}{VH^{N}} = v0 - v1 \cdot r_b^{N} - v2 \cdot r_b^{S} - v3 \cdot i_d - v4 \cdot r_{ee}^{N} - v5 \cdot r_{ee}^{S} + v6 \cdot r_e$$

(75)

$$BT_{Nb}^{E} = BT^{E} - BT_{Nh}^{E} - BT_{Sh}^{E} - BT_{Sb}^{E}$$

(76)

$$BT_{Nb}^{E} = BT_{b}^{E} \left(Y^{N} / \left(Y^{N} + Y^{S} \right) \right)$$

(77)

Simulations and adjustment mechanisms

Adjustment mechanisms and the stabilising role played by the federal budget and eurobonds can be analysed as previously by focusing on shock of loss of competitiveness due to intra-European exchange rate misalignments. Results are given with the simplified version of the model where the interest rates are constant and the rates of growth of equity prices are exogenous. We use three successive model versions in order to identify the stabilisation effects specific to each factor:

- The basic model (model 1) is without federal budget and without eurobonds.
- The model 2 includes a federal budget of approximately 3% of euro zone's GDP. This model is divided into two sub-models depending on the parameter β of the equation (72) that describes the federal transfers (FT). In model 2-a, $\beta = 0$. In this case, adjustment is done simply by fiscal transfers. If the small country (S) is affected by a negative shock on its production, it will pay less taxes and the rest of euro zone (N) will pay more taxes. In model 2-b, $\beta = 50$. The adjustment of the shock happens also by transfers from country N to country S in addition to fiscal transfers.
- The model 3 is without a federal budget but with eurobonds to finance European investments projects GE^{N} and GE^{S} in the two countries.

We compare models 2 and 3 with model 1 (that corresponds to the actual euro zone without federal budget and eurobonds). In the foreign trade equations (51) and (52), we introduce, as previously, an exogenous effect of higher unit labour costs in southern countries relative to the North reflecting the overvaluation of the euro for the country S.

This shock deteriorates the current account of country S and improves North's external trade, leading to a decline of the GDP in the South and an increase in the North. Figure 5.3 describes the relative change in GDP of southern countries with the four models. When there is a simple federal budget without transfers (model 2a) the decline of the production in the country S is only slightly mitigated. The country S pays less federal taxes and the country

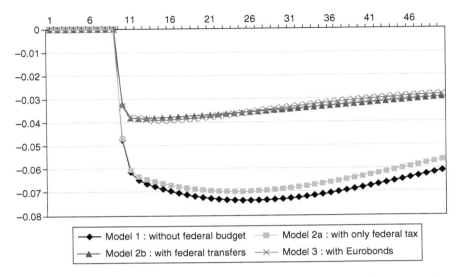

Figure 5.3 Effects on country *S* GDP of a loss of competitiveness without or with a federal budget.

Model 1: without federal budget; model 2a: with only federal tax; model 2b: with federal transfers; model 3: with eurobonds

Source: Authors' computation.

N more but the stabilising effect is limited due to the small size of the federal budget (around 3% of the monetary union GDP). In model 2b, the stabilisation is more important thanks to the transfers financed by the federal budget and received by the country *S*. These transfers are distributed between the two countries according to their relative rates of growth. Each year in average, the country *N* transfers almost 0.4% of its GDP and the country *S* receives transfers equivalent to almost 2% of its GDP. This allows a rather important stabilisation of the initial negative shock for country *S*. In model 3, eurobonds can finance European investments for an annual average amount of 0.9% of the GDP of the whole zone. The loss of competitiveness of the country *S* is compensated by large European projects. This 'growth shock' is mutually beneficial and the growth recovery helps the southern countries. But it is well known that such European investment projects are complex to implement, which can reduce their macroeconomic impact.

The stabilising role played by the federal transfers or the eurobonds after a worsening of the competitiveness in the country *S* can be summarised by the computation of a stabilisation coefficient. This stabilisation coefficient is obtained comparing the relative variation of the GDP compared with the baseline in the model with federal budget and in the model without federal budget (Table 5.5). Without surprise, the stabilisation coefficient is weak when the

Table 5.5 Stabilisation coefficients with a federal budget after a loss of competitiveness in country *S* due to an overvaluation (%)

Stabilisation coefficient = $1 - (\Delta YN/YN)_{Mod\ Fed} / (\Delta YN/YN)_{Mod\ 1}$

$(\Delta YN/YN) = (YN - YN)/YN = (YN\ after\ the\ shock - YN\ before\ the\ shock) / YN\ before\ the\ shock$

t	10	13	20	40	50
Model 2a Federal taxation	1.3	2.9	4.5	7.0	7.8
Model 2b Federalism with transfers	32.5	42.5	48.8	52.9	51.7
Model 3 Eurobonds and European investments	30.3	41.9	47.5	55.3	53.6

Source : Authors' computation.

federal system is limited to simple federal taxation (model 2a). The stabilisation is small at short term (3%) and at long term (7%). On the contrary, with federal transfers (model 2b) the stabilisation is higher at short term (32%) and at long term (52%). It is also the case with eurobonds and European investment programmes (model 3).

The establishment of a federal budget has also the advantage of limiting the rise of the public debt of the southern countries. Figure 5.4 highlights the evolution of public debt in model 1 (without federal budget) and model 2-b (with federal transfers). In the baseline, between periods 10 and 50 the public debt increases up to around 80% of GDP in the South and to 110% in the North. In the scenario with the South's overvaluation and loss of competitiveness, the public debt of southern countries increase further up to 170% of GDP due to the loss of competitiveness which leads to a reduction of GDP growth. But with federal transfers (model 2b), GDP is less affected in country S and the public debt increases less up to only 130%. Without a federal budget, the South public debt increases by 90 % of GDP over forty years. With a federal budget, this relative increase is limited to 50 %.

Adjustment inside the monetary union with eurobonds and intra-European financing

A model with endogenous rates of interest

The new version of the model of the monetary union is no more centred on the fiscal federalism issue but on the intra-European financing and the evolution of interest rates. It appears as an extension of the model already proposed in the previous section and is based on Duwicquet et al. (2018). Several points can be underlined. First, the interest rates on Treasury bills supplied by the state are endogenous. The demand of Treasury bills by private banks is an increasing function of interest rate. Thus, in case of an insufficient demand, this mechanism induces upward pressures on interest rates. Second, the budgetary policy is partially endogenous and is linked to financial markets. When interest rates on

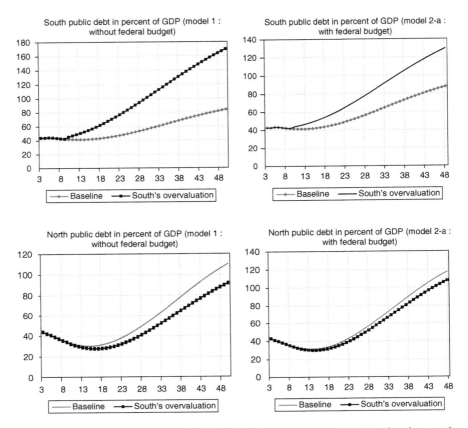

Figure 5.4 Evolution of national public debt in percentage of GDP: baseline and
scenarioswithlossofcompetitivenessandovervaluationintheSouthwithoutorwith
a federal budget.

Source: Authors' computation.

sovereign debt increase, the national governments can reduce public expenditures
in reaction. Third, the possibility to increase intra–zone financing is introduced
in order to reduce the pressure on interest rates. This can be achieved through
foreign banks purchases of public bonds or Treasury bills, through the ESM or
even through direct intervention of the central bank on the public bond market.
Fourth, the role of eurobonds is examined in two ways. On the one hand,
eurobonds are aimed at pooling a part of sovereign debt in the euro zone. On the
other hand, eurobonds could be used to finance European investment projects
in various sectors namely education, innovation, and energetic transition. Last,
the rather traditional policy mix combining tax rebates and expenditures cuts
(roughly the French government strategy) is also discussed.

The government receives taxes from households, firms, and banks; spends
public expenditures; and pays interests. The public deficit is financed by issuance

of bonds ($p_b \Delta B$) and Treasury bills (ΔBT). Supply of Treasury bills balances the gap between public deficit and bonds issuance (eq. (44)).

The central bank provides an unlimited amount of refinancing (RF^N) to commercial banks at the key interest rate (i_b) acting as the lender of last resort (equation 35). The interest rate on bank deposit (i_d) is simply determined with a margin on the key interest rate of the central bank (eq. (41)). Commercial banks supply the entire amount of demanded credit (ΔL^N, eq. (27)). The credit market is open to foreign banks. We suppose that banks of the smaller country (S) do not lend to firms of the rest of the union ($L^N_S = 0$). The interest rates on bank loans (r_l) are now endogenous and depend on the lagged value of Treasury bills' rate of each country (r) and on their own lagged value.

$$r_{lN} = (1-a)\, r_{lN\text{-}1} + a\, r_{N\text{-}1} \tag{78}$$

Treasury bills play a key role in the model. Banks purchase a limited amount of Treasury bills. Bills issued by country S and domestically held by the private sector (BT^S_S) as well as bills held by the rest of the union (BT^S_N) depend on the interest rates differential between the two countries. Thus interest rates become endogenous, as they adjust supply of Treasury bills determined by the public deficit (which has to be financed) and private demand of Treasury bills in each country.

$$BT^S_S /Y^S = a_{1ss}\, r_S - a_{2ss}\, r_N + a_{3ss} \tag{79}$$

$$BT^S_N /Y^N = a_{1ns}\, r_S - a_{2ns}\, r_N + a_{3ns} \tag{80}$$

By summing demands of these two countries, we obtain the global demand for Treasury bills issued by country S (BT^S). The interest rate on Treasury bills issued by the southern country becomes endogenous.

$$r_S = [BT^S + r_N\, (a_{2ss}\, Y^S + a_{2ns}\, Y^N) - a_{3ss} Y^S - a_{3ns} Y^N] / (a_{1ss} Y^S + a_{1ns}\, Y^N) \tag{81}$$

Regarding the rest of the union (country N), we assume that the southern country does not hold bills issued by country N ($BT^N_S = 0$) which finances its public deficit only domestically. The global demand for Treasury bills issued by country N depends on the level of interest rate (r_N) and the national income (Y^N). Consequently, we have the following interest rate determination for country N.

$$BT^N = BT^N_N \tag{82}$$

$$BT^N_N /Y^N = a_{1nn}\, r_N + a_{2nn} \tag{83}$$

$$r_N = (BT^N /Y^N - a_{2nn})/ a_{1nn} \tag{84}$$

An increase of public deficit remains financed by commercial banks. However, the level of interest rates is higher. This tightening of financial conditions is partially transmitted to interest rates on bank loans granted to firms and to interest rates on public bonds which are supposed to be equal to interest rates on Treasury bills.

The main characteristics of the reference scenario with a slow growth around 1% per year are given in Duwicquet et al. (2016). Sensitivity tests have been conducted on the most relevant parameters. They are also available in the same document and two of them are given in Annex 5.2 as an illustration. They show a rather good robustness of the results. From this reference scenario, we simulate as previously an asymmetric loss of competitiveness in country S due to an overvaluation. This can be seen as a shortcut of the current imbalances in the euro zone which have various origins (inflation drift and debt-led growth in southern countries, structural problems of competitiveness).

Alternative scenarios of economic policies

In order to investigate the developments of the euro zone crisis and the alternative economic policies, we compare the effect of this shock in five different scenarios.

Scenario 1: Budget cuts

In this first scenario, public expenditures become endogenous and react to rising interest rates on Treasury bills.

$$G^N = a_{g1} \, G^N_{-1} - a_{g2} \, BT^N_{-1} \tag{85}$$

In line with the objectives of the revised Stability and Growth Pact as well as the aims of the Fiscal Compact, we assume that the government targets to reach a debt-GDP ratio of 70% in period 45. To achieve this challenge, the government progressively reduces its public expenditures. The speed of public expenditures reduction is governed by the evolution of interest rates. The year of the shock, public expenditures decrease by 0.2% of GDP relative to the baseline scenario. In the baseline scenario, public expenditures amount to 19.5 % of GDP in period 45. They drop to 12% of GDP in period 45 in this first scenario.

Scenario 2: Intra-zone financing

We investigate implications of financial support granted by the northern country to the southern country. In the wake of a loss of competitiveness in the southern country, the issuance of public securities will rise to finance an increasing deficit. We assume that private banks of the northern country will sustain a supplementary demand to bring down interest rates. This scenario can also be seen as an illustration of the ESM where northern countries grant loans with low rates of interest to southern countries. Similar effects are also expected if the central bank purchases directly Treasury bills of southern countries. In each case, the debt remains to be paid by the southern country but the debt burden is reduced substantially thanks to the financial aid.

Scenario 3: Issuance of eurobonds

In this scenario, eurobonds are issued in order to mutualise partially sovereign debt of southern countries. We assume that there is a threshold (a debt-GDP ratio of 60 %) from which eurobonds (BT^{ES}) are issued to finance public debt in the euro zone as a substitute to national debt. Nevertheless, national governments have to pay interest on issued eurobonds. Southern countries are committed to stabilise their public debt.

If $D^S/Y^S < 0.6$

$$\Delta BT^S = G^S + r_S\, BT^S_{-1} + B^S_{-1} - T^S - T^S_b - T^S_f - T_{eB}^{\ S} + ST^S - CL^S - p_b^{\ S}\, \Delta B^S + r_e\, BT^E_{S\text{-}1} \tag{86}$$

If $D^S/Y^S > 0.6$

$$\Delta BT^{ES} = G^S + r_S\, BT^S_{-1} + B^S_{-1} - T^S - T^S_b - T^S_f - T_{eB}^{\ S} + ST^S - CL^S - p_b^{\ S}\, \Delta B^S + r_e\, BT^E_{S\text{-}1} \tag{87}$$

We obtain the aggregate supply of eurobonds by adding supply in both countries. Demand for eurobonds simply depends on the interest rate (r_e) and the level of GDP of the entire euro zone ($Y^E = Y^N + Y^S$). Consequently, we have the following determination of interest rate on eurobonds.

$$BT^E = BT^{ES} + BT^{EN} \tag{88}$$

$$BT^E/Y^E = a_{1e}\, r_e + a_{2e} \tag{89}$$

$$r_e = (BT^E/Y^E - a_{2e})/a_{1e} \tag{90}$$

Scenario 4: Issuance of eurobonds and European projects

To complete the previous scenario, eurobonds are used as a tool to finance European investment projects in growth sectors. Southern countries as well as northern countries can use eurobonds in order to stimulate their economic growth.

Scenario 5: Tax rebate and public expenditures cuts

This scenario describes roughly the French CICE which is a tax credit for competitiveness and employment given to firms without any counterpart. The government reduces the social contributions paid by the firms to partly compensate the loss of competitiveness due to the overvaluation. In the import equations we introduce in scenario 5 at period 10 an exogenous reduction of the unit labour cost of country S ($W^S + TI - TR^S/Y^S$) with $TR^S/Y^S = 0.015$ compared to $TI/Y^S = 0.1$. The firms' profit is increased of an equivalent amount. To avoid an increase of the public debt, public expenditures are cut in the same proportion in scenario 6 ($G^S = a_g\, G^S_{-1} - TR^S$ in period 10). However, these measures are not sufficiently devoted to the tradable sector and the effect on employment, which is the other main target, is uncertain. That is why the government toolkit includes also industrial policy measures such as innovation and technology policy or relocation policy. These measures are complex to design and to manage and their effects are only in the long run. As an illustration and in an optimistic way, it is assumed that after period 30 the non-price competitiveness of country S is improved (the import income elasticity of country S, μ_{1s} declines from 1 to 0.98 while the import income elasticity of country N, μ_{1n} increases from 1 to 1.02 in scenario 7).

Simulations

In Figure 5.5, we can observe the evolution of interest rates and public debt in country S in the baseline scenario (overvaluation and loss of competitiveness in country S) and in the first four scenarios. In the baseline scenario, we assume that any adjustment mechanism is implemented to face the loss of competitiveness. Thus, this loss of competitiveness widens the external deficit and in the same time increases the need of external financing. In addition, the negative impact of trade deficit on the GDP implies a diminution of taxes collected by the government and thus an increase of the public deficit. On the Treasury bills market, interest rates increase alongside the debt increase and the slowdown of GDP. This 'snowball' effect implies a tremendous increase of debt levels (140% of GDP in period 45) and of interest rates (4.5% in period 45).

In order to eschew another 'Greek drama', European authorities can react by implementing various economics policies to achieve more sustainable adjustments. In the first scenario, the government tries to reduce the public expenditures in order to prevent an increase of interest rates. The long run purpose of this policy is to reach a debt-to-GDP ratio limited to 70%. However, due to the Keynesian multiplier effect, public expenditures reduction puts a huge strain on economic activity as we can see in Figure 5.6. The GDP of the southern country decreases by 30% at long term. Interest rates are reduced compared with the baseline scenario but still rise in the medium run and reach 2.8% in period 45 due to a smaller demand of Treasury bills induced by the decline of the activity.

In the second scenario, we assume that intra-zone financing is large thanks to an eased demand from private banks of the northern countries or to the implementation of an ESM. This helps to keep interest rates at low level (2.4% in period 45) in spite of a huge increase of public debt-to-GDP ratio (130% in period 45). The negative impact on economic growth is largely offset in the long run but the competitiveness problem is not solved (see Figure 5.6). We notice that the Treaty ratified in March 2012 which gives an institutional background to the ESM stipulates that member states must reach a debt-to-GDP ratio of 60% in the medium run. The results of the second scenario will be greatly affected if the objective fixed by the ESM was respected. In such a case the result in terms of relative growth rates would be largely similar to those of the first scenario.

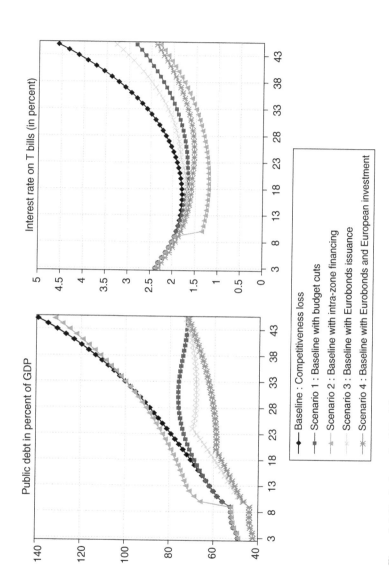

Figure 5.5 Evolution of public debt and interest rate in country S (competitiveness loss and scenarios 1 to 4).
Source: Duwicquet et al. (2018).

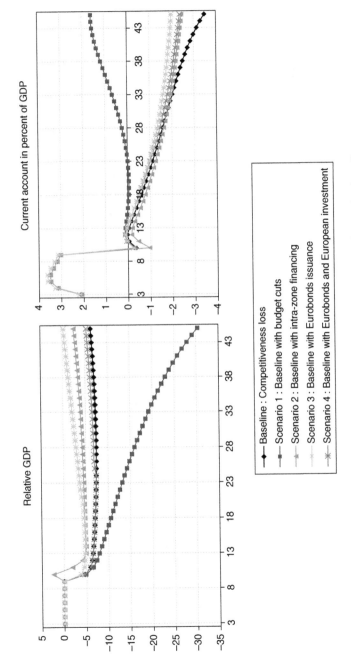

Figure 5.6 Relative GDP and current account in country S (competitiveness loss and scenarios 1 to 4).

Source: Duwicquet et al. (2018).

The third and the fourth scenario analyse the impact of an issuance of eurobonds in the euro zone. We can observe that interest rates increase less rapidly in the fourth scenario than the third scenario (Figure 5.7). In the fourth scenario, eurobonds finance investments in growth sectors therefore economic growth is stronger and upward pressures on interest rates are weaker. These growth gaps can be observed in Figure 5.6. Initially, the GDP drops after the negative competitiveness shock. The implementation of European projects financed by eurobonds (scenario 4) absorbs completely the competitiveness loss in the long run as GDP returns to its value before the shock in period 45. Eurobonds issuance to mutualise partially sovereign debt (scenario 3) permits a partial adjustment. We can notice that intra-zone financing (scenario 2) appears to be more efficient than eurobonds issuance alone (scenario 3). The implementation of an ESM aimed at providing low interest rates to governments and firms stimulates investment. In terms of relative growth, the worst case is the first scenario where governments implement drastic budget cuts in order to achieve a debt-to-GDP ratio of 70% in the long run. The slowdown of economic activity induces a decrease of imports and a massive adjustment of the current account balance. Without any policy reactions after the competitiveness loss, external deficits of the southern country steadily increase and reach 3.5% of GDP in period 45. In other scenarios, we observe a stabilisation of the external deficit around 2% in the long run.

In Figure 5.6, we can analyse the consequences of the various scenarios in the northern country in terms of growth and public debt. Drastic budget cuts in the southern country have negative impact on economic activity even in the northern country. In the long run, the fall of GDP will bring public debt to 65% of GDP. In other scenarios, public debt increases less thanks to a stronger growth, particularly in the fourth scenario.

According to our numerical simulations, the emission of eurobonds constitutes a useful tool to reignite growth in the entire euro zone. Figure 5.7 shows levels of public debt and evolution of interest rates on Treasury bills and eurobonds in the third and the fourth scenario. As growth is stronger in the fourth scenario, interest rates on national T-bills are lower when eurobonds play a role in financing the real economy. Conversely, the interest rate on eurobonds is slightly higher in the fourth scenario (1.9%) than in the third scenario (1.6%). Regarding the levels of public debt, again, European debt in eurobonds is higher in the fourth (20% of GDP) relatively to the third scenario (10% of GDP). Nevertheless, European indebtedness remains sustainable as well as national indebtedness in spite of the fact that national governments have to pay interests on these issued eurobonds.

We now move towards the last scenarios with tax rebate and public expenditures cuts. In scenario 5, the reduction of the social contributions paid by firms partly offsets the effect of overvaluation of the euro for southern countries and their loss of competitiveness. The GDP fall is less pronounced but the balance trade deterioration remains while the public deficit and debt increase a lot, inducing a substantial increase of interest rates (see Figure 5.9). To avoid

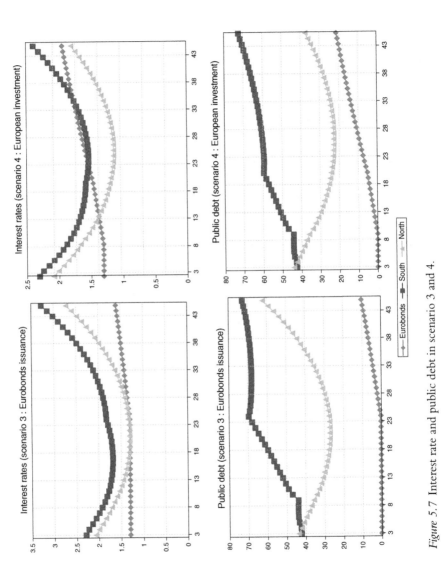

Figure 5.7 Interest rate and public debt in scenario 3 and 4.
Source: Duwicquet et al. (2018).

this unsustainable worsening of the public finance, public expenditures are cut of an amount equivalent to the tax rebate (scenario 6). This limits partly the rise of the public debt and of the interest rate but at the detriment of the GDP growth which returns to the depressed baseline scenario. This strategy of the French CICE uses simultaneously the accelerator and the brake and can have only a limited effect. The initial tax rebate represents a high cost for the public finances without being targeted on the tradable sector, mainly due to European competition rules. The only way of escape would be the success of industrial and innovation policies able to improve at medium term the non-price competitiveness, as it is illustrated in scenario 7. This can be seen as a relevant perspective, but it would face many institutional and political obstacles.

Conclusion

The chapter has analysed in two ways the alternative economic policies that are put forward to overcome the blockages of the euro area: first, the consistency of the different alternatives has been discussed; second, a two-country SFC model of the monetary union has been used to evaluate the macroeconomic impact of these alternatives. Several typical alternative structures have been suggested: reaffirmation of the no bail-out clause for the national governments, fiscal federalism, eurobonds, creation of a Euro Treasury. These alternatives, and some more pragmatic ones, raise many problems and are, in many cases, hardly realistic in political terms.

The simulations with a two-country SFC model of the monetary union have assessed these alternative economic policies and compared them with the current situation of the euro zone. Contrary to what the 'international risk-sharing' approach asserts, the stabilisation effects of portfolio diversification appeared weak and those of intra-zone credit nonexistent in the absence of credit rationing. Intra-zone credit can have a stabilisation effect when non-resident banks, unlike domestic ones, finance without restriction, but this stabilisation remains also limited. When interest rates increase due to the reluctance of the financial markets, intra-zone finance from the rest of the union can have an increasing cost and lead to a cumulative slowdown. On the contrary, the creation of a federal budget, even of a small size around 3% of GDP, but with a redistributive mechanism and federal transfers, could have an efficient stabilising role to face asymmetric evolutions inside a monetary union characterised by huge heterogeneity. A European Unemployment Insurance System could be an illustration of such a mechanism. However the obstacles are numerous, both technical (choice of taxes raised at the federal level, harmonisation of national institutions in order to avoid differentiated effects) and political (there is no will due to the lack of solidarity).

Without the creation of a federal budget the launching of European investments financed by eurobonds could also contribute to reduce the imbalances and lead to a recovery. Investments devoted to the energetic transition and the reduction of the carbon dependency are often mentioned.

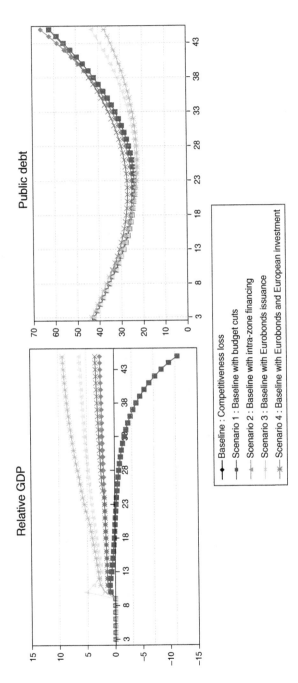

Figure 5.8 Relative GDP and current account in the northern country (competitiveness loss and scenario 1 to 4).

Source: Duwicquet et al. (2018).

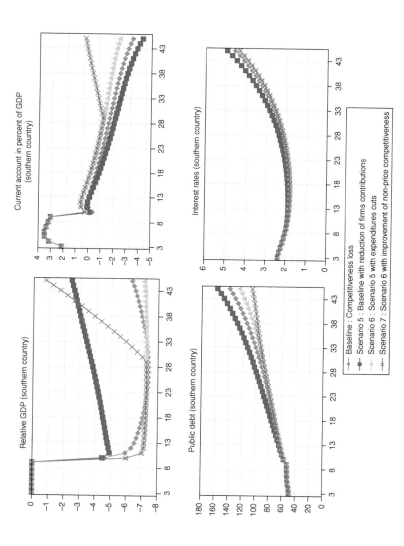

Figure 5.9 Tax rebate and public expenditures cut (scenarios 5 to 7).
Source: Duwicquet et al. (2018).

Investments in infrastructures in new technologies, transports but also education and research are another illustration of programmes which could be defined at the level of the whole European Union. The difficulty is to implement concretely and control such European investments at a large scale in order to have a significant impact at the macro level. Specific programmes of a more limited scale could be more easily proposed but would appear as a kind of extension of what exist already at the European Investments Bank.

The issuance of eurobonds could be used to mutualise the share of public national debts above the threshold of 60% of GDP. It would help to reduce the interest rates and the national debts, especially in the southern countries, with in counterpart a rising European debt. Such a European debt would be useful to define a more balanced monetary policy at the European level. But the eurobonds would not solve the problem of stabilisation, neither the problem of unequal competitiveness of the different countries. Moreover a substantial control of national budgets would be necessary to prevent the risk of slippage in less disciplined countries. This could be obtained whether with a technocratic procedure (a new independent institution) or a democratic one (a new euro zone parliament). In any case the political problems raised by such a transformation could not be underestimated. All this explains that the project of eurobonds seems rather unlikely.

The enlargement of financial support by the northern countries in favour of the southern ones is another possibility. It could be done through the ESM in order to grant loans with lower interest rates to governments facing imbalances. It would contribute to stabilisation, but without reducing sufficiently the level of the national public debts. The results would be all the more limited as the rules of the Stability Pact would impose to reduce more the public debt through budgetary cuts.

On the whole the alternative economic policies are whether unlikely (federal proposal, eurobonds) or hardly feasible (European investments) or with limited impact (eurobonds, northern financial support). The lender of last resort function of the ECB could be enlarged but the acceptance of all national government debts considered as sustainable would need a preventive approach based on fundamentals analysis which would be politically complex to implement. The status of the ECB without the counterpart of a European public debt is difficult to improve.

However the euro zone could survive with marginal ameliorations (plan Juncker bis to stimulate the investments, mini budget of the euro zone reduced to a simple line of a skimpy EU budget) but would remain in a poor shape. The general framework would remain unchanged. The belonging to a monetary union where the single currency is a foreign currency for each country implies the continuation of liberal adjustment policy. National budgetary policies remain under strict control. National public debts exert strong constraints as there is no room for manoeuvre like in the United States with the possibility of intervention of the FED or like in Japan where the outstanding public debt (more than 200% of GDP) is held by domestic agents, mainly the central bank and public financial institutions that reverse to the state the interests they receive. In spite of its weaknesses the euro zone system could resist as, if there are losers, there are also winners, the German block and the European elite. The public debt appears as an efficient weapon to question the social model which was at the heart of many (but not all) European countries. The pension system and the health system are particularly concerned in southern countries like France or Italy. They can be at the source of large public expenditures cuts, reducing the public system to a minimum while opening the rest to private financing for people who can afford it. This project is more coherent than it is sometimes said but can meet resistance that potentially can lead to a burst of the monetary regime. In this perspective a comparison can be made with alternative frameworks where the possibility of intra-European exchange rate adjustments would be reintroduced thanks to a new type of monetary regime.

Annex 5.1 Value of the main parameters

Consumption *Cash* *Tax, social contribution*

a_1	a_2	λ_0	θ	θ_f	θ_b	τ	θ_f^N	θ^N	θ_{Nf}^E	θ_{Nh}^E
0.75	0.04	0.15	0.13	0.35	0.175	0.35	0.35	0.125	0.055	0.10

North households' bonds demand   *South households' bonds demand*

v_0	v_1	v_2	v_3	v_4	v_5	v_0	v_1	v_2	v_3	v_4	v_5
0.047	2	2	0.2	0.1	0.1	0.031	2	2	0.2	0.1	0.1

North households' North equities demand   *North households' South equities demand*

v_0	v_1	v_2	v_3	v_4	v_5	v_0	v_1	v_2	v_3	v_4	v_5
0.476	0.01	0.01	0.2	0.02	0.02	0.213	0.01	0.01	0.2	0.02	0.02

South households' South equities demand   *South households' North equities demand*

v_0	v_1	v_2	v_3	v_4	v_5	v_0	v_1	v_2	v_3	v_4	v_5
0.625	0.01	0.01	0.2	0.02	0.02	0.031	0.01	0.01	0.2	0.02	0.02

Firms' investment   *Depreciation*

k_0^N	k_0^S	k_1^N	k_2^S	k_3^N	k_3^S	k_4^N	k_4^S	k_5^N	k_5^S	δ
0.055	0.057	0.525	0.525	0	0	0.1	0.1	0.375	0.475	0.05

Wage share   *Undistributed profit*

ρ s_f
0.646   0.419

External trade

μ_0^N	μ_0^S	μ_1^N	μ_1^S	μ_2^N	μ_2^S
-1.39	-3	1	1	0.5	0.5

Banks' demand of country S T-bills   *Banks' demand of country N T-bills*

a_{1ss}	a_{2ss}	a_{1ns}	a_{2ns}	a_{3ss}	a_{3ns}	a_{1nn}	a_{2nn}
0.3	1.3	1	1.3	0	0	5	-1.5

Annex 5.2 Sensitivity tests

Sensitivity tests on some crucial parameters.

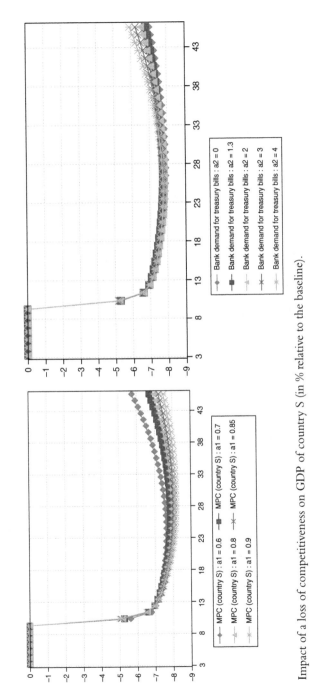

Impact of a loss of competitiveness on GDP of country S (in % relative to the baseline).

Source: Authors' computation.

Demand of Eurobonds

a_{1e} a_{2e}

6.7 –1.33

Interest rate on banks' loans

a

0.1

Government expenditures

a_{g1}

1.018

a_{g2}

0

6 Alternative exchange rate regimes for the euro zone

Jacques Mazier and Sebastian Valdecantos

Introduction

The analysis of the euro zone crisis in the two previous chapters has shown how the reforms often adopted in emergency have brought partial solutions to avoid a break-up. But a deeper transformation of the institutional framework remains necessary. The way of adjusting internal imbalances is still asymmetrical. Deficit countries alone are obliged to adjust. Wage deflation and restrictive policies have replaced exchange rate adjustments and competitive devaluations. The alternative policies have been presented and evaluated. They appeared rather unlikely in the political context or with a limited impact or difficult to implement. Furthermore, these proposals would not solve the real problem, that is, the structural differences that make it impossible for southern countries to compete against the German block at the same nominal exchange rate parity. Adjusting the real exchange rate through the so-called internal devaluations may imply an unacceptable social cost. However, the status quo could prevail with only marginal inflexions and would remain fragile. A last alternative can be explored, a calling into question of the single currency itself, to regain rooms of manoeuvre. The re-introduction of an adjustment of nominal exchange rates within the euro zone may imply a positive competitiveness shock that may help some of the troubled countries. This is the idea of what may be called a multi-speed euro zone which could take two forms.

The first one would be a multiple-euros regime with a global euro acting as an international currency combined with national euros or with a euro zone without the current surplus countries. Thanks to the re-introduction of more flexibility, the countries would be closer to reaching both internal and external equilibrium. The second form would be based on a euro-bancor system inspired by the Keynes' plan of an International Clearing Union to reduce the imbalances (Keynes, 1941). This approach is interesting since, as Cesaratto (2013) and Lavoie (2015) have pointed out, the TARGET2 system that is already in place has many of the features that Keynes imagined during the years that preceded the Bretton-Woods conference.

The aim of this chapter is to examine the different ways in which this reform of the monetary regime could be implemented. To do so, we make use of a four-country SFC model designed to represent the institutional structure of the euro area. In a first section, we explain in detail how each proposal of a multiple-euros regime would work and how the model can be modified to simulate each scenario. We run some simulations aimed at assessing the macroeconomic viability of these potential solutions. In a second section we show how the Keynes' proposal could be adapted to the current setting of the euro area and how it can be represented in the SFC model. Then we present some simulations aimed at examining the performances of each euro-bancor alternative. A last section concludes.

A multiple-euros regime: alternative closures

In this section we present different ways in which the current institutional setting of the euro zone could be reformed in order to yield more sustainable macroeconomic dynamics. We use an SFC model in the lines of the three-country model already presented in Chapter 3. The model is composed of four countries: Germany (representing the surplus countries of the euro area), Spain (representing the deficit countries of the euro area), the United States and the rest of the world. The fourth country has been introduced in the model in order to study other issues such as the future of the international monetary regime or other regional integration process (see Chapters 7 and 8). The institutional agents and the financial assets and liabilities that constitute their balance sheet can be found in Table 6.1. Since we are not coming up with any innovation regarding the behaviour of institutional agents and the general structure of the model, we only give a brief presentation of its main features. The complete description of the model can be found in Mazier and Valdecantos (2014b, 2015).

Table 6.1 The balance sheet of Germany

Households	Firms	Banks	Government	Central Bank	ECB
Hd^{GE}				$-Hs, cb^{GE}$	
Md^{GE}		$-Md^{GE}$			
	K^{GE}				
	$-L^{GE}$	L^{GE}			
		R^{GE}		$-R^{GE}$	
		$-A^{GE}$		A^{GE}	
		Bd, b^{US}_{GE}		Bd, cb^{US}_{GE}	Bd^{US}_{ECB}
		Bd, b^{RW}_{GE}			
		Bd, b^{SP}_{GE}			Bd^{SP}_{ECB}
		Bd, b^{GE}_{GE}	$-Bs^{GE}$	Bd, cb^{GE}_{GE}	Bd^{GE}_{ECB}
$-Vh^{GE}$	$-Vf^{GE}$	$-Vb^{GE}$	$-Vg^{GE}$	$-Vcb^{GE}$	$-V_{ECB}$

Source: Authors' construction.

Each national economy is composed of households, firms, government, commercial banks and a central bank. Households distribute their wealth (V_h) into two types of assets: cash (H) and banking deposits (M). They earn wages (W) and interests ($r_d M_{-1}$) and pay taxes (T_h). They follow a traditional consumption function that depends of disposable income and a wealth effect. Firms accumulate fixed capital (K) and finance their investment (I) through profits (P_f) and loans provided by the banks (L). The wage share and prices are assumed to be constant. Firms can obtain all the credit demanded without rationing. Commercial banks define the structure of their portfolio according to a Tobinesque equation that states that the demand for each type of bonds (domestic and foreign) is a function of their relative return. Banks are required to hold a certain proportion of deposits under the form of reserves (R) at the central bank. Banks' make profits (P_b) out of two sources: interest earnings/payments and valuation effects due to exchange rate movements. The totality of the banks' profits is transferred to the government under the form of taxes. If, at the end of the day, banks lack the funds to back up the stock of deposits with the required amount of reserves, they can get advances (A) from the central bank. The short-term interest rate (r) is constant and fixed by the central bank. The long-term interest rate (r_b) is also kept constant. Government finances its public expenditures (G) and interest payments on its debt ($r_b B_{-1}$) through taxes (T) paid by households, firms and banks. In case the financing needs are positive, the government may fill the gap by issuing bonds (B). Rather strong assumptions have been made in some cases. More realistic specifications can be found in other papers with credit rationing (Duwicquet and Mazier, 2012) or with endogenous long-term rate of interest in the two-country SFC model of the EMU of Chapter 5. These specifications have not been introduced in order to keep the model more manageable and focused on the question of alternative multiple-euro regimes.

The main difference with the previous models is that the portfolio decision regarding how many bonds to buy from each government is attributed to commercial banks of each country instead of households, which seems closer to reality. However, this has no impact on the results of the simulation, mainly because in our model commercial banks are rather passive. This may not be the case if we dealt with the dynamics associated to financialization. Another difference with the model of the monetary union of Chapter 5 can also be underlined. As we introduce the possibility of exchange rate adjustments inside the euro zone, intra-European exchange rates are no more constant and their determination has to be explained. Furthermore, we take into account the relations with the United States and the rest of the world and the exchange rates of the euro and of the European currencies against the dollar become an important issue.

The notation of the financial assets (Bd, cb_{SP}^{US} for example) is the standard notation used in these models. The superscript (US) stands for the country issuing the bond, the subscript (SP) for the country holding the bond. The subscript (d) corresponds to the demand of the bond measured in the currency of the country holding the bond, the subscript (s) to the supply measured in the currency of the issuing country (Bs, b_{US}^{SP} for another example). The last subscripts (b or cb) stand for the institution (commercial bank or central bank) holding the bond. For the sake of simplicity, the size of the four countries is identical. The differences lay in the equations that had to be modified in order to represent the alternative closures that describe each of the proposals for the reform of the euro area into a multi-speed system. The value of the main parameters is given in Annex 6.1.

We begin by a baseline closure of the euro area with the single currency corresponding to the current situation. Then, we consider three exchange rate regimes. The first one combines a global euro which is preserved and national (or regional) euros in each country which are introduced. The second one is a simple return to the European Monetary System where the euro is no more an international currency but a simple unit of account (the former ECU) with national currencies in each country. The third one corresponds to a euro zone which is preserved in the south, but with an exit of the surplus countries of the north.

A baseline closure of the euro area

The following expressions are used for the exchange rates that are presented in the following closures: 1\$ = E1 GE, which is the German euro/dollar exchange rate, 1\$ = E2 SP, which is the Spanish euro/dollar exchange rate. From these definitions we can derive the Spanish euro/German euro exchange rate E3 = E2/E1 (1GE = E3 SP). However, under the current setting there are no specific exchange rates for Spain and Germany as they are engaged in a fixed exchange rate arrangement, the euro zone. Thus, E1 = E2 and E3 =1. Since the European Central Bank (ECB) allows the euro to float freely, the euro/dollar exchange rate will adjust for any imbalances between the supply and demand for bonds denominated in euros (eqs. (1)–(2)). The balance sheet of each national central bank is equilibrated through central bank purchases/sales of domestic bonds (eqs. (3)–(4)). These equations suggest that the national central banks intervene in domestic bond markets which could have been suspected as monetary financing prior to the start of the quantitative easing. This has been debated a lot and is not contrary to the rules of the ECB (Godley and Lavoie, 2007b). The euro government deficits can be financed indirectly by the ECB and the euro system which is, de facto, not different from a direct financing. As neither Spain nor Germany is engaged in a fixed exchange rate arrangement, there is no reserve accumulation (eqs. (5)–(6)), the only possible change in foreign reserves may be due to valuation effects when reserves are expressed in euros (eqs. (7)–(8)). We assume that the rest of the world fixes its currency to the dollar. Hence the domestic bond market is equilibrated through interventions of the domestic central bank. The equilibrium in the balance sheet of the central bank of the rest of the world is ensured by the purchases/sales of foreign reserves (which are necessary to keep the exchange rate fixed).

Finally, the central bank of US purchases/sells domestic bonds to ensure the equilibrium in the domestic bond market. The balance sheet identity of the central bank of the United States is the redundant equation.

$$E1_t = E2_t = \frac{\begin{array}{c} Bs_t^{GE} + Bs_t^{SP} - Bs, b_{SP_t}^{GE} - Bs, b_{RW_t}^{GE} - Bs, b_{GE_t}^{SP} - Bs, b_{RW_t}^{SP} - Bd, b_{GE_t}^{GE} - \\ Bd, b_{SP_t}^{SP} - Bd, cb_{SP_t}^{SP} - Bd, cb_{GE_t}^{GE} - Bd_{ECB_t}^{GE} - Bd_{ECB_t}^{SP} \end{array}}{Bd, b_{US_t}^{GE} + Bd, b_{US_t}^{SP}}$$

$$(1\text{-}2)$$

$$\Delta Bs, cb_{SP}^{SP} = \Delta R^{SP} + \Delta H^{SP} - \Delta A^{SP} - \Delta Bd, cb_{SP}^{US} \tag{3}$$

$$\Delta Bs, cb_{GE}^{GE} = \Delta R^{GE} + \Delta H^{GE} - \Delta A^{GE} - \Delta Bd, cb_{GE}^{US} \tag{4}$$

$$Bs, cb_{SP}^{US} = \overline{Bs, cb_{SP}^{US}} \tag{5}$$

$$Bs, cb_{GE}^{US} = \overline{Bs, cb_{GE}^{US}} \tag{6}$$

$$\Delta Bd, cb_{SP}^{US} = Bs, cb_{SP_{-1}}^{US} . \Delta E2 + \Delta Bs, cb_{SP}^{US} . E2 \tag{7}$$

$$\Delta Bd, cb_{GE}^{US} = Bs, cb_{GE_{-1}}^{US} . \Delta E1 + \Delta Bs, cb_{GE}^{US} . E1 \tag{8}$$

We present only the essential features of the euro regime. The TARGET2 balances are not explicitly described in this version of the current institutional setting. This question will be developed more in detail in the next section. We assume also that the balance sheet of the ECB is constant over time. It could be modified in order to study more precisely the relations between the ECB and the national central banks, without changing the main results of the model. In the next subsections, we show how this simple structure can be changed to model how the different exchange rate arrangements that have been put forward could work.

A euro zone combining a global euro and regional euros

As shown in Chapter 4, there are reasons to think that the introduction of the euro worked as a source of real exchange rate misalignments within the euro area. If we consider this a reasonable argument, then it makes sense to examine what would happen if these misalignments were reduced. This would not require that each country regained its monetary and exchange rate policy, but that the euro zone split into two blocks, each of them gathering countries that are more or less similar. For instance, it seems more reasonable that Portugal shares a common exchange rate with Greece than with Germany or Finland. Thus, what we propose in this sub-section is a scenario where there are two regional euros, each of them associated to a certain sub-region within the euro zone (we keep the classification where Spain represents the deficit countries while Germany represents the surplus countries). Moreover, there would also be a global euro aimed at supporting the role of the current euro in financial markets as an international store of value.

The exchange rate of the global euro vis-à-vis the US dollar would be determined, as usual, as a result of the interaction between supply and demand for euro-denominated bonds (eq. (9)). We call the global euro/dollar exchange rate E9, in order to keep E1 and E2 as the exchange rates between Germany and Spain vis-à-vis the United States. Unlike the current setting of the euro area, where Spain and Germany only issue bonds denominated in euros, in this case we assume that the issuances to foreign creditors are denominated in global euros (for instance, $Bs, b_{GE_t}^{SP, €}$ is the supply of Spanish bonds in global euros to German banks) whereas domestic banks purchase domestic bonds denominated in national currency ($Bs, b_{SP_t}^{SP,SP}$) . Moreover, we keep the assumption that the ECB holds a certain pre-existing stock of German and Spanish bonds, which are denominated in global euros.

$$E9_t = \frac{Bs_t^{GE,€} + Bs_t^{SP,€} - Bd, b_{SP_t}^{GE,€} - Bd, b_{RW_t}^{GE,€} - Bd, b_{GE_t}^{SP,€} - Bd, b_{RW_t}^{SP,€} - Bd_{ECB_t}^{GE,€} - Bd_{ECB_t}^{SP,€}}{Bd, b_{US_t}^{GE,€} + Bd, b_{US_t}^{SP,€}} \quad (9)$$

As the government debt could be denominated in national euros, in this institutional framework each sub-region would regain its monetary sovereignty. As mentioned before, the only institutional agent that can purchase domestic bonds in local currency are the home banks. But it should be born in mind that those countries that do not issue reserve currencies (like the national euros would be) might encounter limits to get external financing by issuing bonds denominated in domestic currency. In those cases, the gap between the financing needs (B_t^{SP}, for instance) and the total demand for bonds denominated in domestic currency (Bd, b_{SP}^{SP}) is filled with issuances of bonds denominated in a reserve currency. In this case, should there be any gap, it would be filled with issues of bonds denominated in global euros ($Bs_t^{SP,€}$). These supplies are the ones that enter equation (9). Since the total supply of bonds in each country is expressed in domestic currency (either Spanish or German euros), it is required to transform this stock of debt into global euros. To do so, we divide by the bilateral exchange rate of Spanish and German euros to global euros (E7 and E8, respectively, which are defined in eqs. (12)–(13)).

$$Bs_t^{GE,\epsilon} = \frac{Bs_t^{GE} - Bs, b_{GE_t}^{GE} - Bs, cb_{GE_t}^{GE}}{E7_t} \qquad (10)$$

$$Bs_t^{SP,\epsilon} = \frac{Bs_t^{SP} - Bs, b_{SP_t}^{SP} - Bs, cb_{SP_t}^{SP}}{E8_t} \qquad (11)$$

The multi-speed feature of this model implies that Germany and Spain can have adjustable exchange rates according to their external performance vis-à-vis their regional trading partner. Thus, we define the Spanish euro/global euro and German euro/global euro exchange rate based on the intra-European current account (CA). We have chosen this variable as the criterion determining the intra-European exchange rate since it reflects the overall performance of the Spanish (German) external sector vis-à-vis the German (Spanish) counterpart. The criterion consists of keeping exchange rates fixed as long as the intra-European current account is in surplus or, if in deficit, only for a certain period of time. We base this criterion on the fact that in principle a country cannot accumulate persistent balance of payments deficits indefinitely. In practice, it has been observed that deficit countries in the euro area have accumulated persistent negative stocks of TARGET2 balances. From our point of view, the crisis itself and the austerity policies that have been implemented in deficit countries thereafter are a sign that show that the euro system is not willing to finance deficits on a permanent basis. If a bad external performance yields a balance of payments deficit for five consecutive periods, then the national currency is adjusted. Once these intra-European exchange rates have been defined, it is also possible to derive the exchange rates vis-à-vis the dollar (eqs. (14)–(15)) as well as the bilateral exchange rate between Spain and Germany (eq. (16)).

$$E7_t = \begin{cases} E7_{t-1} & if \dfrac{CA_{SP_{t-i}}^{GE}}{Y_{t-i}^{SP}} \geq 0 \quad \forall i = 1,2,3,4,5 \\[4mm] E7_{t-1}\cdot(1+\pi) & if \dfrac{CA_{SP_{t-i}}^{GE}}{Y_{t-i}^{SP}} < 0 \quad \forall i = 1,2,3,4,5 \end{cases} \qquad (12)$$

$$E8_t = \begin{cases} E8_{t-1} & if \dfrac{CA_{GE_{t-i}}^{SP}}{Y_{t-i}^{GE}} \geq 0 \quad \forall i = 1,2,3,4,5 \\[4mm] E8_{t-1}\cdot(1+\pi) & if \dfrac{CA_{GE_{t-i}}^{SP}}{Y_{t-i}^{GE}} < 0 \quad \forall i = 1,2,3,4,5 \end{cases} \qquad (13)$$

$$E1_t = E8_t.E9_t \tag{14}$$

$$E2_t = E7_t.E9_t \tag{15}$$

$$E3_t = E2_t / E1_t \tag{16}$$

As Spain and Germany are now engaged in a fixed (but adjustable) exchange rate arrangement where bilateral nominal exchange rates indeed exist (unlike in the current situation, where there are no nominal exchange rates within the euro zone), national central banks must intervene in the foreign exchange markets in order to ensure that the parity holds over time. These interventions are carried out via purchases/sales of foreign reserves. We make the assumption that both countries accumulate these reserves under the form of dollar-denominated bonds issued by the United States. As it is normal in stock–flow consistent models with fixed exchange rates, the central bank intervention that keeps the exchange rate constant is such that its balance sheet identity holds at every point of time (eqs. (17)–(18)). Then, the process of reserve accumulation needs to take into account the possible valuation effects that result from exchange rate movements (eqs. (19)–(20)).

$$\Delta Bs, cb_{SP_t}^{US} = \frac{\Delta R_t^{SP} + \Delta H_t^{SP} - \Delta A_t^{SP} - \Delta Bs, cb_{SP_t}^{SP}}{E2_t} \tag{17}$$

$$\Delta Bs, cb_{GE_t}^{US} = \frac{\Delta R_t^{GE} + \Delta H_t^{GE} - \Delta A_t^{GE} - \Delta Bs, cb_{GE_t}^{GE}}{E1_t} \tag{18}$$

$$\Delta Bd, cb_{SP_t}^{US} = Bs, cb_{SP_{t-1}}^{US}.\Delta E2_t + \Delta Bs, cb_{SP_t}^{US}.E2_t \tag{19}$$

$$\Delta Bd, cb_{GE_t}^{US} = Bs, cb_{GE_{t-1}}^{US}.\Delta E1_t + \Delta Bs, cb_{GE_t}^{US}.E1_t \tag{20}$$

These equations ensure that the model is consistent. With regard to the ECB, no changes are introduced with respect to the model described in the previous section since, as described above, we are not allowing for the interventions that it could eventually make. In the next section we will run some simulation experiments in order to assess the economic viability of this proposal.

A return to the European Monetary System (EMS)

In a similar line to the one proposed in the previous scenario, the ideas embedded in the EMS could be taken up in order to give the euro area a higher degree of stability. The proposal would consist of a split-up of the euro zone into two sub-regions (as we did in the previous case) but, instead of keeping a global euro that would be used as an international currency, there would be a European Currency Unit (ECU) that would only play the role of being a unit of account. As it did in the past, it would be the reference to which the national currencies are pegged. Hence, the ECU could be written as follows (eq. (21)), where β represents the share of Germany in total output of the euro area:

$$\frac{1}{E9_t} = \beta \cdot \frac{1}{E1_t} + (1 - \beta) \cdot \frac{1}{E2_t} \tag{21}$$

The way that the ECU is constructed implies that it is a basket currency constituted partly by the German currency and partly by the Spanish currency. It is expressed in ECUs with respect to units of US dollars, that is, $1\$ = E9$ ECU. The determination of each European currency vis-à-vis the ECU would be the same as the one described in the previous scenario and would depend on the external performance of each country (eqs. (22)–(23), which are identical to eqs. (12)–(13)). However, even if Spain and Germany's currencies were pegged to the ECU, they would float against the US dollar. This implies that the bilateral nominal exchange rate could adjust in such a way that the domestic bond market is in equilibrium (eqs. (24)–(25)). With regard to the exchange rates of the Spanish currency against the US dollar and the German currency, they can be deduced from the other exchange rates (eq. (26)).

$$E7_t = \begin{cases} E7_{t-1} & \text{if } \dfrac{CA_{t-i}^{SP}}{Y_{t-i}^{SP}} \geq 0 \quad \forall\, i = 1,2,3,4,5 \\[2em] E7_{t-1} \cdot (1 + \pi) & \text{if } \dfrac{CA_{t-i}^{SP}}{Y_{t-i}^{SP}} < 0 \quad \forall\, i = 1,2,3,4,5 \end{cases} \tag{22}$$

$$E8_t = \begin{cases} E8_{t-1} & \text{if } \dfrac{CA_{t-i}^{GE}}{Y_{t-i}^{GE}} \geq 0 \quad \forall\, i = 1,2,3,4,5 \\[2em] E8_{t-1} \cdot (1 + \pi) & \text{if } \dfrac{CA_{t-i}^{GE}}{Y_{t-i}^{GE}} < 0 \quad \forall\, i = 1,2,3,4,5 \end{cases} \tag{23}$$

$$E1_t = \frac{Bs_t^{GE} - Bs, b_{GE_t}^{GE} - Bs, cb_{GE_t}^{GE} - Bs, b_{SP_t}^{GE} - Bs, b_{RW_t}^{GE}}{Bd, b_{US_t}^{GE}} \qquad (24)$$

$$E2_t = E1_t.E3_t \qquad (25)$$

$$E3_t = E7_t/E8_t \qquad (26)$$

The adjustment of E1 ensures that the German bond market is always cleared. It is also important to note that this closure implies that the changes in E1 and E2 are such that E3 is constant. This must me the case, since this institutional arrangement of the EMS that we are examining implies that intra-European parities are fixed. Hence, if the movements of E1 and E2 were such that E3 changed continuously, the definition E3 = E7/E8 would be violated. Given that E2 is being determined endogenously by the other exchange rates in order to ensure consistency between all exchange rates, it cannot adjust in such a way that the Spanish bond market is in equilibrium. It is the Spanish central bank which, via its purchases/sales of domestic bonds, clears the bond market (eq. (27)). Finally, since the central banks of Spain and Germany are engaged in a fixed exchange rate arrangement with respect to the ECU, they intervene in the foreign exchange markets via purchases/sales of foreign reserves as in the previous scenarios (eqs. (28)–(31) are identical to eqs. (17)–(20)).

$$Bd, cb_{SP_t}^{SP} = Bs_t^{SP} - Bs, b_{SP_t}^{SP} - Bs, b_{US_t}^{SP} - Bs, b_{GE_t}^{SP} - Bs, b_{RW_t}^{SP} \qquad (27)$$

$$\Delta Bs, cb_{SP_t}^{US} = \frac{\Delta R_t^{SP} + \Delta H_t^{SP} - \Delta A_t^{SP} - \Delta Bs, cb_{SP_t}^{SP}}{E2_t} \qquad (28)$$

$$\Delta Bs, cb_{GE_t}^{US} = \frac{\Delta R_t^{GE} + \Delta H_t^{GE} - \Delta A_t^{GE} - \Delta Bs, cb_{GE_t}^{GE}}{E1_t} \qquad (29)$$

$$\Delta Bd, cb_{SP_t}^{US} = Bs, cb_{SP_{t-1}}^{US}.\Delta E2_t + \Delta Bs, cb_{SP_t}^{US}.E2_t \qquad (30)$$

$$\Delta Bd, cb_{GE_t}^{US} = Bs, cb_{GE_{t-1}}^{US}.\Delta E1_t + \Delta Bs, cb_{GE_t}^{US}.E1_t \qquad (31)$$

A euro zone without the current surplus countries

One of the alternatives that has been put forward, is a situation in which Germany leaves the euro zone and lets its currency float, while the remaining European countries keep the euro, which could either be pegged to the German currency or float freely. The examination of this alternative does not require many changes with respect to the set up that we presented in the previous scenarios. First, it is required to delete the notion of the global euro or the ECU, E9, and its associated exchange rates E7 and E8. Second, the German currency/dollar exchange rate, E1, which in the case of the global euro combined with regional euros, was defined implicitly using E8 and E9, can now be defined explicitly as the ratio of the supply of German bonds to the United States and the demand for German bonds by the United States (as we did in the EMS scenario). Finally, what we called the Spanish currency/German currency exchange rate, E3, can be now be called euro/German currency exchange rate and could either be pegged or float freely. Let us first analyse the case where the euro is pegged to the German currency (1 GE = E3 euro).

$$E1_t = \frac{Bs_t^{GE} - Bs, b_{GE_t}^{GE} - Bs, cb_{GE_t}^{GE} - Bs, b_{SP_t}^{GE} - Bs, b_{RW_t}^{GE}}{Bd, b_{US_t}^{GE}} \tag{32}$$

$$E3_t = \begin{cases} E3_{t-1} & if \ \dfrac{CA_{SP_{t-i}}^{GE} + FA_{SP_{t-i}}^{GE}}{Y_{t-i}^{SP}} \geq 0 \quad \forall i = 1,2,3,4,5 \\[4mm] E3_{t-1} \cdot (1+\pi) & if \ \dfrac{CA_{SP_{t-i}}^{GE} + FA_{SP_{t-i}}^{GE}}{Y_{t-i}^{SP}} < 0 \quad \forall i = 1,2,3,4,5 \end{cases} \tag{33}$$

This new setting requires some small changes in the closure of the model. Basically, the German central bank would no longer purchase foreign assets since there is no exchange rate to be defended. Thus, its balance sheet would be closed through purchases/sales of domestic bonds (eq. (35)). Since the exchange rate would be floating, the domestic bond market would be cleared in the process of the determination of the exchange rate (eq. (32)). With regard to the central bank of Spain, there would be no major changes since its exchange rate would still be fixed. Thus, the monetary authority would keep on purchasing/selling US bonds in such a way that the exchange rate is fixed at every point of time (eq. (34)).

$$\Delta Bs, cb_{SP_t}^{US} = \frac{\Delta R_t^{SP} + \Delta H_t^{SP} - \Delta A_t^{SP} - \Delta Bs, cb_{SP_t}^{SP}}{E2_t} \tag{34}$$

$$\Delta Bs, cb_{GE_t}^{GE} = \Delta R_t^{GE} + \Delta H_t^{GE} - \Delta A_t^{GE} \tag{35}$$

$$\Delta Bd, cb_{SP_t}^{US} = Bs, cb_{SP_{t-1}}^{US}.\Delta E2_t + \Delta Bs, cb_{SP_t}^{US}.E2_t \tag{36}$$

Another way in which this alternative institutional framework could be introduced is one in which instead of being fixed, the euro floats against both the German currency and the US dollar. This alternative should ensure that every external imbalance is automatically corrected via exchange rate adjustments, thereby releasing the central bank from the task of accumulating reserves in order to defend an exchange rate. The drawback of this scenario is that one of the main reasons why the euro was introduced, to avoid the permanent fluctuations of intra-European exchange rates, with the associated adverse effects on international trade, would not be fulfilled. However, all the countries that stay in the Eurozone would still be having a fixed exchange rate arrangement (since they would share the same currency), which means that at least between them the benefits of a stable exchange rate on international trade would still be reaped. Adapting the model to this possible alternative is quite simple. We just need to let the euro/German currency exchange rate, E3, float. In this case, the euro-bond market would be automatically cleared via exchange rate movements and the central bank would ensure the equilibrium in its balance sheet through purchases/sales of domestic bonds. The rest of model would be closed as in the fixed exchange rate case.

To summarize the different proposals that we have been presenting, Table 6.2 describes how each of the equations implicit on the crucial roles and columns of the flow of funds would be satisfied. The first three columns describe which variable ensures the equilibrium in the market of Spanish, German, and European bond markets. The last two columns show which asset adjusts in such a way that the balance sheet identity of the central banks of Spain and Germany holds at every point of time.

Table 6.2 Alternative closures of the model

Model	B^{SP}	B^{GE}	B^{EZ}	CB^{SP}	CB^{GE}
Current setting	$E1 = E2$	$E1 = E2$	–	Bd, cb_{SP}^{SP}	Bd, cb_{GE}^{GE}
Multiple euros	Bd, b_{SP}^{SP}	Bd, b_{GE}^{GE}	$E9$	Bd, cb_{SP}^{SP}	Bd, cb_{GE}^{GE}
EMS	Bd, cb_{SP}^{SP}	$E1$	–	Bd, cb_{SP}^{US}	Bd, cb_{GE}^{US}
Without surplus (fixed)	Bd, cb_{SP}^{SP}	$E1$	–	Bd, cb_{SP}^{US}	Bd, cb_{GE}^{GE}
Without surplus (flexible)	$E3$	$E1$	–	Bd, cb_{SP}^{SP}	Bd, cb_{GE}^{GE}

Source: Authors' construction.

Assessing the viability of a multiple-euros regime

After presenting several alternatives in which a multiple-euros regime could work, the aim of this sub-section is to present a comparative analysis of the different scenarios after a negative competitiveness shock in Spain (which is due to the overvaluation of the euro for the Spanish economy and its undervaluation for the German economy, in line with the evidence shown in Chapter 4).

The current euro zone system

The adoption of the euro by Spain and the fixity of intra-European exchange rates implied, as mentioned before, a loss of competitiveness due to a whole set of structural factors (housing bubble, debt-led growth, decline of non-price-competitiveness due to weak gains of productivity in Spain, wage deflation in Germany). This can be represented in our model through an increase in the autonomous component of Spain's imports equation and a decrease in the same component of German imports. This shock has a direct effect on the trade balance (see Figure 6.1). As it was observed during the years that preceded the crisis, the lack of self-correcting mechanisms prevented the Spanish economy from reaching the long-term external equilibrium. As a result, persistent current account deficits started to accumulate, which in turn implied an increase in the stock of debt, in some cases, like Greece, the debt was mostly public, whereas in other cases, like Spain, the debt was issued by the private sector.

The impact on the exchange rate of the euro against the dollar is null (see Figures 6.2 and 6.3), as what is lost by Spain is gained by Germany, thereby leaving the overall current account of the euro zone unaffected. The determination of the euro–dollar exchange rate is explained by factors that concern Spain and Germany together. In the case of a small open economy that issues its own currency, following some years of current account deficits the exchange rate would depreciate. But the particular configuration of the euro zone prevented this from happening, since the current account deficits of the south were compensated by the surpluses of the north. In fact, most of these imbalances were internal and were compensated by financial flows going from the north to the south. The recessive impact of the loss of competitiveness in Spain can be observed in Figure 6.4, which plots Spain's GDP in national currency. As a result of the deterioration of the trade balance Spain's GDP drops by 1% and does not recover since there are no mechanisms that allow for a reversal of the recessionary impact of the loss of competitiveness. This produces a negative effect on the level of employment, investment, and aggregate demand.

The multiple-euros scenario

The first proposal is one in which national currencies are restored and coexist with the euro. The advantage of this setting is that each country (or group of countries, which would be grouped according to their economic structure)

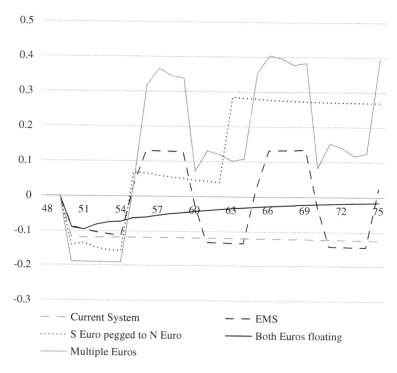

Figure 6.1 Trade balance of Spain (US dollars).
Source: Mazier and Valdecantos (2015).

would have more degrees of freedom to conduct its fiscal and monetary policy. This gain of economic sovereignty would not come at the cost of destroying the achievements of the process of economic integration that took place during the last decades. In other words, the benefits of the unification would be kept, while the drawbacks would be replaced for newly designed institutions.

The negative impact of the competitiveness shock on Spain's GDP can be observed in Figure 6.4, most of which is explained by the deterioration of the trade balance (see Figure 6.1). Figure 6.5 shows that the effect is the opposite in Germany, that is, the trade balance goes into surplus, which in turn increases the rate of growth. Since the positive impact in Germany is neutralized by the negative effect in Spain, there is no impact in the rate of growth of the global economy. Thus, the global euro remains unchanged vis-à-vis the US dollar.

However, the negative competitiveness shock implies that Spain starts to accumulate current account deficits. After five consecutive periods of deficits, the Spanish currency is devalued against the global euro. This adjustment is also observed in the exchange rate vis-à-vis the US dollar (see Figure 6.2).

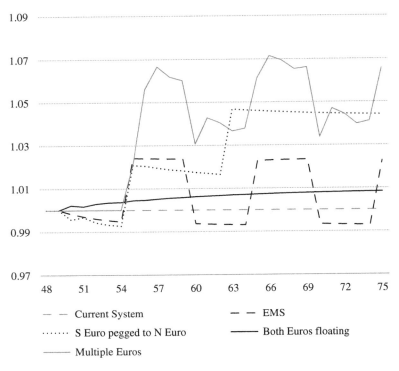

Figure 6.2 Spanish currency against US dollar.
Source: Mazier and Valdecantos (2015).

This devaluation restores Spain's competitiveness, bringing the trade balance into surplus and the growth rate to a positive path. As a result of the higher level of activity, the government starts running a surplus, which implies that the supply of bonds decreases (since the financing needs of the Treasury decrease). This lower supply of bonds denominated in euros translates into an appreciated global euro (recall eq. (9)), which also appreciates the German currency (recall that the German currency is pegged to the global euro).

The adjustment of the Spanish currency erodes Germany's competitiveness to such an extent that some periods later the German currency needs to be devalued (according to eq. (13)). This improves Germany's trade balance but worsens that of Spain. As a result, after some periods the Spanish currency is devalued once again. These dynamics are repeated infinitely. This implies that this setting does not produce stable results over time.

In an extended version of this model (Mazier and Valdecantos, 2014b) we tried out different adjustment criteria for equations (12)–(13). In some cases, instead of setting the adjustment threshold equal to a 0% deficit, we allow for small deficits. This modification helps to stabilize the dynamics, but such a scenario could not last too much since it would imply a continuous loss of foreign reserves. We also set an alternative adjustment criterion that states that the exchange rate is kept fixed as long as the stock of reserves is positive. In this case, balance of payments deficits can persist depending on the initial stock of foreign reserves.

The EMS scenario

In the EMS scenario Spain has the capacity to devalue its currency against the ECU (and hence to the German currency) after some periods of accumulating current account deficits. Figure 6.2 shows that the immediate impact of the competitiveness shock is such that the Spanish currency appreciates. At first sight, this would seem counterintuitive since Spain is running a trade and current account deficit. However, it should be noted that the shock has an overall positive effect on global economic growth, thereby increasing the wealth of the private sector of all the countries except for Spain. As a result, portfolio investment increases, including the demand for bonds issued by the Spanish government. As long as the financial account surplus resulting from the demand for Spanish assets is larger than the current account deficit that arises from the loss of competitiveness, the exchange rate will appreciate. This is, indeed, what explains the downward movement of the exchange rate that is observed between periods 50 and 54. A similar behaviour is observed for the case of the German currency.

According to the institutional setting of this model, Spain is allowed to devalue its currency against the ECU if it registers five consecutive periods of balance of payments deficits. Hence, in period 55 a devaluation of 2% vis-à-vis the ECU is introduced. This gain of competitiveness against Germany improves its trade surplus (see Figure 6.1), thereby inducing an increase in the domestic level of activity (see Figure 6.4). With regard to Germany, the appreciation of its currency vis-à-vis the Spanish currency erodes its competitiveness, thereby reducing its trade, current account, and fiscal surpluses. As a consequence, the German government increases the supply of bonds (or reduces the pace at which bonds are withdrawn from the market, in the case the government is running a surplus), which is reflected in a slight depreciation of the German currency (see Figure 6.3). The global appreciation of the dollar that results from these movements ends up bringing about a larger devaluation of the Spanish currency vis-à-vis the US dollar, compared to the devaluation against the German currency(see Figures 6.2 and 6.3)

The main conclusion that is drawn from this experiment is that in a context in which Spain is allowed to devalue its currency with respect to the ECU (and hence, to the German currency as well) the initial loss of competitiveness can be easily corrected, thereby preventing first a process of unsustainable current account deficits financed by financial account surpluses and, more importantly, the recessionary effect that the trade deficit may have on the level of activity

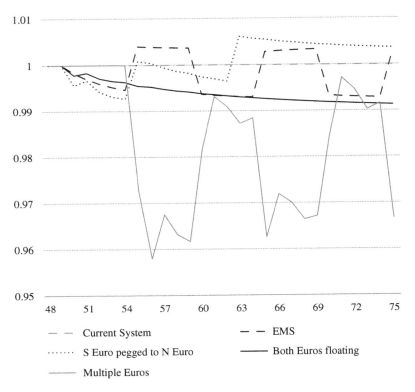

Figure 6.3 German currency against US dollar.
Source: Mazier and Valdecantos (2015).

and employment. Another point that it is worth making is the instability of such a monetary regime. As it is observed in the figures, imposing an adjustment criterion on the exchange rate that is based on the bilateral performance of the current account is prone to generating cycles of continuous devaluations of the intra-European parities. During the times of the EMS, this was considered a drawback of the system, mainly because of the difficulties that imposes on international trade.

The euro zone without Germany scenario

There are, in principle, two relevant experiments to be tested: one in which the euro is pegged to the German currency and another in which both currencies float. If the euro is pegged to the German currency, after having accumulated five consecutive balance of payments deficits Spain is allowed to devalue its currency 2%. It should be noted that in this case there is a slightly larger appreciation of the European currencies after the shock and before the adjustment of the Spanish currency. This is explained by the fact that in the present scenario the shock produces a relatively higher growth effect in Germany (compared to the EMS scenario), which in turn improves the German fiscal balance (due to increased tax collection). As a result, the supply of bonds decreases. In a context where both the United States and the rest of the world are growing and exhibiting an increasing stock of wealth, there will be an excess demand for German bonds. This disequilibrium is solved through an appreciation of the German currency, which is larger than in the EMS scenario since public finances are better in the current case. With regard to the euro, since it is pegged to the German currency, it will follow the trajectory of the latter.

The evolution of the rest of the variables (GDP, trade balance, and public debt) until the adjustment that takes place in period 55 is the same as the one observed in the EMS scenario. Once the Spanish currency is devalued, a positive effect on the trade balance (see Figure 6.1) and economic growth (see Figure 6.4) is observed. It should be noted that, following the expansion brought

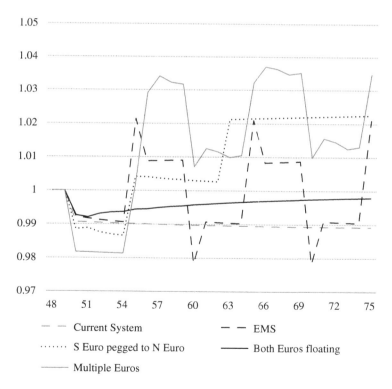

Figure 6.4 GDP of Spain (national currency).
Source: Mazier and Valdecantos (2015).

about by the devaluation, there is a contraction of GDP. This is explained by the positive income effect on imports, which slightly erodes the trade balance. After this adjustment has been made, Spain's overall trade balance is in surplus but deteriorating. However, the bilateral trade balance with Germany is in deficit. From this situation, it could be deduced that a 2% devaluation is not enough to bring the intra-European exchanges rates back to equilibrium. Thus, in period 63, a new devaluation is introduced, after which the same effects that had occurred after period 55 take place. The only difference is that in this case the new exchange rate parity is sufficient to restore Spain's initial competitiveness. No more adjustments take place.

Compared to the two previous scenarios, the case where Germany leaves the euro zone and the remaining countries are pegged to the German currency seems to provide the whole system with a higher level of stability and sustainability in the medium-long run. Moreover, as shown in Figure 6.5, this higher stability in the south does not come at the cost of a recession in Germany, which exhibits a lower level of growth with respect to the baseline scenario, but positive growth still. The conclusion that can be drawn from this exercise is that a situation in which Germany leaves the euro zone and the south is allowed to adjust its currency to a level that is more consistent with its external equilibrium can be beneficial for all: the south would not find itself immersed in a long-lasting recession with associated high levels of unemployment and Germany would grow at a slower pace but it would avoid the politically uncomfortable subsidizing of troubled countries. Compared to a pure fiscal union or a scenario where Germany finances the bail-out of the deficit countries, the institutional setting that was described in these simulations would also save Germany significant fiscal burdens.

Finally, we can examine the last institutional setting where Germany leaves the euro zone and the euro (now the currency of Spain) floats freely. As Figure 6.2 shows, soon after the competitiveness shock the euro starts to depreciate as a result of the current account deficits. The opposite behaviour is observed in the case of the German currency. As it may be intuited, an exchange rate arrangement where everything floats freely is prone to produce situations where the variables return to equilibrium. This is indeed what happens, since the initial trade deficit of Spain is progressively corrected as the euro depreciates. Eventually, the trade balance reaches equilibrium and the exchange rate stabilizes.

To sum up, a four-country SFC model that represents the euro zone has been used to examine the hypothetical scenario of a split-up of the euro into different possible institutional settings, each of them consistent with the equilibrium exchange rate of the corresponding sub-regions. Our simulations show under which conditions such an institutional framework could work. We find that there are different alternatives to solve the causes that explain the external fragility to which southern countries were exposed and that finally materialized under the form of the euro zone crisis. A multiple-euros framework combining

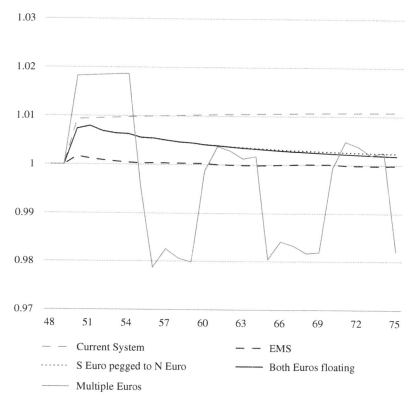

Figure 6.5 GDP of Germany (national currency).
Source: Mazier and Valdecantos (2015).

a global euro with national (or regional) euros or a take-up of the EMS would
help to compensate negative asymmetric shocks but might produce a recurrent
instability, unless the system allows for persistent, but small, deficits. The results
would be better if Germany and other northern European countries belonging
to the German block left the euro area, but this would come at the cost of the
loss of many of the benefits of the process of integration as a whole. Facing
the lack of solidarity between the two blocks, more balanced results could be
obtained thanks to the re-introduction of exchange rate adjustments between
the German block and a euro zone reduced to the southern European countries. Beyond these results describing permanently established exchange rate
regimes, the transition period putting them into effect would raise several sets
of problems that will be discussed in conclusion of the chapter. Before, another
exchange rate regime based on a euro-bancor system will be proposed and
simulated with a new version of the SFC model.

The euro-bancor system

Among the several proposals for the reform of the euro area that have been raised in the recent years to counter the intra-European imbalances and distribute the burden of adjustment more equally between creditor and debtor countries, the reference to Keynes's plan imagined during the years that preceded the Bretton-Woods conferences seems particularly relevant. What makes the Clearing Union proposed by Keynes a useful source of inspiration for the reform of the EMU is the fact that it was designed by Keynes with the view to contrast the build-up of current account imbalances and to avoid the restrictive pressures implied by other monetary arrangements (Fantacci, 2013). The proposal is especially adapted as the TARGET2 system that is already in place has many of the features of Keynes's plan. However, as we will see, some other important points are lacking. The proposal to reform the EMU along the lines of Keynes's Clearing Union building on TARGET 2 was first advocated by Amato and Fantacci (2014). More recently, Amato et al. (2016) have focused on a simple reform of the TARGET2 system introducing symmetric and increasing charges on positive and negative TARGET2 balances. Before discussing the euro-bancor proposal, a more precise presentation of the TARGET2 system is necessary.

The European Monetary Union and the TARGET2 system

The adoption of the euro implied the delegation of monetary and exchange rate policies of each member country to the European Central Bank (ECB). Together with the national central banks of the 19 countries that have adopted the euro, the ECB constitutes the Eurosystem, which is the monetary authority of the euro zone. The main goal of the Eurosystem is price stability. However, financial stability and integration are also part of its mandates. In order to achieve these objectives, the Eurosystem conducts the monetary policy of the euro zone. Additionally, since the introduction of the euro as a medium of exchange, the Single Euro Payments Area (SEPA) has been established with the aim of integrating payments within the euro zone. It was expected that the SEPA will contribute to improve the efficiency in both goods and financial markets.

The interaction between commercial banks, national central banks, and the ECB is ruled by the SEPA. In practice, the system that ensures the automatic clearing of all payments, real and financial, within the Eurosystem is called TARGET 2 (Trans-European Automated Real-time Gross Settlement Express Transfer System). These payment transactions can be either real or financial. Whenever the banks of a given country receive (make) payments from another economic agent of the euro zone, the national central bank in question records a positive (negative) TARGET2 balance. This represents a claim (liability) not on another national central bank but on the ECB, which acts as a clearing house that settles transactions among national central banks (Mayer et al., 2012).

Since the introduction of the SEPA the number of operations that were undertaken within this system has been increasing steadily. Until 2008, TARGET2 balances were rather stable as current account deficits (surpluses) were matched by financial account surpluses (deficits). In other words, current account surpluses were 'recycled' and used to finance economic growth in deficit countries. However, since the beginning of the crisis of 2008 TARGET2 balances have shown the market's perception regarding the vulnerability of deficit countries. Much of the surplus (deficit) registered in the TARGET2 balances of northern (southern) countries in the years after the crisis is explained by the 'flight to quality' effect.

The TARGET2 system can be introduced in the SFC model of the euro zone already presented. The euro/dollar exchange rate is determined in the same way and clears the euro-denominated bond market (eqs. (1)–(2)). The national central banks purchase/sell domestic bonds to equilibrate their balance sheets (eqs. (37)–(38) instead of eqs. (3)–(4)). The balance sheet identities of the central banks of Spain and Germany have a new component: the TARGET2 balances. These balances arise as a result of real and financial transactions within the Eurosystem and constitute an asset for national central banks and a liability for the ECB.[1] However, this does not imply that in practice a national central bank cannot have a negative stock of TARGET2 balances as it has been the case for the southern European countries. As equations (39)–(40) show, the change in TARGET2 balances can simply be defined as the sum of all the intra-European transactions in a given period. In this model the transactions are given by exports, imports, interest payments, and portfolio investment. TARGET2 balances algebraically add to zero in this model. It does not cover the recent negative TARGET2 balances accumulated by the ECB as a consequence of its purchases of extra-Eurozone bonds under the Quantitative Easing which are not described in our model. The rest of the model remains unchanged.

$$\Delta Bs, cb_{SP}^{SP} = \Delta R^{SP} + \Delta H^{SP} - \Delta A^{SP} - \Delta Bd, cb_{SP}^{US} - \Delta TG2^{SP} \tag{37}$$

$$\Delta Bs, cb_{GE}^{GE} = \Delta R^{GE} + \Delta H^{GE} - \Delta A^{GE} - \Delta Bd, cb_{GE}^{US} - \Delta TG2^{GE} \tag{38}$$

$$\Delta TG2^{SP} = X_{SP}^{GE} - IM_{SP}^{GE} + r_{-1}^{GE}.Bd, b_{SP_{-1}}^{GE} - r_{-1}^{SP}.Bd, b_{GE_{-1}}^{SP}$$
$$+ \Delta Bs, b_{SP}^{GE} - \Delta Bd, b_{SP}^{GE} \tag{39}$$

$$\Delta TG2^{GE} = X_{GE}^{SP} - IM_{GE}^{SP} + r_{-1}^{SP}.Bd, b_{GE_{-1}}^{SP} - r_{-1}^{GE}.Bd, b_{SP_{-1}}^{GE}$$
$$+ \Delta Bs, b_{GE}^{SP} - \Delta Bd, b_{GE}^{SP} \tag{40}$$

The euro–bancor model

The euro–bancor model takes what we consider the most useful features of each of the systems that found implementation in Europe during the last decades. First, we borrow from the EMS the existence of a unit of account to which national currencies are pegged. This unit of account currency, which in the EMS was called ECU, was called bancor in Keynes' proposal. In this model, the euro–bancor is determined in the same way as the ECU was determined in the EMS, that is, as a basket currency of national currencies, all measured with respect to the US dollar. It is worth specifying that the Keynes's bancor was not a basket of national currencies but a unit of account in which the balances of the national central banks at the International Clearing Union (ICU) were measured. The same choice could have been done in the model without changing the results. Second, in Keynes' proposal countries accumulated bancor balances according to their external performance, whereas those countries that exhibited trade surpluses registered an increase in their bancor account at the ICU, countries running trade deficits registered a decrease in their stock of bancors or increased drawing on their overdraft line. The idea of accumulating balances of the unit of account as a result of international transactions is the same that we observe in the current TARGET2 system. It implies that most of the institutions that are required to implement a regime of this nature (a clearing union, an international unit of account and a system that registers the transactions within the region) already exist (the ECB could play the role of the ICU and the SEPA is the system that registers all the transactions) or have existed and could easily be restored (the ECU, that would play the role of the bancor). This euro–bancor model is close to the Keynesian ICU (International Clearing Union) proposed by Whyman (2018).

We first describe the basic closure of the euro–bancor model and then show how other aspects of Keynes' idea can be introduced. As mentioned before, the euro–bancor is a basket currency constituted by European currencies (E9 with respect to the US dollar in eq. (41)). Unlike Keynes' proposal, where all the countries in the world are engaged in the bancor framework and thus have all fixed, but adjustable, exchange rates, in this case European currencies are pegged to the euro–bancor (thereby fixed with respect to each other) but they float against the currencies of the rest of the world. This feature of the system is also borrowed from the EMS. The adjustment criterion of European currencies vis-à-vis the euro–bancor (E7 for Spain and E8 for Germany) depends on the intra-regional external performance of each country (eqs. (42)–(43)), as the euro–bancor system is concerned by the intra-zone imbalances. It differs from the case of the EMS where the stability of the system was more depending of the global performance of each country (eqs. (22)–(23)) and not only of the intra-zone imbalances.[2] The external performance of each country is evaluated taking a certain sustainability threshold for the bilateral current account, as it was proposed by Keynes with its limitations on the overall balances. The exchange rate of Germany against the US dollar (E1) is such that the ex post equilibrium in the domestic bond market is ensured (eq. (44)). Spain's exchange rate against the dollar follows the movements of the German currency (eq. (45)).

This definition of the Spanish exchange rate still entails an asymmetry with respect to the fully symmetric system where all countries' exchange rates are determined in the same manner (as was the case in Keynes' proposal). This asymmetry implies that Spain's currency is not only pegged to the German currency (through their mutual engagement in the euro-bancor system) but also follows the movements of the latter with respect to the dollar. This kind of asymmetry seems to be unavoidable from the time that the institutional setting is such that exchange rates are fixed within a certain area and one of the currencies of the area floats freely against the currency of an extra-regional country, thereby becoming the 'leading currency'. In order for the model to be consistent, only one of the currencies of the euro-bancor system can float freely against an extra-regional currency. This conclusion remains even in the case where the euro-bancor is a simple unit of account and not a basket of national currencies. This is also the case in a model with more than two European countries. For example, if 1 euro-bancor = E7 SP = E8 GE = E9 FF (E7, E8, E9 fixed but adjustable), GE, SP, and FF are floating against the dollar with 1\$ = E1 GE = E2 SP = E3 FF. Then 1 euro-bancor = E7/E2 \$ = E8/E1 \$ = E9/E3 \$. The asymmetry remains. One currency (GE for instance) is acting as the leading currency and the other currencies follow. The exchange rate E2 of the currency SP against the dollar is equal to E1 E7 /E8. Similarly the exchange rate E3 of the currency FF against the dollar is equal to E1 E9/ E8.

In the times of the EMS, the leading currency was the Deutsch mark. The key motivation for the euro was to overcome the EMS asymmetry and its recurrent instability. But, with the lack of any adjustment mechanism to face shocks in heterogeneous countries (except wage deflation and restrictive policies), huge current imbalances have reappeared within the euro zone at the benefit of Germany. The euro-bancor proposal would allow a reduction of these imbalances thanks to the re-introduction of national currencies and the possibility of exchange rate adjustments. Like the EMS, the euro-bancor system is symmetric in its principle but would work in an asymmetric way. Germany would remain in a dominant position. The German and Spanish or Italian debts would not be equivalent for the markets. However, this asymmetry would be less pronounced in practice. Germany would not have the power to impose austerity measures in southern countries. As it will be explained later in this chapter, the euro-bancor system would include specific rules which would allow more symmetric adjustments.

With regard to the balance sheet identity of national central bank of Germany, even though it is engaged in a fixed exchange rate arrangement, it does not need to accumulate foreign reserves. Since there is no euro-bancor market, the central bank does not need to defend a certain exchange rate. Thus, the stock of dollar-denominated bonds held by the German central bank is constant (eq. (48)). The situation is different for the central bank of Spain, which has to hoard reserves in order to make the necessary interventions in the foreign exchange market that allow its currency to keep the peg against the German currency (eq. (47) instead of eq. (37)). When expressed in domestic currency the stock of foreign reserves held by the central bank may be subject to changes due to variations in the exchange rate (eqs. (49)–(50)).

$$\frac{1}{E9} = \frac{Y^{GE}}{Y^{GE} + Y^{SP}} \cdot \frac{1}{E1} + \frac{Y^{SP}}{Y^{GE} + Y^{SP}} \cdot \frac{1}{E2} \tag{41}$$

$$E7 = \begin{cases} E7_{-1} & if\ CA^{SP}_{GE_{t-i}} \geq T\ \ for\ all\ i = 1,\ldots,5 \\ E7_{-1} \cdot (1 + \varepsilon) & if\ CA^{SP}_{GE_{t-i}} < T\ \ for\ all\ i = 1,\ldots,5 \end{cases} \tag{42}$$

$$E8 = \begin{cases} E8_{-1} & if\ CA^{GE}_{SP_{t-i}} \geq T\ \ for\ all\ i = 1,\ldots,5 \\ E8_{-1} \cdot (1 + \varepsilon) & if\ CA^{GE}_{SP_{t-i}} < T\ \ for\ all\ i = 1,\ldots,5 \end{cases} \tag{43}$$

$$E1 = \frac{Bs^{GE} - Bd, b^{GE}_{GE} - Bd, cb^{GE}_{GE} - Bs, b^{GE}_{RW} - Bs, b^{GE}_{SP}}{Bd, b^{GE}_{US}} \tag{44}$$

$$E2 = E1 \frac{E7}{E8} \tag{45}$$

$$E3 = \frac{E7}{E8} = \frac{E2}{E1} \tag{46}$$

$$\Delta Bs, cb^{US}_{SP} = \frac{\Delta R^{SP} + \Delta H^{SP} - \Delta A^{SP} - \Delta Bd, cb^{SP}_{SP} - \Delta EB^{SP}}{E2} \tag{47}$$

$$Bs, cb^{US}_{GE} = \overline{Bs, cb^{US}_{GE}} \tag{48}$$

$$\Delta Bd, cb^{US}_{SP} = Bs, cb^{US}_{SP_{-1}} . \Delta E2 + E2 . \Delta Bs, cb^{US}_{SP} \tag{49}$$

$$\Delta Bd, cb^{US}_{GE} = Bs, cb^{US}_{GE_{-1}} . \Delta E1 \tag{50}$$

We have already introduced some of the main features of Keynes' bancor proposal, that is, the existence of an international unit of account and a system that registers all the transactions undertaken within the domain of this institutional arrangement. We can now introduce another key feature of this system: the clearing union. This is the institution where all the payments are cleared. Thus, every country would have an account at the clearing union. This account would be an asset for each national central bank and a liability for the clearing union, just as it happens in the current TARGET2 system. *Stricto sensu*, the International Clearing Union does not hold an account in its own name but only account in the name of member countries (positive or negative and adding to zero). This does not differ from what is written in the model. TARGET2 imbalances become a true (joint) liability for the ICU (or remaining members) when a deficit country exits without settling its negative balance.

However, unlike the current system, euro-bancor balances would not only be composed of international trade and portfolio investment within Europe, but there would also be some specific flows characterising Keynes' proposal. First, in order to make the external adjustment process more symmetric than it is today, this system would make both debtor and creditor countries share the burden of the debts. Thus, all countries would pay interests on their bancor balances, should they be positive or negative. This rule should encourage countries to make their accounts at the clearing union be as close to zero as possible, since it would always be better to consume a real good (an import) or buy an income-earning asset than paying an interest that entails no consumption at all.

A second flow that must be incorporated in the accumulation of euro-bancor balances is the one related to the distribution of the funds collected by the clearing union, which result precisely from the aforementioned interest payments on euro-bancor balances. We call these flows resulting from the redistribution process 'intra-European adjustment' (IEA). The sum of all these flows determines the change in the stock of euro-bancors (EB) held by each country's central banks. The sum of all the interest payments on euro-bancor balances determines the profit of the clearing union (P^{CU}), which distributes these funds to member countries according to the performance of the current account of each member country. If Spain's current account with respect to Germany (CA_{SP}^{GE}) is below a threshold (θ), Spain will get all the funds/profit of the clearing union. If not, the funds will be shared (eqs. (54)–(55)). In that sense, we have a transfer union from creditor to debtor country. Finally, we ensure that the balance sheet identity of the central banks of Spain and Germany holds through the purchases/sales of domestic bonds (eqs. (56)–(57)). The structure of these equations is different because of the asymmetry embedded in the model (whereas Spain needs to hold foreign reserves, Germany does not).

$$\Delta EB^{SP} = X_{SP}^{GE} - IM_{SP}^{GE} + r_{-1}^{GE}.Bd, b_{SP_{-1}}^{GE} - r_{-1}^{SP}.Bd, b_{GE_{-1}}^{SP} + \Delta Bs, b_{GE}^{SP}$$
$$- \Delta Bd, b_{SP}^{GE} - \left| r_{-1}^{EB}.EB_{-1}^{SP} \right| + IEA^{SP}.E7 \tag{51}$$

$$\Delta EB^{GE} = X_{GE}^{SP} - IM_{GE}^{SP} + r_{-1}^{SP}.Bd, b_{GE_{-1}}^{SP} - r_{-1}^{GE}.Bd, b_{SP_{-1}}^{GE} + \Delta Bs, b_{SP}^{GE}$$
$$- \Delta Bd, b_{GE}^{SP} - \left| r_{-1}^{EB}.EB_{-1}^{GE} \right| + IEA^{GE}.E8 \tag{52}$$

$$P^{CU} = \left| r_{-1}^{EB} \cdot \frac{EB_{-1}^{SP}}{E7} \right| + \left| r_{-1}^{EB} \cdot \frac{EB_{-1}^{GE}}{E8} \right| \tag{53}$$

$$IEA^{SP} = \begin{cases} P^{CU} & if \ \dfrac{CA_{SP}^{GE}/E7}{\dfrac{Y^{SP}}{E7}} < \theta \\[4ex] 0.5\,P^{CU} & if \ \dfrac{CA_{SP}^{GE}/E7}{\dfrac{Y^{SP}}{E7}} \geq \theta \end{cases} \tag{54}$$

$$IEA^{GE} = P^{CU} - IEA^{SP} \tag{55}$$

$$Bd, cb_{SP}^{SP} = Bs^{SP} - Bs, b_{SP}^{SP} - Bs, b_{US}^{SP} - Bs, b_{RW}^{SP} - Bs, b_{GE}^{SP} \tag{56}$$

$$\Delta Bd, cb_{GE}^{GE} = \Delta R^{GE} + \Delta H^{GE} - \Delta A^{GE} - \Delta Bd, cb_{GE}^{US} - \Delta EB^{GE} \tag{57}$$

Complementary adjustment mechanisms

Another closure implying a real-side adjustment could consist in the utilisation of the flows of redistributed interests by the clearing union to finance the imports of capital goods that would increase the stock of capital and eventually change the productive structure of the economy, thereby increasing competitiveness and, in the long run, reducing the demand of imported goods. This would require the augmentation of Spain and Germany's import equations by the amount of 'intra-European adjustment' flows received from the clearing union (eqs. (58a)–(59a)). The amount of imported capital goods that results from these flows of 'aid' would be added to the traditional investment function used in SFC models (eqs. (60a)–(61a)). As is shown in the simulations presented in the next section, the structural change effect is introduced as a gradual decrease in the income elasticity of imports of the deficit country.

$$ln(IM_{SP}^{GE}) = \mu_0^{SP} + \mu_1^{SP}.ln\left(Y^{SP}\right) + \mu_2^{SP}.ln\left(\frac{1}{E3}\right) + \mu_4^{SP}.ln[1+IEA^{SP}.E7] \tag{58a}$$

$$ln(IM_{GE}^{SP}) = \mu_0^{GE} + \mu_1^{GE}.ln\left(Y^{GE}\right) + \mu_2^{GE}.ln\left(E3\right) + \mu_4^{GE}.ln[1+IEA^{GE}.E8] \tag{59a}$$

$$\frac{I^{SP}}{K_{-1}^{SP}} = \gamma_0^{SP} + \gamma_1^{SP}.\frac{P^{SP}}{K_{-1}^{SP}} + \gamma_2^{SP}.\frac{r_{-1}^{SP}.L_{-1}^{SP}}{K_{-1}^{SP}} + \gamma_3^{SP}.u_{-1}^{SP} + \mu_4^{SP}.ln[1+IEA^{SP}.E7] \tag{60a}$$

$$\frac{I^{GE}}{K^{GE}_{-1}} = \gamma^{GE}_0 + \gamma^{GE}_1 . \frac{P^{GE}}{K^{GE}_{-1}} + \gamma^{GE}_2 . \frac{r^{GE}_{-1} . L^{GE}_{-1}}{K^{GE}_{-1}} + \gamma^{GE}_3 . u^{GE}_{-1} + \mu^{GE}_4 . \ln[1 + IEA^{GE} . E8]$$

(61a)

If the structural change process is satisfactory, it would be expected to observe that after some periods the deficit country starts being able to substitute imports, thereby reducing the dependence on foreign goods. In order to model this particular scenario we either endogenize the productive structure or we introduce structural change as an exogenous shock that gradually takes place some periods after the country has started to import the capital goods that will contribute to the process of import substitution. For the sake of simplicity, in this model we treat structural change as exogenous.

Finally, there is a last feature that derives from Keynes' proposal that could be introduced. In the previous paragraph we mentioned that in Keynes' proposal countries are encouraged to use their positive bancor balances to increase imports, since otherwise they would be progressively wasting these balances by paying interests on them. This incentive to increase imports can be modelled by expanding the standard import equations. Normally, these equations depend on domestic income and the real exchange rate. In this case, as shown in equations (58b)–(59b), we add an additional term that depends on the burden of the stock of euro-bancors. The intuition behind this term would be that the higher the burden (represented by the interest payments associated to them) the higher the incentive to increase imports. Now, if imports are increased it needs to be specified what sector is going to purchase this additional flow of goods from abroad. In this model we assume that it is the government, since in principle it is the only agent that could internalise the loss that the central bank would incur if euro-bancor balances were gradually extinguished due to the payment of interests to the clearing union. Thus, we augment the traditional public spending equations, which consider government consumption exogenous, to incorporate this additional flow of imports (eqs. (60b)–(61b)). In order to be consistent with Keynes' case for a non-recessionary adjustment process, the import equation is only augmented when euro-bancor balances are positive. This implies that whereas surplus countries are forced to pursue more expansive policies, deficit countries are not forced to undertake a contractionary fiscal policy that restores the long-term balance of payments equilibrium through a recession. There is an asymmetry in the adjustment process in favour of reflation.

$$\ln(IM^{GE}_{SP})$$

$$= \begin{cases} \mu^{SP}_0 + \mu^{SP}_1 . \ln\left(Y^{SP}\right) + \mu^{SP}_2 . \ln\left(\frac{1}{E3}\right) + \mu^{SP}_3 . \ln\left[1 + \left(r^{eb} . EB^{SP}_{-1}\right)\right] & \text{if } EB^{SP}_{-1} > 0 \\ \\ \mu^{SP}_0 + \mu^{SP}_1 . \ln\left(Y^{SP}\right) + \mu^{SP}_2 . \ln\left(\frac{1}{E3}\right) & \text{if } EB^{SP}_{-1} \leq 0 \end{cases}$$

(58b)

$$ln(IM_{GE}^{SP}) =$$

$$\begin{cases} \mu_0^{GE} + \mu_1^{GE}.\ln\left(Y^{GE}\right) + \mu_2^{GE}.\ln\left(E3\right) + \mu_3^{GE}.\ln\left[1 + \left(r^{eb}.EB_{-1}^{GE}\right)\right] & \text{if } EB_{-1}^{GE} > 0 \\ \mu_0^{GE} + \mu_1^{GE}.\ln\left(Y^{GE}\right) + \mu_2^{GE}.\ln\left(E3\right) & \text{if } EB_{-1}^{GE} \leq 0 \end{cases}$$

(59b)

$$G^{SP} = \begin{cases} G_0^{SP} + G_{-1}^{SP}.(1+\rho) + \mu_3^{SP}.\ln\left[1 + \left(r^{eb}.EB_{-1}^{SP}\right)\right] & \text{if } EB_{-1}^{SP} > 0 \\ G_0^{SP} + G_{-1}^{SP}.(1+\rho) & \text{if } EB_{-1}^{SP} \leq 0 \end{cases}$$

(60b)

$$G^{GE} = \begin{cases} G_0^{GE} + G_{-1}^{GE}.(1+\rho) + \mu_3^{GE}.\ln\left[1 + \left(r^{eb}.EB_{-1}^{GE}\right)\right] & \text{if } EB_{-1}^{GE} > 0 \\ G_0^{GE} + G_{-1}^{GE}.(1+\rho) & \text{if } EB_{-1}^{GE} \leq 0 \end{cases}$$

(61b)

These equations complete the closure of the euro-bancor model. We are now able to turn to the simulation experiments, in order to assess the advantages and disadvantages that this system may have in comparison to the previous experiences that took place in Europe. It should be noted that some of these proposals for a euro-bancor regime could be implemented within the current institutional setting of the Eurosystem, without a break-up of the euro. Both the interests paid on the euro-bancor balances (currently the TARGET2 balances) and their redistribution through intra-European adjustments (IEA), and the launch of more expansionary policies in the surplus countries, as well as the utilisation of IEA funds to finance supply side policies improving the non-price-competitiveness of southern European countries could be implemented with no major changes in the current setting of the Eurosystem. However, agreement on such proposals requires a strong and unlikely political will.

Simulations of the euro-bancor model

We intend to show how the different versions of the euro-bancor system react to asymmetric shocks as they happened within the monetary union since the introduction of the euro in 1999. Like previously, our experiment consists of an introduction of a competitiveness loss in Spain due to the overvaluation of the euro for the Spanish economy and its undervaluation for the German economy. This can be represented in the model through an increase in the autonomous component of Spain's imports equation and a decrease on the same component of German imports, both reflecting the effects of the exchange rate misalignments.

The first euro-bancor model, which we label euro-bancor 1, consists of the introduction of the clearing union and interest-bearing euro-bancor balances. These interests are collected and distributed by the clearing union. The devaluation threshold is lax (meaning that only when the current account deficit becomes too large the exchange rate is allowed to be adjusted) and is never reached. The second closure, which we label euro-bancor 2, is identical to the previous one, but with a stricter threshold on the devaluation rule (meaning that a persistent current account deficit of 1% is enough to trigger an exchange rate adjustment), such that after an initial adjustment of the Spanish exchange rate no exchange rate adjustments take place (because after the adjustment all current account balances are not negative enough to trigger a devaluation). The third closure, which we label euro-bancor 3, considers a very strict threshold: no current account deficits are allowed at all. As a result, a devaluation of the currency of Spain is followed by a devaluation of the German currency and so forth. The scenario that we call euro-bancor 4 is the one where countries use the 'aid' provided by the clearing union (i.e. the redistribution of interests by the clearing union) to purchase imported capital goods that in the medium term allow for a higher degree of import substitution (eqs. (58a)–(61a)). This is represented by assuming that after five periods of importing capital goods the country's income elasticity of imports starts to decrease gradually for ten periods, remaining constant thereafter. We refer to this process as 'structural change'. Finally, the model euro-bancor 5 introduces the additional terms on the imports equations, in order to represent the higher incentive to import that surplus countries may have in this institutional setting. As mentioned before, these imports are computed as part of government consumption (eqs. (58b)–(61b)). For the euro-bancor 4 and 5 cases we have introduced the lax devaluation threshold, in order to prevent exchange rates from adjusting. This will allow us to study the specific effect of the mechanisms embedded in these two proposals.

Figure 6.6 represents the reaction of each model to the competitiveness shock (loss of competitiveness in Spain, gain in Germany). The case of the economic and monetary union (EMU), already studied in the first section, is used as a reference. Following the negative shock, the current account of Spain is deteriorated without any adjustment mechanism within the monetary union. In euro-bancor 1, the initial deterioration in the current account is followed by an immediate improvement, which results from the transfers of the interests that the clearing union collects (in this framework the clearing union collects interests on euro-bancor balances and transfers them to member countries according to their external performance). Since in the periods after the shock it is Spain whose current account is in deficit, the clearing union transfers the totality of the interests to Spain. However, the Spanish current account remains in deficit, but in euro-bancor 1, the threshold allows for so large deficits that no devaluation takes place.

With regard to euro-bancor 2 and 3, the initial trajectories are rather similar. After the shock, the deterioration in the current account is followed by an improvement which results from the transfers of the interests by the clearing union. But this is not sufficient to bring the current account balance above the threshold (neither the stricter nor the laxer one). Thus, the Spanish currency is devalued in period 55. The immediate effect is an increase in the current

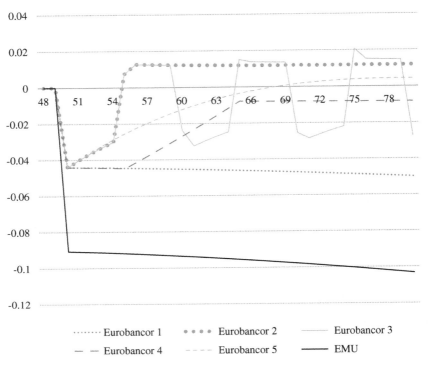

Figure 6.6 Current account of Spain with respect to Germany.
Source: Mazier and Valdecantos (2019).

account balance, to the extent that it turns into surplus. Hereafter, the trajectories of euro-bancor 2 and 3 diverge, owing to the effect that the predetermined threshold has on Germany's current account.

In euro-bancor 3, where the threshold is stricter (only small deficits are tolerated), the devaluation of the Spanish currency and the consequent current account surplus of Spain turns Germany's current account into deficit, eventually falling below the threshold and triggering an exchange rate adjustment. This brings the German current account into surplus, at the expense of Spain. From then on, the dynamics are similar to the ones observed in the European Monetary System (see the first section) where one exchange rate adjustment followed another. We concluded that these dynamics were not desirable. As a matter of fact, European policy-makers decided to abandon the EMS for this reason. Model euro-bancor 2 shows more stable dynamics for the simple reason that the devaluation threshold is higher. This implies that Germany 'accepts' the current account deficit with respect to Spain brought about by the devaluation of the Spanish currency and no more exchange rates adjustments take place.

It is worth noting that this scenario implies that in the long run Spain runs a current account surplus vis-à-vis Germany. Germany's overall current account could still be in surplus if its competitiveness is such that its current account against the rest of the world outpaces its deficit with respect to its European partners.

Finally, euro-bancor 4 and 5 seem to provide the more stable adjustment processes. In the case of euro-bancor 4, after the initial shock that brings Spain's current account into deficit, the accumulation of euro-bancor balances and the subsequent redistribution of interests by the clearing union imply an 'aid' to Spain that is used to purchase imported capital goods. This additional flow of imports, which is added to the one produced by the initial shock, prevent Spain's current account from reaching equilibrium in the short run. However, after some periods, the effects of structural change take over and the country starts to substitute imports. This is reflected in the gradual improvement of Spain's current account until it finally reaches a position that is close to equilibrium.

With regard to euro-bancor 5, after the initial shock the accumulation of positive euro-bancor balances by Germany produces an incentive to increase its purchases of goods from Spain. These imports are purchased by the government. In the long run, this produces a trend to balance the external positions at the same time that potential flows of effective demand do not leak from the system. We consider that the trajectories described by euro-bancor 4 and 5 are the ones that Keynes had in mind when designing the proposal of an international clearing union that he presented at the Bretton-Woods conference, which aimed at 'the substitution of an expansionist, in place of a contractionist, pressure on world trade' (Keynes (1941)).

Let us take a quick look to the behaviour of the Spanish currency vis-à-vis the US dollar under each of these alternative institutional settings, which can be seen in Figure 6.7. In the case of euro-bancor 1, the exchange rate of the Spanish currency vis-à-vis the dollar floats, replicating the movement of the German currency vis-à-vis the dollar (eq. (45)). Even though the shock has a positive impact for Germany's current account, its currency registers a slight depreciation. With the euro-bancor system the country in deficit (Spain) benefits from a redistribution process through the intra-European adjustments (IEA) which are paid by the clearing union (eqs. (54)–(55)) but are equivalent *in fine* to transfers from the surplus country government (Germany) to the deficit one (through the taxes paid by the central banks to their governments). Consequently, the issue of German bonds increases while the issue of Spanish bonds decreases. This implies a depreciation of the German currency (eq. (44)) and also of the Spanish one (eq. (45)). This depreciation is amplified by the fact that the accumulation of euro-bancor balances by the German central bank implies the sale of government bonds (eq. (57)).[3] Since the Spanish currency replicates this trajectory, the short-run impact of the shock is such that its currency is slightly depreciated with respect to the dollar. This depreciation compensates (insufficiently) the initial competitiveness shock.

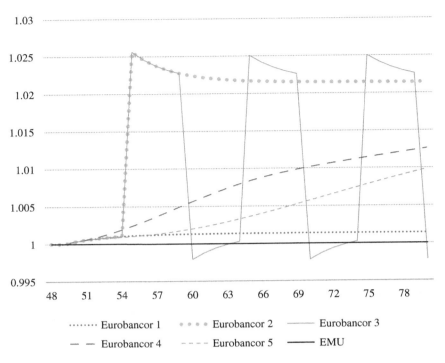

Figure 6.7 Spain's currency versus the US dollar.
Source: Mazier and Valdecantos (2019).

The cases of euro-bancor 2 and 3 are identical to euro-bancor 1 until a first adjustment in the exchange rate of the Spanish currency against the euro-bancor takes place in period 55. When this happens, the current account reverses its sign, thereby producing an appreciation. As the trade surplus boosts economic growth, imports increase further. This not only erodes the new trade surplus but also produces an upward pressure on the exchange rate towards depreciation of the Spanish currency (see the evolution of the exchange rate in euro-bancor 2 and 3 in 56–59 in Figure 6.7). From then on, it is observed that whereas the exchange rate remains stable in euro-bancor 2, it starts fluctuating in euro-bancor 3 (for the reasons that have already been described).

The cases of euro-bancor 4 and 5 exhibit a larger depreciation with respect to the euro-bancor 1 scenario. In order to understand the reasons underlying this trajectory we need once again to analyse the behaviour of the German currency with respect to the dollar. The salient features of the euro-bancor 4 and 5 proposals are their expansionary impulse. The stimuli embedded in these proposals imply a higher level of activity with respect to the previous cases, where only exchange rate adjustments or flows of 'aid' were coming into play. This higher GDP growth also implies a higher level of endogenously created liquidity in each domestic monetary system (banks grant more credit, households demand more money, etc.). Consequently, banks require more advances from the central bank. The central bank of Germany absorbs the excess liquidity by selling domestic bonds. Recalling the equation that describes the balance sheet identity of the German central bank (eq. (57)) we observe that added to the increase in the euro-bancor balances that arise from the initial shock (as it happened in the euro-bancor 1 scenario) the increase in advances induce a tendency to reduce the stock of domestic bonds. The sale of domestic bonds by the central bank produces an excess supply of German bonds that is adjusted through an upward movement of the German currency (and of the Spanish one) with respect to the dollar. This devaluation of the German and Spanish currencies could be less pronounced if adjustment in German central bank's repo auctions had more occurred than bond market interventions.

Finally, the euro-bancor alternatives need not imply a permanent loss for Germany, currently the sole winner under the present configuration of the euro zone. Figures 6.8 and 6.9 show the dynamic trajectory of the Spanish and German GDP. Even though the alternatives where internal disequilibria are corrected through exchange rate adjustments (euro-bancor 2 and 3) or internal

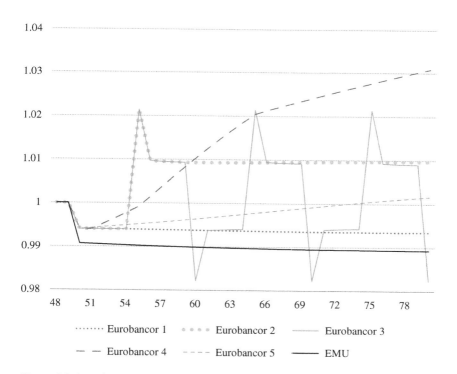

Figure 6.8 Spain's GDP.
Source: Mazier and Valdecantos (2019).

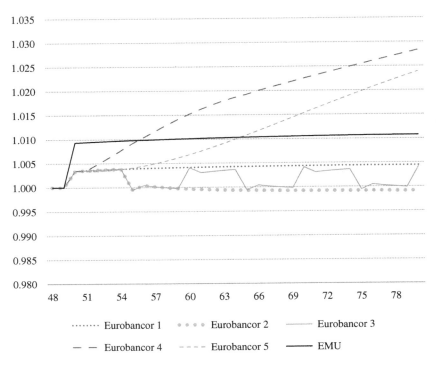

Figure 6.9: Germany's GDP.
Source: Mazier and Valdecantos (2019).

transfers of 'aid' (euro-bancor 1) seem worse in terms of economic growth than the current institutional setting, the expansionary ways out of the crisis appear to be better in the long run. In the euro-bancor 4 scenario, in the short run the German growth remains positive due to the increasing imports of capital goods by Spain. In the medium run German GDP is further benefited from the improvement of the Spanish growth (and hence higher demand for imported goods). In the euro-bancor 5 scenario, the performance is also better in the long run in Germany thanks to the positive impact on the Spanish growth of the increasing imports of Spanish goods through the German public spending policy. In sum, according to these simulations, either the euro-bancor 4 or 5 alternatives (or a combination of both) would bring about a stronger and more sustainable growth regime for European countries.

As it has been explained previously, some of the euro-bancor regimes could be compatible with the current institutional setting of the Eurosystem. It is the case when, as a result of a lax devaluation threshold (exchange rates are devalued only when external imbalances are too high), no exchange rate adjustment is triggered. The euro-bancor 1 model, based on intra-European transfers, is the simplest one. Compared with the current Eurosystem (EMU), it allows an improvement of the performances of the southern European countries in terms of growth and current account, with a slight negative impact on the German growth rate. The euro-bancor 4 and 5 models, based on increasing investment and improvement of non-price-competitiveness in Spain, as well as on more expansionary policies in Germany, would be benefit for both countries. However, the current political context in the Euro zone suggests that it would be difficult to promote such institutional changes. On the contrary, in the euro-bancor 2 and 3 models, exchange rate adjustments can occur as a result of stricter devaluation thresholds (just a small external imbalance is enough to trigger an exchange rate adjustment). Even though the simulations illustrate the effectiveness of exchange rate adjustments to improve the economic performances of southern countries without having to implement ambitious structural policies, the successive exchange rate adjustments that they entail have proven to be undesirable. Indeed, one of the cases in favour of a single currency was to prevent national currencies from excess volatility.

To sum up, the current payments system in the euro area is rather close to the one that Keynes proposed for the reform of the international monetary system at the beginning of the 1940s in spite of some important differences. First, in Keynes's proposal exchange rates are fixed, but adjustable in case of too large imbalances to be managed. Second, in order to make the external adjustment process more symmetric, all the countries pay interests on their bancor balances, shall they be positive or negative. These two points have been reintroduced in our model. Third, in the 1940s capital movements were limited and under control. Keynes's plan was focused on current imbalances. This remains a big difference. We tried to model how the clearing union proposal, associated to an international unit of account that is only used for the settlement of European payments, could be modelled in the framework of an SFC model. The euro system already has many of the institutions that would play a key role under such a regime. Our model shows in which way the existing institutions should be modified in order to make the euro zone an area less prone to producing large imbalances. The simulations presented illustrate the dynamic behaviour that each institutional setting would bring about. In many simulations the threshold for currency adjustments seems to be critical. If it is too small there will be instability associated with repeated devaluation/revaluation. If it is too large, this instability is avoided but instead stock imbalances can build up over time, forcing delayed readjustment at some later time. The key point to emphasise is that country members must avoid persistent competitiveness and current account imbalances to prevent these instabilities from arising. By means of a SFC model we found that Europe could move towards a more sustainable growth cycle, should there be the political will either to reduce the structural heterogeneity within the area (through supply side policies that help develop the productive structure of southern countries) or to allow for exchange rate adjustments when external imbalances within the area become unsustainable.

Conclusion

In the absence of either a system of fiscal transfers between regions or a central bank that can provide unlimited liquidity to deficit countries, the euro zone will suffer recurrent crises. To prevent such instabilities from arising, two types of alternative exchange rate regimes have been proposed and simulated.

The first one is based on a multiple-euro system with a global euro remaining at the international level and national (or regional) euros which would be reintroduced. These national euros would not be internationally convertible and would be only for domestic uses. They would be in fixed exchange rates with the global euro but exchange rate adjustments could occur in case of unsustainable current imbalances. Another variety of multiple euro could be a split of the euro zone with a north euro for the countries of the German block (a resurrected Deutschmark) and a south euro in a remaining euro zone gathering the southern European countries. The north and south euro could float or the south euro could be in a fixed, but adjustable, exchange rate with the north euro.

The second type of exchange rate regime relies on a euro-bancor which would be a simple basket currency and on national currencies which would also be reintroduced and would be in a fixed, but adjustable, exchange rate with the euro-bancor. The ECB would be transformed in a clearing union and new rules would be settled with both debtor and creditor countries paying interests on their euro-bancor balances at the clearing union.

Each alternative has its strengths and its weaknesses. The multiple-euro system has the advantage to preserve the ECB and the euro as an international currency. This could be considered as an asset for the European Union in the prospect of a reconstruction of the international monetary system (see Chapter 8). But the coexistence with national currencies reduced to a simple role of domestic currencies which would not be convertible at the international level might be a source of problems. The international euro might be weakened as it would not be used for domestic transactions. The domestic currencies might be hurt by their non-convertibility, paving the way to potential speculations. The euro-bancor regime also preserves the SEPA and the ECB but reduces it to a simple clearing union. There is no more European currency able to play a role of key currency at the world level. But the system appears more stable than the multiple-euro one as the national currencies would be floating and convertible at the international level.

The split between a north euro (around Germany) and a south euro would contribute to solve one of the main sources of imbalances within the euro zone (the excessive competitiveness of the German block and the undervaluation of the euro for this zone) but it would leave the southern countries in a kind of peripherical position compared to the northern ones. France would face a difficult choice, trying to remain in the German block with the risk to be condemned to a slow death or joining the south in a more comfortable position but with a risk of marginalisation.

In all the cases the re-introduction of exchange rate adjustments when external imbalances within the euro zone become unsustainable appears as a key point. If their macroeconomic and structural impact must not be underestimated, they are not the panacea. To a large extent, structural policies (industrial and innovation policies, education, and infrastructures) aiming to solve the heterogeneity of the euro zone would be preferable but they are complex and difficult to implement. For lack of such policies, the risk of a progressive decline would be great if there is not the support of exchange rate adjustments. The ideal would be to combine both.

Renewal of structural policies

Exit from the euro could help to lay the foundations for a more viable growth regime at the European level but would by no means represent a sufficient condition. Exchange rate adjustment would bring about an important transfer to the advantage or disadvantage, according to its direction, of the exposed sector. This would help to strengthen positions which have become fragile, as in France or Italy. It would also contribute to the take-off of an export sector in Greece or Portugal. But exit from the euro would have to be complemented by structural policies in several fields (industry, research, infrastructure, education, transition to sustainable energy sources, urban regeneration) through the mobilisation of European programmes, national policies, and local initiatives.

National structural policies, principally industrial policy and regional policy, would recover more autonomy as against a less dominant European competition policy. Aid from the public sector would be less subject to Commission control and would take different forms according to the country (for example, more at state level in France, more at regional level in Germany or Italy). More generally, industrial policies would be organised in different ways in different countries (national investment banks, national champions, industrial development funds). Specific cooperation agreements would be developed among certain member states according to their particular strengths and their specificities (European agencies with a limited number of participants, shared investment programmes around specific large-scale projects).

The diversity of social models would continue without institutional convergence (no European minimum wage, a range of different pension systems, varying importance of trade unions and of collective bargaining). But a limited convergence could come about as the weaker economies catch up and growth is more sustained. The federal budget would continue at its present very low level (1% of European GDP) in order to ensure the continuation of certain European policies in the fields of agriculture and research. European regional policies or budgetary transfers across regions would no longer be needed because of the adjustments which could be brought about through modification of intra-European exchange rates.

Transition period

Once permanently established, these new European monetary regimes would ensure that the structural heterogeneity of the euro zone was dealt with in a much better way. However, putting them into effect would raise several sets of problems. Apart from France and Italy most of the southern European countries which had to adjust their real exchange rates have already done so at enormous cost. Misalignments of intra-European real exchange rates are much less pronounced than they were in 2009 (see Table 4.1). The main exception is Germany for whom the euro is largely undervalued. The decline of the euro against the dollar, although it does nothing to correct misalignments within the zone, has provided some room for manoeuvre while giving Germany truly massive advantages on international markets. The country in most difficulty, Greece, is in a specific situation. Relative to its small size, it is not a very open economy and this means that both monetary devaluation and real deflation are less effective than elsewhere. Portugal was in a close situation but has been able to develop more widely its external sector.

The change in monetary regime would have differentiated effects on the countries of the euro zone. With the end of the single currency, Germany and the associated northern countries would lose the implicit subsidy from which they benefit through the undervaluation of the euro, their current account surpluses would be reduced and their output, measured in domestic currency, would fall. A part of their credits on the southern countries could also be lost in the framework of a restructuring of debts. But to compensate for this, Germany would not be involved in a move towards a federal budget to which it would have been a major net contributor. In time it could also benefit from the improved economic situation in Europe and the recovery which would result. But maintaining the status quo, from which it is the main beneficiary, could seem more advantageous to it in a short-run view, even though the stagnation of the euro zone penalises Germany as well in the longer run.

As for the countries of the South, they would benefit from the depreciation of their currencies and would gain in price-competitiveness. This is a necessary but not sufficient condition to help to resolve the structural problems which they face, in particular by making it easier to finance the redeployment of resources across different economic activities. In the medium term, growth could be restored on a new basis. The main difficulties would be the transition period, the restructuring of external debt which would have to be negotiated, and the risks of monetary instability and banking crises which would have to be controlled.

In fact, the introduction of a new monetary regime would be perilous. There would be capital outflows in anticipation of the depreciation of the new currencies. Capital controls would have to be introduced and temporary bank closures might prove to be necessary. 'Incomes policies' should be used to ensure that the return of inflation, induced initially by the increase in import prices, remained under control. An end to deflation and a moderate rate of inflation are desirable, especially in order to reduce the burden of accumulated debt. But if the benefits of depreciation are to be maintained it would be necessary to avoid accelerating inflation. From this point of view, one cannot envisage exit from the euro being combined with a significant rise in wages to start with. Finally, it must be emphasised that although growth and employment would be certainly stimulated by depreciation, national income in terms of international purchasing power would be severely reduced in the south.

One of the most sensitive questions is the management of external, euro-denominated, debt. Where such debt is governed by national legislation, repayment could take place in depreciated national euro without any increase. The fraction of the debt governed by national legislation varies a lot over countries and different economic agents (Durand and Villemot, 2017). The vulnerable countries and sectors subject to foreign legislation are not numerous (public sector debt in Greece and Portugal and the debt of the Greek financial sector where, in any case, debt sustainability is problematic; the debt of the financial sectors of small open economies where large-scale depreciation will not be needed). The public debt of France is almost entirely subject to national legislation.

In practice, the way in which such problems are managed would depend on which monetary regime was adopted. If it was the system with national euros and an overall euro (only the latter being convertible) debt redemption would have to be in overall euro, with no penalty for the creditor but with an increased burden for the debtor. If it was either the bancor-euro system or a eurozone without Germany, repayment could be made, where conditions permitted, in national euros, that is with a reduction for the creditors but without additional costs for the debtor countries. However, in such circumstances the interest rates on the debt could be raised which would increase the burden of the debt. On the other hand, these costs have to be considered relative to overall balance sheets, that is, taking into account both liabilities and assets. In terms of net external positions, the costs of depreciation would be lower for France (net external position -15% of GDP in 2015) and for Italy (-30%) than for Spain (-45%) but the Spanish euro would not need, a priori, to depreciate. It may be recalled that the United Kingdom and Poland had big devaluations in 2010 and the United Kingdom again in 2016. Their economies did not collapse.

Annex 6.1 Value of the parameters

Firms' investment
$\gamma_0 = 0$ $\gamma_1 = 0.2$ $\gamma_2 = -0.1$ $\gamma_3 = 0.05$

Households' consumption
$\alpha_0 = 0$ $\alpha_1 = 0.8$ $\alpha_2 = 0.05$

Households' cash demand (% wealth)
$c = 0.025$

Tax rate on income
$\theta = 0.1$

Tax rate on profit
$\theta_F = 0.35$

Wage share
$\lambda = 0.7$

Rate of depreciation
$\delta_K = 0.05$

Importations
$\mu_0 = -1$ $\mu_1 = 0.6$ $\mu_2 = 0.5$ $\mu_3 = 0.05$

Banks' portfolio choice
$v_0 = 0.7774$ $v_1 = 0.6$ $v_2 = -0.2$ $v_3 = -0.2$ $v_4 = -0.2$

Banks' reserves (% deposits)   Public expenditures (rate of growth)
$q = 0.05$ $\rho = 0.02$

Notes

1   For the sake of simplicity, we omit the equations that describe the ECB, especially
    the Intra-European-Adjustment-Accounts which arise as a result of the difference
    between the effective issuance of banknotes. These equations can be found in Mazier
    and Valdecantos (2014a), where the full description of the model is presented.
2   Although it is not presented, we have tried another specification where the external
    performance of each country is measured through the overall balance of payments
    instead of taking only the current account. However, since in this model the weight
    of the financial sector is smaller in comparison to the real side of the economy, the
    inclusion of the financial account into the criteria for the adjustment of the exchange
    rate ends up having negligible effects.
3   It can be noted that this accumulation of euro-bancor balances differs from the actual euro
    events. Following the emergency policy of the ECB to rescue the deficit country banks,
    German external claims moved from German banks' balance sheet to German central bank
    balance sheet in the form of TARGET2, but the Bundesbank has not been selling anything.

Part III

Enhancing regional and international monetary stability

7 Exploring monetary cooperation in East Asia

Jacques Mazier, Jamel Saadaoui, and Sebastian Valdecantos

Introduction

Beyond the single currency trap in the euro zone, the world economy remains under the threat of several destabilising forces. In general terms a financial crisis is likely as the mechanisms at work before the crisis of 2008 have not been fundamentally changed. A deep downturn can be expected in 2020 thanks to cumulative factors. US growth appears unsustainable with the progressive exhaustion of the effects of the tax cuts, the increasing public and external deficits, the impact of the trade war in some sensitive sectors and the instability of the financial markets. Only the boom of the US oil sector has widened the room for manoeuvre. Some large emerging countries (Brazil, Argentina, Turkey) are facing huge imbalances. East Asia is more resilient and China has launched a new recovery plan based on credit. The globalization has been marked by a turning point since 2008 under the effect of structural factors. The increasing implementation of robotization in production processes combined with the rising unit labour cost in China and other emerging countries have eroded the advantages of global value chains from the EU or the United States to China. The current trade war between the United States and China reinforces this evolution. This could contribute to launch some relocation of activities in the industrialized countries and transform the global economy into a more regionalized one.

At the level of the international monetary system the persistence of a hybrid dollar standard is the most likely with dominant international financial markets and high capital mobility, even if measures in favour of capital controls are more often defended. The dollar remains the key currency of the system. The euro is a regional currency with a relatively high weight in the real and financial transactions but not able to really compete with the dollar. The yuan is in a different position. It is propelled by the rising power of China but its internationalization is far from being achieved and is a long-term project.

Without analysing all the challenges to which is confronted the world economy, two points will be examined more specifically. First, the future of monetary cooperation in East Asia will be explored in this chapter to understand how China can organize its monetary area in an efficient way at the level of the whole East Asia. Second, in a more ambitious perspective we will analyse in the following chapter how a global reform of the international monetary system could contribute to stabilise a world economy threatened by financial crisis and deep downturn. Based on a deepening of the role of the Special Drawing Rights (SDR) its objective will be to stabilise the international monetary system by providing liquidity in case of financial crisis. Regular SDR allocations could also play a role to support the world demand.

The Asian crisis of 1997 has shown the limits of a simple dollar peg policy and of a market driven regional integration without formal institutions. During the 2000s a lot of efforts have been devoted to improve monetary and financial cooperation at the regional level, especially with the Chiang Mai and the Asian Bond Market initiatives. But results have been limited, mainly due to political issues associated to the competition between China and Japan. The financial crisis of 2008 has given new interest to the question of monetary cooperation at the regional level (Asian Monetary Fund, Asian Currency Unit (ACU), yuan block).

The Chinese increasing role in the world economy has raised new issues. The nature of the yuan has been progressively changing at the international level. In 2005 the exchange rate system of China officially shifted to a managed floating regime, which consisted of a flexible exchange rate within some predetermined limits given by a basket of currencies mainly composed of the dollar, euro, yen, and won. After 2005 the yuan has gradually appreciated against the dollar, except for a period between July 2008 and June 2010 when the Chinese central bank pegged the yuan against the dollar in the context of the global financial crisis. The limits the yuan's daily movements against the dollar due to the narrow trading band and the control of international capital movements made the Chinese exchange rate system closer to a fixed regime rather than to a floating system. Despite the appreciation of the yuan against the dollar, the yuan remained undervalued until the beginning of the 2010s (see Chapter 2). Since 2010 the peg of the yuan to the dollar has been transformed into a more flexible regime using a basket of currencies as reference with an intra-day fluctuation band, which has been enlarged in 2012. The huge foreign reserves of the Chinese central bank allowed it to keep the yuan parity under control with a target of real moderate appreciation in the medium term. However since 2014 China has faced financial crunch with large capital outflows ($700 billion until the end of 2015) and a limited depreciation against the dollar which has only partly compensated a real effective revaluation of nearly 20% since 2012. Chinese authorities have hesitated between different kinds of exchange rate policy. A large devaluation to boost the exports, which would be a major shock at world level, is no more an option, even in the context of trade war with the United States. It would not help the Chinese economy to upgrade its international specialization and adopt a new growth regime more devoted to domestic demand. Two possibilities can be considered: a progressive devaluation which would have the default of encouraging more capital outflows; a strengthening of capital controls to stabilise the yuan's value which would be in conflict with the past effort to raise the yuan's international status. The internationalization of the yuan and its convertibility has been a long-term project. They suppose huge institutional transformations. Internationalizing a currency means authorizing non-residents to hold domestic and foreign assets denominated in national currency and allowing their conversion in foreign currencies without restriction. China has a long way to go in this regard.

Since the burst of the financial crisis in 2008 the development of monetary and financial cooperation in East Asia has gained interest. First, some measures aimed at giving more formal structures to the Chang Mai initiatives have been taken. Second, the project of an Asian Monetary Fund to face short term adjustment problems has been re-launched. However, the great heterogeneity of East Asia, both in terms of level of development and of countries' size, pleads for keeping an adjustable exchange rate system in the future monetary regime, at least for a long transition period (Jeong et al., 2012). To go beyond the present system based on managed floating with various forms according the different countries, two main forms of monetary cooperation have been proposed, one based on a common currencies basket (Williamson, 1998), the other based on the Asian Currency Unit (ACU).

The ACU project is the more ambitious. Since the end of the 2000s, in the context of financial crisis, it has gained some interest (Shimizutani, 2009). It is a long-term project. The first step would be centred on the re-building of the institutions created with the Chiang Mai initiative and on the reinforcement of financial supervision. The second step, to be taken after 2020, would be the settlement of the ACU composed of the yen, yuan, won, and other East Asian currencies and its promotion for public and private uses. These years would be used to achieve the financial liberalization and reinforce the financial regulation before the transition to an exchange rate regime based on the ACU in the 2030s. Even at this long term, the perspective of a single currency seems problematic at the level of an area which will always be characterized by huge heterogeneity. On the contrary, the use of the ACU in an East Asian monetary regime where the national currencies would be preserved and would be in a system of fixed, but adjustable, exchange rates against the ACU, would be a more realistic project. The nature of the ACU remains open. It could be, as it is now planned, a currency basket. It could also be a new international currency floating against the dollar and the euro.

A possible alternative to the ACU in the long term could be the yuan, once it has become fully convertible and the Chinese banking and financial system have been restructured and consolidated. Another possibility could be a 'yuan block', where the yuan would be used as an anchor for the other East Asian currencies, while the yen would be in a position rather similar to the one of the pound sterling against the euro. The point in debate is what should be the level of rigidity or flexibility of this regime. Whereas a rigid one would mean that this block yuan would be close to a yuan zone with fixed exchange rates (which would not be suitable with the heterogeneity of the zone) a more flexible one would give more room of manoeuvre to face asymmetric economic performances.

The problem raised by these flexible monetary regimes, whether with an anchor on the yuan or an ACU, is the risk of instability associated to capital flights and recurrent exchange rate adjustments. Hence, some form of capital controls would have to be maintained to provide the system with more stability. This question of capital controls is more debated than it was as the financial crisis of 2008 has shown the limits of a full liberalization and the need of tighter regulation. Last, it can be noted that these flexible monetary regimes would be all the more stable as exchange rates would be close to equilibrium values and would avoid misalignments.

The comparison with the European case is enlightening. The economic and monetary integration has followed a completely different path in Europe. The march towards monetary union has resulted of a strong political will from the Werner report in 1970 to the Maastricht Treaty in 1992. However the road has not been without accident, as we have seen. The contrast is clear with East Asia where the heterogeneity between countries is higher than within the EU. The intra-regional integration is high at the level of ASEAN+3 and has increased but there is no political will in favour of more monetary integration. After the Asian crisis of 1997, more pragmatic exchange rate regimes have been adopted and exchange rate misalignments have been more limited during the 2000s than in the European case, with one main exception, the undervaluation of the yuan during a rather long period.

The chapter is organized as follows. A first section analyses the exchange rate regimes which have prevailed in East Asia since the 1990s using a FEER approach. It appears that exchange rate misalignments are more limited in East Asia in the current period than during the 1990s, in clear contrast with what has been observed between the European countries. A second section evaluates alternative exchange rate regimes for the future, such as the ACU regimes or the yuan block to go beyond the pragmatic regimes which have prevailed since the 2000s. To investigate these regimes a four-country SFC model of East Asia is proposed with two versions. The first one, based on a simple structure China, East Asia, the United States, and rest of the world, gives a rough description of the East Asian monetary regimes, as they have been observed in the past: the dollar pegged regime during the middle of the 1990s, the hybrid regime of the end of the 1990s and the beginning of the 2000s, the more flexible regime of the 2010s. Last, two regimes corresponding to rather long-term scenarios are examined, the yuan zone where the East Asian currency is anchored to the yuan which is floating or managed against the dollar, the yuan block where the East Asia/yuan parity is managed and not fixed. The second set of SFC models with a split between China, Japan, and East Asia is used to analyse more formalized exchange rate regimes like the ACU regimes, the Asian bancor regimes based on a clearing union, and the global ACU regime which implies the launching of a new international currency, the global ACU. On the whole, the ACU regimes, thanks to the possibility of exchange rate adjustments, allow a progressive reduction of imbalances and appear well adapted to a heterogeneous area like East Asia.

Exchange rate regimes and misalignments in East Asia

East Asian exchange rate arrangements covered and still cover a wide range of regimes from the dollar peg of the 1990s to the managed floating of Malaysia, Indonesia, and Thailand or the more freely floating of Japan and Korea. A large difference exists between de jure regime and de facto one. A vast literature has tried to build de facto classification (IMF, 2008; Reinhart and Rogoff, 2004). The main conclusion is that East Asian countries have a preference for intermediate regimes with pragmatic inflexions in case of necessity.

Methodology

In order to assess the exchange rate policies of the East Asian countries since the 1990s, the concept of equilibrium exchange rate will be used once again as a reference. It allows the estimation of exchange rate misalignments with periods of overvaluation or undervaluation. The FEER methodology has been presented in Chapter 2. Exchange rate misalignment is defined as the gap, in percentage, between observed exchange rates and equilibrium exchange rates. The Fundamental Equilibrium Exchange Rate (FEER) is the exchange rate prevailing when the economy simultaneously reaches the external equilibrium (a sustainable current account determined by structural parameters) and the internal equilibrium (full utilization of the productive potential). The analysis is conducted in two steps. First, at the word level, a multinational model describing the foreign trade of the main countries and of the rest of the world is used to calculate the main currencies (dollar, euro, yuan, yen, and pound sterling) equilibrium exchange rates (see Chapter 2). Second, at the level of each East Asian country, an equilibrium exchange rate is estimated, using a simple national model of foreign trade (Aflouk et al., 2010). It is not necessary for a relatively small country at the world scale to use a multinational model to estimate equilibrium exchange rates. The same methodology has been used for the European countries in Chapter 4.

Exchange rate policy and misalignments in East Asia

From the 1980s to the Asian crisis of 1997

In order to avoid exchange rate misalignments between countries increasingly integrated a dollar peg policy has been implemented in most of the East Asian countries at the end of the 1980s. Simultaneously financial liberalization has been developed during the 1990s, facilitating the finance of large current deficits. It has also induced short term indebtedness in dollars, especially of the banking sector, which has appeared highly constraining when the crisis burst. The peg to the dollar of East Asian currencies led to large overvaluation in nominal terms, but less in real effective terms in the 1990s, in relation with important current deficits (see Figure 7.1). The case of China and Japan has already been presented in Chapter 2 and will not be discussed again here.

Thailand, Philippines, and Malaysia present some similarities with respect to exchange rate policy during the 1980s. The early 1980s were marked by the end of economic boom with current account deficit and overvaluation. The peg to the dollar in the middle of the 1980s allowed a real depreciation and an improvement of their current account, leading to an undervaluation of their currencies between 1985 and 1988, especially in Philippines and to a lesser extent in Malaysia where the ringgit was close to its equilibrium value. A reversal took place at the end of the 1980s where economic recovery was related to the reappearance of important current deficits. Thailand was the most affected while the phenomenon was less marked in Philippines where the growth was more modest and current deficit more contained. The Malaysian ringgit remained as before close to equilibrium, as Malaysian economy was more trade open, which reduced misalignments' amplitude. Vietnam, as an economy in transition during the 1990s, has followed a specific path with a large overvaluation during the first half of the 1990s.

Indonesia, as an oil-exporting country, presents also some specificity. The counter-oil shock in 1986 has degraded its current account, leading to overvaluation of its currency at the beginning of the 1990s. At that time, with sustained growth and current account more under control, overvaluation became weak and did not seem to have played a large role in the crisis of 1997. However the currency the most affected by the crisis has been the Indonesian rupee, which might be explained more by political reasons and other economic imbalances. The devaluation of the Indonesian rupee was of the most important amplitude among the East Asian countries, in real and nominal terms. It resulted in a rather limited amelioration of the current account and in an undervaluation of the rupee which could be regarded as modest, compared with the amplitude of the shock. This result could reflect the destructive effects of the crisis on the Indonesian productive system.

In Korea, a period of undervaluation of the won during the 1980s, linked to the export growth strategy, was followed by a rather marked overvaluation, both in nominal and real terms. But, at the opposite of the Japanese case, this occurred after a real depreciation during the first half of the 1980s and, then, a stable dollar-won parity. This overvaluation of the won has been regarded as one of the factors explaining the Korean crisis in 1997.

Over-accumulation, diffusion of the slowdown through high economic interdependency, contagion effects, and capital flights have played a major role to explain the generalization of the Asian crisis. The stabilisation plans imposed by the IMF have amplified the economic slowdown and given a new impulsion to the financial liberalization and the deregulation. The lack of appropriate tools to solve the liquidity problems has been underlined while East Asia, as a whole, had sufficient reserves and net foreign assets to face the problems of the countries in deficit. It can also be noticed that intra-East Asia imbalances were too generalized at that time and made the intra-zone finance more complex to organize.

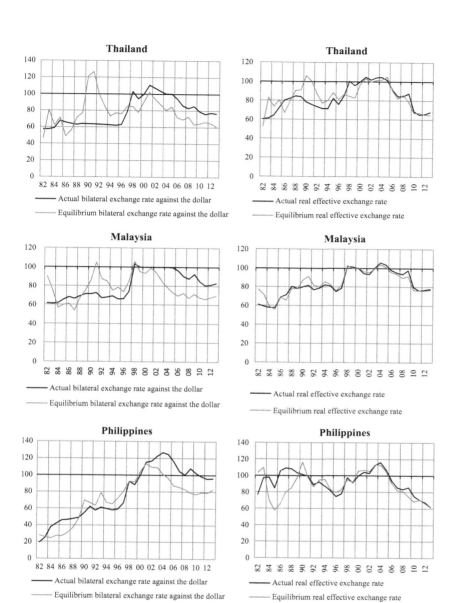

Figure 7.1 Actual and equilibrium real effective and bilateral exchange rates of ASEAN+Korea (base 100 in 2000).

Source: Authors' calculation, IFS for bilateral exchange rates, provisional data for 2013.

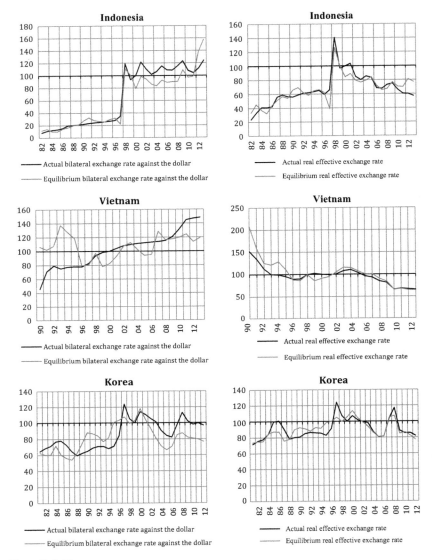

Figure 7.1 Cont.

From the 2000s to the financial crisis of 2008

The recovery has been rather quick after the Asian crisis, thanks partly to large devaluations that boosted exports. After these huge devaluations, pragmatic exchange rate policies were implemented with more diversity between countries than before, from rather strict dollar peg in Malaysia and China until 2005 to more floating regime like in Korea. The result has been, on the whole, a general undervaluation against the dollar and, even if it is less marked, in real effective terms. This was very different from the 1990s and has given more room of manoeuvre to East Asian economies, with large current account surpluses, but at the expense of the rest of the world. Actually the relative positions of various countries were rather contrasted.

The large devaluations following the Asian crisis contributed to the reconstitution of important current surpluses in Thailand and Malaysia, but not durably in Philippines and Vietnam. The bath, the dong and, to a less extent, the ringgit became undervalued, but not the Philippine peso as Philippines faced more structural problems at that time. The situation in Indonesia has been progressively normalized afterwards, the country taking advantage of the rising oil prices during the 2000s. The undervaluation of the Indonesian rupee against the dollar was in line with the other East Asian countries at the end of the 2000s, but slightly less pronounced in real terms. The Korean won was the less undervalued East Asian currency, following a rather sharp appreciation in nominal and real terms after 1999. The Korean exchange rate policy, with a won more freely floating, was more equilibrated from a global point of view, but put more constraints on the Korean economy.

During the 2000s, in spite a general movement of appreciation, the East Asian currencies remained undervalued against the dollar (around 20–30%), but much less in real effective terms. Compared with the Chinese yuan, they appeared far less undervalued, which induced a bias in the international competition among East Asian countries. Beyond this general undervaluation against the dollar, the relative divergence between East Asian currencies reflected that the pragmatic exchange rate policy adopted did not avoid some distortions between area's countries.

The East Asian countries have undertaken two main initiatives at the regional level in order to be able to mobilize local resources in case of countries facing problems of payments, the Chiang Mai initiative, signed in 2000 at the level of the ASEAN+3, and the Asian Bond Market initiative in 2002. Its aims were multiple: to give a regional alternative to the finance of national economies; to avoid the asymmetric in currencies (which implies to borrow in foreign currency for financing the economy in local currency) and the asymmetric of maturity (which refers to short term borrowing for supplying long-term loans);

and to help the ASEAN's small countries whose size is too limited to develop bonds markets.

After the financial crisis of 2008

The impact of the financial crisis of 2008 on East Asia has been more limited than ten years before, although significant at short term and unequal according to the countries. Most of the ASEAN currencies slightly appreciated against the dollar, except the Vietnamese dong which depreciated progressively, while stabilising its real exchange rate. In 2008 the Korean won has depreciated sharply, both against the dollar and in real terms. Indeed, the Korean economy has been badly affected by the crisis and has suffered, more than others East Asian countries, of capital flights in 2008. The regional institutions, especially the Chiang Mai initiative, were unable to contribute to solve the problems of the Korean banking sector. Loans from the FED, the Japanese and Chinese central banks were necessary. The won depreciation, under markets' pressure, helped the export sector, with a financial cost for the banks, and was followed by a stabilisation, which, on the whole, preserved a slight real undervaluation.

On the whole, the divergence between East Asian nominal exchange rate evolutions must not be overestimated since the 2000s. In some countries (Malaysia, Philippines, Thailand, and China since 2005) the currencies have appreciated while in others (Vietnam and, partly, Indonesia) a depreciation is observed. In terms of real effective exchange rates the appreciation trend is more general. Korea and Japan appeared rather specific with larger fluctuations of their currencies, both in nominal and real terms, reflecting a more floating regime, which doesn't exclude targeted interventions. Regarding exchange rate misalignment, East Asian currencies remained undervalued against the dollar during the 2000s. This has lasted since the burst of the financial crisis, except in Indonesia. However, in term of real effective rates, which is the more pertinent concept, exchange rate misalignments are more limited than before, even for the yuan whose real undervaluation has been vanished. The only exceptions seem to be Indonesia, where the real overvaluation appears important since 2009, and Vietnam during the 2000s.

These reduced exchange rate misalignments for East Asian countries are in sharp contrast with what is observed in the euro zone since the 2000s. In spite of an euro only slightly undervalued for the whole euro area, overvaluation of the euro in Southern European countries (Spain, Portugal, Greece, France) has been opposed to the undervaluation of the euro in the German block (see Chapter 4). The euro zone crisis has illustrated the failure of a rigid single currency system without appropriate adjustment mechanisms or forms of fiscal federalism. On the contrary, East Asian countries have adopted intermediate exchange rate regimes with a rather wide spectrum (crawling peg, managed floating, more freely floating). These exchange rate managements are rather asymmetric. By 'fear of appreciation', East Asian countries have tried to limit the appreciation trend of their currencies and have accumulated huge foreign reserves, thanks to the current surpluses. But these current surpluses have been reduced after the burst of the financial crisis of 2008 and the world slowdown. These pragmatic exchange rate regimes have given useful room of manoeuvre to each country. On the opposite, there is a need of more exchange rate coordination due to the high level of economic and financial integration and to the risk of contagious crisis. There is no consensus on the form. But the experience of the 1990s, the high heterogeneity of the East Asian zone and the failure of the euro zone show that a too rigid exchange rate system and a fortiori a project of monetary union are not appropriate. This question of the economic consequences of alternative exchange rate regimes in East Asia will be re-examined using a four-country SFC model of East Asia. The configuration of the 1990s and 2010s will be compared and alternative scenarios for the future of ASEAN integration will be discussed.

East Asian exchange rate regimes and SFC model

To study the impact of various exchange rate regimes on East Asian economies, we construct a four-country SFC model that includes four areas (China, East Asian countries, the United States, and the rest of the world) in a first version. The simulations analyse the adjustment mechanisms following demand or supply shocks. Various forms of exchange rate regimes are considered for East Asian currencies (fixed, floating or managed). A second set of models is based on a more detailed decomposition of East Asia with a split between Japan and the rest of East Asia while the USA are gathered with the rest of the world for more simplicity. It allows for the study of more elaborated flexible exchange rate regimes (fixed but adjustable beyond a certain threshold) and based on alternative forms of the ACU (ACU as a currency basket, global ACU as an international currency, ACU bancor or even ACU as a single currency). The theoretical background is the same as previously in Chapters 3 and 6.

Exchange rate regimes in East Asia and SFC model: the basic alternatives

The world economy is divided in four areas: the United States, China, East Asia, and the rest of the world. Each area has its own currency, dollar ($), yuan (¥), East Asia (₩), and the rest of the world (#). The whole structure of the SFC model is close to the one used in Chapter 6 and will not be described in detail (see Aflouk et al., 2016; Mazier et al., 2018). All of the equations are presented in Mazier et al. (2014). The public bonds are the main international financial assets and the bonds issued by the US government work as the unique foreign reserves. The emphasis is put on alternative exchange rate regimes within Asia. The dollar and the currency of the rest of the world are supposed to be freely floating. Regarding East Asia and China we considered four basic regimes, where the Asian currencies are either fixed or freely floating against the dollar, and four intermediate regimes with more managed exchange rate policies.

Alternative closures of the four basic exchange rate regimes

In SFC models the exchange rate determination is based on the adjustment between supply and demand of bonds on the different markets. Since there are four areas, six bilateral exchange rates should be determined for fulfilling transactions: $1\$ = E_1 \#$ (between US and RW), $1\$ = E_2 \yen$ (between US and China), $1\# = E_3 \yen$ (between RW and China), $1\$ = E_4 \W$ (between US and East Asia), $1\W = E_5 \yen$ (between East Asia and China), $1\# = E_6 \W$ (between RW and East Asia).

The dollar peg regime XX

The starting point is the regime XX where the exchange rates between both the yuan E_2 and the East Asian currency E_4 against the dollar are fixed. This regime can be interpreted as the one prevailing in the middle of the 1990s, when the yuan was anchored to the dollar after a long period of devaluation and adjustment, while most of the East Asian currencies were also pegged to the dollar. This anchorage of the East Asian currencies on the dollar was regarded as a de facto form of regional cooperation for countries already economically integrated. As a consequence, the exchange rate of the East Asian currency against the yuan is also fixed ($E_5 = E_2 / E_4$). The dollar and the rest of the world currency (E_1) are floating.

To keep fixed their exchange rates against the dollar (E_2 and E_4), the Chinese and East Asian central banks adjust their foreign reserves and purchase or sell bonds issued by the US government. The Chinese and East Asian bond markets are cleared by the demand of the domestic bonds by the central banks. Since the exchange rate between the United States and the rest of the world (E_1) is floating, the US bonds held by the central bank of rest of the world, which represent their foreign currency reserves, remain constant while the equilibrium of the rest of the world central bank balance sheet determines the level of the domestic bonds it holds.

The regime XL (yuan/dollar fixed, East Asia/dollar floating)

We now turn to the regime XL where the yuan remains fixed against the dollar while the East Asian currency floats against the dollar. This situation corresponds roughly to what prevailed during the end of the 1990s and the beginning of the 2000s. The modelling of this new regime is simple. Since the exchange rate between the East Asian currency and the dollar (E_4) is floating, it is defined in the same way as the case of E_1. Foreign reserves held by the East Asian central bank are constant while its balance sheet equilibrium determines the domestic bonds it holds. E_4 is determined by equalizing the demand of East

Asian bonds by US banks and the supply of these bonds to US banks given by the equilibrium of their market.

The floating regime LL

The regime LL is a rather hypothetical regime where the yuan and the East Asian currencies are supposed to be freely floating. This could be thought as a situation where the yuan has achieved its long transition period towards its internationalization and is floating against the dollar. As in the regime XL, the East Asian currency floats. This regime would correspond to a world economy dominated by the financial liberalization. By modifying the basic model, we can model the exchange rate of the yuan against the dollar E_2 determined under the floating regime. The foreign reserves of the Chinese central bank are now constant while its balance sheet equilibrium determines the domestic bonds it holds. E_2 is determined by equalizing the demand of Chinese bonds by US banks and the supply of these bonds to US banks given by the equilibrium of their market.

The yuan zone regime LX

The regime LX is another long-term scenario where the yuan is also floating after a complete liberalization. But the East Asian currency would now be pegged to the yuan. In other words the regional cooperation between Asian countries would be sufficiently developed in a long-term perspective in order to form a yuan zone with fixed exchange rates. The modelling of the floating yuan has already been presented and requires no change. The modelling of the yuan area with fixed exchange rate E_5 between the East Asian currency and the yuan implies variable foreign reserves for the East Asian central bank. The exchange rate E_4 between East Asia and dollar is no more constant but is derived from the exchange rate E_2 between yuan and the dollar ($E_4 = E_2 / E_5$).

Table 7.1 shows the alternative closures for each basic exchange rate regime. The first three columns refer to variables that ensure the equilibrium with respect to each country's bond market. The last three columns indicate the variables which ensure the equilibrium of each central bank's balance sheet. We can recall, first, that the US bonds market is always equilibrated by the domestic bonds held by the US central bank $B_{cb}{}^d{}_{US}{}^{US}$, and second, that the equilibrium of the US central bank balance sheet is not written as it is the missing equation of the model.

The closure of the intermediate regimes

Beyond these corner regimes, intermediate monetary regimes can be considered reflecting more managed floating exchange rate policies. Without analysing all the possible combinations, four cases will be distinguished.

Table 7.1 Alternative closures of the basic East Asian exchange rate regimes

	Variable determined in bond market			Variable determined by CB		
	B^{RW}	B^{CH}	B^{EA}	CB^{RW}	CB^{CH}	CB^{EA}
Regime XL E_2 fixed, E_4 floating	E_1	$Bcb^{d\mathrm{CH}}_{\mathrm{CH}}$	E_4	$\Delta Bcb^{d\mathrm{RW}}_{\mathrm{RW}}$	$\Delta Bcb^{d\mathrm{US}}_{\mathrm{CH}}$	$\Delta Bcb^{d\mathrm{EA}}_{\mathrm{EA}}$
Dollar peg XX E_2 and E_4 fixed	E_1	$Bcb^{d\mathrm{CH}}_{\mathrm{CH}}$	$Bcb^{d\mathrm{EA}}_{\mathrm{EA}}$	$\Delta Bcb^{d\mathrm{RW}}_{\mathrm{RW}}$	$\Delta Bcb^{d\mathrm{US}}_{\mathrm{CH}}$	$\Delta Bcb^{d\mathrm{US}}_{\mathrm{EA}}$
Floating regime LL E_2 and E_4 floating	E_1	E_2	E_4	$\Delta Bcb^{d\mathrm{RW}}_{\mathrm{RW}}$	$\Delta Bcb^{d\mathrm{CH}}_{\mathrm{CH}}$	$\Delta Bcb^{d\mathrm{EA}}_{\mathrm{EA}}$
Yuan zone LX E_2 floating, E_3 fixed	E_1	E_2	$Bcb^{d\mathrm{EA}}_{\mathrm{EA}}$	$\Delta Bcb^{d\mathrm{RW}}_{\mathrm{RW}}$	$\Delta Bcb^{d\mathrm{CH}}_{\mathrm{CH}}$	$\Delta Bcb^{d\mathrm{US}}_{\mathrm{EA}}$

Source: Authors' construction.

Regime XA (yuan/dollar fixed; East Asia/dollar managed)

In regime XA the yuan is still pegged to the dollar, but the East Asian currency is now in a managed regime against the dollar, instead of being purely floating like in the regime XL. It is another illustration of the regime of the end of the 1990s and the beginning of the 2000s. This regime can be constructed by modifying the exchange regime that determines E_4 from the basic model XX. We can use two kinds of targeting. The former is based on the foreign reserves held by the East Asian central bank and uses the ratio of US bonds held by central bank to GDP $(Bcb^{d\mathrm{US}}_{\mathrm{EA}} / Y^{\mathrm{EA}})$ as a target, the later uses simply the ratio of the current account to GDP $(CA^{\mathrm{EA}} / Y^{\mathrm{EA}})$. The last equations are the same as in regime XX with variable foreign reserves of East Asia.

$$E_4 = E_{4-1} + \gamma_1 \cdot \left(Bcb^{d\mathrm{US}}_{\mathrm{EA}} / Y^{\mathrm{EA}} - \left(Bcb^{d\mathrm{US}}_{\mathrm{EA}} / Y^{\mathrm{EA}} \right)^e \right) \tag{1}$$

$$E_4 = E_{4-1} + \gamma_2 \cdot \left(CA^{\mathrm{EA}} / Y^{\mathrm{EA}} - \left(CA^{\mathrm{EA}} / Y^{\mathrm{EA}} \right)^e \right) \tag{2}$$

Regime AL (yuan/dollar managed, East Asia/dollar floating)

In the regime AL the Chinese monetary authorities follow a managed regime against the dollar with a target for their foreign reserves or their current account surplus while East Asia is floating against the dollar. This regime is close to the current monetary regime of the 2010s. The system of equations is equivalent to the basic model XL with variable Chinese foreign reserves, except for the equation giving the yuan /dollar exchange rate E_2 which is replaced by one of the following equations.

$$E_2 = E_{2-1} + \gamma_1 \cdot \left(Bcb^{dUS}_{CH} / Y^{CH} - \left(Bcb^{dUS}_{CH} / Y^{CH} \right)^e \right) \tag{3}$$

$$E_2 = E_{2-1} + \gamma_2 \cdot \left(CA^{CH} / Y^{CH} - \left(CA^{CH} / Y^{CH} \right)^e \right) \tag{4}$$

The yuan zone regime AX (yuan/dollar managed, East Asia/yuan fixed)

Regime AX is another version of the yuan zone where the yuan follows a managed exchange regime against the dollar and the East Asian currency is in the fixed regime with the yuan. The Chinese financial liberalization is supposed to be less advanced and the Chinese authorities keep the yuan more under control. Equations are the same as in the fixed regime XX, except for the yuan-dollar exchange rate E_2 which is under control like in regime AL while the Chinese foreign reserves are variable. However the East Asian currency is no more anchored on the dollar, but on the yuan (E_5 is constant instead of E_4).

The yuan block regime LA (yuan/dollar floating, East Asia/yuan managed)

Regime LA describes the situation where the East Asian monetary authorities are engaged in a managed floating regime with the yuan, while the yuan is floating against the dollar. This regime can be labelled a yuan block as the yuan plays a role of anchor, but in a more flexible way than in a yuan zone with a fixed East Asian currency/yuan exchange rate. The equations are the same as in regime LX, except for the exchange rate E_5 (EA/yuan) which is adjusted by the intervention of East Asian monetary authorities to meet the target on the foreign reserves or the current account. East Asian foreign reserves are variable, but under control.

$$E_5 = E_{5-1} + \gamma_1 \cdot \left(Bcb^{dUS}_{EA} / Y^{EA} - \left(Bcb^{dUS}_{EA} / Y^{EA} \right)^e \right) \tag{5}$$

$$E_5 = E_{5-1} + \gamma_2 \cdot \left(CA^{EA} / Y^{EA} - \left(CA^{EA} / Y^{EA} \right)^e \right) \tag{6}$$

Simulations of the basic and intermediate regimes

We focus on an asymmetric supply shock inside the whole East Asia area which is the main challenge for East Asian monetary regimes and we consider a gain of competitiveness of China against East Asia (the income elasticity in equation giving the Chinese imports from East Asia is reduced from 0.6 to 0.5). Figure 7.2 gives the main results for China and East Asia (in relative difference from the baseline).

GDP of China

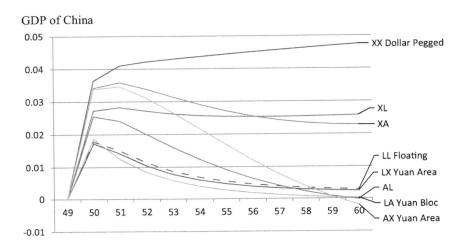

GDP of East Asia

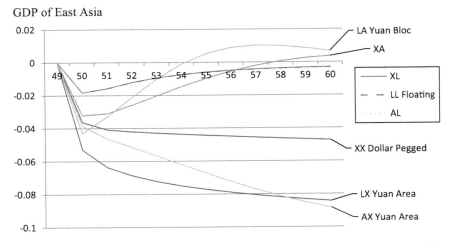

Figure 7.2 Improvement of the competitiveness of China towards EA (in relative difference from the base line).

Source: Authors' simulation.

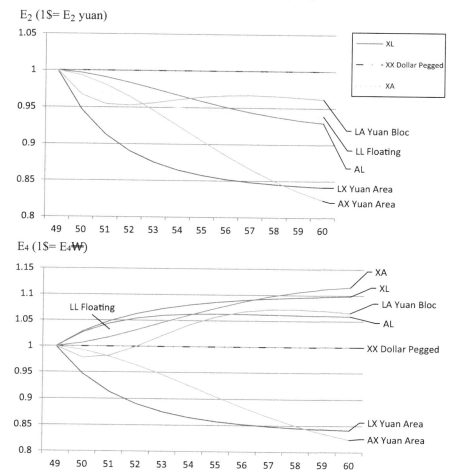

Figure 7.2 Cont.

The basic regimes

We start with regime **XX** (dollar pegged) which corresponds roughly to the middle of the 1990s with a de facto cooperation between East Asian countries by the anchorage on the dollar and also with the interventions of the Chinese monetary authority to limit the fluctuations of the yuan and anchor the yuan on the dollar. It is a kind of dollar standard with only the rest of the world floating against the dollar. The gain of Chinese competitiveness against East Asia induces a boom of Chinese GDP and trade surplus at the expense of East Asia, which suffers from symmetric losses. With fixed exchange rates, there is no mechanism of adjustment. Imbalances between China and East Asia remain without adjustment.

Regime XL (yuan/dollar fixed, East Asia/dollar floating) corresponds to the end of the 1990s and beginning of the 2000s when Chinese monetary authority limited the fluctuation of exchange rates within a certain range while the East Asian currencies were more floating against the dollar. The gains of competitiveness of China against East Asia induce a boom in China with increasing current surplus to the detriment of East Asia. But the floating exchange rate of East Asia absorbs the shock with a devaluation against the dollar which reduces the current deficit and the slowdown in East Asia to the detriment of the United States.

The main characteristic of the floating regime LL is the existence of adjustment mechanisms alleviating the persistent imbalances through flexible exchange rates. In case of an improvement of Chinese competitiveness against East Asia the current account surplus or deficits which occur in the early periods after the competitiveness shock are reduced gradually, as the exchange rates are adjusted. Chinese current account surplus makes the yuan appreciate against the dollar while the currency of EA depreciates.

Regime LX (yuan/dollar floating, East Asia/yuan fixed) is representative of a yuan zone with the East Asian currency anchored on the yuan which floats freely after a long period of liberalization. Although this regime is rather unlikely, it is worth studying it. In case of gains of Chinese competitiveness against East Asia, this is another illustration of the negative effect of fixed exchange rates when asymmetric shock occurs. Thanks to the gains of Chinese competitiveness the yuan appreciates against the dollar, followed by the East Asian currency which is pegged to the yuan. The East Asian slowdown and current deficit are amplified without mechanism of rebalancing. The United States appears as the main winner of this evolution.

The intermediate regimes

In the managed exchange rate equation, we introduce only the version using the ratio of US bonds held by central bank to GDP. Even though results are a little bit different depending on the selected target variable, it will be sufficient to show the feature of adjustment mechanisms. The shock corresponds as previously to a loss of East Asian competitiveness against China (see Figure 7.2).

In regime XA (yuan/dollar fixed, EA/dollar managed) the results are very similar to regime XL where the yuan/dollar was fixed and the EA/dollar floating. The only significant difference is that the movements of exchange rates are slower to meet the target value. Both regimes XL and XA are representative of the end of the 1990s and the beginning of the 2000s.

In regime AL (yuan/dollar managed, EA/dollar floating) the features are rather similar to the floating regime LL. The velocity of adjustment in the early periods is slower than in the case of pure floating system. Consequently, the simulation shows that the scale of the fluctuation in current account is enlarged. China is able to better preserve its gains in terms of growth and current surplus thanks to a reduced appreciation of the yuan. Regime AL corresponds broadly to the 2010s.

Regime AX (yuan/dollar managed, EA/yuan fixed) is another version of the yuan zone where, instead of having a pure floating yuan as in regime LX, the yuan follows a managed regime, while the East Asian currency remains anchored rigidly to the yuan. Without surprise, the results resemble to those of regime LX. However, once again, Chinese results in terms of growth and trade are better preserved due to the more limited appreciation of the yuan at short term. The evolution is also less unfavourable to East Asia at short-medium term, thanks to the more limited appreciation of the yuan (and of the East Asian currency) and the better situation of China. But the rigid anchorage on the yuan remains highly painful.

Regime LA (yuan/dollar floating, East Asia/yuan managed) is another version of a yuan block which is a more flexible regime. The exchange rate of EA currency/yuan is managed and no more rigid, as in the yuan zone. The results for China are close to those of the floating regime LL or to the yuan zone LX, but with a more reduced yuan appreciation, as Chinese surpluses increase less due to the depreciation of the East Asian currency. Thanks to this depreciation, a recovery and an improvement of the current account are observed in East Asia. On the whole this is the more favourable regime for East Asia facing a shock of competitiveness from China.

A first assessment

This first set of simulations has given a rough description of East Asian monetary regimes as they have been observed in the past or could evolve in the future. It is of course a highly simplified representation but it describes the interdependency between real and financial spheres in stocks and flows in a consistent way at the world and regional levels. The focus has been put on the Chinese gain of competitiveness against East Asia which has been and still is an important issue for the region. Other shocks could be simulated like a stronger Chinese rate of accumulation, a gain of Chinese competitiveness against the United States or a revaluation of the yuan (see Mazier et al., 2014 for the main results).

On the whole, these simulations illustrate that floating exchange rates are a powerful tool to reduce international imbalances. But the large instability is the intrinsic drawback of this exchange rate system and some form of capital controls should be implemented to preserve the stability. A managed exchange rate system could be a feasible political alternative as an intermediate stage, even though the adjustments are realized more gradually and the scale of the fluctuations is larger compared to the case of the pure floating system. Comparing with the current situation, two points must be underlined. The yuan is not floating and the managed exchange rate of the yuan is under control of the Chinese central bank. All of the East Asian currencies are not freely floating and various forms of managed exchange rate regimes have been adopted. However since the end of the 2000s the East Asian current surpluses have been reduced significantly.

For the future, a yuan zone with the East Asian currencies anchored to the yuan which is floating or managed against the dollar (regimes LX and AX) is a long-term scenario which could be achieved after a difficult process of economic and politic integration in East Asia. Although unlikely, it was worth being examined, especially in case of asymmetric shocks. Following a stimulation of Chinese investment, China and East Asia benefit of the yuan depreciation which improves both the current account and the GDP growth. On the opposite the United States suffer large losses due the dollar appreciation. In this demand shock East Asia benefits of Chinese recovery. But in case of Chinese gains of competitiveness against the United States, the induced growth leads to an appreciation of the yuan and of the East Asian currency which penalizes the East Asian growth and deteriorates its current account. Conversely, the US benefit of the dollar depreciation. The same results have been observed in case of an increasing Chinese competitiveness against East Asia. Asymmetric shocks in a fixed exchange rates regime (the yuan zone) induce divergent evolutions which are difficult to manage in the absence of exchange rate adjustments. This is a well-known result, although it is often forgotten. Even if a yuan zone is a long-term perspective, these results do not play in its favour, especially since this yuan zone would be characterized by strong structural heterogeneities between the participant countries.

On the opposite, a yuan block is another long-term scenario for East Asia where the exchange rate of the East Asian currency against the yuan is managed and no more rigid (regime LA). In case of Chinese gains of competitiveness against East Asia, the results for China are close to those of the floating regime LL. Thanks to the depreciation of the East Asian currency, a recovery and an improvement of the current account are observed in East Asia. On the whole this is the more favourable regime for East Asia facing an increasing competitiveness of China. It can be considered as a useful target for a future East Asian exchange rate regime.

Exchange rate regimes in East Asia: the ACU regimes

A second set of models allows for the study of more elaborated intermediate monetary regimes using alternative forms of Asian Currency Unit (ACU): traditional ACU as a currency basket, ACU bancor, global ACU as an international currency, or even ACU as a single currency. They are based on a more detailed decomposition of East Asia with a split between Japan and the rest of East Asia while the USA are gathered with the rest of the world for more simplicity. Consequently, in this SFC model the world economy is divided in four areas: China, Japan, the rest of East Asia and the rest of the world. The whole structure of the SFC model remains the same (see Mazier et al., 2014, 2018).

The traditional ACU regime

The traditional ACU is a currency basket composed of the yuan, the yen, and the East Asian currency ($1UC^{RW} = E_{10}$ ACU) which is used only as a unit of account. The ACU/rest of the world exchange rate (E_{10}) is built as a weighted average of the yen (E_1), the yuan (E_2), and the East Asian currency (E_4) compared to the rest of the world currency.

$$\frac{1}{E_{10}} = \frac{Y^{JP}}{Y^{JP}+Y^{CH}+Y^{EA}} \cdot \frac{1}{E_1} + \frac{Y^{CH}}{Y^{JP}+Y^{CH}+Y^{EA}} \cdot \frac{1}{E_2}$$
$$+ \frac{Y^{EA}}{Y^{JP}+Y^{CH}+Y^{EA}} \cdot \frac{1}{E_4} \tag{7}$$

The yen, the yuan, and the East Asian currency are floating against the rest of the world currency and are pegged to the ACU (1 ACU= E_7 yen =E_8 yuan= E_9 UC^{EA}). For sake of simplicity it is supposed there is no fluctuation margin but these exchange rates are adjustable when the current account in percentage of GDP is permanently under a certain threshold. The yuan/rest of the world exchange rate (E_2) is determined in a floating regime and the yuan is acting as anchor of the whole system. The East Asian currency/yuan and the yen/yuan exchange rates are fixed, but adjustable within the ACU regime. Consequently, the East Asian currency/rest of the world (E_4) and the yen/rest of the world (E_1) exchange rates can be simply deduced from the yuan exchange rate (E_2). Under this hybrid regime the East Asian and Japanese central banks accumulate foreign reserves under the form of bonds issued by the rest of the world government (Bcb^{sRW}_{JP} and Bcb^{sRW}_{EA}).

$$E_{7t} = E_{7t-1} \cdot (1+\varphi), \text{ if } \frac{CA^{JP}_{t-i}}{Y^{JP}_{t-i}} < -0.001, \forall i = 1,2,3,4,5 \tag{8}$$

(same equations for E_8 and E_9)

$$E_1 = E_2.E_7/E_8 \text{ and } E_4 = E_2.E_9/E_8 \tag{9}$$

$$Bcb^{sRW}_{JP} = Bcb^{dRW}_{JP} / E_1 \tag{10}$$

$$\Delta Bcb^{dRW}_{JP} = \Delta RSV^{JP} + \Delta H^{d^{JP}} - \Delta A^{JP} - \Delta Bcb^{dJP}_{JP} \tag{11}$$

$$Bcb^{dJP}_{JP} = B^{sJP} - Bb^{dJP}_{JP} - Bb^{sJP}_{RW} - Bb^{sJP}_{CH} - Bb^{sJP}_{EA} \tag{12}$$

(same equations for East Asia)

The ACU regime can also be organized without Japan or China which would prefer to preserve their autonomy. In the ACU regime without Japan, the yen floats against the rest of the world. This regime is very similar to the previous one. The yuan is still the anchor of the ACU regime (E_2). The only difference is the determination of the yen /rest of the world exchange rate (E_1) which is now floating.

$$\frac{1}{E_{10}} = \frac{Y^{CH}}{Y^{CH} + Y^{EA}} \cdot \frac{1}{E_2} + \frac{Y^{EA}}{Y^{CH} + Y^{EA}} \cdot \frac{1}{E_4} \tag{13}$$

$$E_{8t} = E_{8_{t-1}} \cdot (1 + \varphi), \text{ if } \frac{CA^{CH}_{t-i}}{Y^{CH}_{t-i}} < -0.001, \forall i = 1,2,3,4,5 \tag{14}$$

(same equations for E_9)

$$E_4 = E_2.\, E_9/E_8 \tag{15}$$

$$Bcb^{dRW}_{JP} = constant \tag{16}$$

$$Bcb^{sRW}_{JP} = Bcb^{dRW}_{JP} / E_1 \tag{17}$$

$$\Delta Bcb^{dJP}_{JP} = \Delta RSV^{JP} + \Delta H^{dJP} - \Delta A^{JP} - \Delta Bcb^{dRW}_{JP} \tag{18}$$

$$E_1 = \left(B^{sJP} - Bb^{dJP}_{JP} - Bb^{sJP}_{CH} - Bb^{sJP}_{EA} - Bcb^{sJP}_{JP} \right) / Bb^{dJP}_{RW} \tag{19}$$

In the ACU regime without China, this country remains outside the system to preserve its autonomy and the yuan floats alone against the rest of the world (E_2). This regime is similar to the previous ones. The yen becomes the new anchor of the ACU regime (E_1).

$$\frac{1}{E_{10}} = \frac{Y^{JP}}{Y^{JP} + Y^{EA}} \cdot \frac{1}{E_1} + \frac{Y^{EA}}{Y^{JP} + Y^{EA}} \cdot \frac{1}{E_4} \tag{20}$$

$$E_{7t} = E_{7_{t-1}} \cdot (1 + \varphi), \text{ if } \frac{CA^{JP}_{t-i}}{Y^{JP}_{t-i}} < -0.001, \forall i = 1,2,3,4,5 \tag{21}$$

(same equations for E_9)

$$E_4 = E_1.\, E_9/E_7 \tag{22}$$

The ACU bancor

A more ambitious regime would borrow some of the ideas proposed by Keynes (1941) in his report on an international monetary reform. An Asian bancor would be introduced and would in practice be very similar to the traditional ACU, a basket currency of the national currencies. More important, an Asian clearing union would be created and the participant countries would accumulate bancor balances (AB) at this clearing union according to their external performances, both in terms of current account and capital movements. A surplus country would register an increase in its bancor account at the clearing union whereas a country in deficit would register a decrease in its stocks of bancors. The East Asian currencies would be pegged to the Asian bancor with a system of fixed, but adjustable, exchange rates. The adjustment criterion of each East Asian currencies vis-à-vis the Asian bancor would depend on the intra-regional external performance of the associate country ($CA_{CH}^{JP} + CA_{EA}^{JP}$, for instance). But the East Asian currencies would float against the currency of the rest of the world, with one of them acting as an anchor for the whole system (the yuan for instance). Its exchange rate against the rest of the world (E_2) would be determined by the supply and demand of its domestic bonds markets, while its central bank would keep constant its foreign reserves (Bcb^{sRW}_{CH}). As the other East Asian currencies are pegged to the Asian bancor and engaged in a fixed exchange rate system, their exchange rates against the rest of the world can be simply deduced while their central banks accumulate foreign reserves (Bcb^{sRW}_{JP} and Bcb^{sRW}_{EA}).

$$1 \text{ Asian bancor} = E_7 \text{ yen} = E_8 \text{ yuan} = E_9 \text{ UC}^{EA} \tag{23}$$

$$\frac{1}{E_{10}} = \frac{Y^{JP}}{Y^{JP} + Y^{CH} + Y^{EA}} \cdot \frac{1}{E_1} + \frac{Y^{CH}}{Y^{JP} + Y^{CH} + Y^{EA}} \cdot \frac{1}{E_2}$$
$$+ \frac{Y^{EA}}{Y^{JP} + Y^{CH} + Y^{EA}} \cdot \frac{1}{E_4} \tag{24}$$

$$E_{7_t} = E_{7_{t-1}} \cdot (1 + \varphi), \text{ if } (CA_{CH}^{JP} + CA_{EA}^{JP}) / Y^{jp}$$
$$< 0.001 \text{ (same equation for E8 and E9)} \tag{25}$$

$$E_2 = \left(B^{sCH} - Bb^{dCH}_{CH} - Bb^{sCH}_{JP} - Bb^{sCH}_{EA} - Bcb^{sCH}_{CH} \right) / Bb^{dCH}_{RW} \tag{26}$$

$$Bcb^{sRW}_{CH} = \text{constant} \tag{27}$$

$$\Delta Bcb^{dRW}_{CH} = Bcb^{sRW}_{CH-1} \Delta E_2 \tag{28}$$

$$E_1 = E_2 . E_7/E_8 \text{ and } E_4 = E_2 . E_9/E_8 \tag{29}$$

Every East Asian country would have an account at the clearing union. This account would be an asset for each national central bank and a liability for the clearing union. However Asian bancor balances (AB) would also include specific flows characterizing Keynes' proposals. First, in order to make the adjustment process more symmetric within East Asia, the rule would make both debtor and creditor countries share the burden of the debts. Thus, all countries would pay interests on their bancor balances, positive as well as negative ($r^{JP}_{-1} \cdot \left| AB^{JP}_{-1} \right|$, for example). This rule would encourage countries to make their account at the clearing union be as close to zero as possible. A second flow incorporated in the bancor balances would be the one related to the distribution of the funds collected by the clearing union and resulting from the interest payments on the bancor balances (the profit of the clearing union PAB). This intra-Asian adjustment (IAA) would be distributed to member countries according to their external performance. Last, the balance sheet identity of the East Asian central banks holds through the purchases or sales of foreign reserves.

$$\Delta AB^{JP} = \Delta CL^{JP} + r^{JP}_{-1} \cdot \left| AB^{JP}_{-1} \right| + IAA^{JP} \cdot E_7 \tag{30}$$

$$\Delta CL^{JP} = CA^{JP}_{CH} + CA^{JP}_{EA} + KA^{JP}_{CH} + KA^{JP}_{EA} \tag{31}$$

$$PAB = r^{JP}_{-1} \cdot \left| AB^{JP}_{-1} \right| / E_7 + r^{CH}_{-1} \cdot \left| AB^{CH}_{-1} \right| / E_8 + r^{EA}_{-1} \cdot \left| AB^{EA}_{-1} \right| / E_9 \tag{32}$$

$$\Delta Bcb^{d\,RW}_{JP} = \Delta RSV^{JP} + \Delta H^{d^{JP}} - \Delta A^{JP} - \Delta Bcb^{d\,JP}_{JP} - \Delta AB^{JP} \tag{33}$$

Finally, in Keynes' proposals surplus countries are encouraged to use their positive bancor balances to increase imports, since otherwise they would be wasting their balances. Consequently, it is assumed that the government of surplus country augments its public expenditures to purchase imported products from other member countries. This adjustment process is non-recessionary as only surplus countries would be pushed to pursue more expansive policies.

$$\begin{cases} \psi^i_t = \mu \cdot log\left(1 + r \cdot AB^i_{t-1}\right), \ if \ AB^i_{t-1} > 0 \\ \qquad \psi^i_t = 0, elsewhere. \end{cases} \text{, for } i = \text{JP, CH, EA} \tag{34}$$

$$G^i_t = G^i_0 \cdot (1 + gr^i)^t + \psi^i_t, \text{ for } i = \text{JP, CH, EA} \tag{35}$$

The global ACU as a new international currency

In a more ambitious perspective the ACU would not be a simple basket currency, but a true international currency, the global ACU (AG), acting as an international store of value. East Asian governments would issue bonds in national currencies (yen, yuan, EA) which would be purchased only by national agents (domestic banks in the model). The gap between the financial needs of the government ($B^{s\,JP}$ for instance) and the demand for bonds denominated in domestic currency ($Bb^{s\,JP}_{JP}$) would be filled by issuance of bonds denominated in global ACU ($B^{s\,JP,AG}$) and purchased by foreign creditors to get external financing ($Bb^{s\,JP,AG}_{CH} + Bb^{s\,JP,AG}_{EA} + Bb^{s\,JP,AG}_{RW} + Bb^{s\,JP,AG}_{ACB}$). This global ACU would float at the world level and its exchange rate against the rest of the world currency ($1UC^{RW} = E_{10}\,AG$) would be determined as usual by the interaction between supply and demand of global ACU-denominated bonds.

$$B^{s\,JP,AG} = \frac{B^{s\,JP} - Bcb^{s\,JP}_{JP} - Bb^{s\,JP}_{JP}}{E_7} \tag{36}$$

$$E_{10} = \frac{B^{s\,JP,AG} + B^{s\,CH,AG} + B^{s\,EA,AG} - Bb^{s\,JP,AG}_{CH} - Bb^{s\,JP,AG}_{EA} - Bb^{s\,CH,AG}_{JP} - Bb^{s\,CH,AG}_{EA} - Bb^{s\,EA,AG}_{JP} - Bb^{s\,EA,AG}_{CH} - Bb^{s\,JP,AG}_{ACB} - Bb^{s\,CH,AG}_{ACB} - Bb^{s\,EA,AG}_{ACB}}{Bb^{d\,JP,AG}_{RW} + Bb^{d\,CH,AG}_{RW} + Bb^{d\,EA,AG}_{RW}} \tag{37}$$

In order to give flexibility to this exchange rate regime, the exchange rates of the national currencies (yen, yuan, EA) against the global ACU ($1\,AG = E_7$ yen $= E_8$ yuan $= E_9\,UC^{EA}$) are fixed, but can be adjusted according to the external performance vis-à-vis their trading partners. A rule similar to the one used in the traditional ACU regime can be retained. Once the intra-East Asian exchange rates are defined, it is possible to derive the exchange rates of the national currencies vis-à-vis the rest of the world ($E_1 = E_{10}.E_7$; $E_2 = E_{10}.E_8$ and $E_4 = E_{10}.E_9$).

The same type of clearing union as in the bancor regime is adopted. Each national central bank has a balance at the clearing union equal to its current account and portfolio balance with the other countries' participants (CL^{JP}). As the global ACU is floating and as the national central banks accumulate these balances at the clearing union in global ACU, they have no need of foreign reserves which are supposed to be constant, with the possibility of valorization effects. Last, the balance sheet identity of the East Asian central banks holds through the purchases or sales of domestic bonds.

$$\Delta CL^{JP} = CA^{JP}_{CH} + CA^{JP}_{EA} + KA^{JP}_{CH} + KA^{JP}_{EA} \tag{38}$$

$$\Delta Bcb^{d\,JP}_{JP} = \Delta RSV^{JP} + \Delta H^{d\,JP} - \Delta A^{JP} - \Delta Bcb^{d\,RW}_{JP} - \Delta CL^{JP} \tag{39}$$

$$Bcb^{s\,RW}_{JP} = cst \tag{40}$$

$$\Delta Bcb^{d\,\text{RW}}_{\text{JP}} = Bcb^{s\,\text{RW}}_{\text{JP}-1}.\Delta E_1 \tag{41}$$

The ACU as a single currency

This monetary regime is rather unlikely as it supposes a strong political will to accept the settlement of a monetary union between all the East Asian countries which would remain highly heterogeneous and would be dominated by one of them, China. Unlike the traditional ACU, which is a basket currency, the new ACU would be a true currency in which real and financial transactions would be denominated. There are no more national currencies and all national Asian bonds are denominated in ACU. The ACU floats against the rest of the world and the traditional flexible exchange rate closures prevail. The ACU/rest of the world exchange rate clears the ACU-denominated bond market and the national central banks purchase/sell domestic bonds to balance their balance sheet. There is no foreign reserves accumulation by the East Asian countries (they are kept constant) with only valuation effects when the reserves are expressed in ACU.

Table 7.2 Alternative closures of ACU exchange rate regimes

	Variable determined in bond market			Variable determined by CB		
	B^{CH}	B^{EA}	B^{JP}	CB^{CH}	CB^{EA}	CB^{JP}
ACU regime Floating, fixed but adjustable	E_2	$Bcb^{d\,\text{EA}}_{\text{EA}}$	$Bcb^{d\,\text{JP}}_{\text{JP}}$	$\Delta Bcb^{d\,\text{CH}}_{\text{CH}}$	$\Delta Bcb^{d\,\text{RW}}_{\text{EA}}$	$\Delta Bcb^{d\,\text{RW}}_{\text{JP}}$
ACU regime without JP Floating, fixed but adjustable	E_2	$Bcb^{d\,\text{EA}}_{\text{EA}}$	E_1	$\Delta Bcb^{d\,\text{CH}}_{\text{CH}}$	$\Delta Bcb^{d\,\text{RW}}_{\text{EA}}$	$\Delta Bcb^{d\,\text{JP}}_{\text{JP}}$
ACU regime without yuan Floating, fixed but adjustable	E_2	$Bcb^{d\,\text{EA}}_{\text{EA}}$	E_1	$\Delta Bcb^{d\,\text{CH}}_{\text{CH}}$	$\Delta Bcb^{d\,\text{RW}}_{\text{EA}}$	$\Delta Bcb^{d\,\text{JP}}_{\text{JP}}$
Bancor ACU	E_2	$Bcb^{d\,\text{EA}}_{\text{EA}}$	$Bcb^{d\,\text{JP}}_{\text{JP}}$	$\Delta Bcb^{d\,\text{CH}}_{\text{CH}}$	$\Delta Bcb^{d\,\text{RW}}_{\text{EA}}$	$\Delta Bcb^{d\,\text{RW}}_{\text{JP}}$
Global ACU	$B^{s\,\text{CH,AG}}$	$B^{s\,\text{EA,AG}}$	$B^{s\,\text{JP,AG}}$	$\Delta Bcb^{d\,\text{CH}}_{\text{CH}}$	$\Delta Bcb^{d\,\text{RW}}_{\text{EA}}$	$\Delta Bcb^{d\,\text{JP}}_{\text{JP}}$
ACU single currency	$E_2{=}E_4{=}E_1$	$E_2{=}E_4{=}E_1$	$E_2{=}E_4{=}E_1$	$\Delta Bcb^{d\,\text{CH}}_{\text{CH}}$	$\Delta Bcb^{d\,\text{RW}}_{\text{EA}}$	$\Delta Bcb^{d\,\text{JP}}_{\text{JP}}$

Source: Authors' construction.

Table 7.2 shows the alternative closures for the different ACU regimes. As previously, the first three columns refer to variables that ensure the equilibrium with respect to each country's bond market. The last three columns indicate the variables which ensure the equilibrium of each central bank's balance sheet. We can recall first, that the rest of the world bonds market is always equilibrated by the domestic bonds held by the rest of the world central bank, second that the equilibrium of the rest of the world central bank balance sheet is not written as it is the missing equation of the model.

Simulations of the ACU regimes

As previously, we focus on asymmetric supply shocks inside the whole East Asia area and consider, as an example, a loss of competitiveness of East Asia against Japan (the income elasticity in equation giving the Japanese imports from East Asia is reduced from 0.6 to 0.5). Figures 7.3 and 7.4 give the main results (in relative difference from the baseline) for the traditional ACU regimes and for the bancor ACU and global ACU regimes. Regime XL (yuan pegged to the dollar, East Asia, and Japan floating) and the single currency regime are used as reference regimes.

A loss of competitiveness of East Asia against Japan induces a negative shock with a slowdown and current deficit. With fixed exchange rate regimes like regime XX (all the East Asian currencies pegged on the rest of the world) or the single currency, there is no adjustment mechanism. The slowdown and the current deficit remain on the long term. On the contrary more flexible regimes like the ACU regimes with or without the yen allow a progressive adjustment by successive steps with a recovery and a reduction of the current deficit thanks to a depreciation of East Asian currency. More surprisingly, an ACU without the yuan gives negative results with a more dramatic GDP decline and current deficit. This can be easily understood, since, in this regime, the Japanese currency is the new anchor of the ACU regime and appreciates strongly due to the gains of competitiveness. The East Asian currency follows this appreciation which increases the initial negative shock. An adjustment is observed only in the long term. Also surprisingly, in the ACU regime, in spite of the gain of competitiveness of the Japanese economy the yen depreciates against the dollar, which leaves a large advantage to Japan in terms of growth. This is due to the fact that the yuan is the anchor in this regime and slightly depreciates, inducing also the yen depreciation. These mechanisms reflect the fact that the ACU regime gives some flexibility in the adjustments but is not well adapted to face asymmetric shocks between the country participants.

We now turn to Asian bancor regimes with the same type of shock, a loss of competitiveness of East Asia against Japan. A bancor regime without exchange rate adjustment (due to restrictive criterion) allows almost no correction and the initial decline of East Asian GDP remains at the advantage of Japan. When exchange rate adjustments are introduced, a devaluation of the East Asian currency by successive steps allows a progressive rebalancing. Last, a bancor regime

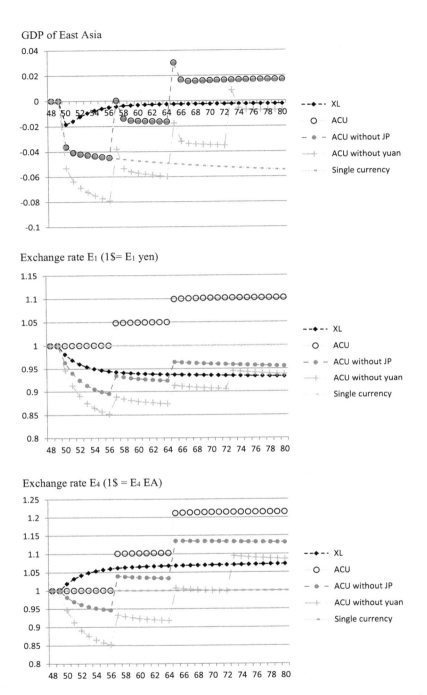

GDP of East Asia

Exchange rate E₁ (1$= E₁ yen)

Exchange rate E₄ (1$ = E₄ EA)

Figure 7.3 Loss of competitiveness of East Asia against Japan for ACU regimes (in relative difference from the base line).

Source: Authors' simulation.

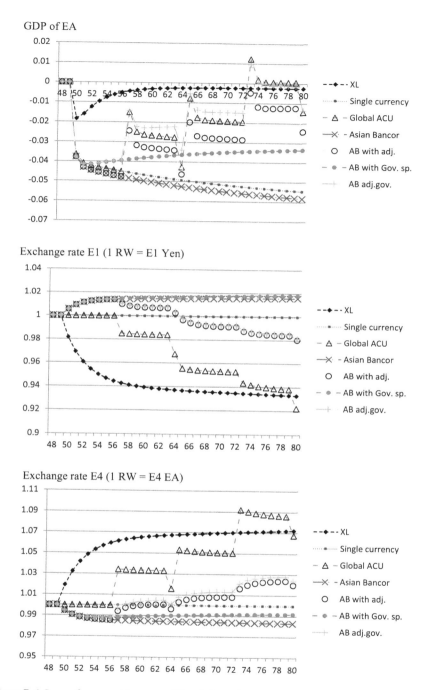

Figure 7.4 Loss of competitiveness of East Asia against Japan for Bancor and global ACU regimes (in relative difference from the base line).

Source: Authors' simulation.

where the surplus country is supposed to increase its public expenditures and imports more from the rest of East Asia gives the best performance, especially when it is combined with exchange rate adjustments. But this hypothesis of rebalancing policy by the surplus country is rather exigent and would need important improvement of coordination at the level of East Asia (Figure 7.4).

In the global ACU regime the rebalancing are larger than those observed with the Asian bancor and the traditional ACU regimes. In case of a loss of competitiveness of East Asia against Japan, the global ACU is floating and remains stable. The intra-East Asian exchange rate adjustments (devaluation of the East Asian currency and revaluation of the yen) are more limited than with the ACU, but more efficient. In the ACU regime the devaluation of the East Asian currency is indeed partly offset by a devaluation of the ACU and of the yen. Finally, the case of the ACU as a single currency is worth to be examined although it seems very unlikely. Without surprise the single currency regime appears as the less adapted to face asymmetric shocks. There is no mechanism to compensate the initial loss of competitiveness and the GDP of the country negatively shocked remains durably depressed.

Conclusion

The current exchange rate regime in East Asia is characterized by a progressive liberalization of the yuan and pragmatic managed floating regimes for the other currencies. With the increasing economic and financial regional integration, monetary and financial cooperation has been debated a lot since the 2000s without clear improvement. New issues have been raised by the financial crisis of 2008 and the increasing role of China at the regional and world level. The aim of this chapter has been to assess the pragmatic exchange rate regimes adopted in East Asia since the 2000s and to evaluate alternative monetary regimes such as the ACU regime or the yuan block. A clear opposition has appeared with the European case where more rigid monetary regimes have been implemented since the end of the 1970s, from the EMS to the launching of the euro. An estimation of the exchange rate misalignments since the 1990s has shown that these misalignments were more limited in East Asia during the current period than in the 1990s, in contrast with what has been observed between the European countries. To investigate these exchange rate regimes a four-country SFC model of East Asia has been proposed. It is of course a highly simplified representation but it describes the interdependency between real and financial spheres in stocks and flows in a consistent way at the world level. In this SFC approach there is no opposition between a determination of the exchange rates by the capital flows and by the current account. Both are taken into account simultaneously. Two versions of the SFC model have been used.

The first one, based on a simple structure China, East Asia, the United States, and rest of the world, has given a rough description of the East Asian monetary regimes as they have been observed in the past. The dollar pegged regime during the middle of the 1990s has shown its limits with the lack of adjustment mechanisms and the persistent international imbalances. The hybrid regime of the end of the 1990s and the beginning of the 2000s has introduced more flexibility to absorb the asymmetries and reduce exchange rate misalignments thanks to the managed or floating East Asian exchange rates against the dollar but the yuan pegged on the dollar was a source of disequilibrium. The more flexible regime of the 2010s, where the yuan/dollar parity is managed and the East Asia/dollar parity more floating, has been able to limit the consequences of major international imbalances. Its main drawback is its potential instability and the necessity to implement some forms of capital control to make it more resilient. Pure floating remains a rather theoretical regime. Last two regimes corresponding to rather long-term scenarios have been examined. The yuan zone where East Asia currency is anchored to the yuan which is floating or managed against the dollar is rather unlikely as it could be achieved only after a long process of political and economic integration in East Asia. The difficulty to manage the shocks in an area characterized by strong structural heterogeneity between participant countries remains a major problem which has been clearly observed in the euro area during the 2000s and the 2010s. A yuan block where the East Asia/yuan parity is managed (and not fixed) is also a long-term scenario but it allows a better absorption of asymmetric shocks. It seems a more promising perspective in the case where the yuan would strengthen its position at the world and regional level.

The second set of SFC models with a split between China, Japan, and East Asia has been used to analyse more formalized exchange rate regimes. In general, the ACU regimes, thanks to the possibility of exchange rate adjustments, allow a progressive reduction of imbalances and appeared well adapted to heterogeneous area like East Asia. However, they are very sensitive to the currency acting as anchor and to the countries participating or not to the ACU basket. On the whole they present the same advantages and limits than the EMS in the European case. The Asian bancor regimes, based on a clearing union, are more exigent in terms of institutions and bancor balances play a key role. But the amplitude of the adjustments is more limited than in the traditional ACU regimes. The bancor regime becomes more efficient when it is supposed that surplus countries are engaged in public expenditures policy to increase their demand and reduce their surplus. Although desirable, such an engagement would be difficult to obtain.

Last, the global ACU allows larger rebalancing effects than the bancor or ACU regimes. It is more balanced than the ACU regime as the global ACU is floating vis-à-vis the rest of the world. It could appear as an attractive compromise but it is rather exigent as it implies the launching of a new international currency (the global ACU) and the limitation of the role of the national East Asian currencies. The East Asia context is on that point very different from the European experience where the euro is equivalent to the global ACU and exists already. In the euro zone case the challenge is to reintroduce the possibility of exchange rate adjustments.

The case of the ACU as a single currency, although very unlikely, illustrates the negative effects of the lack of any exchange rate adjustment to face asymmetric evolutions in an heterogeneous area. It confirms the results already observed with the so called yuan area. On this respect East Asia seems in the exact opposite situation compared with the euro area. The single currency has been launched since 1999 without the institutional changes which would have been necessary, but were almost impossible to implement due to political reasons (mainly the very limited solidarity between European countries and the refuse to go towards fiscal federalism). Its failure has been particularly clear since the burst of the euro crisis. It confirms how unwise it would be for East Asian countries to go towards this kind of monetary regime.

8   Enhancing the role of the SDR

Jacques Mazier and Sebastian Valdecantos

Introduction

In the aftermath of the 2008 crisis many proposals were raised to reform the functioning of the international monetary system. Some of these proposals concerned the deepening of the Special Drawing Rights (SDR) as a reserve asset in order to provide liquidity in times of financial turmoil. It was even put forward that regular SDR allocations could be useful to support the development of low-income countries regardless of the phase of the business cycle in which the global economy may find itself. Some of these proposals were gathered in the *Stiglitz Report* (Stiglitz, 2009). Other contributions have been made by the IMF (2011) itself. The debate faded later on with more urgent problems like the euro zone crisis and then with the progressive recovery of the world economy. Since the election of Donald Trump in the United States and the decline of the multilateralism, these proposals could appear as offset. But the likely return of a new world downturn and the depletion of the traditional tools of economic policy (both at the fiscal and monetary levels) could give new impetus to such coordinated actions.

In this chapter, as in the previous ones, we examine these issues using the same approach based on a Stock Flow Consistent (SFC) model. The model consists of four-country blocks (the United States, euro zone, China and the rest of the world) with a structure similar to the Chapters 3 and 7. It is assumed that China and the rest of the world peg their currencies with respect to the dollar, while the euro floats freely. The accumulation of foreign reserves is initially made under the form of US Treasury bills. In order to test the effects of the introduction of the SDR as a reserve asset we run different types of simulations. The chapter is organized as follows. A first section gives a brief historical background of the international monetary reforms undergone since the end of the 1960s and of their inability to face the rising financial instability. A second section summarizes the proposals to enhance the role of the SDRs after the financial crisis of 2008. A third section presents the four-country SFC model with three alternative closures: the dollar pegged regime, the pure floating regime and the SDR regime. In a fourth section two sets of simulations are presented. A first one attempts to compare the current system (organized upon the US dollar as the key currency) with a scenario where there is a coordinated decision to enhance the role of the SDRs as a reserve asset with regular emission. The second set of simulations aims at comparing the current system with one where SDRs are issued counter-cyclically in times of global recession. In all our simulations the SDRs are defined as the IMF currently defines them, namely as a reserve asset that is no-one liability, but a potential claim on the currencies of its members. A last section concludes.

Historical consideration

The SDRs were created in 1969 to support the Bretton-Woods fixed exchange rate system. Under this institutional arrangement countries committed to keep their exchange rates pegged to the dollar, which in turn was fixed to gold (at a rate of $35 per ounce). In order to do so, countries needed to hoard an amount of reserves that was able to guarantee the convertibility of their national currencies to the dollar. The growing needs of liquidity by the global financial system raised doubts on capacity of the United States to provide the world with the necessary amount of reserves and, eventually, on the soundness of a system where the key currency was at the same time a national currency. This debate came to be known as the Triffin dilemma, in a reference to Triffin's (1960) contributions. For this author, when the international reserve currency is issued by a single country, the United States in the Bretton-Woods system, the international demand for reserves in that currency may not be compatible with the domestic targets for monetary policy in the issuing country. In order to prevent the system from suffering a liquidity crisis, the international community decided the creation of an international reserve asset, whose value was based on a basket of five reserve currencies, issued by a supranational institution (the IMF). However, the allocations of SDRs (only two until the extraordinary allocation of 2009) were insufficient to give this asset a real international status: the first allocation was for a total amount of SDR 9.3 billion, distributed in 1970–1972, and the second for SDR 12.1 billion, distributed in 1979–1981.

After the collapse of the Bretton-Woods agreements in 1971 exchange rates acquired a larger degree of flexibility and were mostly determined by market forces. However, the lack of an international set of rules regarding the coordination of exchange rate policies allowed countries to manage their exchange rates through interventions and other types of regulation. As a result, while Europe chose a floating regime vis-à-vis the US dollar (although currencies within the region were pegged in the framework of the European Monetary System), Asian countries opted for an administrated regime that tended to keep the exchange rate relatively stable until the Asian crisis of 1997.

There were, however, some attempts to build a more coordinated set of rules that govern international monetary relationships. In 1972–1974, the Committee of Twenty established within the IMF, started studying the possible implementation of a substitution account. The plan would allow official reserve holders (creditor countries) to replace a portion of their foreign exchange reserves with SDRs issued by a special account overseen by the IMF. This would imply a substitution of the debtor – instead of owing liabilities (under the form of Treasury bills) to creditor countries, the United States would owe its debt to the IMF who, in turn, would issue the SDR balances under which creditor countries would hold their reserves. It was not clear, however, what would be the cost that the United States would have to face under this alternative regime in comparison to the prevailing situation, where it had to pay the interest rate on the Treasury bills. Thus, the United States preferred to keep an open mind to the need of transforming reserves while an emphasis was put on the necessity to introduce mechanisms that promoted symmetric adjustments of current account imbalances. As a result of the lack of agreement on the interests payable on assets and liabilities under this alternative framework combined with the need to focus on more urgent problems (mainly the oil crisis and the context of stagflation) the proposal of the Committee of Twenty was dismissed (McCauley and Schenk, 2014).

The second attempt to rule the working of the international monetary system took place in 1978–1980, when two new projects for a substitution account were proposed. These projects suggested that developed countries (including the United States) deposit an amount of dollars equivalent to the amount of SDRs they were allocated into a substitution account in order to increase the proportion of global reserves denominated in SDRs. The IMF would then invest the proceeds in long-term US Treasury securities. According to McCauley and Schenk (2014) these attempts failed for several reasons: first, the reluctance of the US government to create a rival to the dollar as the reserve currency; second, the lack of agreement regarding the return on SDR assets in the substitution account; third, the need for the United States to take on a major burden of any of the proposed schemes; last, the desire of Europeans that the United States amortize theirs obligations. Kenen (2010) seems to share this view when he states that:

> the proposal was widely discussed at the time but was not adopted for two reasons: the strengthening of the dollar in foreign exchange markets at the start of the 1980s and, more importantly, the refusal of the United States to take sole responsibility for maintaining the dollar value of the SDR–denominated claims on the proposed account.

Furthermore, the idea of the substitution account would have been rather heavy to implement and would not have solved the underlying problems of the international monetary system. The fundamental mechanism would have remained unchanged.

The third attempt to coordinate monetary and exchange rate policies at the international level took place in the second half of the 1980s, with the signing of the Plaza and Louvre Accords in 1985 and 1987, respectively. The strong appreciation that the US dollar registered between 1980 and 1985 against the currencies of Japan, Germany, France and the United Kingdom widened current account imbalances. This implied that creditor countries were hoarding massive stocks of American debt. Moreover, the lack of competitiveness of US manufacturing sector (explained in part by the appreciation of the dollar) was laying the foundations for protectionist laws. In order to prevent potential problems in the domain of international trade, the US government started negotiations with the remaining big countries to let the dollar depreciate. After the Plaza Accord, signed in 1985, the depreciation of the dollar was possible because central banks coordinated their interventions in a way that was predictable to the market.

As a result of the sharp depreciation of the dollar the Louvre Accord was signed in 1987. This agreement entailed the coordination of exchange rate policies and attempted to coordinate domestic fiscal and monetary policies in such a way that imbalances were reduced. But, by the end of 1987, the fears of inflation in Germany led the Bundesbank to raise the short-term rate of interest, which was followed by the monetary authorities of the remaining countries. The inability to commit to the rules of the agreement put an end to the Louvre Accord.

All these failed attempts to build a universally accepted monetary arrangement left the global economy without real monetary order and the drawbacks of the international monetary system remained unsolved. As a result, the global adjustment process was ineffective, meaning that there were no either self-correcting or imposed mechanisms that tended to reduce current account imbalances. When imbalances became unsustainable, only deficit countries were forced to pursue 'structural adjustment policies' or 'structural reforms'. Thus, the burden of the adjustment was born only by the debtors. Also, the lack of financial regulation produced large amounts of liquidity that reduced countries' ability to meet their domestic policy goals, simultaneously increasing financial fragility. This led to a series of financial crisis since the middle of the 1900s with the Mexican peso crisis in 1995, followed by the Asian crisis in 1997, then by the Russian and the Argentine ones in 2001. In order to reduce the degree of vulnerability many countries (mainly emerging and developing) started to pursue a policy of reserve accumulation that could have otherwise been used to finance development and attain higher levels of demand and employment both at the domestic and global level.

Some proposals to enhance the role of the SDR

After the financial crisis of 2008 the debate about the reform of the international monetary system has experienced some renaissance. Enhancing the role of the SDRs as a reserve asset has been proposed with the possibility of providing liquidity in case of financial crisis, but also with the idea of regular SDR allocation to support the development independently of the phase of the business cycle. Some of these proposals can be found in the *Stiglitz Report* (Stiglitz, 2009), which benefited from the contributions of several economists that have been largely working on the problems of the current international monetary system. In this section we take what we consider the most relevant features of the proposal concerning the deepening of the role of the SDRs as it was laid down in that report. This is not, however, the only contributions that have been made in this regard. Other contributions have been made by the IMF itself, for example in the report 'Enhancing international monetary stability: a role for the SDR?' (IMF, 2011).

According to the IMF, 'the SDR is neither a currency, nor a claim on the IMF. Rather, it is a potential claim on the freely usable currencies of IMF members'. There are in principle two ways in which holders of SDRs can obtain these currencies. Either they can arrange voluntary exchanges with other members, or the IMF can designate members with strong external positions to purchase SDRs from members with weak external positions. Thus, SDR allocations are made *ex nihilo*, with no 'backing' whatsoever. These (eventual) allocations are distributed according to each country's quota in the capital of the IMF. In terms of accounting, when the stock of SDRs is increased (as it happened in 2009 with an extraordinary allocation of SDRs) the net worth of the IMF remains unchanged since SDRs are not a liability for it, but 'a potential claim' on the central banks of its members (especially on those whose currencies constitute the basket on which the SDR is based). Thus, SDR allocations imply an increase in the net worth of the central banks of the member countries with no balancing entry at all. This is why we believe that this reserve asset has a great potential to bring about a better functioning of the international monetary system.

In the *Stiglitz Report* there are, broadly speaking, two proposals aimed at enhancing the role of the SDR. The first one entails that countries agree to exchange their own currencies for SDRs and vice-versa, in a way that could be described as a system of worldwide swaps among central banks. In this case the emissions of SDRs would be fully backed by a basket of the currencies of member countries, in which case SDR allocations would imply no change in the net worth of central banks. Since nowadays, as mentioned in the previous section, SDR allocations are made *ex nihilo* we prefer to focus on the second proposal put forward in the *Stiglitz Report*. It basically consists of taking the present system and introducing some modifications, on the one hand the establishment of either regular SDR allocations or a system of countercyclical allocations (unlike the current situation, where only three allocations have taken place in more than 50 years), and on the other the modification of the distribution criterion, in such a way that developing countries receive a larger share of every allocation. Table 8.1 summarizes the different alternatives that can be derived from the *Stiglitz Report*, for each of which we attempt to build a model that reproduces the economic dynamics that would result should they be implemented.

Table 8.1 Alternative SDR-based reforms of the international monetary system

Distribution criterion Emission criterion	Regular emissions (annual, every five years, etc.)	Countercyclical emissions (only in times of global recession)
According to each country's quota	Model 1	Model 2
According to each country's demand for reserves	Model 3	Model 4

Source: Authors' construction.

SDR regime and SFC modelling of the international monetary system

The SFC model of the world economy used to study the international monetary system is similar to those of the previous chapters. The world economy is divided in four countries, United States, euro zone, China and the rest of the world. Imports are determined on a bilateral basis from GDP and the exchange rate, since we assume fixed prices in this version of the model. Six bilateral exchange rates are used in the model between the four currencies: US dollar (\$), euro (€), yuan (¥) and rest of the world (#): 1 \$ = E1 € = E2 ¥ = E4 #; 1 € = E6 # = E3 ¥; 1 # = E5 ¥. The production is demand determined. The functional distribution of income is the wage bill, together with interest and dividends paid by banks. They determine household income, which is taxed by the government. Households spend out of disposable income and the residual saving determines the end-of-period stock of household wealth, which can be held under the form of money or bank deposits. Non-financial firms have to pay taxes and interests on the existing stock of loans. Retained earnings are available for investment, which is determined by the profit rate, the cost of servicing the debt and an accelerator term. The demand for loans is given by the desired investment which cannot be financed by retained earnings. These loans are provided on demand, with no credit rationing. Banks distribute all of their profits to households. Additionally, banks are required to hold reserves as a share of deposits and ask for advances from the central bank whenever the amount of liquidity from deposits, or eventually own capital, is insufficient to provide loans plus satisfying their demand for domestic and foreign bills. The central bank is assumed to transfer its profits to the government and to provide advances to commercial banks on demand with no restriction on credit. The government deficit is obtained as the difference between expenditures on goods and services, which grow at a constant rate, plus interest payments and tax receipts. Any deficit is financed by issuances of new bills. Table 8.2 gives the balance sheet of the rest of the world with the main assets and liabilities.

Three alternative closures of the model can be proposed in order to describe three different monetary regimes at the world level. The first one corresponds to the dollar peg regime where the yuan and the currency of the rest of the

Table 8.2 Balance sheet of the rest of the world

Asset/Liability	Households	Firms	Banks	Government	Central Bank
Capital		$+K^{RW}$			
Central Bank Money	$+Hd^{RW}$				$-Hs^{RW}$
Deposits	$+Md^{RW}$		$-Md^{RW}$		
Loans		$-Ld^{RW}$	$+Ls^{RW}$		
Advances			$-Ad^{RW}$		$+As^{RW}$
Reserves			$+Rd^{RW}$		$-Rs^{RW}$
U.S. Bills			$+Bd, b_{RW_t}^{US}$		$+Bd, cb_{RW_t}^{US}$
Eurozone Bills			$+Bd, b_{RW_t}^{EZ}$		
Chinese Bills			$+Bd, b_{RW_t}^{CH}$		
RoW Bills			$+Bd, b_{RW_t}^{RW}$	$-Bs^{RW}$	$+Bd, cb_{RW_t}^{RW}$
SDR					$+SDRd^{RW}$

Source: Authors' construction.

world are pegged to the dollar. The second is the rather theoretical regime where all the currencies are freely floating. These two models have already been presented in Chapters 3 and 7 with very similar specifications. The third one is a SDR regime which illustrates the Stiglitz's proposals and goes beyond the simple substitution account.

The dollar pegged regime

This regime where the euro and the dollar are floating while the yuan and the rest of the world currency are pegged to the dollar corresponds roughly to the hybrid regime which settled after the collapse of the Bretton-Woods regime. The exchange rate E1 is floating and clears the euro-denominated bonds market.

$$E1_t = \frac{Bs_t^{EZ} - Bs, b_{EZ_t}^{EZ} - Bs, cb_{EZ_t}^{EZ} - Bs, b_{CH_t}^{EZ} - Bs, b_{RW_t}^{EZ}}{Bd, b_{US_t}^{EZ}} \tag{1}$$

Foreign reserves of the ECB under the form of US bonds ($Bs, cb_{EZ_t}^{US}$) remain constant and the central bank's demand for domestic bonds in the euro zone adjusts the balance sheet identity.

$$\Delta Bd, cb_{EZ_t}^{EZ} = \Delta H_t^{EZ} + \Delta R_t^{EZ} - \Delta A_t^{EZ} \tag{2}$$

The yuan and the rest of the world currency are pegged to the dollar (E2 and E4 fixed) and the central banks of China and rest of the world adjust their foreign reserves (kept under the form of US bonds).

$$\Delta Bs, cb_{CH_t}^{US} = \frac{\left(\Delta H_t^{CH} + \Delta R_t^{CH} - \Delta A_t^{CH} - \Delta Bd, cb_{CH_t}^{CH}\right)}{E2_t} \tag{3}$$

$$\Delta Bs, cb_{RW_t}^{US} = \frac{\left(\Delta H_t^{RW} + \Delta R_t^{RW} - \Delta A_t^{RW} - \Delta Bd, cb_{RW_t}^{RW}\right)}{E4_t} \tag{4}$$

The domestic bond markets of China, the rest of the world and the United States are equilibrated by the purchases of the central banks which absorb as many bonds as necessary.

$$Bd, cb_{CH_t}^{CH} = Bs_t^{CH} - Bs, b_{CH_t}^{CH} - Bs, b_{EZ_t}^{CH} - Bs, b_{US_t}^{CH} - Bs, b_{RW_t}^{CH} \, \in \tag{5}$$

$$Bd, cb_{RW_t}^{RW} = Bs_t^{RW} - Bs, b_{RW_t}^{RW} - Bs, b_{EZ_t}^{RW} - Bs, b_{CH_t}^{RW} - Bs, b_{US_t}^{RW} \, \in \tag{6}$$

$$Bd, cb_{US_t}^{US} = Bs_t^{US} - Bs, b_{US_t}^{US} - Bs, b_{EZ_t}^{US} - Bs, b_{CH_t}^{US} - Bs, b_{RW_t}^{US} - Reserves_t \tag{7}$$

$$Reserves_t = Bs, cb_{EZ_t}^{US} + Bs, cb_{CH_t}^{US} + Bs, cb_{RW_t}^{US} \tag{8}$$

The balance sheet of the US central bank is not written, as it is the missing equation.

The dollar regime with pure floating

This regime, rather theoretical, would correspond to an achievement of the financial liberalization. The exchange rates of the yuan (E2) and rest of the world (E4) are now floating and are clearing the bond markets of China and rest of the world while foreign reserves are kept constant. The balance sheet identity of the central bank of China and rest of the world are modified consequently.

$$E2_t = \frac{Bs_t^{CH} - Bs, b_{CH_t}^{CH} - Bs, cb_{CH_t}^{CH} - Bs, b_{EZ_t}^{CH} - Bs, b_{RW_t}^{CH}}{Bd, b_{US_t}^{CH}} \tag{9}$$

$$E4_t = \frac{Bs_t^{RW} - Bs, b_{RW_t}^{RW} - Bs, cb_{RW_t}^{RW} - Bs, b_{EZ_t}^{RW} - Bs, b_{CH_t}^{RW}}{Bd, b_{US_t}^{EZ}} \tag{10}$$

$$Bs, cb_{CH_t}^{US} = \overline{Bs, cb_{CH}^{US}} \tag{11}$$

$$Bs, cb_{RW_t}^{US} = \overline{Bs, cb_{RW}^{US}} \tag{12}$$

$$\Delta Bd, cb_{CH_t}^{CH} = \Delta Hd, h_{CH_t}^{CH} + \Delta Rd, h_{CH_t}^{CH} - \Delta Ad_t^{CH} \tag{13}$$

$$\Delta Bd, cb_{RW_t}^{RW} = \Delta Hd, h_{RW_t}^{RW} + \Delta Rd, h_{RW_t}^{RW} - \Delta Ad_t^{RW} \tag{14}$$

The SDR regime

An introduction of SDRs derived from the *Stiglitz Report* (2010) is proposed and based on the structure of Valdecantos and Zezza (2015). The fact that SDRs as defined by the IMF do not constitute a liability for anyone, but just a 'potential claim' on the currencies of advanced economies, goes against one of the principles of SFC modelling, which states that every financial asset must have a financial liability as its balancing entry. In SFC models only real assets, like the stock of capital, can be created without the creation of a liability of equal size. In this model we attempt to reproduce the working of SDRs as it is in reality, even though that can seem not fully consistent to the ones that are familiar with this literature. The SDRs that each central bank is allocated (as assets) are matched by a transfer of money from the central banks of the advanced economies (here, the United States and the euro zone) to the IMF (SDRs being liabilities for IMF), in such a way that the idea of a 'potential claim' is represented. This specification seems more reasonable from a SFC modelling viewpoint, but does not reflect the accounting criteria adopted by the IMF and central banks around the world.

In this regime, the euro floats freely while China and the rest of the world peg their currencies with respect to the dollar. The exchange rate E1 is floating and clears the euro-denominated bonds market.

$$E1_t = \frac{Bs_t^{EZ} - Bs, b_{EZ_t}^{EZ} - Bs, cb_{EZ_t}^{EZ} - Bs, b_{CH_t}^{EZ} - Bs, b_{RW_t}^{EZ}}{Bd, b_{US_t}^{EZ}} \tag{15}$$

Foreign reserves of the ECB under the form of US bonds ($Bs, cb_{EZ_t}^{US}$) remain constant and the central bank's demand for domestic bonds in the euro zone adjusts the balance sheet identity.

$$\Delta Bd, cb_{EZ_t}^{EZ} = \Delta Hs_t^{EZ} + \Delta Rs_t^{EZ} - \Delta As_t^{EZ} - \overline{\Delta Bd, cb_{EZ_t}^{US}} - \Delta SDRd_t^{EZ} \tag{16}$$

The yuan and the rest of the world currency are pegged to the dollar (E2 and E4 fixed) and the central banks of China and rest of the world adjust their foreign reserves (kept under the form of US bonds).

$$\Delta Bs, cb_{CH_t}^{US} = \frac{\Delta Hs_t^{CH} + \Delta Rs_t^{CH} - \Delta As_t^{CH} - \Delta Bd, cb_{CH_t}^{CH} - \Delta SDRd_t^{CH}}{E2_t} \tag{17}$$

$$\Delta Bs, cb_{RW_t}^{US} = \frac{\Delta Hs_t^{RW} + \Delta Rs_t^{RW} - \Delta As_t^{RW} - \Delta Bd, cb_{RW_t}^{RW} - \Delta SDRd_t^{RW}}{E4_t} \tag{18}$$

$$\Delta Bd, cb_{US_t}^{US} = \Delta Hs_t^{US} + \Delta Rs_t^{US} - \Delta As_t^{US} - \Delta SDRd_t^{US} \text{ (not written)} \tag{19}$$

The domestic bond markets of China, the rest of the world and the United States are equilibrated by the purchases of the central banks which absorb as many bonds as necessary.

$$Bd, cb_{CH_t}^{CH} = Bs_t^{CH} - Bs, b_{CH_t}^{CH} - Bs, b_{EZ_t}^{CH} - Bs, b_{US_t}^{CH} - Bs, b_{RW_t}^{CH} \text{ €} \tag{20}$$

$$Bd, cb_{RW_t}^{RW} = Bs_t^{RW} - Bs, b_{RW_t}^{RW} - Bs, b_{EZ_t}^{RW} - Bs, b_{CH_t}^{RW} - Bs, b_{US_t}^{RW} \text{ €} \tag{21}$$

$$Bd, cb_{US_t}^{US} = Bs_t^{US} - Bs, b_{US_t}^{US} - Bs, b_{EZ_t}^{US} - Bs, b_{CH_t}^{US} - Bs, b_{RW_t}^{US} - Reserves_t \tag{22}$$

The SDR is defined with respect to the dollar as a basket currency given in equal terms by the dollar and the euro.

$$1\$ = E7 \text{ SDR} \tag{23}$$

$$1/E7 = 0.5 \ (1/E1) + 0.5 \tag{24}$$

Following the proposals laid down in the *Stiglitz Report* we define two alternatives for the emissions of SDRs. The first one consists of an issuance on a regular basis, where z is an exogenous predetermined rate of growth:

$$SDRs_t = SDRs_{t-1} \cdot (1 + z) \tag{25}$$

The second possibility is to establish a rule according to which a certain amount of SDRs, λ, are issued every time the global economy enters a recession.

$$SDRs_t = \begin{cases} SDRs_{t-1} & \text{if } \dfrac{\Delta Y_t^W}{Y_{t-1}^W} > 0 \\[2em] SDRs_{t-1}.(1+\lambda) & \text{if } \dfrac{\Delta Y_t^W}{Y_{t-1}^W} \leq 0 \end{cases} \qquad (26)$$

Finally, two alternatives for the allocation criteria can also be considered. A first possibility could be given by the current criterion, according to which each country receives an amount of the newly issued SDRs based on its quota at the IMF. This can be simply modelled defining each country's quota, q, as its share on global GDP.

$$q_t^i = \frac{Y_t^i}{Y_t^W} \quad \forall i = US, EZ, CH, RW \qquad (27)$$

Another possibility could consist of the establishment of a criterion based on the relative demands for foreign reserves. This would benefit emerging and developing countries, whose demand for reserves is larger for the self-insurance motive. There are several ways to design the formula that defines the allocation criterion based on the relative demand for reserves. In order to keep things as simple as possible we assume that SDR are equally allocated among the countries whose reserve-to-GDP ratio was larger than 10% in the previous period. The combination of these two emission and allocation criteria yields four different models, as shown in Table 8.1.

Last, since the spirit of SDR proposals are Keynesian, we assume that the SDR allocations are made to allow the government to increase its consumption with no fear of creating tensions in its balance of payments, on the exchange rate and on the financial stability of the country. The government consumption equation, which stated that expenditures grew at a constant rate, is augmented to include an additional term that is equal to the SDR allocation that is made on the corresponding period. This can be interpreted, depending on the simulation experiment, either as a higher room for countercyclical fiscal policies in times of recessions or as foreign aid for the investments that are needed for the development of the country.

$$G_t^i = G_{t-1}^i.(1+g) + \Delta SDR, d_t^i \quad \forall i = US, EZ, CH, RW \qquad (28)$$

Assessment of the different international monetary regimes

The nature of the adjustment mechanisms in the different international monetary regimes which have been considered can be analysed using exogenous shocks as in the previous chapters, first a restrictive fiscal policy in the United States, second a reduction of the public spending in the four countries inducing a global recession.

The dollar pegged regime

The dollar pegged regime, where only the euro and dollar are floating, illustrates the regime which has prevailed after the collapse of the Bretton-Woods system until the end of the 1990s. It has already been analysed in Chapter 3 with the three-country model and Chapter 7 with the model more devoted to East Asia. A restrictive US policy induces a slowdown in the United States with a dollar appreciation against the euro and a negative impact in China and the rest of the world leading to a world slowdown. Current account imbalances in the United States, China and the rest of the world appear without any adjustment mechanism (Figures 8.1, 8.2 and 8.3). The euro area is less affected thanks to the euro depreciation and the European current balance is close to equilibrium.

The SDR regime

In order to examine the impact of the four alternative SDR regimes we compare these models with the model that represents the current functioning of the international monetary system. We first analyse the SDR regime with regular emissions (models 1 and 3), then the SDR regime with countercyclical emissions (models 2 and 4).

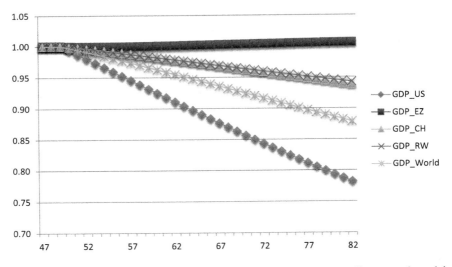

Figure 8.1 Restrictive fiscal policy in the US, impact on GDP – Dollar pegged model (with respect to the base line).

Source: Authors' simulation.

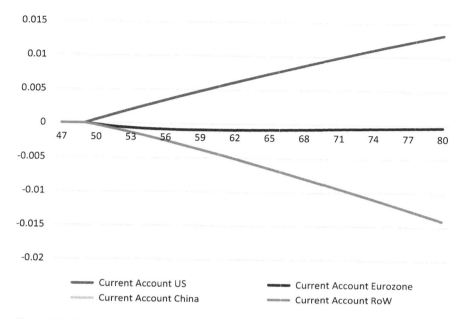

Figure 8.2 Restrictive fiscal policy in the US, impact on current account – Dollar pegged model (with respect to the base line).

Source: Authors' simulation.

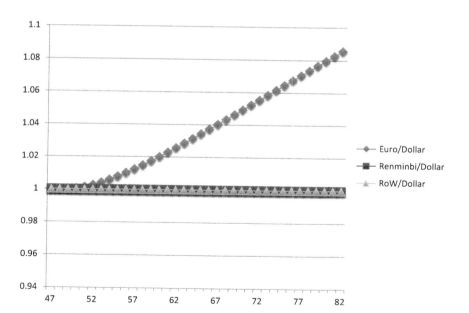

Figure 8.3 Restrictive fiscal policy in the US, impact on exchange rate – Dollar pegged model (with respect to the base line).

Source: Authors' simulation.

The SDR regime with regular emissions

Figure 8.4 plots the trajectories of the global GDP both in the model that represents the current system and in the two scenarios where the SDR is given a larger role through regular emissions according to each country's quota (model 1) or according to each country's demand for reserves (model 3). In the left axis we measure the growth of the global GDP. The sudden issuance of SDRs in period 50 entails an impulse to the global economy, since the recipient countries find themselves with more room to launch more expansionary fiscal policies. Figure 8.4 shows that a sudden allocation of SDRs not only produces an expansionary effect in the period when it takes place, but that its impact is also long-lasting thanks to the fact that thenceforth new emissions of SDRs are made in every period. Thus, the results of these simulations (models 1 and 3) show that higher levels of global demand could be attained by means of the creation of reserve assets *ex nihilo* that countries can use to back up the pursuit of more expansionary fiscal policies without incurring in macro-financial inconsistencies.

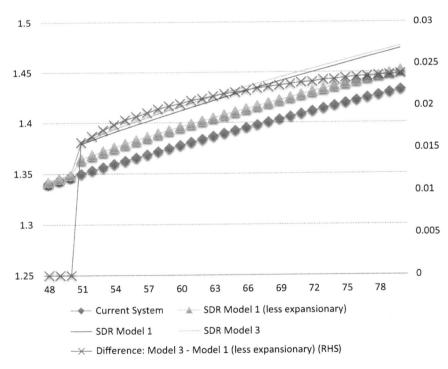

Figure 8.4 Impact of regular emissions of SDRs on the growth of global GDP.
Source: Authors' simulation.

The same simulation can be made but assuming that only China and the rest of the world use the SDRs to pursue expansionary policies. Figure 8.4 reproduces also the situation where the United States and the euro zone do not launch an expansionary fiscal policy after the emission and distribution of SDRs. Not surprisingly, the rate of growth that the global economy attains is lower than in the previous scenario, since in this case only two country blocks start pursuing more expansionary fiscal policies after the emission of SDRs. Nevertheless, the global economy finds itself growing at a faster pace with respect to the situation where the international monetary system remains unchanged. Also, the difference between model 1 (less expansionary), that is, the one where only China and the rest of the world pursue expansionary policies after the allocation of SDRs and model 3 (the one where SDRs are allocated according to the demand for reserves) seems to reflect why many economists think that the extraordinary allocation of SDRs in 2009 was insufficient to boost the global economy: because the larger amount of SDRs were given to the countries that needed them the less.

The SDR regime with countercyclical emissions

In order to assess the contribution that SDRs could have to mitigate the effects of a global recession we assume that at a certain point of time there is an exogenous reduction in the autonomous component of public spending in the four-country blocks. This leads to a global recession that, following the specification of models 2 and 4, trigger the emission of SDRs. Figure 8.5 shows the trajectories of global GDP in these two models and in the model that represents the international monetary system as it is today. The results of the simulations must be interpreted as the ratios with respect to the baseline scenario (i.e., where no shock is introduced).

The main result of this simulation is that after the shock, which has a negative effect in the three models, global GDP recovers faster at short term when the distribution of SDRs is made according to the demand for reserves of each country (model 4) than when SDRs are allocated according to the quotas (model 2). This is explained by the fact that, when it is the demand for reserves the criterion that prevails, China and the rest of the world receive the totality of the SDRs emission, which in turn leads to a higher fiscal impulse in these countries. These expansionary fiscal policies induce a higher demand for European and US goods that improves the current account of the United States and the EU. Since the yuan and the currency of the rest of the world are pegged to the dollar, the euro appreciates and the dollar depreciates in all the cases, but much more in case of distribution of SDRs according to the demand for reserves (model 4, Figures 8.6–8.8). This implies that the enhancement of the SDR as a reserve asset for times of global recession is good *per se*. However, their countercyclical impact in the short run is larger when the allocation criterion is given by the demand for reserves. This is due to the fact that the stronger expansionary fiscal policies launched by China and the rest of the world benefit

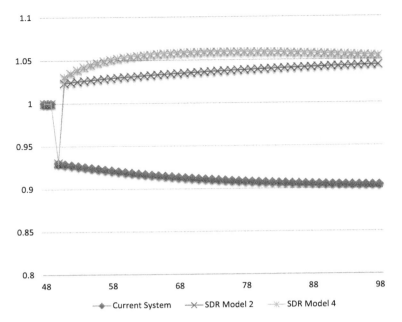

Figure 8.5 Impact of countercyclical emissions of SDRs on the growth of global GDP (with respect to the base line).

Source: Authors' simulation.

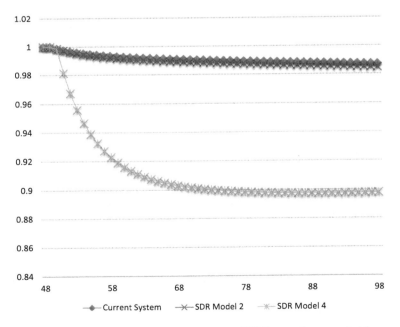

Figure 8.6 Impact of countercyclical emissions of SDRs on the euro (with respect to the base line).

Source: Authors' simulation.

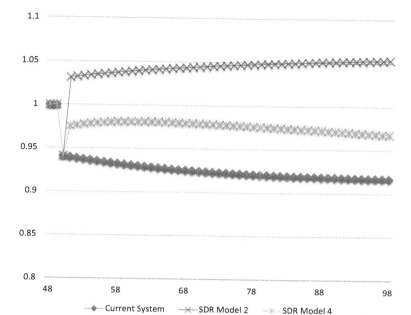

Figure 8.7 Impact of countercyclical emissions of SDRs on the GDP of the US (with respect to the base line).

Source: Authors' simulation.

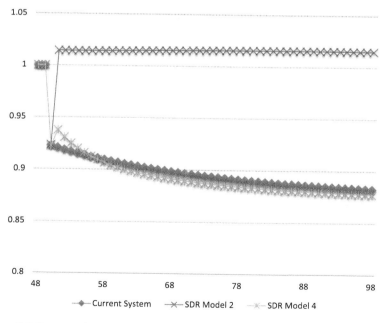

Figure 8.8 Impact of countercyclical emissions of SDRs on the GDP of the Eurozone (with respect to the base line).

Source: Authors' simulation.

more to the United States than to the EU thanks to the dollar depreciation and the increasing US competitiveness.

Conclusion

Two sets of simulations using SFC international models have been presented to show how SDR regimes could be modelled in order to assess their impact on international regulation mechanisms. At the world level the hybrid regime with free floating for the euro/dollar and a dollar pegged for the other currencies, close to what has been observed during the 1980s and 1990s, has been simply characterized. It appeared to be marked by large world imbalances without appropriate adjustment mechanisms.

A scenario based on SDRs has been proposed with two alternatives for the emission criterion of SDRs, one with regular emissions, the other with countercyclical emissions and two alternatives for the distribution criterion of SDRs, one according to each country quota, the other according to each country's demand for reserves. These preliminary results show that emission of SDRs could be used to support more expansionary fiscal policies and to mitigate the effects of global recession. These expansionary fiscal policies play a key role to support growth at the world level. In itself the emission of SDRs is not sufficient to bring about a recovery. It gives room of manoeuvre to national governments when they wish to implement more expansionary policy, but this has to be done and is not automatic.

The SDRs could have another important role. They could contribute to monetary stability at two levels. First, an enlarged use of new SDR-denominated assets would contribute to stabilize the international financial markets. Second, instead of the dollar, the SDR could be used as an anchor by the central bank of the emergent countries (the rest of the world in the model). This would also induce a more stabilized exchange rate regime, as it could be shown within the SFC model.

Last, a comparison can be made with a more ambitious reform based on the Keynes' project of the creation of a euro-bancor at the world level with an international clearing union and proposed by Zezza and Valdecantos (2015). This reform has been tested using the same type of four-country SFC model. It would imply the elimination of the dollar or other financial asset as the international currency. Both debtor and creditor countries would pay interests on their bancor balances at the international clearing union, which would encourage countries to reduce these bancor balances. Two adjustment mechanisms are introduced. First, the funds collected by the clearing union through the interests paid would be redistributed as foreign aid to developing countries. This aid would finance additional imports and an increase of investment of these countries. Second, the surplus countries, instead of accumulating useless bancor balances, would pursue expansionary fiscal policies to reduce these imbalances. In the bancor regime, these two adjustment mechanisms are key points to explain how a trend towards more balanced position of the different countries can be obtained. The bancor balances and the international clearing union give the framework but, as in the previous SDR regime, there is a need of an explicit expansionary policy. It can be added that, as in the Keynes' proposal, the exchange rates are fixed but could be adjusted by mutual agreements in case of persistent imbalances.

On the whole, the two proposals are in the same logic. Both suppose that more expansionary policies would be implemented thanks to the room of manoeuvre given by the issuance of SDR or the redistribution of bancor balances. The bancor proposal underlines the necessity of active policies to induce the surplus countries to share the cost of readjustment. But the SDR proposal relies more on existing institutions which just have to be more developed and mobilized while the bancor proposal implies a radical transformation of the international monetary system which is rather unlikely.

Conclusion

Jacques Mazier

Two sets of conclusions can be drawn from this study. The first one concerns the methodology and the theoretical background, the second the operating mode of the financial growth regime that has settled since the late 1980s and the future of this regime, both at the regional (especially European) and international levels.

The theoretical background

The theoretical background has relied on two complementary approaches, a Stock Flow Consistent (SFC) modelling in order to formalize the main macroeconomic forces which are at work, and a Fundamental Equilibrium Exchange Rate (FEER) methodology in order to give a synthetic view of world imbalances. The SFC modelling approach has been proposed for a closed economy in a first step, at the world level in a second step with a three-country model, at the regional level in a third step with different multinational models. The framework is macroeconomic without microeconomic foundations, based on national accounts in real and financial terms. The real side of the economy cannot be understood independently from the monetary/financial side. Accounting consistency imposes strict constraints, especially balance sheet constraints and revaluation effects, with capital gains and losses that play an important role in the finance-led regime. Short-term equilibrium is obtained through price adjustments in financial markets and through output adjustments to balance investment and saving. The sequence of these short-term equilibria generates long-term trends without any specification of productivity growth or of the supply side. Long-run equilibrium is defined by stable stock–flow ratios. If such stable ratios cannot be reached, the system appears unsustainable.

The finance-led regime is characterized by financial cycles and large international imbalances, both in terms of current account and capital flows. Periodic crises appear as its normal adjustment mode. Some of the main characteristics of the cycles of the 1990s and 2000s can be reproduced by a simple SFC model for a closed economy. Compared to the usual SFC models, the firms' behaviour has been completed by two relations, a financial accumulation with the financial rate of return as the main driver and a credit demand increasing function of the rate of return and decreasing of the interest rate. The adjustment mechanisms can be briefly recalled. An increase of firms' debt reduces the issuance of equities, leading to a rise of the equities' price and of the financial rate of return. This higher profitability sustains a financial boom with capital gains which reinforces the upward movement. In a first step firms' investment is reduced to the benefit of the financial accumulation but is stimulated in a second step with the upswing in the rate of profit. However, a reversal takes place in financial markets. Equities' issuance is increased to finance the boom, leading to a fall in equities' price. Financial cycles continue without a lasting real recovery. Similarly, a decline of the wage share, as it has been observed since the 1980s, implies a higher rate of profit which sustains real and financial accumulation with a larger access to credit. Firms issue less equities which in turn drives a rise of equities' price. The financial boom is amplified. Capital gains and wealth effects preserve consumption and a real recovery appears. But a turning point occurs once again. In order to finance real and financial accumulation, firms issue more equities which deteriorates equities' price and the financial rate of return decreases. With reduced wages and capital losses consumption declines, inducing a downturn. Firms' investment and equities' issuance are reduced. This allows a new upturn of equities' price afterwards.

These adjustment mechanisms by equities' price clearing the market are schematic, even if they have played a role in the financial crises observed in 1992, 2001, and 2008. Other components of the finance-led regime would have to be incorporated in more complex SFC models. First, rising income inequality is rather simple to tackle with a split of households between capitalists and workers. Two mechanisms contribute to enlarge the imbalances before the burst of the crisis in 2001 and 2008, the increasing indebtedness of the poorest households and the rising demand of financial assets by the richest ones. Second, the housing bubble driven by households' indebtedness is another face of the growing imbalances during the 2000s. Third, land capital must also be considered separately with speculative movements inducing large capital gains before the downturn and losses afterwards. The negative impact on productivity and the rate of profit of the total capital (productive and land) has also magnified imbalance factors. Fourth, financialization has considerably enlarged in gross terms the balance sheet of the financial sector with growing wholesale lending between financial institutions which has been facilitated by financial innovations. The empirical SFC modelling of this issue, especially of the price of the derivatives, is currently in progress.

The increasing global imbalances, both at the real and financial levels, have been another main feature of the 1990s and 2000s. They can be partly enlightened with multi-country SFC models connecting domestic economies with foreign ones. The exports of one country are the imports of the others. The agents hold assets and assume liabilities issued both in their country and abroad. They receive and pay income abroad according to the foreign denominated assets and liabilities they hold. Financial assets of some are the liabilities of others whether they are denominated in domestic or foreign currency. Capital gains or losses are generated by swings in domestic and foreign assets' prices, including exchange rate variations. The exchange rate against the dollar is determined endogenously to clear the supply and demand of US bills or, equivalently, to clear the flow of international transactions for goods and financial assets. In this approach there is no opposition between a determination of the exchange rates by capital flows and by the current account. Both are taken into account simultaneously. This SFC approach seems better adapted than the traditional general equilibrium models or portfolio models, given that it provides a more comprehensive description of the real and financial flows and stocks at the world level, can integrate most of the ingredients of the general equilibrium models (including the valuation effects) and do not presuppose, as it is often done despite mounting evidence of the contrary, that adjustments are limited to relative prices.

A three-country SFC model has allowed a preliminary analysis. At the world level the hybrid regime with free floating for the euro-dollar and dollar pegged for the other currencies, close to what has been observed during the 1980s and the 1990s, has been marked by large world imbalances without appropriate adjustment mechanisms. The analysis has focused on the US deficit and the Asian surpluses and on the exchange rate regimes between the dollar and the yuan. A fixed dollar-yuan parity, as it has prevailed from 1995 to 2005–2010, has limited the adjustments at the benefit of China and at the expense of the United States. A diversification of Chinese foreign reserves towards the euro would be favourable to the US economy, but international imbalances would remain important. A freely floating dollar-yuan could contribute to reduce these imbalances but is unrealistic and would encounter problems of financial stability. However, more managed floating regimes, with target of the People's Bank of China expressed in percentage of GDP for the foreign reserves or the current account, could give rather similar adjustment mechanisms. A target for the foreign reserves would give more stable results. The original model formulated with fixed prices has been enlarged by introducing flexible prices and wages and the main results have been confirmed.

These simple multi-country models have been combined with the original SFC model for a closed economy and have been the origin of two-country models of the European monetary union which have been used to analyse the single currency trap. Firstly, they have allowed a critique of the "international risk sharing" approach. Contrary to the main conclusion of the latter, well integrated capital markets do not constitute a powerful adjustment mechanism. Secondly, a model with fixed or endogenous interest rates has been used to analyse the euro zone crisis and alternative economic policies (fiscal federalism, euro bonds, European financing).

More broadly, larger four-country models have studied alternative exchange rate regimes at the regional level, for the euro zone (with multiple euros or euro-bancor regimes) and for East Asia (with ACU regimes or yuan block regimes). Lastly, at the world level, more ambitious reforms of the international monetary system with an enlarged role of the SDRs have been analysed.

Throughout the book, the SFC modelling approach has been useful to enlighten some of the main issues of the finance-led regime and to evaluate alternative economic policies at the regional and world levels. However, a considerable amount of work remains to be done to achieve a more satisfactory model of world imbalances. The world economy is dominated by a global financial cycle in capital flows and asset prices that is not explained by the simple SFC models analysed so far. This global financial cycle is disconnected from countries' specific macroeconomic conditions and largely determined by the US monetary policy (Rey, 2018). However, if the statistical correlations are well documented, the underlying mechanisms are less clearly described. This could be done with a three-country SFC model interconnecting the national equities' markets and where adjustments would pass through equities' prices and exchange rates.

This SFC modelling has been combined with the synthetic view of the international imbalances given by the FEER methodology which estimates the exchange rate misalignments. The FEER is defined as the level of the exchange rate which allows the economy to reach internal and external equilibrium. Based on a model of the world trade for the United States, the euro zone, the United Kingdom, Japan, China, and the rest of the world, a FEER has been estimated for the main currencies and has enlightened the successive waves of global imbalances from the 1980s to the post-crisis period of the 2010s. With simple national models connected to the previous world trade one, the FEER approach has also been used to estimate exchange rate misalignments at the regional levels. First, for the euro zone where intra-European exchange rate misalignments have been a key issue before and after the launching of the euro. Second, for East Asia where monetary cooperation and exchange rate regimes have been hotly debated since the Asian crisis of 1997 in a context of increasing economic and financial integration.

The operating mode of the finance-led regime

Some stylized facts have been recalled concerning the finance-led regime that settled since the 1980s in most developed countries. Despite the restoration of the rate of profit, the recovery of the non-financial rate of accumulation has been rather limited. This can be linked to a less favourable evolution of profitability when a broader notion of capital, which includes land, is used since a boom of property prices has been further fuelled by financial liberalisation. On the contrary, financial accumulation has been stronger with the financial rate of return as its main driver, and financial markets are regulated by periodic crises. The increasing indebtedness of firms has been masked by valuation effects with the boom of the property price and of the equities' price. However, the risk of over-indebtedness has remained and can appear in case of a reversal in financial markets. The SFC modelling has given a first illustration of the adjustment mechanisms which have been at work in the financial cycles of the 1990s and 2000s with the equities' price clearing the market. But the explanation remained partial, even when complementary factors have been taken into account, like the over-indebtedness of the poorest households, the rising demand of financial assets by the richest ones and the housing bubble.

Global imbalances have been another feature of the finance-led regime. Our theoretical framework has shed some useful, though limited, light on this. The increase of the international imbalances at the beginning of the 1980s has been contained by the Plaza-Louvre agreements in 1985–1987, far from free floating and leading to a depreciation of the dollar and an appreciation of the yen and of the European currencies. In the second half of the 1990s, the US deficit and Asian surpluses have been on the rise, partly due to the fixity of the dollar-yuan parity and to the undervaluation of the yuan. From 2005 to 2008, the appreciation of the yuan against the dollar has been rather limited, and exchange rate misalignments were important before the 2008 crisis. After the burst of the crisis, only the yen has appreciated and the revaluation of the yuan after 2010 has remained limited. China did not play the role of Germany during the 1970s and of Japan during the 1990s who had accepted large revaluations in order to contribute to reduce global imbalances. Although China has refused such a large revaluation, the undervaluation of the yuan has progressively disappeared thanks to a depreciation of the equilibrium exchange rate of the yuan induced by the settlement of a new Chinese growth regime, turned more towards the domestic market and by the boom of the Chinese tourists' expenditures. For the future, a pragmatic Chinese exchange rate policy, based for example on a target of current account or of foreign reserves and combined with a limited capital liberalisation, could help to preserve a more balanced world growth regime. However, since the beginning of 2019 with the new climate of trade war the Chinese leaders may be tempted to use exchange rate policy to deal with imports tariff increases.

The euro has been a different case. Before the 2008 crisis the European current imbalance was relatively limited, and the euro was close to its equilibrium parity. But the huge intra-European imbalances and the institutional fragility of the euro zone have led to a depreciation of the euro against the dollar which appeared as a safe haven. It induced huge European surpluses, mainly German, and contributed to perpetuate global imbalances. However, during the second half of the 2010s the exchange rate misalignments remained limited and focused around the yen (again undervalued due to the active quantitative easing policy) and the German euro. The dollar was paradoxically close to its equilibrium value before the beginning of the trade war against China and the EU.

The single currency trap

The settlement of a monetary union between heterogeneous countries, both at structural and institutional levels, with no adjustment mechanism (no fiscal federalism, no political agreement to allow the ECB to guarantee the national public debts), except competitive wage deflation, could only lead to divergent evolutions with recurrent crisis. Reforms have been adopted in emergency to avoid a break-up (creation of the European Stability Mechanism, procedure of Outright Monetary Transactions, launching of the Quantitative Easing) but remain unfinished (Banking Union) or ill-adjusted (Fiscal Treaty). The way of adjusting internal imbalances is still asymmetrical. Deficit countries alone are obliged to adjust. Wage deflation and restrictive policies have replaced exchange rate adjustments and competitive devaluations. In spite of a macroeconomic improvement in 2016–2017, unemployment remains high in southern Europe and income inequalities are wide. There is an increasing polarisation around the German block and a split between northern and southern Europe. Unsurprisingly, social tensions are rising.

The necessity of a deep institutional reform has been reaffirmed with several typical alternatives: a reaffirmation of a no bail-out clause for member state governments; the fiscal federalism; the mutualisation of public debt; the creation of a Euro Treasury. These alternatives raise serious problems and are hardly realistic politically. More hybrid proposals have been put forward: the CEPR one, rather technocratic and unconvincing; the IMK one, more pragmatic but difficult to implement; the proposal of complementary (or fiscal) currencies with an European clearing union, which could be useful but with rather limited macroeconomic impact; an enlargement of the role of the EIB to finance the ecological transition; more traditionally a simple European unemployment insurance system. A political union of some core countries ready to accept a major leap forward is also defended. Nevertheless, the most likely scenario is maintaining the status quo with only marginal inflexion so that, if there are many losers, there are also winners (the German block and the European élite).

This status quo would remain fragile and a last alternative can be explored, a calling into question of the single currency itself to regain rooms of manoeuvre with three conceivable regimes: a system of national euros with a global euro which would be preserved; a euro zone without Germany or a northern euro combined with a southern euro; a euro-bancor system. Once established, any of these new monetary regimes would provide, combined with structural policies, an appropriate response to the heterogeneity of the euro zone but the transition period would be perilous. Capital controls would be necessary, and the external euro-denominated debt would require specific treatments.

Simulations with SFC models have confirmed this general assessment. First, contrary to the "international risk sharing" approach, well integrated capital markets with portfolio diversification and intra-zone credit do not constitute a powerful adjustment mechanism. Holding foreign assets has a stabilising role but the capital income stabilising coefficient is small. More importantly intra-zone credit seems to have no specific stabilisation effect. Second, the creation of a federal budget, even of a small size but with federal transfers, could have an efficient stabilising role, as could be illustrated by a European Unemployment Insurance System. But the obstacles are numerous, both technical and political. The launching of European investments financed by euro bonds could also contribute to reduce the imbalances and lead to a recovery. The difficulty is to implement concretely such European investments at a large scale to have a significant macroeconomic impact. Third, the issuance of euro bonds could be used to mutualise a share of public national debts. It would help to maintain low interest rates and reduce national debts, especially in southern countries. But the euro bonds would not solve the problem of stabilisation, nor the problem of unequal competitiveness of the different groups of countries. Moreover, a strict control of national budgets would be necessary, which would raise political issues. Fourth, the enlargement of financial support by northern countries in favour of the southern ones is another possibility, through the ESM for instance. It would contribute to reduce the imbalances but it would not sufficiently lessen the level of national debts, and would be accompanied by fiscal cuts imposed by the Fiscal Treaty. On the whole, the alternative economic policies are whether unlikely or hardly feasible or with a limited impact. The status quo could prevail but would meet resistance.

A last alternative based on a break-up of the monetary union has been simulated. The first version is a multiple-euro system with a global euro remaining at the international level and national euros that would eventually be reintroduced. They would not be internationally convertible and would be in a fixed exchange rate with the global euro. But exchange rate adjustments could occur in case of unsustainable current account imbalances. The second version relies on a euro-bancor that would be a simple basket currency and on national currencies that would also be reintroduced and floating at the international level. The ECB would be transformed into a clearing union with new rules, especially a symmetric treatment between debtor and creditor countries. The national euros would be in a fixed but adjustable exchange rate with the euro-bancor. Each system has its strengths and weaknesses. The simulations have shown that, once established, these new European monetary regimes could ensure a better management of the structural heterogeneity of the euro zone than the current monetary union, but they would not be a panacea.

Enhancing the international monetary regime

Beyond the persistent blocking of the euro zone, the world economy remains on the threat of a new recession. The dollar is still the key currency of the system and the euro is mainly limited to a regional role. The yuan is propelled by the rising power of China, but its internationalization is currently underway (thus incomplete). Since the beginning of 2019 with the increasing trade war, the multilateral system seems fragile. Despite this context two questions have been explored in terms of international monetary issues, the first one at the level of East Asia, the second at the world level.

First, the future of monetary cooperation in East Asia has been analysed as new issues have been raised by the financial crisis of 2008 and the rising importance of China. With a more fragmented multilateral system, China may be interested in enhancing regional monetary cooperation. Pragmatic floating regimes have been implemented in East Asia since the 2000s and exchange rate misalignments have been more limited during the current period than during the 1990s (with the exception of the yuan until 2010) in contrast with what has been observed in the euro zone where the march towards the single currency has been decided in 1992, and where the intra-European exchange rate misalignments have been important. A first version of a four-country SFC model of East Asia has reproduced the exchange rate regimes observed in the past, the rigid dollar pegged regime of the 1990s which has led to persistent imbalances, the hybrid regime of the end of the 1990s and of the beginning of the 2000s where the yuan pegged on the dollar was still a source of disequilibrium, the more flexible and managed regime of the 2000s. For the future two scenarios have been built, a yuan zone too rigid and unlikely, a yuan block where the anchor on the yuan of the other East Asian currencies is managed (and not rigid), which seems a more promising perspective. A second version of SFC models has analysed more elaborated exchange rate regimes, the ACU regime, the Asian bancor regime or the global ACU regime which would suppose the launching of a new international currency (the global ACU). The simple ACU regime, where the latter remains a basket currency, has appeared rather well adapted to the heterogeneity of the area but would be more exigent in institutional terms than the yuan block.

Second, at the world level, with the mounting threat of a new deep downturn, the efficiency of a new international monetary system based on SDRs' emission was interesting to assess, although it would need a high level of multilateralism which is rather unlikely under current circumstances. Based on a four-country SFC model various scenarios have been proposed with two alternatives for the emission of SDRs, one with regular emission, the other with countercyclical emission, and two alternatives for the distributive criterion of SDRs, one according to each country's quota, the other according to each country's demand for reserves. Convergent results have shown that the emissions of SDRs gave room of manoeuvre to national governments to implement more expansionary policies to combat a world slow down but were not by themselves enough to foster the recovery. An active policy is facilitated by the issuance of SDRs, but they have to be implemented by the national governments. The SDRs could also contribute to monetary stability at two other levels. An enlargement of the use of SDRs denominated assets could help to stabilise the international financial markets. They could also be used as an anchor by central banks of emerging countries, instead of the dollar, in order to increase the stability of their exchange rate regimes.

References

Aflouk, N., Jeong, S.-E., Mazier, J. and Saadaoui, J. (2010), 'Exchange rate misalignments and world imbalances, a FEER approach for emerging countries', *International Economics*, 124, pp. 31–74.

Aflouk, N. and Mazier, J. (2013), 'Exchange rate misalignments and economic growth: a threshold panel approach', *Economics Bulletin*, 33(2), pp 1333–1347.

Aflouk, N., Mazier, J. and On, M. (2016), 'Impact of monetary regimes and exchange rates on ASEAN economic integration' in *ASEAN Economic Community: A model for Asia wide integration*, ed. B. Jetin and M. Mikiz, London, Palgrave Macmillan.

Aglietta, M. (1998), 'Le Capitalisme de demain', Notes de la fondation Saint-Simon, no. 101.

Ahearne, A., Cline, W.R., Lee, K.T., Park, Y.C., Pisani-Ferry J. and Williamson, J. (2007), Global Imbalances: time for Action, *Policy Brief 07-4, March, Peterson Institute for International Economics*, Washington

Amato, M. and Fantacci, L. (2014). *Saving the market from capitalism*, Policy Press, Cambridge.

Amato, M., Fantacci, L., Papadimitriou, D. and Zezza, G. (2016). Going forward from B to A? Proposals for the Eurozone crisis, Levy Economics Institute, Working paper no. 866, May.

Asdrubali, P., Sorensen, B. and Yoshua, O. (1996), 'Channels of inter-state risk sharing: United States 1963- 1990', *Quarterly Journal of Economics*, 111, p 1081–1110.

Asdrubali, P. and Kim, S. (2004), 'Dynamic risk sharing in the United States and Europe', *Journal of Monetary Economics*, 51, pp. 809–836.

Bensassy-Quéré, A., Ragot, X. and Wolf, G. (2016), 'Quelle union budgétaire pour la zone euro?', *Notes du Conseil d'Analyse Economique*, 29, February.

Benassy-Quéré, A. et al. (2018), 'Reconciling risk sharing with market discipline: a constructive approach to euro area reform', *CEPR, Policy Insight*, 91, January.

Bibow, J. (2016), 'Making the euro area viable, the Euro Treasury Plan', *European Journal of Economics and Economic Policies, Intervention*, 13(1), pp. 72–86.

Blanchard, O. and Katz, L. (1992), 'Regional evolutions', *Brookings Papers on economic activity*, 1, pp. 1–75.

Blanchard, O. Giavazzi, F. and Sa, F. (2005), 'The US current account and the dollar', *Brookings Papers on Economic Activity*, 1.

Blinder, A. and Solow, R. (1973), 'Does fiscal policy matter?', *Journal of Public Economics*, 2(4), pp. 319–337.

Boyer, R. (1999), 'Le gouvernement économique de la zone euro', Rapport du Commissariat Général du Plan, La Documentation Française.

Boyer, R. (2000), 'Is a finance-led growth regime a viable alternative to Fordism? A preliminary analysis', *Economy and Society*, 29(1), pp. 111–145.

Brainard, W.C. and Tobin, J. (1968), 'Pitfalls in financial model building', *American Economic Review*, 58(2), pp. 99–122.

Bresser-Pereira, L.C. (2010), *Globalization and competition*, Cambridge, Cambridge University Press.

Bresser-Pereira, L.C., Oreiro, J.L. and Marconi, N. (2014), *Developmental macroeconomics*, London, Routledge.

Brillet, J.L. (2000), *A workbook for the use of the Chinese annual model*, INSEE, Paris.

Cadiou, L., Guichard, S. and Maurel, M. (1999), 'Ajustements sur les marchés du travail en Europe', Working paper CEPII no. 99–11.

CEPII-OFCE-MIMOSA (1994), 'Lutter contre le chômage de masse en Europe', *Revue de l'OFCE*, 48, July.

Cesaratto, S. (2013), The implication of TARGET2 in the European balance of payments crisis and beyond, *European Journal of Economics and Economics Policies: Intervention*, 10(3), pp. 359–382.

Chinn, M.D. and Prasad, E.S. (2003), Medium term determinants of current accounts in industrial and developing countries: an empirical exploration, *Journal of International Economics*, 59, Elsevier, pp. 47–76.

Clark, P.B. and MacDonald, R. (1998), Exchange Rates and Economic Fundamentals: A Methodological Comparison of BEERs and FEERs, Working Paper 98/00, March, International Monetary Fund, Washington.

Clévenot, M. and Duwicquet, V. (2011), 'Partage du risque inter-régional', *Revue de l'OFCE*, 119, October.

Clévenot, M., Guy, Y. and Mazier, J. (2010), 'Investment and the rate of profit in a financial context: the French case', *International Review of Applied Economics*, 24(6), pp. 693–714.

Clévenot, M., Guy, Y. and Mazier, J. (2012), 'Financiarisation de l'économie française et modélisation postkeynésienne', *Économie appliquée*, 65(4), pp. 39–78.

Cline, W.R. (2008), Estimating Consistent Fundamental Equilibrium Exchange Rates, Working Paper 08-6, July, Peterson Institute for International Economics, Washington.

Cline, W.R. (2014), Estimates of Fundamental Equilibrium Exchange Rates, Policy Brief 14–25, November, Peterson Institute for International Economics, Washington.

Cline, W.R. and Williamson, J. (2008), New Estimates of Fundamental Equilibrium Exchange Rates, Policy Brief 08-7, July, Peterson Institute for International Economics, Washington.

Couharde, C. and Mazier, J. (2001), 'The equilibrium exchange rates of European currencies and the transition to euro', *Applied Economics*, 33(14), pp. 1795–1801.

Couharde, C., Delaite, A.L., Grekou, C., Mignon, V. and Morvillier, F. (2017), EQCHANGE: a world database on actual and equilibrium effective exchange rates, Working Paper CEPII no. 2017-14, July.

Davanne, O. (1998), 'L'instabilité du système financier international', Rapport du Conseil d'analyse économique, no. 14, La Documentation Française.

Davis, E.P. (1987), 'A Stock-Flow Consistent macro-econometric model of the UK economy' (parts I and II), *Journal of Applied Econometrics*, 2.

Dées, S. (1999), The Role of External Variables in the Chinese Economy; Simulation from a Macroeconomic Model of China, Working Paper no. 1999-09, juin, CEPII, Paris.

Dos Santos, C.H. and Zezza, G. (2008), 'A simplified, 'benchmark', stock-flow consistent Post-Keynesian growth model', *Metroeconomica*, 59(3), pp. 441–438.

Durand, C. and Villemot, S. (2017), 'Balance sheets after the EMU: An assessment of the redenomination risk', *OFCE*, January.

Duwicquet, V. and Mazier, J. (2010), 'Financial integration and macroeconomic adjustments in a monetary union', *Journal of Post Keynesian Economics*, 33(2), pp. 331–368.

Duwicquet, V. and Mazier, J. (2012), 'Financial integration and stabilization in a moneatry union without or with bank rationing', in *Contributions in Stock-Flow Modelling, Essays in Honor of Wynne Godley*, New York, Palgrave Macmillan.

Duwicquet, V., Mazier, J. and Saadaoui, J. (2012), 'Exchange rate misalignments, fiscal federalism and redistribution; how to adjust in a monetary union?', Working Paper CEPN 2012–04.

Duwicquet, V., Mazier, J. and Saadaoui, J. (2013), 'Désajustements de change, fédéralisme budgétaire et redistribution', *Revue de l'OFCE*, 127, Debates and policies, pp. 57–93.

Duwicquet, V., Mazier, J. and Saadaoui, J. (2016), Interest rates, Eurobonds and intra-European exchange rate misalignments: the challenge of sustainable adjustments in the Eurozone, BETA Working paper 2016–19.

Duwicquet, V., Mazier, J. and Saadaoui, J. (2018), 'Dealing with the consequences of exchange rate misalignments for macroeconomic adjustments in the EMU', *Metroeconomica*, 69(4), pp. 737–767.

Eichengreen, B. and Wyplosz, C. (1994), 'Pourquoi le SME a explosé et comment le relancer?', *Revue Economique* no.3, May.

European Commission (1988), '1992: the new European economy', *European Economy* no.35, March.

European Commission (1990), 'Single market, single currency', *European Economy* no.44, October.

European Commission (1996), 'The 1996 Single Market review. Background information for the Report of the Council and European Parliament', Commission Staff Working Paper, 16 December.

European Commission (2007), 'Quaterly report on the euro area', no. 3.

European Commission (2018), A new, modern Multinational Financial Framework for the EU that delivers efficiently on its priorities post-2020, *Communication from the European Commission to the European Parliament, the European Council and the Council*, 23 February.

Fantacci, L. (2013). Why not bancor? Keynes's currency plan as a solution to global imbalances in Marcuzzo M.C., Mehrling P. and Hirai T. (eds) *Keynesian reflections, effective demand, money, finance and policies*, Oxford University Press.

Faruqee, H. and Isard, P., Editors (1998), Exchange Rate Assessment: Extensions to the Macroeconomic Balance Approach, IMF Occasional Paper no.167, International Monetary Fund, Washington.

Fontagné, L., Freudenberg, M. and Péridy, N. (1998), 'Intra-industry trade and the single market: quality matters', CEPR Discussion Paper no. 1953.

Fuest, C., Heinemann, F. and Schroder, C. (2016), 'A viable insolvency procedure for Sovereigns in the euro area', *Journal of Common Market Studies*, 54(2), pp. 301–317.

Gerlach, S. and Yiu, M.S. (2004), Estimating Output Gaps in Asia: a Cross-Country Study, *Journal of the Japanese and International Economics*, 18(1), pp. 115–136.

Godley, W. (1999), 'Money and credit in a Keynesian model of income determination', *Cambridge Journal of Economics*, 23(4), pp. 393–411.

Godley, W. and Cripps, F. (1983), *Macroeconomics*, Oxford University Press.

Godley, W. and Lavoie, M. (2005), 'Comprehensive accounting in a simple open economy macroeconomics with endogenous sterilization or flexible exchange rates', *Journal of Post-Keynesian Economics*, winter, 28(2), pp. 241–276.

Godley, W. and Lavoie, M. (2007a), *Monetary Economics: An Integrated Approach to Credit, Money, Income, Production and Wealth*, Palgrave Macmillan.

Godley, W. and Lavoie, M. (2007b), 'A simple model of three economies with two currencies: The eurozone and the USA', *Cambridge Journal of Economics*, January, 31(1), pp. 1–24.

Goodwin, R.M. (1967), 'A growth cycle' in *Socialism, capitalism and economic growth*, p 54–8, Cambridge University Press, Cambridge.

Gourinchas, P.O. and Rey, H. (2005), 'International financial adjustment' Working Paper 11155 Cambridge, Mass. NBER, February.

Hein, E. (2012), *The macroeconomics of finance-dominated capitalism- and its crisis*, Edward Elgar.

Hervé, K. (2000), Comparaison des Comportements d'Exportations entre la Zone Euro, les États-Unis et le Japon, Note, B2-00-145/KH, Direction de la Prévision, Paris.

International Monetary Fund (2008), 'De facto classification of exchange rate regimes and monetary policy frameworks', Washington DC, IMF.

International Monetary Fund (2011): 'Enhancing international monetary stability: a role for the SDR?', prepared by the Strategy, Policy and Review Department, January.

Italianer, A. and Pisani-Ferry, J. (1992), 'Systèmes budgétaires et amortissements des chocs régionaux: implications pour l'Union économique et monétaire', *Economie internationale*, no. 51, 3rd quarter.

Jacquet, P. and Pisani-Ferry, J. (2000), 'La coordination des politiques économiques dans la zone euro: bilan et propositions', dans '*Questions européennes*', Rapport du Conseil d'analyse écconomique no. 27, La Doccumentation Française, pp. 17–40.

Jeong, S.-E. and Mazier, J. (2003), Exchange Rate Regimes and Equilibrium Exchange Rates in East Asia, *Revue Économique*, 54, September, Presses de Sciences Po, Paris, pp. 1161–1182.

Jeong, S.-E., Mazier, J. and Saadaoui, J. (2010), Exchange rate misalignments at world and European levels; a FEER approach, *International Economics*, 121, pp. 25–58.

Jeong, S-E., Mazier, J. and Saglio, S. (2012), 'Given the heterogeneity of Asian countries, is a monetary integration or coordination possible?' in *Diversity and transformation of Asian capitalisms* ed. R. Boyer, H. Uemura and A. Isogai, London, Routledge.

Kalecki, M. (1965), *Theory of economic dynamics*, London, Allen and Unwin.

Keen, S. (1995). Finance and economic breakdown: modeling Minsky's 'financial instability hypothesis', *Journal of Post Keynesian Economics*, 17(4) pp. 607–635.

Keen, S. (2013). A monetary Minsky model of the great moderation and the great recession, *Journal of Economic Behavior* 86 pp. 221–235.

Keen, S. (2014). Endogenous money and effective demand, *Review of Keynesian Economics*, 2(3), pp. 271–291.

Kenen, P.B. (2010): Reforming the global reserve regime: the role of a substitution account, *International Finance* 13(1), pp 1-23.

Keynes, J.M. (1941), 'Proposals for an International Clearing Union'. 15 December 1941, in *Collected Writings*, Macmillan and Cambridge University Press 25, p. 74.

Koo, R. (2008), *The Holy Grail of Macroeconomics: lessons from Japan's great recession*, Singapore, John Wiley & Sons.

Koo, R. (2015), *The escape from balance sheet recession and the QE trap: a hazardous road for the world economy*, Wiley.

Kwack, S.Y., Ahn, C.Y. and Lee, Y.S. (2007), Consistent Estimates of World Trade Elasticities and an Application to the effects of Chinese Yuan (RMB) Appreciation, *Journal of Asian Economics*, 18, Elsevier, pp. 314–330.

Lane, P.R. and Milesi-Ferretti, G.M. (2007), The External Wealth of Nations Mark II: Revisited and Extended Estimates of Foreign Assets and Liabilities, 1970–2004, *Journal of International Economics*, 73, Elsevier, pp. 223–250.

Lavoie, M. and Daigle, G., (2011), 'A behavioural finance model of exchange rate expectations within a stock-flow consistent framework', *Metroeconomica*, 62 (3), pp. 434–458.

Lavoie, M. and Godley, W. (2001), 'Kaleckian growth models in a stock and flow monetary framework: a Kaldorian view', *Journal of Post Keynesian Economics*, 24(2), pp. 277–312.

Lavoie, M. (2015), The euro zone crisis: a balance of payments problem or a crisis due to a flawed monetary design?, *European Journal of Economics and Economics Policies: Intervention*, 44(2), pp. 57–60.

Lavoie, M., and Zhao, J. (2010), 'A study of the diversification of China's foreign reserves within a three country stock-flow consistent model', *Metroeconomica*, 61(3), pp. 558–592.

Le Heron, E. and Mouakil, T. (2008), 'A Post-Keynesian stock flow consistent model for the dynamic analysis of monetary policy shocks on banking behavior', *Metroeconomica*, 59(3), pp. 405–440.

Mayer, T., Mobert, J. and Weistroffer, C. (2012) 'Macroeconomics imbalances in EMU and the Eurosystem' in *CESIfo Forum Special Issues*, pp. 35–42.

Mazier, J., Oudinet, J. and Saglio, S. (2002), « La flexibilité des pris relatifs et la mobilité du travail en Union monétaire : une comparaison Europe-Etats-Unis », *Revue de l'OFCE*, October. 83, pp. 325–388.

Mazier, J. and Saglio, S. (2008), 'Interdependency and adjustments in the European Union', *International Review of Applied Economics*, 22(1), pp. 17–44.

Mazier, J. and Tiou-Tagba Aliti, G. (2009), 'World imbalances and macroeconomic adjustments: a stock flow three countries model', Working paper CEPN no. 19–2009, CNRS- Université Paris Nord, http://www.univ-paris13.fr/CEPN/IMG/pdf/wp2009_19.pdf.

Mazier, J. and Tiou-Tagba Aliti, G. (2012), 'World imbalances and macroeconomic adjustments: a three-country stock-flow consistent model with fixed or flexible prices', *Metroeconomica*, 63(2), pp. 358–388.

Mazier, J. and Valdecantos, S. (2014a), A detailed representation of the Eurosystem and the current crisis of the Euro zone: A stock flow consistent approach, Working paper CEPN no. 2014-02.

Mazier, J. and Valdecantos, S. (2014b), A multispeed Europe: Is it viable? Working paper CEPN no. 2014-03.

Mazier, J. and Valdecantos, S. (2015), 'A multispeed Europe: is-it viable? A Stock Flow Consistent approach', *European Journal of Economics and Economic Policies: Intervention*, 12(1), pp. 93–102.

Mazier, J. and Valdecantos, S. (2019), 'From the European Monetary Union to a euro-bancor: a Stock Flow Coherent assessment', *European Journal of Economics and Economic Policies: Intervention*, February.

Mazier, J., On, M. and Valdecantos, S. (2014): 'East Asian monetary regime: a SFC approach', CEPN, Working Paper, No. 2014-11.

Mazier, J., On, M. and Valdecantos, S. (2018), 'East Asian monetary regimes and comparison with the European case: A Stock Flow Consistent approach' in R. Boyer, H. Uemura, T. Yamada and L. Song ed. *Evolving diversity and interdependence of capitalisms*, Springer, Japan.

Mazier, J. and Reyes, L. (2014), 'Financialized growth regime: lessons from Stock Flow Consistent Models', *Recherche et Régulation,* 16, 2nd Semester.

Mazier, J., Clévenot, M. and Duwicquet, V. (2016), *Quand les crises reviennent*, Paris, Economica.

McCauley, R.N. and Schenk, C.R. (2014), Reforming the IMF in the 1970s and 2000s: Would an SDR substitution account have worked? Working paper BIS, March.

McKinnon, R. (1993), 'The rules of the game: International money in historical perspectives', *Journal of Economic Literature,* 31(1).

Melitz, J. and Zumer, F. (1998), "Redistribution régionale et stabilisation par le gouvernement central", *Economie Internationale*, 75, 3rd Quarter.

MIMOSA (1996), La Nouvelle Version de MIMOSA, Modèle de l'Économie Mondiale, *Revue de l'OFCE*, 58(1), pp. 103–155.

Midelfart-Knartik, K.H., Overmann, H.G., Redding, S.J. and Venables, A.J. (2000), 'The location of European industry', *Economic papers*, 142, European Commission.

Minsky, H. (1986), *Stabilizing an Unstable Economy*, McGraw-Hill.

NIESR (1997), The World Model NIGEM, juillet, NIESR.

Nikiforos, M. (2016), 'A non behavioral theory of saving', *Journal of Post-Keynesian Economics*, 39(4), pp. 562–592.

Nikiforos, M. and Zezza, G. (2017), 'Stock-flow consistent macroeconomic models: A survey', *Journal of Economic Surveys*, 30 October, pp. 1204–1239.

Nikolaidi, M. (2015), 'Securitization, wage stagnation and financial fragility: A stock-flow consistent perspective', *Greenwich Papers in Political Economy* 14078, Greenwich Political Economy Research Center.

Obstfeld, M. and Rogoff, K. (2005), 'Global current account imbalances and exchange rate adjustments', *Brookings Papers on Economic Activity*, no. 1.

OECD (2016), Economic Outlook.

Pain, N., Mourougane, A., Sédillot, F. and Le Fouler, L. (2005), The New OECD International Trade Model, OECD Working paper no.440, August, OECD, Paris.

Papadimitriou, D.B., Nikiforos, M. and Zezza, G. (2014), Prospects and policies for the Greek economy, Levy Economics Institute Strategic Analysis, February.

Papadimitriou, D.B., Nikiforos, M. and Zezza, G. (2016), How long before growth and employment are resorted in Greece?, Levy Economics Institute Strategic Analysis, January.

Piketty, T. et al. (2018), 'Manifeste pour la democratisation de l'Europe', *Le Monde*, 11 December.

Reinhart, C. and Rogoff, K. (2004), 'A modern history of exchange rate regimes: a reinterpretation', *Quarterly Journal of Economics*, 119(1), pp. 1–48.

Rey, H. (2018), 'Dilemna not trilemna: the global financial cycle and monetary policy independence', NBER Working Paper 21162.

Sawyer, M. and Passarella, M.V. (2017), 'The monetary circuit in the age of financialisation; a stock-flow consistent model with two fold banking sector', *Metroeconomica*, 68(2), pp. 321–353.

Shimizutani, S. (2009), 'Asian Common Currency as a driving force of economic integration in East Asia: A prospect', *Asia Pacific Review,* 16(2), pp. 26–41.

Sterdyniak, H. (2018), 'L'aveuglement européen', *Les économistes atterrés*, Working Paper, January.r.

Stiglitz, J.E. (2009): Report of the Commission of experts of the President of the United Nations General Assembly on reforms of the International Monetary and Financial System, September.

Stockhammer, E. (2004), Financialisation and the slowdown of accumulation, *Cambridge Journal of Economics*, 28(5), pp. 719–742.

Taylor, L. (2004) *Reconstructing macroeconomics. Structuralist proposals and critiques of the mainstream*, Harvard University Press.

Taylor, L. (2012), 'Growth, cycles, asset prices and finance', *Metroeconomica*, 63(1), pp. 40–63.

Théret, B. and Coutrot, T. (2018), 'Monnaie fiscale complémentaire: sortir des impasses européiste et souverainiste', https//blogs.mediapart.fr/Thomas-coutrot/blog/260618/.

Tobin, J. (1969), 'A general equilibrium approach to monetary theory', *Journal of Money, Credit, and Banking*, 1(1), pp. 15–29.

Trichet, J.C. (2007), 'Le processus d'intégration européenne', Fondation Jean Monet pour l'Europe, European Central Bank, Communication Department.

Triffin, R. (1960), *Gold and the dollar crisis*, New Haven, Yale University Press.

Valdecantos, S. and Zezza, G. (2015): Reforming the international monetary system: a SFC approach, *Journal of Post-Keynesian Economics*, 38(2), pp. 167–191.

Von Treek, T. (2008), Reconsidering the investment-profit nexus in finance-led economies: a ARDL approach, *Metroeconomica*, 59. no 3: 371–404.

Watt, A. and Watzka, S. (2018), Overcoming euro area fragility, *IMK report* 139, June.

Whyman, P.B. (2018), *Rethinking economic and monetary union in Europe, a post-Keynesian alternative*, London, Routledge.

Williamson, J. (1983), The Exchange Rate System. 1st edition, 2nd edition 1985, Institute for International Economics, Washington.

Williamson, J. (1998), 'The case for a common basket peg for East Asian currencies' in Collignon S., Pisani-Ferry J. and Park Y.C. (eds) *Exchange rate policies in emerging Asian countries*, Routledge.

Wren-Lewis, S. and Driver, R.L. (1998), Real Exchange Rates for the Year 2000, May, Institute for International Economics, Washington

Zezza, G. (2008), 'US growth, the housing market and the distribution of income', *Journal of Post-Keynesian Economics*, 30(3), pp. 379–405.

Index

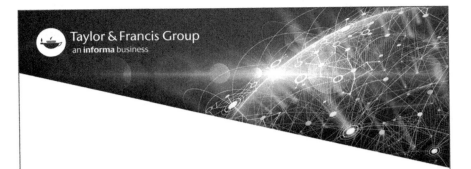

Printed in the United States
by Baker & Taylor Publisher Services